Managing Virtual Web Organizations in the 21st Century: Issues and Challenges

Ulrich J. Franke
Cranfield University, UK

 **Idea Group Publishing**

 **Information Science Publishing**

Hershey • London • Melbourne • Singapore • Beijing

Acquisitions Editor:	Mehdi Khosrowpour
Managing Editor:	Jan Travers
Development Editor:	Michele Rossi
Copy Editor:	Beth Arneson
Typesetter:	LeAnn Whitcomb
Cover Design:	Deb Andree
Printed at:	Integrated Book Technology

Published in the United States of America by
    Idea Group Publishing
    1331 E. Chocolate Avenue
    Hershey PA 17033-1117
    Tel: 717-533-8845
    Fax: 717-533-8661
    E-mail: cust@idea-group.com
    Web site: http://www.idea-group.com

and in the United Kingdom by
    Idea Group Publishing
    3 Henrietta Street
    Covent Garden
    London WC2E 8LU
    Tel: 44 20 7240 0856
    Fax: 44 20 7379 3313
    Web site: http://www.eurospan.co.uk

Library of Congress Cataloging-in-Publication Data

Managing virtual web organizations in the 21st century / [editor] Ulrich J. Franke.
    p. cm.
  Includes bibliographical references and index.
   ISBN 1-930708-24-6 (cloth)
   1. Virtual reality in management. 2. Organization. 3. Electronic commerce. I. Franke, Ulrich J., 1965-

  HD30.2122 .M35 2001
  658'.054678--dc21
                                             2001039655

British Cataloguing in Publication Data
A Cataloguing in Publication record for this book is available from the British Library.

NEW from Idea Group Publishing

Managing Virtual Web Organizations in the 21st Century: Issues and Challenges

Table of Contents

SECTION I:
Virtual Web Management Challenges:
What Are The Challenges of Managing Virtual Web Organizations and How Can Those Challenges Be Tackled?

SECTION II:
Virtual Web Management Issues:
Special Issues and Possible Solutions of Managing Virtual Web Organizations

Preface

With the development of the Internet and modern information and communication technology (ICT), new ways of conducting business have been evolved. The term e-commerce has become a buzzword and Internet applications such as virtual marketplaces, Internet auctions and Internet procurement platforms are becoming more and more popular with companies in purchasing and selling products and services in virtual space and in the global marketplace. However, e-commerce does not create any value on its own; it basically improves the market transparency, and it increases competition and provides companies with an extended potential customer base.

On the other hand, e-business aims to improve the value creation process between companies or company units by making use of Inter- and intranet applications. Thus, B2B e-business seeks to generate synergies between value chain elements through the fast and detailed exchange of data and information along the supply chain. Theoretically, e-business is a way to organize cooperations between individual parts of value chains without geographical limitations and to generate benefits for all parties involved.

However, despite the differences, both e-commerce and e-business have to be integrated on the company and intercompany level. Both concepts, the kinds of e-relationships within the supply chain and towards the external environment, are interrelated and constitute the emerging global e-economy.

Today, many e-commerce and e-business concepts promise economic benefits through ad-hoc market transaction, short-term ones of collaborations and almost unlimited access to global resources. All these e-solutions are short-term driven and exploit the immediate global market opportunities. This short-term thinking and opportunistic behavior lead to uncertainty and mistrust between the value chain elements and consequently to unsatisfied final customers. The main criticism is that these e-solutions lack sustainability, neglects long term strategies, and hinder the generation of synergies through cooperations. Basically, the businesses become opportunity driven.

In contrast, the virtual Web organization is a different and particular form of an e-business organization model with long-term prospects. Like other e-business models the virtual Web concept aims to improve the collaboration between independent economic actors. However, in addition it focuses on the fast and flexible configuration and operation of dynamic value chains. Similar to other new forms of organizations the main drivers of virtual Web organizations are customer orientation and globalization facilitated by the global spread of the Internet and efficient ICT applications. The main difference compared to traditional and other new forms of organizational arrangements is the different business understanding of the partnering virtual Web member firms. On the one hand, the tendency towards concentrating on core competencies has been resulting in the fact that individual companies cover smaller parts of the total value creation process. This tendency increases the need of companies to be included in many different value chains in order to market and exploit their specialization and core competencies. On the other hand, this development increases the dependency on other, more powerful value chain partners, as well as the need to coordinate the activities along the supply chain. The different business understanding of virtual Web partner firms is integration and cooperation with other partner firms in dynamically formed and temporally operated virtual corporations. Basically, it is the openness of partner firms for 'real' cooperation, which means the preparedness of partner firms to share costs, risks, benefits and profits. The competitive advantage of such interorganizational virtual organizations (virtual corporations/virtual enterprises) is the dynamic and flexible configurations of (world-class) value chains.

However, the major concerns of partnering companies are how to find suitable partner companies with complementary (core-) competencies, how to establish a trust-based partnership in a very short period of time and how to coordinate the activities of the geographically and organizationally dispersed independent partner companies.

The virtual Web organization, as an e-business organization model, provides an organizational framework that facilitates the coordination and cooperation between virtually partnering companies. Basically, the virtual Web concept incorporates three sub-concepts: the virtual Web platform, the virtual corporation, and the Net-broker.

First, the virtual Web platform is a pool of independent companies that generally agree to cooperate. This virtual Web platform provides the environmental condition, such as trust and coordination mechanisms and tools, necessary for the dynamic configuration of market and customer-driven value chain constellations.

Thus, deriving from the rather stable virtual Web platform, virtual corporations are temporary operational units that are configured on market opportunities and/or customer needs. Moreover, virtual corporations are characterized not by close but integrated cooperation between independent and dispersed partner firms. Virtual corporations can take the form of supply chains, joint R&D projects and any other form of vertical or horizontal partner cooperation. Both the relatively stable virtual Web platform and the dynamic virtual corporations are integrated and constitute the virtual Web organization.

The third organizational element of the virtual Web concept is the management organization, the so-called net-broker (management service company) that acts as a inter-firm network facilitator. Basically, the net-broker initiates the virtual Web platform, maintains the relationships between the Web partner companies and facilitates the formation of market and customer driven temporary virtual corporations. Modern interorganizational ICT applications and a common business understanding of partnering companies facilitate the collaboration between the virtual Web partner firms.

This book and its individual chapters aim to provide readers with a better understanding of this new kind of e-business organization concept. Thus, this book deals with issues and challenges of managing virtual Web organizations. Besides introducing the organizational concept of virtual Web organizations, the individual chapters provide theoretical background, practical examples and guidance on how to manage virtual Web organizations. The different book contributions view and investigate the virtual Web organization from different managerial perspectives, identify issues and challenges about the management of the stable virtual Web platform and, in particular, the deriving dynamic virtual corporations (virtual enterprises) as well as introduce management models, concepts and tools that are suitable to operationalise virtual Web organizations. In general, this book can be regarded as a handbook – guidance for the management of a new kind of b2b e-business organization, namely the virtual Web organization.

The first part of this book reviews the particular challenges in respect to managing virtual Web organizations and proposes possible solutions on how to tackle those challenges by applying a number of distinct managerial models, concepts and tools developed to facilitate the management of dispersed and independent partner firms in virtual space and real day-to-day business performance.

The first chapter of this book introduces the organizational concept of virtual Web organizations that encompasses three organizational elements, namely the relatively stable virtual Web platform from which dynamic virtual corporations derive. The third element of this organizational construct is the management organization that initiates and maintains the stable virtual Web platform as well as forms and facilitates the operation of dynamic virtual corporations. In order to provide readers with a better understanding of how virtual Web organizations are managed, the author introduces a competence-based management model of virtual Web management organizations. Based on empirical research across six different virtual Web organizations this competence-based model provides an overview of a set of competencies virtual Web management organizations employ to initiate and manage stable virtual Web platforms and facilitate the dynamic formation of temporary virtual corporations.

In Chapter Two, Malcolm Warner and Morgen Witzel argue that interorganizational virtual organizations are a powerful strategic option for firms attempting to extend the scope and reach of their operations. However, physical dispersal of organizations brings with it many associated problems of management and control. The authors argue that management in virtual organizations still requires attention to the fundamentals of management. 'Going virtual' should be seen as a strategic option which requires firms to achieve the optimal mix of physical and virtual elements and systems. In particular, they argue that a mastery of the skills of knowledge management is necessary in order to manage virtual systems and structures and if firms fail to develop these skills they will run significant risks when taking the virtual option.

Chapter Three deals with one of the key challenges in virtual organizations, namely, trust between the dispersed and independent partner firms. The authors regard virtual corporations as new organizational forms to ensure knowledge sharing and innovation. They argue that in virtual corporations a shared identity and mutual trust between participating partners are of paramount importance to innovation. Virtual corporations are in fact balancing on a tightrope. They have to create an identity which is strong enough for the participants to trust each other. At the same time the identity shared by the participants of the virtual corporation must not become so strong that very promising innovative avenues are blocked. Besides the development of knowledge-creating competencies, the authors place emphasis on information and communication technology (ICT) that will fulfil an important function aiming to support the social relations between virtual corporation participants.

Chapter Four outlines some of the constraining forces and suggests the parameters in which a business strategy and a course of action can be devised as a pathway to the future. Richards and Makatsoris note that a process of turbulent change is taking place in which companies shape up to deal with the unremitting global competition for which there is an uncertain outcome. Businesses have to look at the wider horizons and dynamics of both their supply chains and markets to discover new ways of working with both customers and suppliers to grow and remain viable. The authors state that a number of opportunities exist to advance a business to dynamic trading networks and also market to virtual corporations. The future path is cut according to business strategic goals and on the ability to determine the right course of action by a strong capable leadership. Strategy can change at any time to set a company on the right path with respect to its business partners in dynamic supply chains and eMarkets. It will be essential for short term stepwise actions to ensure company benefits that progress toward a larger landscape for business with an ability to deal with the real dynamic world in synchrony with the supply chain and market need. The authors conclude that ultimately all companies will strive to be part of dynamic trading networks and/or virtual corporations.

In Chapter Five, Chandrashekar and Schary constitute that the virtual Web-based supply chain is emerging as a new form of industrial organization. Their contribution discusses the concept as a juncture of three forces: the virtual organization, Web-based communication and the application service provider (ASP). They state that the virtual organization is a familiar concept in many industries and that Web-based communication provides access and networks with new institutions. The third element is the ASP, which makes rapid change and flexible connections feasible. Together they establish focus, flexibility and rapid response to change in demand and customer requirements. Therefore, by casting this in a strategic framework of structure, process and organization, it provides a basis for projecting the future.

Wade, Lewis, Brook and Donnelly state that a key element in successful e-Commerce / e-Business operation is the improved integration and management of the e-Business value chains, such as the management of Business-to-Customer (B2C) and Business-to-Business (B2B) chains. In chapter six they criticize that current e-Business managed solutions tend to concentrate on only single aspects of the e-Business integration, e.g., outsourced accounting management or virtual private network (VPN) services. Thus, the authors advocate that e-Business organizations of the future will require a more holistic, integrated approach to e-Business management networks. Such e-Business services would support integrated management solutions across the B2C and B2B value chain. Therefore, this contribution proposes a management component framework to support the rapid and flexible construction of an e-Commerce management infrastructure. This management solution is based on a holistic management approach supporting seamless integration of network and application management services (i.e., vertical), as well as integrating management across distinct functional areas (i.e., horizontal). Furthermore, this contribution presents an analysis of the business model for a provider of such B2B and B2C management and examines the requirements for such management services.

In Chapter Seven, Selz and Klein investigate 'Value Webs'. They argue that the new information infrastructure redefines the roles and relationships between buyer, seller, and middleman, allowing new ways of accessing and tapping information and price arrangements. Most importantly, information about a product or service may be separated from the product or service itself. Thus, their contribution scrutinizes how companies are using these opportunities to establish networked retail businesses and generate customer value in innovative ways. The authors have reconstructed widespread interorganizational arrangements for product and service retailing on the Web, its antecedents, its challenges and its economic logic.

In his contribution, Hugo Meijers introduces a specific type of Web organization in the professional service sector. Due to the knowledge-intensive, project-based and service-centric characteristics, the professional service sector acts as a prime example of this possible new organization model. Chapter Eight provides a general overview of all system elements such a Web organization is based on. This contribution is based on theoretical models, practical experiences out of three cases, as well as the personal involvement of the author as business architect in the formation of Web organizations. The three case studies conducted are described in detail and the author identifies the major lessons learned from each case. The author concludes that whether such organizational structures can survive the complexity of fast-changing environments, cultural differences and general human nature will show the future. Many challenges lie ahead in developing Web organizations; its limitations are not yet clear. However, the first examples are promising.

The support of real collaborative 'Virtual Enterprise' (VE) scenarios sets forward particularly interesting challenges in terms of distributed information management, regarding the proper sharing and exchange of information among pre-existing autonomous enterprises. In order to address these challenges, it is necessary to achieve a comprehensive analysis of advanced information management approaches that can be applied in virtual enterprise platforms. In this context, the authors of chapter nine present a representative survey of several virtual enterprise-related information management standards, technologies, and existing approaches that can be applied to support future virtual enterprise infrastructures. This survey is useful for managers of enterprises that are considering joining virtual organizations, because it describes some of the crucial ICT management issues that will be faced by those companies. In addition this chapter also points out how these issues have been addressed by existing virtual enterprise in order to support platforms in a wide variety of application domains.

The second part of this book deals with special issues and possible solutions with respect to the management of virtual Web organizations. Therefore, each chapter places emphasis on particular virtual Web management issues and provides ideas and management approaches in order to ease the dynamic partnering process and to support the operation of temporal virtual corporations.

Chapter Ten seeks to reach a better understanding of the relationship between virtual organizations and international strategic alliances in manufacturing industry. In the consideration of international strategic alliances and virtual organisations, little attention has been paid to networks devoted to manufacturing and the implication of communication technologies for their structure and operations. Understanding the nature of manufacturing system operating in the emerging global and electronic commercial and communication environment is fundamental to understanding the implications of e-business for manufacturing worldwide. The authors identify the 'Global Manufacturing Virtual Network' (GMVN) as a specific class of manufacturing system and outline its characteristics and potentials. The potential of GMVNs is to enhance company's ability to dynamically generate and exploit competence and thus the authors suggest that the global manufacturing virtual network represents a new form of manufacturing system based on Internet interfirm collaborations.

Tononi and Amorosi present in chapter Eleven an Italian research program. This research program aims to support networks of small-medium sized enterprises (SMEs) in depressed regions of Italy. Their research focuses on experimentation with a business model for SME networks and introduces advanced tools and methods, such as concurrent engineering. The business model, developed within the program, has the basic features of virtual Web organizations. Thus, in this chapter the authors explain the organizational and functional model that has been defined in a framework of a cooperation between the researchers and the SMEs involved in the research program. The authors conclude that, despite the Internet usage, SMEs still prefer to network with others from the same geographical area. It is not a matter of geography but of culture and of sharing the same problems, such as (local) market trends or other (local) environmental problems. Initiatives by the local associations or authorities, aimed at solving shared problems, have proven to be very good enablers for virtual Web organizations consisting of SMEs.

In Chapter Twelve the authors state that the process of core competencies identification has been incorporated by enterprises in their strategic planning. The virtual enterprise, which is a form of cooperation between independent enterprises, is one of the most benefited with this new process, mainly in its formation stage. The identified core competencies, which are deployed in products, process and technology, may support a more agile gathering of the virtual enterprise partners. Chapter Twelve presents a method to identify core competencies, supported by a practical case of successful virtual enterprise formation, where the method was applied and validated.

Similar to Chapter Twelve, Chapter Thirteen focuses on the partner search and dynamic configuration of virtual enterprises (VEs). Vaggelis Ouzounis notes that VEs enable the deployment of distributed business processes among different partners in order to shorten development and manufacturing cycles, reduce time to market and operational costs, increase customer satisfaction, and operate on global scale and reach. Dynamic virtual enterprises are an emerging category of VE where the different partners are being selected dynamically during business process execution based on market-driven criteria and negotiation. Thus, in this chapter the author presents an agent-based platform for the management of dynamic VE. The main contributions of these approaches are the distributed, autonomous agent-based business process management, the XML-based business process definition language, the flexible ontologies, and the dynamic negotiation and selection of partners based on virtual marketplaces. The presented platform has been fully developed using emerging agent and Internet standards like FIPA, MASIF, and XML.

Having selected the suitable virtual enterprise partner firms, Florent Frederix introduces a planning and scheduling methodology for the operation of virtual enterprise. In Chapter Fourteen the author notes that virtual enterprises consisting of geographically dispersed, independent units are a reality in the global economy. These units concentrate on core technologies and create partner networks for the design, manufacturing and sales of their products. Thus, this chapter presents a methodology, more flexible and efficient than the more traditional techniques, to schedule activities in virtual enterprises and enterprise networks. The presented technique that stepwise searches for improved activity schedules has the advantage that in any stage of the iteration process a resource-feasible schedule is available. Investing in network and computation capacity results in more efficient schedules. The virtual enterprise units view the platform as a time phased capacity trading marketplace.

Veil and Hess introduce a basic approach towards cost accounting for virtual Web organizations in Chapter Fifteen. Virtual Web organizations as well as traditional companies require a cost accounting system in order to guarantee the organization's competitiveness in markets. Their contribution outlines the design of a cost accounting system for the management of virtual Web organizations based on cost accounting theory and the cost accounting practice of virtual Web organizations. Specific methods for transfer pricing and order pricing for virtual corporations are shown and discussed. In addition, to assure accurate order pricing decisions, a coordination-cost rate analysis is presented.

Another important issue regarding the management of virtual Web organizations is to evaluate the success of deriving dynamic virtual corporations. Wohlgemuth and Hess state that a fundamental condition precedent to strategic decisions of virtual corporations and their partners is a profound knowledge of the cooperation's success. Thus, in Chapter Sixteen the authors discuss different evaluation methods and elaborate a specific technique for multidimensional appraisals of success. The authors introduce the CONECT-procedure as a specific kind of benefit value analysis that has been adopted in a pilot project with satisfactory results. With this method both the evaluations of the partners and the consolidated assessments of virtual corporations can be ascertained with little expense in installation and transaction. Simultaneously, the procedure allows very sophisticated analysis possibilities through the inclusion of both the main examination levels. The "benefit" of CONECT is the possibility of recognizing early existing dissatisfaction of partners and with that to avoid related costs for the cooperation, like passive or destructive behavior as far as to the withdrawal of the partner.

Claudia Cevenini tackles a different management issue about interorganizational virtual organizations. From a legal point of view she argues that virtual organizations are a complex subject, which requires an interdisciplinary approach. In the absence of a specific legislation, consolidated doctrine and case law, jurists can resort to three main cornerstones: agreements between members and with third parties, analogical application of laws in force, informal rules and trade usage. She proposes that the preliminary step is to define the object of analysis as clearly as possible by building a model definition of 'Virtual Organizations' for the legal research. On the basis of the model's features, the most relevant legal issues are outlined in Chapter Seventeen.

At present, due to the very nature of VOs, no definitive legal solutions are possible. However, this chapter provides some basic indications in order to enable potential and affected partners of VOs and other readers to reach a better understanding of the legal issues and implications in regard to their activities in virtual organizations.

The editor would like to thank all of the authors for their insights and excellent contributions to this book. Most of the authors of chapters included in this book also served as referees for articles written by other authors. Thanks go to all those who provided constructive and comprehensive reviews. In particular, I would like to acknowledge the help of my colleges Jennifer Abley, Joe Peppard, Paul Chapman, Chris Morgan and Otto Jockel at Cranfield School of Management in providing critical and constructive reviews on submitted chapters. A further special note of thanks goes also to all the staff at Idea Group Publishing, whose contributions throughout the whole process from inception of the initial idea to final publication have been invaluable.

Ulrich J. Franke, PhD
Cranfield, Bedfordshire, UK
June 2001

Section I

Virtual Web Management Challenges: What Are The Challenges of Managing Virtual Web Organizations and How Can Those Challenges Be Tackled?

Chapter I

The Competence-Based View on the Management of Virtual Web Organizations

Ulrich J. Franke
Cranfield University, UK

The organizational concept of virtual Web organizations encompasses three organizational elements, namely the relatively stable virtual Web platform from which dynamic virtual corporations derive. Virtual corporations are interorganizational adhocracies that are configured temporally of independent companies in order to serve a particular purpose, such as joint R&D, product development, and production. The third element of this organizational construct is the management organization that initiates and maintains the virtual Web platform as well as forms and facilitates the operation of dynamic virtual corporations. Since the organizational concept of virtual Web organizations is hardly researched this chapter aims to provide readers with a better understanding of the organizational concept of virtual Web organizations and in particular of how such an organizational construct is managed. Based on empirical research the author developed a competence-based management model of virtual Web management organizations. This competence-based view of virtual Web management organizations presents an overview of a set of common sub-competencies underlying the three virtual Web management's main competencies of initiating and maintaining virtual Web platforms and forming dynamic virtual corporations. Furthermore, the developed competence-based management model describes the content of the individual sub-competencies and it explains the purpose, the interrelateness and the temporal dimensions of the virtual Web management's sub-competencies.

INTRODUCTION

Since the early 1990s the concept of "virtual organizations," as a particular form of cooperative networks, has been introduced. Despite Mowshowitz (1986) using the term "virtual organization" in 1986 for the first time, the academic world paid little attention to this new organizational network approach. Only since Davidow and Malone published their book *The Virtual Corporation* in 1992 as well as the landmark *Business Week* article of Byrne in 1993 about virtual corporations was published, have academics around the world become interested in this topic.

Since them, the organizational concept of "virtual organization" has been researched and a number of real "virtual organizations" have been established in practice. However, many authors have created a variety of different terms and definitions to describe this new form of network organization that has caused confusion about the term "virtual organization" and its underlying organizational concept, i.e., terms such as virtual company (Goldman and Nagel, 1993), virtual enterprise (Hardwick et al., 1996), and virtual factory (Upton and McAfee, 1996). Moreover, most of the contributions in the literature of virtual organizations are conceptual and descriptive and some authors even tend to advocate the concept of virtual organizations in a rather idealistic and speculative way.

Basically, one can constitute that the "virtual organization" is a partnership network enabled and facilitated by modern information and communication technology (ICT). The term "virtual" originates from the Latin word "virtus" which basically means "proficiency, manliness" (Scholz, 1994), it defines an attribute of a thing, which is not really existing, but would have the possibility to exist (Scholz, 1996). What does that mean in the context of organizations? Scholz (1997) distinguishes the virtual organization into an intra-organizational and inter-organizational perspective.

Whereby the intra-organizational perspective on virtual organizations refers to a particular form of organization within defined boundaries of a firm (hierarchy), the inter-organizational perspective is about the exchange of resources between firms. The inter-organizational perspective is divided into virtual markets (market transactions) and virtual corporations (transaction through networking). Virtual markets mean e-commerce market transactions between actors using sophisticated ICT, i.e., the Internet. In contrast, virtual corporations are basically partnership networks of independent companies.

Thus, Byrne (1993) defines the virtual corporation as follows: *A Virtual Corporation is a temporary network of independent companies–suppliers, customers, and even rivals–linked by information technology to share skills, costs, and access to one another's markets. This corporate model is fluid and flexible–a group of collaborators that quickly unite to exploit a specific opportunity. Once the opportunity is met, the venture will, more often than not, disband. In the concept's purest form, each company that links up with others to create a virtual corporation contributes only what it regards as its core competencies.*

Technology plays a central role in the development of the virtual corporation. Teams of people in different companies work together, concurrently rather than sequentially, via computer networks in real time (pp. 36-37).

Having a closer look at this definition, it basically means that independent actors, such as companies, are allocated on short-term notice and contribute their best (core competencies) to a partnership of strangers. Furthermore, the constant alternation of the value chain configuration does certainly not improve the level of trust between the acting partners and the willingness to share their knowledge and resources to be exploited by others. In theory, it sounds perfect to switch between the best in class, to constantly alternate the value chain as needed, and to design the perfect value chain to achieve the common goals. But, who is "common;" who carries the benefits away? Is this totally free system of assignment and reassignment of companies to tasks feasible; is it realistic if one considers that each company can be out of the game any time? Does a company contribute its best to a partnership in such an uncertain and turbulent environment? It seems to be fairly obvious that this would not be the case. Hence, the following four fundamental key difficulties have to be addressed in respect to the organizational concept of virtual corporations.

- The search for suitable partner companies that keep the complementary core competencies in order to design a successful value chain.
- The organizational fit of the selected partner companies, technologically and sociologically.
- The necessary level of trust between the partner companies in order to accelerate the partnering process, to shorten the time to market process and to reduce transaction costs.
- The needs for cooperation management in order to coordinate the activities of the dispersed partner companies and to build trustworthy relationships between the partnering companies.

Therefore, Goldman et al. (1995) proposes the organizational concept of "virtual Webs." They define the "Web" as an open-ended collection of pre-qualified partners that agree to form a pool of potential members of virtual corporations. The success of the virtual organization model is tied to the ability of "real" companies to form virtual organizations rapidly to meet an emerging time-based opportunity. The ability to work intensively with other organizations and to be able to trust them from the start of the project is enhanced by prequalification agreements based on company attributes and contractual commitments (Goldman et al., 1995). Basically, the virtual Web organization consists of three organizational elements. First, the virtual Web platform is a pool of independent companies that have agreed to cooperate. This virtual Web platform is a rather stable company network from which dynamically virtual corporations derive. Virtual corporations are inter-organizational adhocracies that are configured temporally of independent companies in order to serve a purpose, such as joint R&D, product development, and production. The third element of this organizational construct is the management organization that initiates and maintains the virtual Web platform as well as forms and facilitates the operation of dynamic virtual corporations.

Since the organizational concept of virtual Web organizations is hardly researched this chapter aims to provide readers with a better understanding of the organizational concept of virtual Web organizations. In particular, this chapter introduces a competence-based view on the management of virtual Web organization. Thus, the author introduces a competence-based management model of virtual Web organizations that has been derived from empirical research. However, first this chapter reviews the organizational concept of virtual Web organizations (VWO); it briefly outlines the theoretical approach of the competence-based view and presents the research methods that were used for the development of the competence-based management model of VWOs. The chapter concludes with a brief discussion about the introduced competence-based management model and its implications on the establishment of virtual Web organizations in practice.

THE ORGANIZATIONAL CONCEPT OF VWOS

Goldman et al. (1995) define the virtual Web platform as an open-ended collection of pre-qualified partners that agree to form a pool of potential partner companies for the formation of virtual corporations. They state, one can imagine organizing a large number of supplier companies into a resource pool from which to draw the number of companies, and the kind of companies, that would be required to provide comprehensive customer services in any industry and that would compete directly with the largest single companies in that industry (Goldman et al., 1995).

Klüber (1997) proposes a two-level model of abstraction to distinguish the virtual Web platform from virtual corporations. The virtual Web platform is basically regarded as the organizational framework on a macro-organizational level, whereby virtual corporations are the actual performing units on the micro-organizational level. On the macro organizational level the virtual Web platform is the institutional framework of companies and their resources, which facilitates the formation of virtual corporations according to market needs. Therefore, it is proposed that the organizational concept of virtual Web organizations consists of three organizational elements. First, the virtual Web platform is a relatively stable network, it can be compared with a resource, capability, and core competence warehouse from which the necessary items are employed to meet customer expectations and market opportunities. Second, a virtual Web management organization (net-broker organization) manages the virtual Web platform and the formation of virtual corporations. The third organizational element is dynamic networks, virtual corporations that derive from the pool of independent companies, which are consolidated on the virtual Web platform. Figure 1 illustrates the concept of virtual Web organizations and its three interrelated organizational elements.

The Virtual Web Platform

In general, one can state that the main purpose of the virtual Web platform is to facilitate the formation of virtual corporations. Therefore, the virtual Web

Figure 1: The virtual Web organization, Franke and Hickmann (1999)

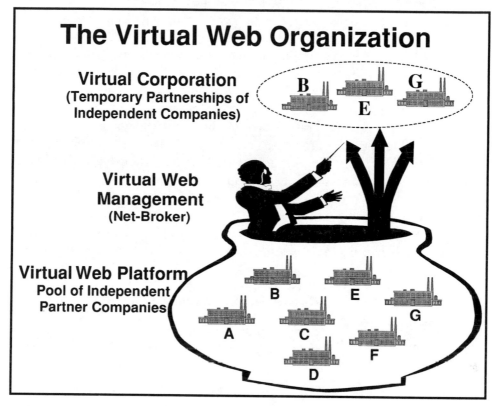

platform is regarded as a relatively stable company network that aims to provide a cooperative environment for its partner companies. The focus of the virtual Web platform is to prepare the conditions for the coordination of virtual corporations, such as to define the flow of information and to agree on coordination mechanisms. In addition, the virtual Web platform is supposed to provide the environment in which trust between partner firms can develop. In general, the virtual Web platform fertilizes the development of cooperation and cooperative behavior of partner firms and their individual employees.

The Virtual Web Management Organization

In the academic literature this central management function of virtual corporations has been interchangeably named as broker, net-broker (Franke, 1999, 2000a) or network broker (Hatch, 1995), network coach (Schuh, 1998), information broker (Upton and McAfee, 1996), network intermediaries (Perry, 1996), and the virtual general manager (Warner and Witzel, 1999). For the purpose of this chapter this central management function is interchangeably named as "net-broker" or the "virtual Web management organization." However, Reiß (1997) assumes that the foremost role of the net-broker of a virtual Web organization is primarily the management of synergy. Hatch (1995) defines the net-broker as a facilitator and catalyst. Net-brokers help companies to form strategic partnerships, organize network activities and identify new business opportunities. Their task is to spread the network concepts, promote cooperation, organize groups of firms, and connect them to the product designers, marketing specialists, training providers, and industry service programs they need to compete successfully. Karnet and Faisst (1997) propose that the net-broker is also the primary point of contact for the customer. The net-broker proposes a suitable virtual corporation configuration and monitors their performance. They suggest that during the operation of a virtual corporation the net-broker acts as moderator and helps resolve possible conflict between partner companies. In respect to virtual Web organizations the management, the net-broker organization, does not only focus on the formation of virtual corporations, but also manages the virtual Web platform. Therefore, the virtual Web management organization takes care of the cooperation management on the stable virtual Web platform and facilitates the formation of dynamic virtual corporations.

The rather normative statements regarding the management of virtual Web organizations (net-brokers) indicate that the view on net-broker organizations is merely based on assumptions rather than on empirical research. Therefore, this chapter presents the competence-based view on the management of virtual Web organizations that is grounded in empirical research.

The Deriving Virtual Corporations

Basically, virtual corporations are temporary partnerships of independent actors, such as individuals, companies, research institutes, etc. The major difference between totally free configured virtual corporations and virtual corporations deriving from virtual Web platforms is that partner firms have established a pre-partnership relationship prior to working together for the first time. Thus, the virtual Web platform can be viewed as a hub of potential partner firms that are selected according to an actual need in order to carry out a given task on a temporary basis. In general, such virtual corporations are value-added partnerships of independent virtual Web partner firms, but depending on their purpose and given circumstances, such deriving virtual corporations also might integrate customers and external suppliers into the temporary value-adding partnership. Figure 2 illustrates a virtual Web organization, the virtual Web platform and its partner firms that form virtual corporations and integrate customers and virtual Web external suppliers.

Furthermore, virtual Web partner companies can be involved in more than one virtual corporation at the same time. However, as soon as the joint project is completed or the customer orders are executed the virtual corporation disbands and the individual partner firms fall back into the pool of companies consolidated on the virtual Web platform. Virtual corporations are value-added partnerships, which can either comprise the vertical or horizontal value chain, or both (Franke, 2000b). In

Figure 2: The virtual Web organization, Franke (1998)

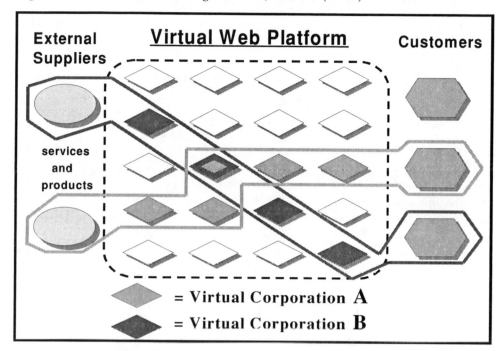

addition, virtual corporations are expected not to be limited to a particular sector or industry. Virtual corporations can be formatted from the service or manufacturing sector, or mix, the partner firms can originate from one and the same industry or partner firms from different industries join their forces. Nevertheless, the direction of virtual corporations might depend on the vision and mission of the virtual Web organization, which means it depends on the kind of companies that are aggregated on the virtual Web platform. Furthermore, it is suggested that besides joint manufacturing or the joint provision of services, the purpose of virtual corporations can also be joint R&D and innovation project (Bund, 1997) or joint learning and education partnerships (Stuart et al., 1998).

In summary, the virtual Web organization and its organizational concept can be defined as follows:

> The organizational concept of "virtual Web organizations" encompasses three interrelated organizational elements, namely the virtual Web platform, the virtual Web management and virtual corporations. The virtual Web platform is a stable company network of pre-qualified independent partner firms that have generally agreed to cooperate in virtual corporations. The virtual Web platform establishes a cooperative environment and prepares the conditions for the formation and operation of dynamic virtual corporations. The management of virtual Web organizations takes care of the cooperation management on the virtual Web platform and facilitates the formation and operation of virtual corporations.

THE COMPETENCE-BASED VIEW

The idea of looking at firms as a broader set of resources goes back to the seminal work of Penrose (1959). She argues that a firm is more than an administrative unit; it is also a collection of productive resources, the disposal of which between different uses and over time is determined by administrative decisions. The essence of the resource-based view of a firm is not to see the firm as a portfolio of products, i.e., Daimler-Chrysler and its product range of cars, trucks and buses. The resource-based theory identifies the firm as a pool of resources, capabilities and competencies needed to accomplish a task, i.e., physical products or intangible services.

The "Resource-Based Theory" literature is mainly divided into two different streams, one group of researchers are concerned with the internal and external resources of a firm, the economic perspective of market, hierarchies and networks, or the different implications of transaction cost theory. The other group of researchers emphasize how to make the best use of the available resources, i.e., core competence theory (Prahalad and Hamel, 1990), asset stock accumulation and sustainability of competitive advantage (Dierickx and Cool, 1989), or the relationship between the firm's resource base and competitive advantage (Grant, 1991).

For the purpose of this chapter the resource-based theory is used as an analytical framework in order to describe the tasks and duties virtual Web management organizations perform. Grant (1991) states that resources and capabilities are the input to a transformation process. On its own, only a few resources and capabilities are productive. To be productive as a team of inputs they need cooperation and coordination. Competencies are the capacity for a team of resources and capabilities to perform some task or activity. In simple terms, competencies are the combination of capabilities and resources. Therefore, a competence is the capacity of combining and coordinating resources and capabilities in a way that it leads to a desired outcome.

To build competencies is not simply a matter of pooling resources; competencies involve complex patterns of coordination between people, knowledge and other resources. To understand the anatomy of a firm's competencies, Nelson and Winter's (1982) concept of "organizational routines" is illuminating. Organizational routines are regular and predictable patterns of activity, which are made up of a sequence of coordinated actions by individuals. Thus, a competence is, in essence, a routine, or a number of interacting routines (Grant, 1991). Furthermore, Grant (1991) states that organizations themselves are a huge network of routines. This statement implies that firms' competencies are employed within a network of many competencies and that the competencies interrelate to each other.

Thus, the competence-based view on virtual Web management organizations portrays the organizational routines, the tasks and duties performed by virtual Web management organizations into order to manage VWOs.

THE RESEARCH METHOD

The competence-based management model of virtual Web management organizations presented in this chapter is based on six case studies conducted about virtual Web organizations and their management. The qualitative data collection contained semi-structured interviews with manager of virtual Web management organizations as well as virtual Web partner firms. The authors conducted more than 40 interviews as well as spent more than six months with a management organization of a virtual Web organization (participant observation case study). Based on the empirical data the author conducted a number of cross-case analyses and constructed the competence-based management model presented in this chapter.

THE COMPETENCE-BASED FRAMEWORK OF VIRTUAL WEB MANAGEMENT ORGANIZATIONS

Besides a theoretical and analytical framework (the competence-based view), the author developed a conceptual competence-based framework for the research project as well. Grant (1991) states that a firm (organization) consists of a network of competencies. Such a competencies network can be structure in main compctencies, sub-competencies and so on. Thus, this conceptual–competence-based framework aims to predetermine the main competencies in order to facilitate the investigation of the underlying level of sub-competencies. The three identified main net-broker competencies derived deductively from the literature review on virtual Web organizations. Thus, the predetermined conceptual framework of main virtual Web managements' competencies provided an initial structure for the empirical field research, data analysis, and the competence-based management model building process. Figure 3 illustrates the developed conceptual framework. The presentation of the competence-based management model of virtual Web management organizations follows this section.

- **Initiation** of the virtual Web platform. The purpose of this main competence is the ability to perform the process of establishing a stable network organization of independent companies. The performance of the initiation competence lays the foundation for the succeeding operation of the virtual Web organization, the maintenance and formation competencies.
- **Maintenance** of the virtual Web platform. This net-broker's competence enables the net-broker to maintain the stable virtual Web platform consisting of independent partner firms. Thus this competence keeps the independent partner companies together and is concerned with the further development of the virtual Web organization. In general, the net-brokers' maintenance competence manages the virtual Web platform and prepares the ground for the dynamic formation of temporary virtual corporations.

Figure 3: Main competencies of virtual Web management organizations

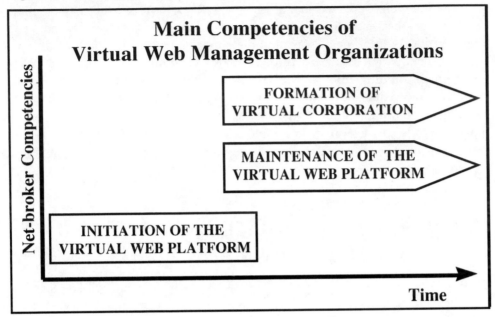

- **Formation** of virtual corporations. The purpose of this net-broker's competence is the ability to form and operate virtual corporations, which are timely or purposely limited partnerships of independent virtual Web partner companies. Based on the literature, the net-broker allocates a purpose for the formation of virtual corporations, whether it is a market opportunity, a customer inquiry, or an opportunity to conduct joint R&D. The net-brokers' main task is to configure a virtual corporation that is based on the virtual Web partners' resource-bases in order to match the allocated opportunity.

THE COMPETENCE-BASED VIEW ON VIRTUAL WEB MANAGEMENT ORGANIZATIONS

Based on the empirical data collected, the author conducted a series of cross-case analyses. The result of the research work is a set of 21 sub-competencies commonly employed by virtual Web management organizations. These sub-competencies support the performance of the three main competencies identified, namely the initiation of virtual Web platforms, the maintenance of virtual Web platforms and the formation and operation of dynamic virtual corporations. In addition, the author identified the temporal dimensions of the sub-competencies employed by virtual Web organizations. Figure 4 illustrates the set of 21 sub-competencies underlying the three main competencies employed by virtual Web management organizations. Additionally, Figure 4 indicates the temporal employment of the individual sub-competencies on an imaginary timescale. This temporal bracketing of virtual Web management organizations' sub-competencies portrays the point of time, the sequence and the duration of sub-competencies employed by virtual Web management organizations.

The following description of each individual sub-competence explains the content and the purpose of each sub-competence. Furthermore, it summarizes the set of sub-competencies underlying each main competence using the predetermined structure of the conceptual competence-based framework introduced in the previous section. The summary of each main competence employed by virtual Web management organizations also states the interrelation between the individual sub-competencies as well as the interrelation between the three main competencies.

Initiating Sub-Competence: Market Research and Business Plan

This sub-competence entails the ability of the VWO management organizations / initiators to conduct market research and to develop a business plan. For the market research the VWO initiators search for information about the markets (national and/ or international), market potentials, competitors, and customers. Furthermore, this sub-competence includes the ability to conduct a structure analysis about the industry, the business field in which the future VWO should be established. In addition, VWO initiators carry out a feasibility study, an assessment which is supposed to indicate the possibility to establish a VWO in the identified business field. Based on this market research information the VWO initiators develop a business plan, which determines the strategic planning of setting up a VWO, the future operation of the VWO as well as defining business and marketing goals. The purpose of the VWO business plan is to guide the establishment and later operation of the VWO.

Initiating Sub-Competence: Development of Organizational Concept

This sub-competence is about the ability of VWO initiators to design an organization concept that is feasible and practical so that it can be operationalized through the participation of partner firms. Thus, this sub-competence is concerned with the design of a new VWO organizational concept and / or the modification of an already existing VWO concept. The VWO initiators have to consider the particular circumstances and the environmental conditions of the emerging VWO. The developed VWO concept describes, for instance, the defined organizational structure, conditions (rules and regulations), and the planned operation of the stable virtual Web platform, the virtual Web management organization as well as the deriving dynamic virtual corporations. This sub-competence serves several purposes. One purpose of developing a new VWO concept or adjusting an existing VWO concept to the particular circumstances is to have guidance for the initiation

Figure 4: Temporal Bracketing of Virtual Web Management Organization's Sub-Competencies

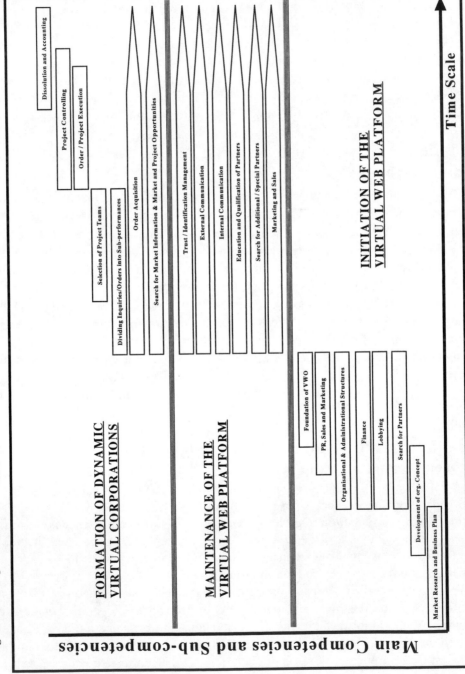

and a blueprint for the operation of the emerging VWO. The second purpose of the organizational concept is to present it to possible partner firms and to convince them to participate in new VWOs. Furthermore, the developed organizational concept can be used to convince private or public investors to provide financial resources for the initiation and operation of VWOs and/or to gain support of different stakeholder groups (lobbying).

Initiating Sub-Competence: Search for Partners

This sub-competence entails the VWO initiators' ability to attract, select, discuss and convince potential partner firms to join the VWO. The sub-competency "search for partners" consists of a number of different tools. First, the VWO initiators define a group of companies they seek to attract. For the selection of partner firms they determined criteria, such as particular industries, geographical limitations, or particular qualification criteria. Secondly, they present the organizational concept and other possible advantages to potential partner firms at information events/workshops or through other media, such as newspapers, journals, or sending out information material to potential partner firms. In addition, they contact potential partner firms directly by telephone or through personal contacts. Thirdly, the VWO initiators get in a personal contact with the candidates, and try to persuade them to join the VWO. Furthermore, the VWO initiators assess the candidates and decide whether the candidates are admitted to become a partner firm of the VWO. The main reason for VWO initiators to employ this sub-competence is to find suitable partner companies that are willing to cooperate with other firms in temporary partnerships. Thus, they search for and select partner firms with similar interests, such as firms from a similar or the same industry, which are willing to contribute their competencies, whether they are similar or complementary, to temporary partnerships, i.e., value-added partnerships, or joint R&D project teams. The purpose of applying qualification criteria for the assessment of candidates is to secure a certain quality standard on the virtual Web platform as well as to admit companies to the virtual Web platform that have the ability to cooperate with other firms. However, the overall aim of this sub-competence is to collect a pool of partner firms on the virtual Web platform from which dynamic virtual corporations can derive.

Initiating Sub-Competence: Lobbying

This sub-competence entails the ability of the VWO initiators to communicate and to convince key persons of stakeholder groups about the VWO concept and visions. Therefore, they present, advertise and convince different stakeholder groups, such as politicians, ministries, industry and trade associations, and chambers of commerce, about the concept and visions of the new VWO. They use different communication channels to stakeholder groups, i.e., meetings and events to present their VWO concept, press conferences and press releases, and in particular, personal meetings with opinion makers in industry and politics. The main objective of this sub-competence is to receive support and 'goodwill' from the different stakeholder groups. This support and/or goodwill is supposed to help with obtaining public funding, implementing long-term relationships with key persons, as well as supporting the credibility of the new VWO in order to ease the search for partners and to establish customer relationships.

Initiating Sub-Competence: Finance

Basically, this sub-competence concerns the ability of the VWO management to obtain and administrate financial resources for the initiation and maintenance of the virtual Web platform. There are a variety of different financing possibilities. For example, the VWO initiators can obtain their venture capital by selling shares to their partner firms and cover the operation costs during the maintenance phase through commissions for executed orders. Another possibility is to obtain public funding and/or to generate income through membership fees partner companies pay to the VWO association. Therefore, the VWO initiators calculate the financial needs of the VWO and determine the yearly membership fees. Besides obtaining financial resources, this sub-competence also involves the ability to make financial plans for the expenditures of the VWO, to develop VWO budgets and long-term financial strategies. The purpose of this sub-competence is to obtain the financial resources and to plan the VWO's financial requirements (budgets) during the initiation and maintenance phase. Such VWO budgets are needed to obtain financial resources such as public funding, membership fees, shareholder capital, and commissions on orders. These financial resources are required in order to cover the costs for providing partner firms with VWO services and, if necessary, to generate profits. Therefore, the overall purpose of this sub-competence is to plan the financial needs (budgeting) and to obtain the financial resources needed to operate the VWO.

Initiating Sub-Competence: Organizational and Administrative Structures

On the one hand, this sub-competence is concerned with implementing and setting up the virtual Web management organization and its infrastructure. Therefore, the VWO initiators search for suitable employees, and purchase, rent or lease infrastructure, such as office space, office furniture, computer hardware and software, telecommunication infrastructure, etc. On the other hand, this sub-competence is concerned with the development, adjustment and implementation of business processes, job descriptions, roles and responsibilities for the virtual Web management organization as well as for the maintenance of the virtual Web platform and the formation and operation of dynamic virtual corporations. The aim is to install an office infrastructure for the virtual Web management organization, as well as to define and implement VWO rules and regulations (processes, roles, responsibilities, etc.) for the management of the virtual Web platform and the deriving dynamic virtual corporations.

Initiating Sub-Competence: PR, Sales and Marketing

The VWO initiator's sub-competence "PR, sales and marketing" consists of performing a number of different activities, such as writing and publishing articles in the daily press and specialized journals and placing advertising campaigns in newspapers. Moreover, this sub-competence entails presenting the VWO at events and trade fairs, showing physical products of the VWO to customers, designing and developing corporate identity (branding), and organizing training for sales representatives of partner firms to enable them to sell VWO products and services. This sub-competence aims to make the emerging VWO known, to present and advertise their product range and to build up an image and reputation (branding) within the target markets and among stakeholder groups. In addition, the early sales activities aim to provide partner companies with a sense of achievement, which is basically supposed to keep or even to increase the level of motivation of partner firms to contribute to the further development of the VWO. Furthermore, the training provided to partners' sales personnel seeks to integrate partner firms into the VWO PR and marketing activities as well as to encourage them to sell the VWO product range, which is intended to be produced by deriving dynamic virtual corporations.

Initiating Sub-Competence: Foundation of VWO

This VWO initiator's sub-competence entails the ability to develop (together with partner firms) a legal framework for the VWO and to register the VWO as a legal entity. Whether the VWO is established as a non-profit organization or as a shareholding company, the VWO initiators (together with partner firms) develop and realize a legal framework for the VWO, such as defining a constitution for the VWO or a partnership agreement, and register the VWO as a legal entity officially. Furthermore, this sub-competence entails the ability to organize an official and formal foundation ceremony of the VWO. The foundation of a legal entity serves several purposes. First, it enables the VWO and its management organization, to do business officially, i.e., to sign contracts with customers and suppliers. Secondly, the VWO as a legal entity enables the VWO initiators to set up the net-broker organization, which means, for example, to rent office space, to lease cars, to invest in office equipment, and to employ a management team. Thirdly, the VWO as a legal entity provides the legal framework for the dynamic formation of temporary virtual corporations. Furthermore, the organization of a foundation ceremony serves as the initial general meeting of members, partners or shareholders in order to apply legal obligations, such as to agree on a constitution or a partnership agreement for the VWO and to elect an executive committee, a supervisory board and/or board members for the virtual Web management organization. Another purpose of the foundation ceremony is to demonstrate the official launch of the VWO. This can be communicated to the external environment (i.e., the press, stakeholder groups) and on the other hand, it is supposed to create a kind of partner's identification with the VWO. Moreover, it is also a social event where partner firms can meet in order to get in touch with each other and to make initial contacts.

Summary of Initiating Sub-Competencies

In summary, the main competence of 'initiating the virtual Web platform' entails the ability of VWO initiators to employ a number of different sub-competencies. The aggregation of the distinct individual sub-competencies aims to establish a virtual Web platform from which dynamic virtual corporations can be formed. Thus, the performance of the initiating sub-competencies lays the foundation for the subsequent maintenance of the virtual Web platform and consequently, for the deriving dynamic virtual corporations. The overall objective of the initiating sub-competencies is to create a stable interorganizational company network (virtual Web platform) that provides a suitable environment and favorable conditions for the dynamic formation of temporary virtual corporations. All individual sub-competencies employed by VWO initiators interrelate each other. Some sub-competencies need the completion, or at least partial completion, of other sub-competencies before they can be employed. Furthermore, some sub-competencies are sequential whereas some others, such as "search for partners," "lobbying," "finance," and "organizational and administrative structure," are employed in parallel (see also Figure 4). In general, one can conclude that all initiating sub-competencies are one-off sub-competencies, interrelating with each other, whereas their employment is partly sequential and partly parallel. The initiation phase of virtual Web platforms is completed with the legal foundation, marked by the foundation ceremony. Moreover, the set of sub-competencies employed during the initiation phase has a strong and direct impact on the succeeding maintenance phase of virtual Web platforms and the formation of dynamic virtual corporations.

Maintaining Sub-Competence: Marketing and Sales

This sub-competence concerns the ability of the virtual Web management organization to do marketing and sales of VWO products and services as well as to support the marketing activities of its partner firms. Thus, the virtual Web management organization has to be able to use a variety of different marketing tools, such as press and advertising campaigns, setting up a VWO homepage, design and development of information material (brochures), direct mailing, attending trade fairs and exhibitions, establishing contacts for partners to customers, designing a VWO logo (branding) and organizing events and presentations. Furthermore, this sub-competence entails the ability of VWO managements to motivate partner firms to do sales and marketing for the VWO. Thus, for example, virtual Web management organizations establish working groups together with partner firms that deal with the sales and marketing activities for VWO products and services. The aim is that the VWO becomes better known to improve its reputation, to inform externals about the VWO and to communicate its potentials. The ultimate purpose of this sub-competence is to sell VWO products and services which consequently leads to the formation and operation of dynamic virtual corporations.

Maintaining Sub-Competence: Search for Additional/Special Partners

Basically, the sub-competence "search for additional/special partners" employed during the maintenance phase by virtual Web management organizations is about the ability to attract additional partner firms, to assess them and to introduce them to the VWO and its partner firms. In general, one can distinguish between an active and passive partner search. Passive partner search basically means that companies contact the VWO management in order to become a member/partner firm. Active partner search means that the VWO management searches actively for new partner firms with particular attributes or distinct competencies. Thus, the virtual Web management organization determines attributes and competencies which are needed on the virtual Web platform. If the VWO managers have detected a suitable candidate they get in contact with this company and try to convince the company to become a partner firm. However, whether a candidate contacts the VWO management or is approached by it, the virtual Web management conducts a candidate assessment and seeks acceptance of the other partner firms, or the executive committee. Furthermore, new partner firms have to attend a seminar where they learn more about the VWO, its structure, rules and regulations. The objective of this sub-competence is to enlarge and to improve the scope and scale of the virtual Web platform with the final aim to improve the competitiveness of the VWO as a whole and its deriving virtual corporations. Furthermore, VWO managers search for new partner firms with specific, additional and complementary competencies in order to substitute partner firms which left the virtual Web platform. In its final consequence, this sub-competence improves the quality of the virtual Web platform and its available scope and scale as well as increases the possible number of combinations for the dynamic formation of virtual corporations.

Maintaining Sub-Competence: Education and Qualification of Partners

This sub-competence concerns the ability of virtual Web management organizations to analyze education and qualification needs of partner firms, to keep contact with universities and research institutes in order to keep updated regarding the latest developments, and to provide partner firms with education and qualification events. The virtual Web management organization might install a working group consisting of partner firms that analyze the need for training programs. Furthermore, this sub-competence consists of planning, organizing, moderating and conducting different kinds of education and qualification events, such as seminars about the VWO organizational structure and culture, seminars about the Internet and the VWO intranet, seminars for marketing and sales managers of partner firms, or seminar with special technical topics. Moreover, the VWO management team organizes so-called workshops in which interested partner companies meet, search for synergies and might initiate a consultant or R&D project. Another kind of event is regional group meetings, which are supposed to facilitate the exchange of information and experiences between partner firms but also where particular topics are presented and discussed. In addition, virtual Web management organizations might organize continuous training programs for partner firm's employees, such as a "business English seminars." The purpose of this sub-competence is to facilitate the cooperation between partner firms and to improve competitiveness of the individual partner firms and consequently of the VWO as a whole. Furthermore, this sub-competence aims to achieve synergies in the area of education and qualification and to develop ideas for the formation of new virtual corporations, i.e., joint R&D projects or value-added partnerships. Another aim is to make partner firms familiar with the VWO organization, its structures and culture, and to fertilize cooperation on the virtual Web platform and to accelerate the formation of virtual corporation.

Maintaining Sub-Competence: Internal Communication

In general, this sub-competence is about the distribution of information from the virtual Web management organization to the partners and the communication between VWO management and partner firms, but also between partner firms. In order to perform this sub-competence, virtual Web management organizations develop a number of communication tools. For example, the virtual Web management organizations maintain an Intranet from which partner firms can retrieve information about the VWO, present projects and project tenders, training and education events, a calendar, partner's profiles and competencies, and so on. Furthermore, the VWO management organizations send regular newsletters by e-mail or postal mail to their partner firms and inform them about VWO news. In addition, virtual Web management organizations organize regular partner meetings or work group meetings in which a smaller group of partner firms meet in order to exchange information and experiences. Besides the regular partner meetings in smaller groups, virtual Web management teams might also organize experience exchange meetings for all partner firms of the VWO every three months. Another tool to improve the communication between partner firms is that virtual Web management teams organize company tours, which means, that one partner company invites other VWO partners to visit its production facilities and learn more about the partner firm. In short, this sub-competence includes the ability to develop and maintain suitable communication tools, such as intranet, newsletters, partner meetings, company visits, etc. One purpose of this sub-competence is to keep all partner firms at the same level of information about the VWO and its activities to inform them about market news and opportunities, new technical possibilities and technical innovations, new project tenders, projects and orders. The second purpose is to establish trust and communication between the virtual Web management organization and the individual partner firms to exchange information, experiences, ideas, proposals and critique. The third purpose of this sub-competence is to establish trust and communication between partner firms in order to improve the cooperation on the virtual Web platform and the formation and operation of virtual corporations.

Maintaining Sub-Competence: External Communication

The sub-competence "external communication" describes the ability of virtual Web management organizations to establish communication and relationships with stakeholder groups other than customers. Virtual Web management teams maintain relationships with universities and other research institutions in order to keep themselves updated about the latest developments, but also to make use of the resources (i.e., expert knowledge for seminars and R&D projects) provided by external institutions. In addition, they establish and maintain relationships with stakeholder groups, such as other lobbying groups, institutions and associations, the press, politicians and financial institutions. The basic tools underlying this sub-competence are PR and lobbying activities as well as personnel contacts. Furthermore, virtual Web management organizations inform their partner firms about the external communication (lobbying) activities. In principle, virtual Web management organizations employ this sub-competence in order to pursue the VWO business goals, such as to do lobbying for their partner firms, to improve the conditions for their particular industries, to secure access to external knowledge, and to improve the virtual Web platform potentials and the competitiveness of deriving virtual corporations.

Maintaining Sub-Competence: Trust/Identification Management

The sub-competence "trust/identification management" concerns the ability of virtual Web management organizations to facilitate and to fertilize the development of trust among all VWO players as well as to achieve that partner firms identify themselves with the vision and mission of the VWO. On the one hand, this sub-competence consists of establishing an information and communication infrastructure that keeps partner firms updated and provides occasions for f2f (face-to-face) meetings, such as regular partner meetings and company visits. Furthermore, this sub-competence also includes joint activities on the virtual Web platform, such as working groups, workshops, and seminars. Another tool to facilitate the development of trust among the VWO players is a clear and transparent VWO concept as well as that partner firms understand and incorporate the VWO's visions and missions. Such a VWO concept defines roles and responsibilities, predetermines business processes, states a code of conduct and provides rules and regulations for the cooperation of partner firms on the virtual Web platform and deriving virtual corporations. Furthermore, this sub-competence also includes the coaching of passive partner firms in order to integrate them into the VWO. The main purpose of this sub-competence is to create a trustworthy environment on the virtual Web platform from which dynamic virtual corporations can derive. Thus, the virtual Web management organization aims to establish a cooperative culture on the virtual Web platform by generating positive experiences partner firms gain through the cooperation with other partners by working together in working groups or other partner meetings. Hence, the objective of this sub-competence is to create the environmental conditions on the virtual Web platform in order to achieve competitive advantages through fast and flexible configuration and close and smooth cooperation in temporary virtual corporations.

Summary of Maintaining Sub-Competencies

The main competence of "maintaining the virtual Web platform" entails the ability of virtual Web management organizations to employ a number of different sub-competencies that aim to establish an environment from which dynamic virtual corporations can be formed. In general, one can distinguish the individually employed sub-competencies into two groups. One group of sub-competencies, such as "search for additional/special partners," "education and qualification of partners," "internal communication," and "trust and identification management" aim to maintain and improve the quality and potentials of the virtual Web platform as a whole and to fertilize the ability and willingness of partner firms to cooperate. On the other hand, the maintaining sub-competencies of "marketing and sales," and "external communication" aim to bridge the VWO towards the external environment. However, all maintaining sub-competencies focus on creating an environment and conditions for the dynamic formation and smooth operation of virtual corporations. The overall purpose of the maintaining sub-competencies employed by virtual Web management organizations is to improve the competitiveness of the individual partner firms for either their own and individual businesses, or, more importantly in respect to the VWO, for their participation in dynamic virtual corporations. In general, all virtual Web managements' maintaining sub-competencies are permanently employed during the maintenance phase of virtual Web platforms whereby some sub-competencies might fluctuate in their intensity depending on the need they are required at certain times. However, all six common maintaining sub-competencies identified are employed in parallel and interrelate with each other. The maintaining sub-competencies start with the completion of the initiation phase and continue until the VWO eventually disbands. In summary, all maintaining sub-competencies aim to maintain or improve the environmental conditions, whether internally or externally, with the objective to facilitate the formation and operation of dynamic virtual corporations.

Forming Sub-Competence: Search for Market Information & Market and Project Opportunities

This sub-competence entails the virtual Web management organization's ability to search for market information, such as market trends and opportunities, local and international tenders, information about political and other environmental changes, public support and subsidies for projects, and technical innovations, and to distribute it to its partner firms. Furthermore, this sub-competence also refers to the ability to detect possible cooperation projects or to develop cooperation ideas based on the information gathered, and to search and find partner companies, which are interested to participate in such joint cooperation projects. There are different ways to allocate VWO cooperation projects. For example, based on the observation of markets and customer contacts, the virtual Web management organization develops ideas for possible cooperation projects and presents those to partner firms. Another possibility is that external experts (i.e., consultants) submit project proposals to the virtual Web management and they decide whether to go ahead with the project proposals. A third possibility is that one or a group of partner firms submits an idea for a cooperation project. If required, the virtual Web management team assists to find other interested partner firms for joint cooperation projects.

Forming Sub-Competence: Order Acquisition

In principle, each partner firm is encouraged to sell VWO products and services. However, this sub-competence concerns the ability of the virtual Web management organization to acquire and analyze customer inquiries, to consult customers and develop customer solutions, to calculate the costs, and to prepare and present quotations to customers. Additionally, this sub-competence involves the ability to negotiate and complete contracts with customers. On the other hand, this sub-competence also refers to the ability of the virtual Web management organization to motivate and encourage partner firms to do sales for the VWO, as well as to employ external sales brokers. Whether partner companies, external sales brokers, or the virtual Web management organization itself acquires inquiries/orders and submits quotations, the purpose of this sub-competence performed by the virtual Web management organization is to complete contracts with customers in order to form and operate virtual corporations.

Forming Sub-Competence: Dividing Inquiries/Orders

This sub-competence refers to the ability of the virtual Web management organization to divide inquiries or orders into a set of different sub-services/sub-performances. These sub-services/sub-performance are then described individually in order to be sent as tenders to partner firms, which keep the required competencies. These partner firms are supposed to submit quotations according to the specifications of tenders sent out. For example, the virtual Web management organization places a tender on the VWO intranet and all partner firms are requested to submit offers for the part of the whole inquiry that they are able to perform. Another possibility is that the virtual Web management team contacts partner firms directly and requests them to submit a quotation. However, based on partners' quotations the virtual Web management organization prepares one quotation to the customer that includes all sub-services/sub-performances. If necessary, the partners' quotations are renegotiated. In addition, this sub-competence also includes the organization of seminars for partner firms regarding the kind of supply chain thinking that is needed to oversee the virtual Web potentials and therefore the sales of complete value chains configured from the pool of competencies available on the virtual Web platform. The purpose of this sub-competence is to make use of the virtual Web platform potentials and to allocate the dispersed potentials available on the virtual Web platform. By dividing complete inquiries/orders into separate performance areas the VWO aims to define smaller and more specialized work units that can be carried out by virtual Web specialists. The use of a tender system aims to allocate virtual Web potentials. The virtual Web management organization applies market mechanisms to the VWO in order to identify the best suitable and most economical partner firm for a particular suborder. However, the definite aim is that the aggregation of suborders, carried out by specialists, provides an economic and qualitative competitive advantage for virtual corporations compared to traditional companies and value chains.

Forming Sub-Competence: Selection of Project Teams

This virtual Web management's sub-competence refers to the ability to search for and to select the most appropriate team of partner firms for a particular order or project. There are different ways project teams' configurations of virtual corporations are determined. Either the virtual Web management organization selects the partner firms that they think are capable to participate in particular projects, or every interested partner company is invited to join the cooperation project, i.e., in the case of joint R&D projects. However, if a project idea is put forward, the virtual Web management team provides assistance in defining the project aims and objectives, development of a detailed project plan, and agreeing on a cooperation contract. A third possibility is that the virtual Web management organization applies a tendering system. Then, the virtual Web management organization administers the tender process and observes the deadlines. Since several partners normally submit offers for one sub-service, the partners' offers are compared and the best offer is selected to be included in the final quotation to the customer. Furthermore, the virtual Web management might benchmark internal quotations against external quotations in order to evaluate their competitiveness. Whether the virtual Web management organization or a partner firm takes over the virtual corporation management, the virtual corporation manager subcontracts the selected partner companies, or if necessary, external suppliers as well. However, virtual Web management organization provides assistance in setting up the virtual corporation. The overall aim of this sub-competence is to search for and to select the most appropriate team of partner firms for the formation and operation of virtual corporations.

Forming Sub-Competence: Order/Project Execution

In general, virtual Web management organizations are not directly involved, as a value-adding partner, in the execution of orders or projects. However, the virtual Web management organization provides the overall project management, which means that they coordinate and monitor all activities along the value chain. The actual order/project execution is performed by the virtual corporation partner companies. There is an appointed virtual corporation manager, either an employee of the virtual Web management organization or a partner firm, who coordinates the activities along the value chain that involves VWO partner firms, external suppliers and eventually customers as well. The virtual corporation manager (a virtual corporation partner firm or the virtual Web management organization) signs a contract with the customer and is liable for the delivery of virtual corporation products and services. Furthermore, the virtual corporation manager signs the contracts with the participating VWO partners and external suppliers. The main reason for the virtual Web management organization to employ this sub-competence is to provide general project management to virtual corporations. The overall aim of the virtual Web management organization is the successful completion of orders and projects. Successful, executed orders/projects improve the reputation of the VWO as a whole, which might lead to additional order/projects. Furthermore, this sub-competence clarifies the legal issues/relationships between the involved parties, such as customers, partner firms, and external suppliers.

Forming Sub-Competence: Project Controlling

This sub-competence refers to the ability of the virtual Web management organization to monitor and control the performance of its virtual corporation and its participating parties. This means that they monitor the quality, keeping the schedule and project plan, as well as cost control. This controlling might involve keeping track of and controlling project interim reports, interim reviews and the final project reports, or joining project meeting without pre-notice. Since the virtual Web management organization has a neutral role, it intervenes only in cases where the project or order execution is interrupted or the defined objectives are not achieved, or in case of conflicts between the participating partner firms. Then, the virtual Web management organization facilitates to solve the problems, so that the project or order can be completed. Furthermore, the virtual Web management organization measures the satisfaction of externals, using such tools as customer surveys, with the performance of virtual corporations and reports the results back to the partner firms. The overall purpose of this virtual Web management's sub-competence is to monitor and control the performance of virtual corporations in order to safeguard the achievement of the defined project objectives and/or the delivery of the agreed products/services to the customers. Furthermore, the virtual Web management organization measures the performance/customer satisfaction after delivery in order to learn and to improve the performance of future virtual corporations.

Forming Sub-Competence: Dissolution and Accounting

Basically, this sub-competence employed by virtual Web management organizations is about the ability to disband virtual corporations when a project is completed or an order is executed and delivered to the customers. Thus, this sub-competence is concerned with the dissolution of virtual corporations and the accounting. In general, the partner firms submit their invoices to the virtual Web management organization or the virtual corporation manager, whereby on the other hand, they submit their invoices for the whole project/order to the customer. This accounting mainly involves bookkeeping and credit control. Furthermore, this sub-competence also includes the distribution of project results, i.e., of R&D projects to other virtual Web partner firms. The overall aim of this sub-competence is the smooth dissolution of virtual corporations, so that no negative implications for future virtual corporations arise. The purpose of making project results available to other virtual Web partner firms is to provide them with a good example of a successful complete project and to make the new/additional knowledge available to other partner firms so that other partner firms can benefit from joint virtual Web partner projects.

Summary of Forming Sub-Competencies

The main competence of "forming virtual corporations" concerns the ability of virtual Web management organizations to form, operate and dissolute dynamic virtual corporations. Certainly, there is a difference between virtual corporations which are temporary value-added partnerships or, for example, temporary R&D partnerships. However, in both cases it is a partnership of independent companies that agreed to cooperate for a limited period of time. Therefore, the individually employed forming sub-competencies aim to facilitate the formation, to ease the operation and to smooth the disbanding of dynamic virtual corporations. The main interest of virtual Web management organizations is the successful completion of virtual corporations. In sum, the aggregation of all forming sub-competencies cover the lifetime of temporary virtual corporations, from the initial idea or market opportunity to dissolution of the partnership and the settlement of invoices. In general, the purpose of the virtual Web management's main competence of "formation of dynamic virtual corporations" is to lead virtual corporations to a positive outcome in order to generate positive examples for others and to improve the VWO's reputation for further projects and/or orders. Thus, there is a strong interrelation between the main competence of "maintaining virtual Web platforms" and "forming and operating virtual corporations." On the one hand, the formation and operation of dynamic virtual corporations depends heavily on the groundwork laid on the virtual Web platform. On the other hand, the performance of dynamic virtual corporations reflects back on the virtual Web platform and, thus, has a strong impact on a number of sub-competencies employed during the maintenance of virtual Web platform. Apart from the two initial sub-competencies, which are employed continuously, all other sub-competencies employed during the formation and operation of virtual corporations are related to individual projects, customer inquiries and/or orders. Therefore, these sub-competencies are employed sequentially as one-off sub-competencies for each project, customer inquiry or order separately and, consequently, are repeated for each formation and operation of virtual corporations.

CONCLUSION

The introduction of this chapter identified four fundamental key difficulties associated with the organizational concept of virtual corporations that are configured as adhocracies of strangers. Thus, in order to overcome such inhibitors and obstacles regarding the formation of dynamic virtual corporations the virtual Web concept has been evolving within the last few years. The organizational concept of the virtual Web organization and its three encompassing organizational elements provides a possible way for the dynamic formation of temporary value chain and/or other temporary limited cooperations of independent companies, such as joint R&D projects. The virtual Web platform, as a stable company network, provides the environmental certainty necessary to establish favorable conditions for the dynamic formation of temporary limited cooperations. The groundwork laid on the virtual Web platform determines the formation and operation process of virtual corporations and consequently their competitiveness and the business success of each individual partner firm. However, besides the stable and the dynamic company networks, the management organization is the third organizational element of virtual Web organizations. Based on six empirically conducted case studies the author developed a competence-based management model of virtual Web management organizations. This competence-based view on the management of virtual Web organizations provides an overview of the sub-competencies employed by virtual Web management organizations to initiate and maintain virtual Web platforms and to facilitate the formation and operation of dynamic virtual corporations. Basically, this competence-based management model describes the content of the individual sub-competencies and it explains the purpose, the interrelateness and the temporal dimension of the virtual Web management's sub-competencies.

In respect to the four identified difficulties of totally free configured virtual corporations, the virtual Web management organization searches for suitable partner companies for the stable virtual Web platform that keep the complementary core competencies in order to be selected for the formation of dynamic virtual corporations. The virtual Web management organization searches for and selects partner firms according to predefined qualification criteria for the virtual Web platform that fit technologically and sociologically with the VWO and its partner firms. In addition, the virtual Web management organization develops and improves the technological and social fit of each individual partner firm and the group of collaborators in general. Furthermore, the virtual Web management organization implements an internal communication infrastructure and conducts trust and identification management in order to fertilize the development of trust between the partner companies, to accelerate the partnering process, to shorten the time to market process and to reduce transaction costs. Finally, the virtual Web management organization provides cooperation management on the virtual Web platform and for dynamic virtual corporations, in order to coordinate the activities of the dispersed partner companies and to build trustworthy relationships between them.

REFERENCES

Bund, M. (1997). Forschung und Entwicklung in der virtuellen Unternehmung. *Wirtschaftsmanagement, 5,* 247-253.

Byrne, JA. (1993, February 8). The virtual corporation. *Business Week*, February 8, 98-102.

Davidow, W. H., and Malone, M. S. (1992). *The Virtual Corporation: Customization and Instantaneous Response in Manufacturing and Service, Lessons from the World's Most Advanced Companies.* New York: Harper Collins.

Dierickx, I., and Cool, K. (1989). Asset stock accumulation and sustainability of competitive advantage. *Management Science*, 35(12), 1504-1514.

Franke, U. J. (1998). The evolution from a static virtual corporation to a virtual Web–What implications does this evolution have on supply chain management. *VoNet: The Newsletter*, 2(2), 59-65. Retrieved MD,Y from the World Wide Web: http://virtual-organization.net.

Franke, U. J. (1999). The virtual Web as a new entrepreneurial approach to network organizations. *Entrepreneurship & Regional Development*, 11(3), 203-229.

Franke, U. J. (2000a). The knowledge-based view (KBV) of the virtual Web, the virtual corporation, and the Net-broker. In Y. Malhotra (Ed.), *Knowledge Management and Virtual Organizations* (pp. 20-42). Hershey, PA: Idea Group.

Franke, U. J. (2000b). Virtual logistics: The vertical co-operation of virtual corporations. In *Conference Proceedings of the International Manufacturing, International and Strategic Network Development* University of Cambridge, UK, September.

Franke, U. J. and Hickmann B. (1999). Is the Net-broker an entrepreneur? What role does the net-broker play in virtual Webs and virtual corporations? *Workshop: Organizational Virtualness and Electronic Commerce*, Zurich, Switzerland. *Proceedings of the 2nd International VoNet-Workshop*, September, 117-134.

Goldman S. L., and Nagel R. N. (1993). Management, technology and agility: The emergence of a new era in manufacturing. *International Journal of Technology Management, 8* (1-2), 18-38.

Goldman S. L., Nagel R. N., and Preiss K. (1995). *Agile Competitors and Virtual Organizations: Strategies for Enriching the Customer.* New York: Van Nostrand Reinhold.

Grant, R. M. (1991). The resource-based theory of competitive advantage: Implications for strategy formulation. *California Management Review*, 33(3), 114-135.

Hardwick, M., Spooner, D. L., Rando, T., & Morris, K. C. (1996). Sharing manufacturing information in virtual enterprises. *Communications of the ACM*, 39(2), 46-54.

Hatch, C. R. (1995). The network brokers handbook. Gaithersburg, MD: U.S.

Department of Commerce, National Institute of Standards and Technology, Manufacturing Extension Partnership.

Kanet, J. J. and Faisst, W. (1997). *The Role of Information Technology in Supporting the Entrepreneur for the Virtual Enterprise: A Life-Cycle-Oriented Description*. Working paper, Clemson University, SC.

Klüber, R. (1997). The need for the function of the promotor. *VoNet: The Newsletter*, 1(4), 3-9. Available on the World Wide Web at: http://virtual-organization.net.

Mowshowitz, A. (1986). Social dimensions of office automation. In M. Yovits (Ed.), *Advances in Computers*, 25, 335-404.

Nelson, R. R. and Winter S. G. (1982). *An Evolutionary Theory of Economic Change*. Cambridge, MA: Harvard Business Press.

Perry, M. (1996). Research note: Network intermediaries and their effectiveness. *International Small Business Journal*, 14(4), 72-79.

Prahalad, C. K. and Hamel, G. (1990). The core competence of the corporation. *Harvard Business Review*, 68(3), 79-91.

Reiß, M. (1997). Virtuelle Organization auf dem Prüfstand. *VDI–Zeitschrift*, 139(1), 24-27.

Scholz, C. (1994). Die Virtuelle Organisation als Strukturkonzept der Zukunft. Arbeitspapier Nr. 30. Lehrstuhl für Betriebswirtschaft. Universität des Saarlandes, Saarbrücken, Germany.

Scholz, C. (1996). Virtuelle Organisationen: Konzeption und Realisation. *Zeitschrift für Organisation*, (4), 204-210.

Scholz, C. (1997). Das Virtuelle Unternehmen–Schlagwort oder echte Vision? *Bilanz Manager*, (1), 12-19.

Schuh, G. (1998). *Virtuelle Fabrik: Neue Marktchancen Durch Dynamische Netzwerke*. München, Germany: Carl Hanser Verlag.

Stuart, I., Deckert, P., McCutcheon, D., and Kunst, R. (1998). Case study: A leverage learning network. *Sloan Management Review*, 39(4), 81-93.

Upton, D. M. and McAfee, A. (1996). The real virtual factory. *Harvard Business Review*, 74(4), 123-133.

Warner, M. and Witzel M. (1999). *The Virtual General Manager*. Working Paper 15/99. The Judge Institute of Management Studies, University of Cambridge, England.

Chapter II

Which Way Is Forward? Direction and Control in Virtual Space

Malcolm Warner
University of Cambridge, UK

Morgen Witzel
London Business School, UK

The virtual organization offers many advantages, and can be a powerful strategic option for firms attempting to extend the scope and reach of their operations. However, it is by no means an easy option. Physical dispersal of the organization brings with it many associated problems of management and control. In this chapter, we look at some of these management issues and some of the options for managing more effectively in virtual space. In particular, we argue that management in virtual organizations still requires attention to the fundamentals of management. "Going virtual" should be seen as a strategic option which requires firms to achieve the optimal mix of physical and virtual elements and systems. In particular, we argue that a mastery of the skills of knowledge management is necessary in order to manage virtual systems and structures. Firms which fail to develop these skills run significant risks when taking the virtual option.

INTRODUCTION

Throughout the past decade, the concepts of virtual organization and knowledge management have both been the subject of a growing literature. Our work over the past few years (Warner and Witzel, 1998, 1999, 2000) has concentrated on showing how these two concepts are to a great extent interlocked, both in terms of theory and practice. Knowledge management takes place in virtual space, we argue, whether that space be created by computer technology or the human mind. Likewise, the virtual organization–and this is particularly true of virtual Web organizations– cannot exist without knowledge. Information technology provides the means by which such organizations are created, but knowledge flows are the process whereby they exist and function.

The virtual organization offers many advantages and can be a powerful strategic option for firms attempting to extend the scope and reach of their operations. However, it is by no means an easy option. Physical dispersal of the organization brings with it many associated problems of management and control. In this chapter, we look at some of these management issues and some of the options for managing more effectively in virtual space, taking our arguments one stage further. In particular, we argue that management in virtual organizations still requires attention to the fundamentals of management. We draw on the elements of management first identified by Henri Fayol (1984) and show how these, with some amendment, remain relevant and important in virtual organizations.

Although this chapter treats the problems of virtual organizations generally, it should be assumed that its comments are even more relevant to virtual Web organizations. In virtual Webs, the problems we discuss–fuzzy boundaries, the need for direction and planning, the difficulties of auditing–are even more crucial. Similarly, the need for knowledge management skills and systems, functioning and well-planned networks of relationships and the need for clear definitions of roles and responsibilities are even more important for success.

We begin by looking at how virtual organizations are situated in time and space and briefly rehearse the relationship between virtual organizations and knowledge management. We show how virtual organization is not an all-embracing concept and how choosing to "go virtual" actually involves developing a strategic mix of virtual and non-virtual components. We then look at how moving into virtual space poses challenges to the way in which the firm is managed and identify the key challenges and responses, using Fayol's scheme and suggesting how it might be modified.

THE ORGANIZATION IN TIME AND SPACE

Most theorizing about the history of "organizational behavior" has implied that organizations exist in time and space (see Warner, 1994); that is, they are subject to the laws of physics and have a concrete existence that evolves over time. However, these organizational dimensions are being transformed by the information revolution, itself driven by advances in communications and information technology. "Time," for example, has become compressed; many activities such as information exchange which formerly took days or weeks now take seconds, and many others such as transportation and distribution are now much faster as well.

"Space" too has been transformed; the organization of today is both shallower and broader than its counterpart of even a few decades ago. In other words, organizational units are tending to be both smaller in and of themselves, and more widely dispersed, with less geographical concentration around the core or headquarters of the organization.

Many important players in the "old economy" are now taking advantage of virtual management. Following the frenzy of dot.com creation, it now looks increasingly that the advantage may go to the large, long-standing, giant MNCs who are taking on new organizational structures relating to, for example, B2B activities (see The Economist, 18 November 2000). This step is a case of evolution, not revolution, as new techniques and capabilities are merged with old ones to create a synthesis.

Evans and Wurster (2000) have noted how adopting high-level information technology networks allows an organization to disperse itself spatially, across a region or across the globe. In other words, the better an organization's communications, the better it is able to compress time. Compressing time in turn allows more spatial dispersion. When communication between departments or divisions took several days, it was necessary to keep operating units close together, to cut down on the time lag in communications; now that they take seconds, the need for geographical concentration begins to fade. And at the same time, individual operating units tend to become "smaller," at least in terms of the amount of the land, real estate or office space they require.

What happens here is not just physical dispersal; the relocation of a department of the firm from Birmingham to Bombay is not just a matter of changing geography. At the same as this physical dispersal takes place, a portion of the firm's activity is shifted into what we may call "virtual space." This virtual activity is activity which used to take place through face-to-face contact, concentrated physical systems and so on, and has now been transferred to remote-access networks. Most activity of this sort concerns the acquisition, exchange and use of knowledge, what we call knowledge management.

This move from real space to virtual space is one of degree rather than one of kind. The change is not a total one; rather, it involves changing the balance of components within the organization. Virtual organizations themselves are not wholly new. Even as early as the Middle Ages, banks and exchanges operating across borders traded in knowledge and information; bills of exchange became a "virtual" representation of money, and it was the traders' own knowledge which was the primary commodity on the market (de Roover, 1949). Later, administrative organizations such as the East India Company, especially after it wound up its commercial activities, were structured virtually, with broad and shallow organizational structures designed specifically for the transmission of knowledge (Drucker, 1989). Economists from Adam Smith and Nassau Senior onwards have increasingly recognized the role that "mental work" or knowledge plays in business organizations and in economies more broadly. Today, the shift is towards still greater emphasis on the knowledge components of work; but, as we shall see below, even the most knowledge-dependent firms retain some physical components.

THE KNOWLEDGE-DEPENDENT ORGANIZATION

Franke (1999, p.2) has commented that 'knowledge is regarded as the key resource to gain competitive advantage'. Many conceptions of the virtual organization (Grenier and Metes, 1995; Goldman et al., 1995; Bleeker, 1998; Papows, 1999; Franke, 1999) show how personal and organizational knowledge are critical to the virtual organization on a variety of levels, and how the exchange of knowledge is the most important competitive factor. Warner and Witzel (1998, 1999) have shown how the virtual organization is to a large extent dependent on its knowledge capital. Here are some of the ways in which knowledge is used:

- it is exchanged between members of the firm, enabling workers and managers to carry out their tasks efficiently and effectively no matter where they are physically located;
- it is exchanged between the firm and its partners and suppliers, enabling these also to work efficiently and effectively and in some cases actually blurring the boundaries of the firm;
- it is exchanged with customers, with knowledge being a key component of virtual products and services, and customers' knowledge in turn feeding back into the firm as part of a process of continuous product improvement and development.

Knowledge, then, is the "glue" that holds virtual organizations together. Technology is important as the means by which organizations exchange knowledge, and recent advances in information technology have made great strides forward in this area, compressing physical space and speeding up transmission. Nevertheless, computers and Internet technology are just that–technology–and to that extent they are no different from parchment and quill pens; they are capable of moving information and knowledge in much greater quantities and much more quickly, but their essential function is the same. And both technologies are useless if they do not have knowledge to transmit. As many firms have discovered to their cost, investing in IT networks does not pay dividends unless the firm can also structure its knowledge capital in such a way that the networks can access and use it (Boisot, 1998). A virtual organization without access to knowledge is both deaf and blind, unable to coordinate the activities of its elements and unable to address the needs of customers. Technology then, is the means, but knowledge management is the process that makes virtual organizations work.

Thus the concepts of virtual organization and knowledge management are to a large extent co-dependent. The virtual organization uses technology to break down the barriers to knowledge transmission created by time, space and organizational structure; the better the technology, the lower these barriers can be dismantled. The virtual organization aims to allow knowledge to circulate more efficiently among the organization's managers, workers, customers and suppliers. Knowledge, in this conception, is a "great leveler" and, as it circulates, also serves to break down not only internal barriers within the firm but also external organizational parameters. The concepts "firm," "supplier" and "customer" start to become fuzzy; instead, all become linked components within a virtual organization or virtual Web, partners and sharers in the same knowledge management system.

THE "DUAL NATURE" OF ORGANIZATIONS

As the above passage suggests, all firms have a dual nature in that they are made up in part of virtual components and in part of physical components. Non-virtual components are what economists would see as the traditional factors of production: land, labor and capital. They include physical facilities, plant, stock and also the firm's employees. Non-virtual components are the firm's intangible assets or, as they have sometimes been described, its "intangible capital." They are things which cannot be seen or touched, but are nonetheless present, including the firm's culture, its reputation and that of its products and brands, and most of all, the knowledge inherent in its people, processes, systems and technologies.

Nor can assets always be strictly classified as virtual or non-virtual. As Adam Smith was the first to point out in the seventeenth century, machines have value not just as objects, but also for the knowledge of their makers and designers, which is built into them. It is vitally important, then, not to confuse knowledge itself with the artifacts that store it or the media that transmit it. People in particular take both forms. A company needs employees partly for the physical force of labor and partly for the intangible force of knowledge, both qualities which are built into each employee or manager. It is important to know how each quality is used and creates value.

Yet, these two components can hardly be separated. As Zeleny (2000) points out, knowledge is a process. "Knowledge" and "knowing" are one and the same thing. Knowledge cannot exist independently; it must inhere in some thing, be that thing a person's mind and memory, a magnetic storage device such as a computer disk, any other piece of technology, printed words on a page, and so on. There is a symbiotic link between knowledge and artifacts: knowledge cannot exist independently of artifacts, artifacts have no function unless knowledge is present which will make them work.

The mix may be quite different for different firms, even those in the same industry or sector. A specific business example may help to show this more clearly. In the retail book industry, W.H. Smith and Amazon.com have chosen two quite different mixes of virtual and non-virtual components in establishing their organizations. The former has adopted what might be termed a "convenience store" approach: it makes itself available to customers at several thousand locations in town high streets, shopping malls and railway stations. Originally a newsagent, W.

H. Smith had continued to use roughly the same distribution model, putting a large variety of books and other merchandise–some related to books and some not–on display so that consumers can make a quick choice. Choice and exchange happen quickly and often on the spur of the moment, and the customer's level of involvement is typically very low. To reflect this low involvement, W.H. Smith has a high physical presence, with a large number of physical facilities, high levels of stock and large numbers of staff. Amazon.com, on the other hand, requires a higher level of involvement from customers, who are less likely to browse and more likely to go to the Web site with a set of specific requirements already in mind. Because of this, Amazon.com has been able to reduce its physical presence, substituting physical facilities and staff for virtual systems deployed over the Internet. Paradoxically, given the differential cost-base, in the short- to medium- term at least, W.H. Smith has been making profits and Amazon.com is hardly in the black as yet.

VIRTUAL OPTIONS

It follows that managers need to develop organizations which have both virtual and tangible components. These components should fit together into an organizational form that is in turn fit for its own purpose and able to achieve its goals.

There are thus two premises. First, "going virtual" is a strategic option, the utility of which depends in part on the organization's capacity and needs, and those of its customers and suppliers. Second, there is no single or unique virtual organizational strategy. Instead, each organization needs to search for a suitable mix of virtual and non-virtual components in order to achieve its ends. It must be born in mind that virtual organization is a means, not an end in itself. Adopting a virtual organization model will not solve all of the firm's problems; in some cases, it may raise as many barriers as it breaks down. Before choosing a virtual organizational strategy, then, the firm should have answered the following questions:

- What is the nature of firm's product/service? Is it a physical, tangible product, or is it invisible and knowledge-based? Here one has to be sure that the whole product is considered. Does Amazon sell books, or does it sell its information and knowledge system over the Web? In fact, of course, it sells both.
- What is the relationship between the firm and its customers? Do customers need a high-contact relationship, and if so, can this be transferred to the Internet or telephone? UK banks, in switching to call centers, are finding that as the level of personal contact between customers and bank managers declines, so the relationship between them deteriorates.
- What is the relationship between the firm and its suppliers? This can also depend on the nature of the goods being supplied. Parts and components which require physical shipment and are sourced on a just-in-time basis are often sourced locally, even from the factory gate. Knowledge and information, on the other hand, are not location-contingent and can be sourced from anywhere. Getting the sourcing mix right is another aspect of the virtual-real continuum.

- What is the relationship between the organizational elements in the firm? How can this relationship be strengthened? The nature of the interdependence between people, teams, departments and so on needs to be examined carefully. Some situations lend themselves easily to virtual working; others do not.
- What kinds of work are done within the firm? Can this be changed to become more efficient? Again, this will vary between departments and teams. A concentrated production team, for example, may not be able to work well virtually and may require close proximity; sales teams, more typically, are scattered physically and work through virtual links.
- What is the relationship between management and employees? How can this too be strengthened? One of the most common problems facing organizations which adopt virtual modes is loss of control and motivation. The removal of the physical proximity of management must be counterbalanced with mechanisms that will ensure relationships remain tight.

THE MANAGEMENT CHALLENGE

It follows that if organizations have both virtual and tangible forms, then so does management. It is possible, and may in many cases be desirable, to manage virtually using virtual Webs or other similar structures even when the organization is largely conventional in form. Indeed, given that management is largely a knowledge-based activity, it might be argued that *all* management should be conceptualized as a virtual activity. However, this may be stretching the concept too far. Managing over distances using virtual media is not the same as working in close proximity. For example group-working and team-working tend to be less effective when the group- or team- members are not in physical proximity, unless all members are skilled and experienced at working in virtual situations. Technological solutions, such as teleconferencing and the video-cam laptop, are being applied to this problem with some success. Nevertheless, working in spatial isolation brings its own special sets of problems.

The new types of virtual organization can, as Papows (1999) has described, eliminate some of the problems caused by time, distance and organizational barriers. But they can also lead to problems of loss of control, lack of monitoring and supervision, poor compliance and, if the systems do not work, misinformation or disinformation creeping into the network (as the Barings and Sumitomo banks respectively found out to their cost in the late 1990s). All these increase transaction costs, in Coasian terms. But how can senior management best assess the impacts which virtual management will have and adapt their own management methods to meet the emerging new model?

The answer to this question lies not in "new" management techniques but in a return to fundamentals. One of the best overarching concepts of the tasks of management is that developed by Henry Fayol in 1917 (Fayol 1984), which classified all management activities under one of seven headings. This system was known by the acronym POSDCORB, the initials standing for *Planning, Organizing, Staffing, Directing, Coordinating, Reporting and Budgeting.*

Fayol's system was designed to manage "traditional" organizations with a high level of tangible assets (specifically, he was interested in the management of large manufacturing firms). Managers contemplating a move to a form of organization with a high level of virtual components should consider how this move will impact on each of these sets of tasks, as follows.

Planning

Planning in conventional organizations is usually a central function. Information may be gathered from many different sources, but the actual process of planning takes place very close to the organizational core, with primary responsibility lying with senior managers and directors. In a virtual Web or other networked organization, the core is much smaller, and in some models is even nonexistent; the question then arises as to who does planning and who takes responsibility for it. Also, given that virtual organizations tend to have fuzzy boundaries, there arises a further question of what entity is actually being planned for.

Both issues are capable of resolution. Many planning models, not just those connected with virtual organizations, argue for more people to be included in the planning process, and a system whereby "everybody plans" may at first sight seem ideally suited to a virtual Web organization. However, practical problems quickly emerge, especially if not all members of the network have the same level of skills or worse, access to the same levels of knowledge. Great care must be taken that members involved in the planning process have access to identical knowledge. Even so, other problems may arise. One of the most common is "groupthink," whereby the members of the Web adopt a compromise planning solution which may not necessarily be the best option.

The boundaries issue is more difficult, especially as members of a virtual organization–even more, a virtual Web–will often be involved in other activities outside the organization. Membership of the virtual Web may not be the only, or even the main, priority. Plans developed for the Web organization may conflict with members' own plans and interests. Reconciling these will not be easy; it will be tempting for the more powerful members of the Web organization to use their power to get their own way and push their own goals to the head of the planning process.

Both problems can be dealt with by establishing clear planning responsibilities from the outset, and by ensuring that one or more parties takes clear formal responsibility for ensuring that planning is done and to a satisfactory level. Such responsibility should be designed into the organization, not simply allowed to evolve.

Organizing

Many of the comments made about planning apply to the principles of organizing. Fuzzy teams mean that members may not have clearly defined roles and may not fit into an organizational hierarchy. Nevertheless, this does not mean that anarchy can ensue. Organizing in the virtual world requires above all a clear focus on the goal; indeed, the goal may be the only thing that is clearly visible in an otherwise unfocused world. We are not suggesting a return to old-fashioned hierarchy is necessary, but we do argue that in any organization, all members must have a clear view of the organization's purpose and their own role in it. Duties and responsibilities need to be made clear, even if only in outline form, when the organization is first designed and established.

Much attention is paid in the literature to the role of the network broker or network hub (other names such as network manager or even net-preneur are also used). Establishing a clear central point of reference within the network can be very valuable in ensuring that information and knowledge flow freely and are accessible to all parties. Great care must be taken, however, that this network broker does not become a gatekeeper or controller, restricting rather than facilitating the flow of knowledge. For, as we saw above, a virtual organization without knowledge flows is literally a dead organism.

Staffing

Not everyone can work in a virtual organization. Only some people have the skills to do so, and only some people are temperamentally suited for doing so. Man (and woman) is a social animal, and many otherwise skilled people find themselves becoming de-motivated and unable to work to full effectiveness unless they receive stimulation and recognition from colleagues and managers, and indeed customers and other stakeholders, in a face-to-face environment. Not everyone who sells books successfully over a counter can do so over the Internet; sets of personal selling skills may require physical proximity to the customer. Internet selling often involves de-skilling, as is the case in call-centers.

Companies switching to virtual modes of operation have two choices: they can recruit staff who have the skills and temperament required to work virtually, or they can attempt to retrain existing staff. The first option brings up issues of selection: how will the firm identify the relevant skills and temperament in potential employees? What tools and knowledge will need to be acquired to do so? The second is a training issue. Along with the relatively straightforward matter of skills provision, there is the question of changing temperament through encouragement, motivation and support. How can the lack of physical contact be compensated for? Periodic physical visits or meetings, regular personal contact by telephone or over the Internet, mentoring systems, even e-discussion groups and bulletin boards for members of staff and management to exchange views are all possible solutions.

Directing

The problems of directing or controlling a virtual organization are probably the most difficult and enduring. Virtual organizations, by their very nature, devolve large amounts of responsibility to individuals, teams and groups. They are highly democratic. This is potentially a good thing, as people are encouraged by the trust shown in them and the responsibility they are given. Most will do more than just maximize utility; that is, they will go beyond the strict confines of doing the job for its rewards (salary, perks) to them individually and will seek to maximize benefits for the firm as well.

Problems tend to arise when the firm can no longer inspire employees to act creatively on its behalf. Proximate causes can include the breakdown of trust between employer and employee, systems failures, negligence, perceived lack of success in meeting personal organizational goals, or even entropy–the creeping boredom of doing the same job over a long period of time can be just as crippling in virtual work as in assembly line production.

When this happens, democratic virtual organizations can be beset with the same kinds of problems that develop in democratic political systems, including factionalism and opting out. In factionalism, members of the organization in effect "take sides" and begin putting the interests of their own group first; they may even seek to actively hinder the efforts of rival factions. Needless to say, although an element of creative tension can at times be useful, over the long run this acts to the detriment of the organization. In opting out, employees cease to identify with the organization's goals and begin putting in less effort; they may also choose to leave the organization and go elsewhere.

Both these problems, factionalism and opting out, occur in conventional organizations as well, but their effect on a virtual organization is more severe. As members divert more of their efforts into internal conflicts or external activities, the impact on the flow of knowledge will be noticeable. In both cases, members may deliberately withhold knowledge from the system, either for political gain or because they no longer care enough to participate. If this happens, then again, the knowledge management system can dry up and the virtual organization ceases to live.

Coordinating

That coordination is more difficult over distance is a well-known axiom of military science, and it applies equally in management. Communications technology has been able to solve many of the problems of coordination over distance, but not all of them. Systems failures are the most common cause of coordination failure, and these can be both human and technical. In 1939, Royal Air Force fighter squadrons operating in northern France were supplied with the wrong crystals for their radios, meaning that above 7,000 feet altitude the pilots could not hear their own controllers at base (they could, however, receive dance music programs on BBC radio with great clarity).

Systems for coordination over distance need to be robust and able to handle the unexpected. They must not be overdesigned–a common fault–as this then requires both greater levels of operator skill and greater cost and time loss should the system fail and need to be repaired. Rather than spending money on a single complex system, the firm should consider simple systems with redundant capacity which can be activated in a crisis. The Royal Air Force again provides a good example. During the

Battle of Britain from July-September 1940, RAF Fighter Command managed an aerial battle spread over many thousands of square miles of airspace, involving input from more than 15 radar stations, 20 airfields and 600 pilots. The coordination system involved multiple telephone lines feeding into several sector command-centers simultaneously, with sector controllers then issuing orders to the fighter squadrons in the air; the sector control-centers used technology no more complex than wooden blocks on a map table. Each control-center was linked to the others, and if one was bombed and put out of action, the others could quickly fill in the gap.

Even more than systems, though, coordination requires skill and ability on the part of those doing the coordinating. As in planning and organizing, above, coordination should be a specific responsibility assigned to a few members of the organization; otherwise, "if everybody does everything, then nobody does anything." Those tasked with coordination should be good at organizing both knowledge and people; a good sense of spatial awareness would be an asset. It may be worthwhile for firms to train or recruit personnel whose sole function is attention to coordination issues.

Reporting

Reporting is both part of the problem and part of the solution. In the recent past, reporting issues have been seen as a critical factor in the business failures of, for example, Barings. Examination of events, however, shows that in most of these cases it is failure to report or reporting of inaccurate information, that it is the essential problem. The answer would to be more and better quality reporting which would allow all essential knowledge to be received throughout the firm. Reports contain knowledge, which as we have seen is essential to the functioning of a virtual organization; failures in reporting bear within them the seeds of organizational failure. It follows that virtual organizations must be transparent and that knowledge must not only be *allowed* to circulate freely, but must even be *compelled* to do so.

Budgeting

As we have discussed in detail in an earlier article (Warner and Witzel 1999), the adoption of virtual forms of organization brings with it a series of financial management issues. Financial managers to some extent have a head start over the rest of the organization when it comes to virtual thinking because (whether they realize it or not) they have long been used to working and thinking in virtual spheres. On the other hand, much of financial management in the past has been driven by the use and management of virtually transmitted and recorded *information* and *data*. There is a key difference between this and the new virtual, *knowledge*-based organization, as we will see below. Financial managers need to transform their own thinking if they are to keep pace with growth of virtual organizations. Since the costs of managing capital also need to be confronted, there is a need for a new look at how to "downsize" their financial infrastructure.

Finance professionals need to become more knowledge-based, more adaptive and more innovative if they are to be effective in a virtual environment. To this end, training programs must be designed to ensure that financial managers are adequately familiar with not only IT developments but also the new organizational and HR practices which are associated with them. The latter practices are still evolving and managers should be flexible in devising solutions to suit their specific organizational requirements and not adopt textbook templates.

Another problem in this area concerns regulation. Governments tend not to like the virtual world very much; they cannot control it and they cannot tax it. Firms operating in a virtual environment are likely to become increasingly under pressure from national and international agencies to make their operations more transparent: "virtual yet visible" may well become the regulatory watchword. The firm's finance professionals are likely to have a key role to play in this regard, helping to ensure that virtual operations remain compliant; and this in a regulatory environment that is likely to undergo rapid change in the near future.

The problem of valuing knowledge as an asset has not yet been satisfactorily solved. It can be argued that the share price of a virtual company (not all Internet stocks are virtual companies, but the two have enough common features to be comparable here), is a reflection of the value of the knowledge that company has in other words, its knowledge capital. But how does an investor make a return if that knowledge cannot be turned into profit? Many Internet companies have not made a profit; many never will. Knowledge is static; investing in knowledge alone is like investing in a pile of rocks. Human capital is required to make that knowledge active and at least potentially profitable.

NEW TASKS FOR VIRTUAL MANAGEMENT

The analysis of the seven tasks above shows a number of gaps between the tasks assigned to conventional management and those required for virtual management. These gaps can be described as the *skills gap*, the *network gap*, the *knowledge management gap*, the *boundaries gap* and the *direction and control gap*.

The skills gap. It is commonly assumed that management in virtual organizations requires an entirely new set of skills which will sweep the old set aside. We would argue rather that new skills need to complement existing skills. The major need in terms of new skills is in the area of knowledge management and relationship management; technical skills are of secondary importance, though important nonetheless.

The network gap. A virtual organization–and in particular a virtual Web organization–is a network and needs to be conceived of as such. Unlike traditional hierarchies, which are static, the network needs to be organic and flexible. This organic nature of the network needs to be built into its design; it cannot be assumed that it will evolve. A new approach to organization design is thus required.

The knowledge management gap. Though knowledge is often discussed in management terms, it is seldom conceptualized as a discrete asset requiring specific management systems. In virtual organizations, this needs to change. Knowledge needs to be seen as the essential core asset of the organization, which must be managed and used to be effective. An organic view of the virtual organization should see it in terms of components being linked by knowledge flows, in much the way that the bloodstream carries blood and its essential components to various parts of the body.

The boundaries gap. The hierarchical view of the firm creates boundaries, which are often designed to exclude as much as to include. Virtual organizations tend to be much less exclusive, and their fuzzy boundaries serve to include many who would not be considered part of a traditional firm. Approaches to planning and reporting, especially, need to be more inclusive and less exclusive than previously.

The direction and control gap. In terms of conventional organizations, the debate has tended to focus on the merits of top-down versus bottom-up control. Neither is really appropriate for virtual organizations which, being fuzzy and dispersed, tend not to have a top and bottom, or indeed other conventional dimensions. Network organizations tend to exercise control from the center outwards. However, as we mentioned above, this kind of control can be restrictive if the central controllers begin to conceive of themselves as gatekeepers rather than facilitators.

To overcome some of these gaps, we believe it is necessary to supplement the original POSDCORB model. The emphasis here must be on the word supplement. We are not suggesting an entirely new model of management, because we are not dealing with an entirely new organizational form; instead, as set out at length above, companies need to create organizational syntheses using both virtual and non-virtual components. The management of the virtual components requires additional tasks, but the tasks in the original model remain as important as ever.

The four additional management tasks required, we believe, are communication, assessment, learning and valuation. A short summary of each now follows.

Communication

The communication task involves ensuring that knowledge flows are efficient and timely, linking all the elements of the organization and its suppliers, customers and other stakeholders. Communication is about rendering the organization both efficient and transparent. By communicating, we exchange knowledge, improve the quality of action and decision, and reduce or remove uncertainty and risk. Communication should be seen as a core part of the management task in virtual organizations. The new technology has now dramatically reduced the transaction costs involved in intra-organizational communication.

Assessment

Assessment in this sense is the matching of the organization's goals with its form and structure on a dynamic basis, and altering or amending that structure when opportunities arise. Because the virtual organization is a flexible and dynamic organizational form, its capabilities must be constantly tested and matched against organizational goals (which, of course, may also be dynamic and evolving). This assessment is not solely a planning function, but should be part of all management functions, and the results of ongoing assessment should be circulated as part of the knowledge management system. In this way the organization can become more self-aware and more able to anticipate and meet change.

Learning

Learning here means the constant replenishment of an organization's stock of knowledge capital through such activities as training and education, research and development, environmental scanning and so on. Learning is a primary element of knowledge management, as it involves the creation and acquisition of new knowledge which is added to that already circulating in the knowledge management system. Using the organic metaphor of organization, learning can be seen as the process of adding "fuel" to the organization, stimulating it into further growth and creativity. Organizational learning is the "new value-added" of our times.

Valuation

Valuation is the continuous and dynamic reassessment of knowledge assets in terms of their present and future value to the firm. Like assessment, this process must be continuous and a part of every manager's task. The valuing of intangible assets is much more than just a process of accounting for them as part of the organizational bottom line. Potential value as well as present-day value needs to be known. It is probably that new valuation measures will need to be developed to meet this need.

CONCLUSION

The upshot is that new managerial skills are needed to deal with the challenges laid out above. A new kind of general management model is required to coordinate and synthesize the strands of virtual activity we have described. The virtual organization offers many advantages and can be a powerful strategic option for firms attempting to extend the scope and reach of their operations. However, it is by no means an easy option. It requires four additional management tasks, we believe, which are respectively communication, assessment, learning and valuation. The new virtual manager will have to combine such qualities and be able to apply them to the new challenges of managing intangibility alongside tangible assets.

REFERENCES

Bleeker, S. E. (1998). The virtual organization. In G. R. Hickman (Ed.), *Leading Organizations*. Thousand Oaks, CA: Sage.

Boisot, M. (1998). *Knowledge Assets: Securing Competitive Advantage in the Information Economy.* Oxford, England: Oxford University Press.

Davis, S., and Meyer, C. (1999). *Blur: The Speed of Change in the Connected Economy.* Oxford, UK: Capstone.

De Roover, R. (1949). *Gresham on Foreign Exchange.* Cambridge, MA: Harvard University Press.

Drucker, P. (1989). *The New Realities.* Oxford,UK: Heinemann.

Drucker, P. (1999). Knowledge-worker productivity: The biggest challenge. *California Management Review,   41*(2), 79-94.

Fayol, H. (1984). *General and Industrial Management.* New York: I. Gray, Trans. (Original work published in 1917 by David S. Lake).

Franke, U. (1999). The virtual Web as a new entrepreneurial approach to network organizations. *Entrepreneurship and Regional Development*, 11, 203-209.

Goldman, S. L., Nagel, R. N. and Preiss, K. (1995). *Agile Competitors and Virtual Organizations.* New York: Van Nostrand Reinhold.

Grenier, R. and Metes, G. (1995). *Going Virtual: Moving Your Organization into the 21st Century.* Upper Saddle River, NJ: Prentice Hall.

Papows, J. (1999). *Enterprise.com.* London: Nicholas Brealey.

Warner, M. (1994). Organizational behavior revisited. *Human Relations*, 47(10), 1151-1166.

Warner, M. and Witzel, M. (1998). General management revisited. *Journal of General Management*, 23(4), 1-18.

Warner, M. and Witzel, M. (1999). The virtual general manager. *Journal of General Management*, 24(4), 71-92.

Warner, M. and Witzel, M. (2000, January-February). Finance and the virtual organization. *Corporate Finance Review*, 1-10.

Zeleny, M. (2000). Knowledge vs. information. In M. Zeleny (Ed.), *The Handbook of Information Technology in Business* (pp. 162-168). London: Thomson Learning.

Chapter III

The Virtual Corporation and Trust: Balancing Between Identity and Innovation

Wendy Jansen, Hans P. M. Jägers and Wilchard Steenbakkers
Royal Netherlands Military Academy, The Netherlands

It is ironic that trust, often criticized by managers as a soft and unmanageable concept, is nevertheless a necessary condition for achieving the competitive advantages related to strategic and structural innovations (Whitener, Brodt, Korsgaard and Werner, 1998)

Virtual corporations are seen as new organisational forms to ensure knowledge sharing and innovation. In this chapter the reason for the knowledge-creating competence of virtual corporations is explained. A shared identity and mutual trust of the participants are of paramount importance to innovation. Virtual corporations are in fact balancing on a tightrope. They have to create an identity which is strong enough for the participants to trust each other. At the same time the identity shared by the participants of the virtual corporation must not become so strong that very promising innovative avenues are blocked. ICT will fulfil an important function here which is mainly aimed at the support of the social relation between the participants.

INTRODUCTION

Why do organizations work together more and more often in the form of networks in general and virtual corporations in particular? Why are terms such as trust, knowledge sharing and innovations used more and more frequently when organizing (virtual) cooperation between organizations? What is the relation between these concepts and from which angle can cooperation between organizations be considered?

We shall examine this in more detail in this chapter and try to shed light on the complex pattern that is related to exchanges between parties and individuals. We maintain that 'trust' is the keyword in cooperation in networks in general and in virtual corporations in particular. This trust, however, is based in the shared identity of those concerned. We shall describe which aspects are important in obtaining and keeping mutual trust in organizations, but especially in virtual corporations. This chapter contains an analytical model, in which the relations between these different aspects of trust are represented. In the discussion of this model in the following paragraphs we shall argue that the virtual corporation is a successful form of organization for operating in an uncertain environment with a high degree of competition. On the one hand we see the traditional organizational form, in which innovation is hampered by the internal hierarchic supervision and the strong organizational culture and identity.

On the other hand, the exchanges of organizations take place on the free market, where the absence of a common culture and identity hampers the sharing of knowledge and the realization of innovation. Virtual corporations have the best of both worlds. However, this does mean that sufficient attention needs to be paid to the issues of trust and identity, which are often labelled as "soft."

RELEVANT APPROACHES

In this paragraph three lines of approach are described for the organization of activities and the relations between the individuals and/or parties concerned here.

The lines of approach are, successively:
- the transactional costs approach;
- the organizational capability approach;
- the social exchange approach.

The transactional costs approach has been chosen because it is a much-discussed theory in the literature to provide an explanation for the organization of activities. Trust, although not mentioned explicitly, plays an important part in this approach. The organizational capability approach embroiders on this. It contends that the transactional costs approach does not suffice for this explanation. Attention to knowledge is necessary as a supplement to the transactional costs approach. Examination from a social exchange point of view instead of the transactional costs theory sheds a clearer light on the dynamic aspects of relations (Whitener et al., 1998). This point of view helps to explain why people are still inclined to trust the other party instead of resorting to control.

The Transactional Costs Approach

The difference between the internal organization of activities and obtaining goods or services by way of the market can be made clear by means of the transactional costs theory (Williamson, 1975). The point of departure here is that if the transactional costs are higher than the (internal) coordination costs, activities will take place within the organization. If the transactional costs are low, goods or services will be acquired by way of the market. As the uncertainty increases, the chance that parties behave differently from what has been predicted also increases. This is also denoted as the principle of discretionary powers. In the event of a high degree of uncertainty trust is necessary to offer resistance to opportunist behaviour. Uncertainty may be defined as the difference between the information that is needed and the information that is present/available (Galbraith, 1976). This information is possibly held by other parties. In the transactional costs theory this is called information asymmetry (Williamson, 1975). One party knows more than another party. For the other party it is difficult to get that information or the cost for the other party is so great that the advantages of having that information make no odds against the chance that it gets more certainty. Imbalance in the information which parties have will also lead to opportunist behaviour of the party which has the most information. Information asymmetry and opportunism are directly interrelated. Both influence each other and lead to uncertainty. Opportunism and information asymmetry are used in the transactional costs theory to explain why activities take place in organizations or by way of the operation of the market mechanism.

Trust decreases the transactional costs, because there is less (fear of) opportunist behaviour (Granovetter, 1985, 1992; Gulati, 1995). This opportunist behaviour of partners becomes most obvious when sharing knowledge. The party with knowledge at its disposal has a position of power based on this in comparison with the other party. Sharing knowledge, one of the main resources of organizations (Hertog and Huizenga, 1997; Weggeman, 1997; Jansen, Jägers and Steenbakkers, 1998) requires a great deal of trust.

The Organizational Capability Approach

The organizational capability (OC) approach embroiders on the transactional costs approach, but attempts to diminish the shortcomings of the latter approach. An organization is no longer seen as a "bundle of transactions or contracts," but as a "bundle of knowledge and the processes on which it is based." This view of knowledge is an important nuance on the transactional costs approach, which assumes that economic activities can always take place by way of the market. Knowledge is unique and not so easy to trade. This partly explains the growing importance of collaborations and in particular of virtual corporations. The decision about the organization of economic activities (within the organization/hierarchy), by way of the market or collaborations) is not only based on the minimization of the (transactional) costs. Certain unique capabilities and knowledge of organizations which enable them to create value must also be taken into account in the decision-making process (Madhok, 1996).

The Social Exchange Approach

This approach is based on the social relationships, contrary to the economic approach with contracts as it takes place in the transactional costs approach. The basic assumption here is that an individual performs something with which he obliges another party to reciprocate. Trust therefore plays a role as a pattern of expectations. Initially, this can produce problems. After all, how can anyone know whether the other party can be trusted? Blau (1964) contends that two factors account for this basis of trust, that is, the fact:

- that relationships often have a repetitive character;
- that achievements increase in importance in the course of time.

The "social exchanges" differ fundamentally from the contractual relationships in the transactional costs approach. In the social exchange approach, also intrinsic advantages can be the subject of the relationship. It does not concern direct economic advantage here, but for example support or friendship. Beside that, the performances in the social exchange approach have not been laid down formally or contractually. This means that trust should be seen in a social context here. Identification of social relationships requires that they are approved of by shared values and standards. Consequently, these relationships are strengthened and sustained.

Just like the organizational capability approach complements the more limited point of view of the transactional costs approach, the social exchange point of view complements both approaches. The strong point of the social exchange approach is not only the attention to the cultural context in which the exchanges between parties take place, but especially the fact that trust is considered as part of the dynamic process of exchange in this. This point of view pays attention to the given that successful exchanges influence the perceptions with respect to the risks of not fulfilling agreements and expectations (opportunism) and mutual trust. The social exchange approach explains why parties which have a strong social bond, built up on the basis of a process of successful exchanges, perceive less of a risk of opportunism than parties to which this does not apply (Whitener et al., 1998, p.515). The creation of such a social bond is therefore of paramount importance in the development and functioning of virtual corporations.

In this chapter our basic assumption is that in relationships among parties within and among organizations, economic factors, knowledge considerations, as well as aspects in the field of values and standards and mutual trust play an important role. Only by considering exchanges from several perspectives will there be a view of the whole.

TRUST AND RISK

Trust in and among organizations is generally considered as especially important (Handy, 1995; Jarvenpaa, Knoll & Leidner, 1998; Jarvenpaa & Shaw, 1998; Lewicki, McAllister & Bies, 1998; Grabowski & Roberts, 1998). Yet one can barely speak of coherent research in the field of trust. One of the reasons for this is that definitions of the concept of trust have brought about more confusion than clarity in the course of time. Among other things, trust has been described as a type of behaviour, an attitude, an expectation, a contingency variable, a structure variable, a social agency variable and an interpersonal variable (McKnight et al., 1998). For some authors trust is a static variable for others trust is the outcome of a process.

In short, the concept of trust is a container concept, in which anyone can find something they like. In this chapter we approach trust from the point of view of the design of organizations. We distinguish four important aspects of trust, the relational aspect, the aspect of the dynamics, the aspect of the mutual dependence and the aspect of dealing with risks. As a starting point, we take the following definition of trust, whereby these aspects come up for discussion:

Trust is the mutual willingness of parties (individuals and/or organizations) to take up a position of mutual dependence with a feeling of relative security, even if negative results are possible.[1]

The Relational Aspect

Trust is not only an attitude of one party vis-à-vis another one, but exists in the relationship between the parties (Whitener, 1998, p. 514). By considering trust as an essential part of a relationship between parties and not a one-sided aspect or a process, justice is done to the fact that all parties must make efforts to develop trust and to deepen it. Beside that, with this we shed light on the fact that the basis of the trust must be shared by the parties. In this chapter we contend that the shared identity of the parties in general and the virtual corporation in particular is of crucial importance for its effective functioning.

The Dynamics Aspect

In paragraph 2 in the discussion of the social exchange approach, attention was already paid to the fact that exchanges between parties and the role of trust in this constitute a dynamic process. Many authors point to the fact that in most cases trust only grows after a considerable period of time and can be lost very quickly (Dasgupta, 1988; Luhmann, 1988). Trust should therefore be considered a dynamic concept, whereby the key question is: "How does trust come about at the beginning of the relationship between parties, what is trust based on and how can it be deepened?" (McKnight et al., 1998).

The Aspect of the Mutual Dependence

Trusting is about dependence. If parties in a relationship do not depend on each other it is not necessary to trust each other. The concept of dependence brings trust into the design theory. Trust is an important "mechanism" to shape the dependence and is even considered to be the new coordination mechanism by some authors (Jarvenpaa & Shaw, 1998). Furthermore, within this framework trust and the coordination mechanism of "control" have been represented as a continuum by a number of authors. On the one hand the dependence can be managed by using stringent control instruments, while on the other hand the control is not necessary if there is sufficient trust (McKnight et al., 1998; Whitener et al., 1998; Das & Teng, 1998).

Dealing With Risks

The possibly negative consequences which trust entails are sometimes called "risks" or "uncertainty" (Gambetta, 1988; Lewicki et al., 1998; McKnight et al., 1998). Precisely because negative consequences are possible, successful exchanges and relationships make trust necessary.

In exchanges between parties a distinction can be made between two types of risks (Ring & Van de Ven, 1994, p. 94; Das & Teng, 1998, p. 25), namely performance risks and relational risks. In exchanges there is always the risk that the other party fails to perform what is expected or agreed.

Performance risk is related to the possibility that the strategic goals of the collaboration cannot be achieved. In virtual corporations, focussed on structural innovation, the outcome of the process is not known beforehand. There is a chance that new products or services can be developed, but this can also fail. The uncertainty about the outcome of the (innovation) process means that trust is necessary between the parties that participate. Trust is then related to the belief in each other's abilities/skills and in the products/services that are to be developed. These skills/abilities which organizations "offer" in interorganizational collaborations can usually be reduced to knowledge (Das & Teng, 1998, p. 23). Trust in each other's performances is also based on the experiences of the participating parties with each other in the past (Thorelli, 1986).

Relational risks are the risks which parties run when the interpersonal relationship cannot progress according to expectations.

Relational risk has to do with the relationships between the cooperating individuals and/or organizations and has direct consequences for the cooperation. Trust between persons, as representatives of the organization, strengthens the common standards and values and simplifies the communication. Consequently, the cooperation takes place more smoothly. Not surprisingly, the risk is more related to the relations between people than to the outcomes of the process. The relational risk exists particularly in interorganizational cooperation (Das & Teng, 1998, p. 26) because this is directly related to opportunist behaviour. This behaviour is focussed on maximizing self-interest, even if this is at the expense of the common interest which parties have in cooperation (Williamson, 1983, 1985; Gulati, 1995). Trust, the conviction that a mutually satisfying relationship continues (Thorelli, 1986), decreases the relational risk and the opportunism (Ring & Van de Ven, 1992; Zaheer & Venkatraman, 1995, p. 379; Kraut, Steinfield, Chan, Butler & Hoag, 1998).

THE ROLE OF TRUST IN HIERARCHIES, MARKETS AND VIRTUAL CORPORATIONS

In this paragraph we present our conceptual model. In this model the role of trust in hierarchies, markets and virtual corporations is highlighted. In each of the three forms, however, the interpretation of the model differs. Discussion of the market as well as the hierarchy is important for the line of reasoning. Therefore, the interpretation of this model for these two situations will come up for discussion for these two situations subsequently. The core of this chapter, however, lies in the discussion of the interpretation of the model for the virtual corporation (see Figure 4). The starting point here is that trust is a necessary condition for knowledge sharing and innovation. It concerns structural innovation here, whereby new knowledge is created, and not so much incremental improvements. Up until now attention has been paid to the need for trust, but the risk that is perceived in virtual corporations has mostly been interpreted as a performance risk. This "top" of the model has been widely discussed in the literature about virtual corporations, among other places in the discussion about the combination of core skills, knowledge sharing, and the power to innovate of virtual corporations (Have et al., 1997; Travica, 1997). We contend that the 'bottom' of this model is at least as important for the successful functioning of the virtual corporation. Trust is the upshot of a social process. The aspects of identity and communication are inextricably bound up with trust. Relational risk and trust go hand in hand here. We will go into that in more detail in the following paragraphs.

Hierarchies

Identity Leads to Knowledge Sharing

An organization (hierarchy) differs from a market because coordination, communication and learning have not only been brought together physically in one location, but also mentally in an identity. Organizations provide the normative field with which members identify themselves. This identification is often described as a process of self-characterization, characterized by distinctive, central and enduring qualities (Kogut & Zander, 1996, p. 509). The identity, which is obtained in a continuous process and is kept in place, is extremely important for organizations. First of all, the identity determines the habits and rules by means of which individuals in the organization coordinate their behaviour and decision making. People know what to expect from the others and what the other members expect from the organization. Identity sees to it that problems are solved in a similar way and that making decisions takes place in the same way and based on the same assumption. Identity, not surprisingly, has the reduction of uncertainty as an important function. (Schein, 1992, Van Hoewijk, 1988)

A second and even more important function is fulfilled by the shared identity in organizations in the process with which learning is developed (Kogut & Zander, 1996, p. 506).

Individuals (participants) share cognitive models of the world based on the same categories through a common identity. Although these images are enduring and robust, this does not mean that these shared images of reality cannot be changed. Organizations can learn and it is easier to learn based on common understanding. Communication between participants who share cognitive models is fruitful because new learning is promoted because of the fact that there is a certain basic knowledge with fixed categories (Kogut & Zander, 1996, p. 510). For this basic knowledge various terms are used, such as meta-knowledge, background knowledge and accepted knowledge protocols (Coleman, 1999, p. 37). In the model represented in Figure 1 the relationship between the concepts is portrayed diagrammatically. There is a process in which the aspects mutually reinforce each other. Identity causes communication through learning. After all, the shared categories (the cognitive models) are acquired through learning and knowledge sharing. As a result of the shared identity, communication, and thereby learning (i.e., knowledge sharing) is made easier, while the common identity is reinforced again through learning and knowledge sharing.

Trust is a crucial aspect in this. Due to the shared identity that is present, with shared expectations and shared understanding, the members of the same organization "know" that the relational risks are limited and that sharing knowledge is supported and welcomed.

Identity Hampers Innovation

Innovation, the creation of new knowledge, does not take place in a vacuum, in an absence of already existing knowledge and skills. Merging, or the increase of the combining capacity is the only way to create new knowledge from existing knowledge (Davenport and Prusak, 1998, Volberda, 1998, Jansen et al., 1998).

Although identity leads to order on the basis of which people can transfer knowledge and learn more easily within organizations, this knowledge sharing and knowledge increase nevertheless remain limited to the existing knowledge.

The fact of the matter is that identity creates order but also lays down rules regarding exceptions. Identity implies that some ideas, logic, or practices are not allowed to come up for discussion in the organization because they do not fit in with the notions which are shared in the identity. That is why there are disadvantages

Figure 1: The role of trust in hierarchies

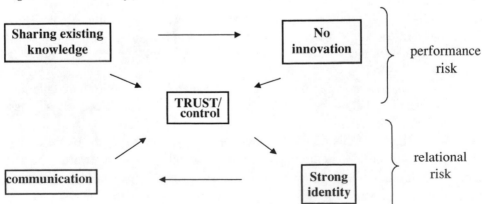

inherent in a shared identity which can cancel out the advantages. Because identity demands consistency, potentially attractive ways for innovation and creativity are kept outside the organization that way.

Identity not only provides a feeling of a shared central character, but also of distinction, what does and does not belong to the domain of the organization.

Precisely because learning is guaranteed in the shared identity, it is impossible for many organizations to innovate. This is also called the problem of the inertia of knowledge (Kogut and Zander, 1992).

The holding on to existing knowledge and patterns of knowledge is explained by the way in which organizations deal with knowledge. Although new information (whether or not in the form of new employees) comes into organizations, in most cases the existing principles of the organization of knowledge and the existing relational structures in the organization are not changed. Organizations are nevertheless open to flows of data, but they are basically closed systems with regard to information and knowledge). What keeps the innovative search limited to the existing knowledge is the fact that knowledge and technologies which fit in with the organizational knowledge and capabilities do not require any changes in the "recipes" for the organization of research and in the organization's meta-knowledge (Kogut & Zander, 1992, p. 392).

The Role of Trust in Markets

There is No Knowledge Sharing in Markets

Trust plays no concrete role in markets. The transactions which have come about through the market mechanism are based on goods or services which are obtained in a competitive situation. This means that the same goods or services can also be supplied by different suppliers. The absence of trust renders knowledge sharing impossible. After all, parties do not trust each other and are afraid that the other party "runs off with the knowledge." As a result of the absence of knowledge sharing, innovation within the relationship between market parties is not possible. Products or services are very easy to specify and contracts will give substance to all aspects which are important for the transaction (terms of delivery, price, quality aspects etc.).

The contracts arrange for the transaction (see Figure 2). Parties therefore do not need to have a common identity because the contracts do not leave anything to be desired with regard to clarity. Not even a common framework of concepts is necessary, because the contract normally specifies the concepts which are important for the transaction. Communication is therefore not necessary to deepen the trust. Performance of the transaction, after all, is not guaranteed by trust, but by contracts and control of them.

The knowledge of an organization or hierarchy has an economical value which rises above market transactions in the sense that identity leads to social knowledge, with which coordination and communication is supported. If an organization

Figure 2: The role of trust in markets

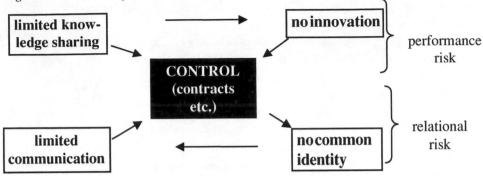

considers innovation to be important, a different form shall need to be chosen for the organization of activities. Markets are not suitable for this. With innovations it is hard or impossible to specify the exchanges in advance. Consequently, specified contracts cannot be drawn up; as a result of which, control is not possible. If trust and control are seen as the ends of a continuum, markets are to be positioned on the side of control.

A qualification is in order here. The fact that trust is not a necessary condition for the achievement of the goals of the organization does not mean that trust plays no role at all in markets. Based on experiences in the past, trust also plays a role in transactions which come about by way of the market mechanism (people also often go back to the same shops, etc.), but it does not play a dominant role in it. The fact of the matter is that there is no obligation to have the next transaction take place in the same way. Subsequent transactions can come about with other parties.

The Role of Trust in Virtual Corporations

Activities can also be organized in other ways than through a hierarchy or market (Das & Teng, 1996, p. 829). Network organizations are a way to cooperate without the hierarchic relations of traditional organizations being necessary for this and without market operation fulfilling its role (Jones, Hesterly & Borgatti, 1997). Albertini (1998) argues that the dependence between organizations keeps becoming greater and this leads to a "variety of hybrid organizational forms ... between markets and hierarchies. This wide population of intermediate structures has been called networks."

Network organizations (Figure 3) are located between markets and hierarchies (Thorelli, 1986; Albertini, 1998). The degree in which opportunism and, directly related to this, the attention to trust play a role depends on the type of network organization. In a virtual corporation the chance of opportunism is great and trust plays a dominant role (Jarvenpaa & Shaw, 1998; Jägers, Jansen, & Steenbakkers, 1998). An important network form is the virtual corporation.

Characteristics of the Virtual Corporation

A virtual corporation is a combination of several, geographically dispersed, parties (persons and/or organizations) that through the combination of mutually complementary core activities and means attempt to achieve a common goal. This virtual corporation has an equal distribution of power of participants. The coordination of these activities is supported by electronic connections (an ICT infrastructure). The virtual corporation can be found in situations of great uncertainty. Participants of the virtual corporation do not try to decrease this uncertainty by means of control or regulation (for example, by means of contracts), but by sharing information and knowledge. An example of this is the cooperation between KPN multimedia and the temporary employment agency START, which was the only temporary employment agency with the courage to share information during the creation of a virtual labour market (the so-called Jobbing Mall) (Jong, 1997).

There is a high degree of mutual dependence between the participants in the virtual corporation. Without the skills and means of the partners the end product or the services cannot be realized. Sharing knowledge takes place because the participants know that they depend heavily on each other and that sharing this is necessary to be able to continue participating in the network (Have et al., 1997).

Figure 3: Networks: Between markets and hierarchies

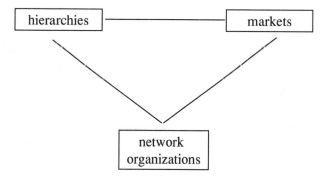

Figure 4: The role of trust in virtual corporations

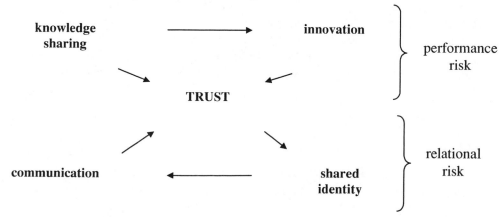

Trust and Identity

Virtual corporations operate in environments that lack certainty. Often they operate on new markets, of which it is uncertain whether the existing knowledge of the individual organizations is applicable. In such situations the organizations are deterred from developing the available knowledge or from imitating the knowledge of other organizations because the organizing principles (i.e., the underlying codes, the meta-knowledge) cannot easily be identified (Kogut & Zander, 1992, p. 395). Beside that, an important characteristic of virtual corporations is that the participants are not physically together. This combination of (extreme) uncertainty and distance seems an insurmountable barrier to knowledge sharing and innovation. Effective virtual corporations, however, meet an essential condition of knowledge sharing. Contrary to participants in a market situation, participants in an effective virtual corporation have a common identity. This identity offers the virtual corporation support in communication and knowledge sharing but is not so strong that the disadvantages of the identity in the more traditional organizations (hierarchy) occur in the form of knowledge inertia and barriers to innovation (see Figure 4). An (often implicitly) common goal of virtual corporations, not surprisingly, is to experiment with new ways in which relationships are structured. The most important function of the shared identity, however, is that this constitutes the basis for the relational trust. Relational trust is a requirement in situations of information asymmetry.

Information Asymmetry

Traditionally, information asymmetry plays an important role in the variety of approaches to organizing. As mentioned earlier, a high degree of information asymmetry has been a reason to keep knowledge sharing within the organization from times immemorial. Virtual corporations are interesting phenomena, because, for the first time, in this way of organizing there is no decrease of information asymmetry or decrease of the related risks of uncertainty (Galbraith, 1976; Williamson, 1975, 1983). It is inherent in the concept of virtual corporations (the sharing of knowledge and the combination of core skills) that information asymmetry exists and is in some cases even promoted. Knowledge sharing in situations of information asymmetry, however, is only possible if there is trust. This trust extends further than merely the expectation of each other that people fulfil agreements and perform. For true knowledge sharing relational trust is essential. There has to be a certain basis of values and standards and of accepted knowledge protocols.

COMMUNICATION AS A POINT OF ACTION

We hold the view that through improvement of the communication, the process of increasing trust and reinforcing the identity can be initiated.

Several "measures" are possible to build up or reinforce a common identity in virtual corporations through communication. Organizational as well as technological (ICT) measures can contribute to this.

Organizational Measures

First of all personal contact can and should be considered. In a virtual corporation the participants will have to get together regularly. The formal as well as the informal meetings will contribute to the common identity. The common identity finds the origin and results in "shared dreams" (Steenbakkers et al., 1998). Since virtual corporations jointly develop a product or service, or introduce it on the market, brands can reinforce the identity ('branding'). The organization of "customer"-days is another possibility to reinforce the common identity. These times offer good possibilities to "make everyone fall into line" in the content-related field, while thoughts can be exchanged also in an informal atmosphere.

Employees who have left the organization (and who have often established companies themselves) can continue to be involved with the organization. They can become a part of the virtual corporation. They know the standards and values of the organization and have partly internalised them.

A virtual corporation does not come to bloom by itself. It is necessary to have a number of "initiators" or "boosters" for this. Who these are is not so important. However, it is important that this group is spirited and passionate about the subject. The "boosters" have to invest a lot of energy in the motivation of the other participants in the virtual corporation.

Training and/or education of participants that are, or are going to, function in a virtual corporation is also a possible measure. Learning a common repertory of concepts can constitute an important part of such training. This could also be applied in a situation in which suppliers and/or customers participate in a virtual corporation.

Technological Measures

Information and communication technology (ICT) plays an increasingly important role in the way organizations function and collaborate. Yet the application of ICT seems to be limited to the support of existing physical processes. Many organizations try to reduce uncertainty that way with the help of ICT. The decrease of information asymmetry is often seen as a goal of the application of ICT in organizations. Also the applications which are developed for knowledge management (intranets and other systems) are usually based on this idea. However, ICT can also play a role in the "bottom" of the model, that is to say the promotion of the communication and the reinforcement of the identity and thereby the trust. This is a condition for cooperation, particularly in virtual corporations.

Because the participants in a virtual corporation are in most cases geographically dispersed, ICT plays an essential role in the realization of the identity, which, however, differs in nature from the often-described role of ICT in innovation. After all, in many virtual corporations ICT is applied in order to support the content-related aspect, the exchange of knowledge and information itself.

Phillips Alaska, for example, a large oil company, has developed a system ("Alaska Drilling Knowledge Transfer") whereby employees, customers, suppliers, and external experts can share knowledge about oil drilling. Not only is knowledge shared by experts within the organization, but also experts outside the organization are involved in the improvement of the processes for oil drilling. Also the experiences of "operators" play a role in the improvement of the drilling process (Pfister, 2000).

Also the applications which are developed for knowledge management (intranets and other systems) are usually based on this idea. Examples of the use of ICT are applications such as e-mail, groupware, and videoconferencing are all focussed on the promotion of the communication and not so much on the content-related aspects.

ICT measures can therefore reinforce the identity. These alone, however, are insufficient to turn a virtual corporation into a success. A mistake which is often made is looking for solutions in technology. Participants in the virtual corporation are responsible for knowledge sharing and keeping the community "lively," not technology. Therefore, when applying ICT, attention shall not only have to be focussed on the establishment of a virtual corporation. This is an important point of attention for the brokers who try to bring the parties in a virtual corporation together, and especially try to keep them together and to help them develop a common identity. In practice it turns out that successful brokers indeed make very great efforts in this field (Bremer et al., 1999). Beside the organizational measures already mentioned ICT can offer possibilities to facilitate and support social relationships within the virtual corporation.

CONCLUSION AND MANAGEMENT CONSEQUENCES

In the discussions of virtual corporations, attention has long been focussed on the aspects of knowledge sharing and innovation. ICT has been considered an important support in this, particularly for the content-related exchange of information between the participants. In this chapter we have indicated that the aspects which are often characterized as the softer aspects of cooperation are playing an increasingly important role. Virtual corporations are the ideal form for optimal knowledge sharing and innovation. They are balancing on a tightrope. They have to have an identity which is strong enough to trust each other and to provide enough meta-knowledge to innovate. At the same time this shared identity cannot become so strong that very promising avenues are blocked, because these require or create knowledge which does not fit in with the collective knowledge models. Those participating in the virtual corporation shall have to become aware of this necessary balance. In the beginning stage of the virtual corporation the shared identity shall have to be created and reinforced. Next, very close attention must be paid to the realization of a shared identity of the network in which their organizations function and to the communication necessary for this. ICT will fulfil a different function here which is mainly aimed at the support of the social relation between the participants in the cooperation. But the participants in the virtual corporation must also keep sufficient freedom to preserve their own separate identities. Only then will the virtual corporation achieve the ideal balance between identity and innovation.

ENDNOTE

1 This definition is largely based on the definition of trust of Knight et al. (1999), in which a party's willingness to adopt a dependent position towards another party is discussed. In this chapter the relational aspect has been added to this definition.

REFERENCES

Albertini, S. (1998, July). *Inter-organizational networks: The conceptual approach and the analytical framework*. Paper presented at the EGOS-14th Colloquium, Maastricht, The Netherlands.

Blau, P. M. (1964). *Exchange and Power in Social Life*. New York: Wiley.

Bradach, J. L., and Eccles, R. G. (1989). Markets versus hierarchies: From ideal types to plural forms. In W.R. Scott (Ed.), *Annual Review of Sociology* (pp. 97-118). Palo Alto, CA.

Bremer, C. F., Mundim, A. P. F., Michilini, F. V. S., Siqueira, J. E. M., and Ortega, L. M. (1999). New product search and development as a trigger to competencies integration in virtual enterprises. In P. Sieber & J. Griese (Eds.), *Organizational Virtualness and Electronic Commerce*: (pp. 205-215). *Proceedings of the 2nd International VoNet Workshop*. Bern, Switzerland: Simowa Verlag.

Das, T. K. and Teng, B. S. (1996). Risk types and inter-firm alliance structures. *Journal of Management Studies, 33*, 827-843.

Das, T. K. and Teng, B. S. (1998). Resource and risk management in the strategic alliance making process. *Journal of Management*, 24, 21-42.

Dasgupta, P. (1988). Trust as a commodity. In Gambetta, D. (Ed.), *Trust*, 49-72. New York: Basil Blackwell.

Davenport, T. and Prusak, L. (1998). *Working Knowledge: How Organizations Manage What They Know*. Boston, MA: Harvard Business School Press.

Galbraith, J. R. (1976). Designing complex organizations. Reading, MA: Addison-Wesley.

Gambetta, D. (1988). *Trust: Making and Breaking Cooperative Relations*. New York: Basil Blackwell.

Grabowski, M. and Roberts, K. H. (1998). Risk mitigation in virtual organizations. *Journal of Computer Mediated Communication*, 3. Retrieved M D, Y from the World Wide Web: http://jcmc.huji.ac.il/vol3/issue4/grabowski.html.

Granovetter, M. S. (1973). The strength of weak ties. *American Journal of Sociology*, 78, 1350-1380.

Granovetter, M. S. (1985). Economic action and social structure: A theory of embeddedness. *American Journal of Sociology*, 91, 481-510.

Granovetter, M. S. (1992). Problems of explanation in economic sociology. In Nohria, N. and Eccles, R. (Eds.), *Networks and Organizations: Structure, Form and Action*. Boston, MA: Harvard Business School Press.

Gulati, R. (1995). Does familiarity breed trust? The implication of repeated ties for contractual choice in alliances. *Academy of Management Journal*, 38, 85-112.

Handy, C. (1995). Trust and the virtual organization. *Harvard Business Review*, 41-50.

Have, S. ten, Lierop, F. van, and Kühne, H. J. (1997). Hoe virtueel moeten we eigenlijk zijn?[Virtuality: To what extent?]. *Nijenrode Management Review*, 85-93.

Hertog, J. F. den, and Huizenga, E. (1997). *De Kennisfactor, Concurreren als Kennisonderneming [The Knowledge Factor: Competing as a Knowledge Corporation]*. Deventer: Kluwer Bedrijfsinformatie.

Hoewijk, R. van. (1988). De betekenis van de organisatiecultuur: Een literatuuroverzicht, (The meaning of organization culture: A literature survey), *M&O*, 42.

Jägers, H. P. M., Jansen, W. and Steenbakkers, G. C. A. (1998). Characteristics of virtual organizations. In Sieber, P. and Griese, J. (Eds.), *Organizational Virtualness*, 65-77. Bern: Simowa Verlag.

Jansen, W., Jägers, H. P. M. and Steenbakkers, G. C. A. (1997). Kennis, macht en informatietechnologie in netwerkvarianten, (Knowledge, power and ICT in network forms). *Management en Informatie*, 5, 4-12.

Jansen, W., Jägers, H. P. M. and Steenbakkers, G. C. A. (1998). Kennismanagement en organisatie-ontwerp, (Knowledge management and organization design). *Management & Informatie*, 6, 30-43.

Jarvenpaa, S. L., Knoll, K. and Leidner, D. (1998). Is anybody out there? Antecedents of trust in global virtual teams. *Journal of Management Information Systems*, 14, 29-64.

Jarvenpaa, S. L., and Shaw, T. R. (1998). Global virtual teams: Integrating models of trust. In Sieber, P. and Griese, J. (Eds.), *Organizational Virtualness*, 35-53. Bern: Simowa Verlag.

Jones, C., Hesterly, W. S. and Borgatti, S. P. (1997). A general theory of network governance: Exchange, conditions and social mechanisms. *Academy of Management Review*, 22, 911-945.

Jong, S. de. (1997). Virtuele arbeidsmarkt geopend, (Creation of a virtual employment market). *Computable*, 11.

Kogut, B. and Zander, U. (1992). Knowledge of the firm, combinative capabilities, and the replication of technology. *Organization Science*, 3, 383-397.

Kogut, B. and Zander, U. (1996). What firms do? Coordination, identity and learning. *Organization Science*, 7, 502-518.

Kraut, R., Steinfield, C., Chan, A., Butler, B. and Hoag, A. (1998). Coordination and virtualization: The role of electronic networks and personal relationships. *JCMC*, 3. Available on the World Wide Web at: http://jcmc.huji.ac.il/vol3/issue4/kraut.html.

Lewicki, R. J., McAllister, D. J. and Bies, R. J. (1998). Trust and distrust: New relationships and realities. *Academy of Management Review*, 23, 438-458.

Luhmann, N. (1988). Familiarity, confidence, trust: Problems and alternatives. In Gambetta, D. (Ed.), *Trust*, 94-107. New York: Basil Blackwell.

Madhok, A. (1996). The organization of economic activity: Transaction costs, firm capabilities, and the nature of governance. *Organization Science*, 7, 577-590.

McKnight, D. H., Cummings, L. L. and Chervany, N. L. (1998). Initial trust formation in new organizational relationships. *Academy of Management Review*, 23, 473-490.

Pfister, M. (2000, May). Lecture presented at the *IRMA Conference*, Anchorage, AK.

Provan, K. G. (1993). Embeddedness, interdependence, and opportunism in organizational supplier-buyer networks. *Journal of Management*, 19, 841-856.

Ring, P. S. and Ven, A. H. van de. (1992). Structuring cooperative relationships between organizations. *Strategic Management Journal*, 13, 483-498.

Ring, P. S. and Ven, A. H. van de. (1994). Developmental processes of cooperative interorganizational relationships. *Academy of Management Review*, 15, 90-118.

Schein, E. H. (1992). *Organizational Culture and Leadership*. New York: Jossey-Bass.

Steenbakkers, G. C. A., Jägers, H. P. M. and Jansen, W. (1998). Prolion: A case study of a virtual organization. Paper presented at the *3rd EGOS Conference*, Maastricht, The Netherlands.

Thorelli, H. B. (1986). Networks: Between markets and hierarchies. *Strategic Management Journal*, 7, 37-51.

Travica, B. (1997). The design of the virtual organization: A research model. *Proceedings of the Americas Conference on Information Systems*, USA, Vol., 417-419.

Volberda, H. W. (1998). *Blijvend Strategisch Vernieuwen: Concurreren in de 21e Eeeuw*, (*Continuing Strategic Renewal: Competing in the 21st Century*). Deventer: Kluwer.

Weggeman, M. (1997). *Kennismanagement*, (*Knowledge Management*). Schiedam: Scriptum Management.

Whitener, E. M., Brodt, S. E., Korsgaard, M. A. and Werner, J. M. (1998). Managers as initiators of trust: An exchange relationship framework for understanding managerial trustworthy behavior. *Academy of Management Review*, 23, 513-530.

Williamson, O. E. (1975). *Markets and Hierarchies*. New York: Free Press.

Williamson, O. E. (1983). Credible commitments: Using hostages to support exchange. *American Economic Review*, 73, 519-540.

Williamson, O. E. (1985). *The Economic Institutions of Capitalism*. New York: Free Press.

Zaheer, A. and Venkatraman, N. (1995). Relational governance as an interorganizational strategy: An empirical test of the role of trust in economic exchange. *Strategic Management Journal*, 16, 373-392.

Chapter IV

The Metamorphosis to Dynamic Trading Networks and Virtual Corporations

Howard D. Richards[1]
MAPS, UK

Harris G. Makatsoris[2]
Orion Logic Ltd., UK

A process of turbulent change is taking place in which companies shape up to deal with the unremitting global competition for which there is an uncertain outcome. Businesses have to look at the wider horizons and dynamics of both their supply chains and markets to discover new ways of working with both customers and suppliers to grow and remain viable. The diverse industrial, commercial and operational practices and processes need to be remolded and target the collaborative aspects of relationships to the advantage of company performance and creation of new opportunities. This chapter outlines some of the constraining forces and suggests the parameters in which a business strategy and a course of action can be devised as a pathway to the future.

INTRODUCTION

Over the last decades of the twentieth century a large number of companies faced the future with trepidation while others lacked a good strategy. This had not happened overnight but had crept upon them over a period of time. Competitive pressures had always been there and many things had been tried, some with success, to stem the loss of market share and even provide market growth. Changes had taken place in the approach to product quality, working practices, and greater customer awareness but making money was becoming more and more difficult. It was a time and climate for dramatic new approaches (Goldman, Nagel & Preiss, 1995). New technologies were replacing old at a faster rate and information technology provided better management and control vision, albeit on a limited local scale. And, push to pull manufacturing (Mertins, 1996) distinctly changed the approach to customers and service. Above all the global reach of customers, manufacturers and service providers keen to exploit the wealth of opportunities in established markets further increased both competitive and economic pressures. Moreover, even players only operating in local markets could not resist the tide of change. As a result many companies and economies (Hutton, 1995) were in a state of upheaval and as a consequence some fell by the wayside. Large companies had to gear up to face the incessant global competition through reorganization, or by stripping to core competencies, or by forming new strategic alliances, or by reducing their product life-cycles, or through changing combinations of these. This was a climate in which start-up companies could flourish and take on the larger, established companies by their sheer agility in markets, their ability to create new markets and their fast use of new technology, their astute design, and their agile management approaches, and at the same time were encouraged by the increasing wealth of venture capital available.

Toward the end of the century it was into this melting pot that a new communications and information technology, pioneered Tim Berners Lee in 1989, emerged. By 1993 the World Wide Web was to produce an environment for a much-needed revolutionary change in industrial approach that was to be far from the former stepwise, cautionary, evolutionary tendency. But like all revolutions a period of chaos exists before a more normal but obviously changed environment is created. During this period of confusion and turbulence there will be survivors and there will be newcomers, the latter entrepreneurial with new ideas and technology to grow their businesses. It is this turbulent period of massive change and uncertainty with its many possible outcomes that is the focus of this chapter; moreover it is the survivors of the old order that are particularly stressed.

METAMORPHOSIS

Metamorphosis as applied here is a process of change from an existing now obsolete way of doing business to a new form but non-predestined state. This is expected to be characterized by an expanding global economy, greater collaboration in supply networks, better deployment of knowledge, greater dynamism, versatility and opportunities in markets, highly dynamic processes, new standards of customer service excellence, and the better use of both capital and human resources.

Philosophical Insights

The greatest obstacle to making progress is complacency. C.G.Zamit states "vested interests and apathy have been the foes to advancement, so strong is the reluctance to change, so great the pain of a new idea, so dominant the power of feeling over reason, of that wish to believe which demands no effort, against the desire to know, which involves strenuous inquiry and application." Max Planck adds a useful insight, "A new scientific truth does not triumph by convincing its opponents, but rather because its opponents die, and a new generation grows up that is familiar with it." Goethe provides further wisdom, "Daring ideas are like chessmen moved forward, they may be beaten, but they may also start a winning game."

Watershed

The 1990s were a watershed. But, it was realized by many in the manufacturing industry and government that skills were the scarcest resource. Nevertheless, the political climate was not all that supportive to ensure both a rapid and highly necessary readjustment to the educational processes. The Cold War had finished and had released massive capital to support industry particularly in the USA, whereas in Europe the single market created massive new opportunities. Time was critical for companies and nation states to capitalize on these altered conditions and it was urgent to change the way things were done. G.W.Possl in his 1991 book *Managing in the new world of manufacturing* wrote, "The keys to leapfrogging competition" are:

- Educate to enhance people's skills and abilities
- Smooth and speed up material and information flow
- Shorten processing cycle times of all activities
- Become more proactive than reactive
- Mount continuous, relentless assaults on all wastes
- Improve teamwork with suppliers and customers

And, directing his attention in particular to the USA states, "The future will be fertile or futile depending on the ability of top level managers in the United States to redirect their efforts in operating manufacturing companies. Manufacturing businesses are not loosely knit confederations of marketing, engineering, finance and manufacturing activities but are with their suppliers and customers, a single entity needing a unified, integrated effort with all functions working closely together utilizing common strategies."

Surge of New Ideas

Such work by Possl and others (Possl, 1991; Warnecke, 1993) both stimulated the debate and commented on the change that was taking place. This helped to focus ideas within the fast mover groups. On the other hand many others did not fully appreciate the vast implications to the way that industry could flourish in the future. They were not convinced followers and were at the same time susceptible to panaceas and the power and glory of the three-letter acronym (e.g., JIT,[3] CIM,[4] ERP,[5] FMS,[6] CRM,[7] etc.) that was pushed by consultants and the technical literature at large. However, some good work was done in improving shop floor systems (Goldratt, 1988; Argello, 1994; PASSE project, 1995; Makatsoris & Besant, 1995), maintenance systems and process control, but an integrated approach to operational and business systems remained weak (Kanet, 1988; PASSE project, 1995). Alvin Toffler commented "one of the most highly developed skills in contemporary Western civilization is dissection: the split-up of problems into their smallest possible components. We are good at it. So good we often forget to put the pieces back together again." Nevertheless, work on IT architectures, frameworks and standards–SEMATECH (Whelan, 1995), NIIIP (Hardwick et al., 1996), EUROFRAME (Ridder et al., 1997) and new software and system approaches (Leachman et al., 1996; Richards et al., 1997) pioneered some new ideas for integrated processes.

Early Setbacks

Missing were more intelligent approaches to IT (Drucker, 1992; Macintosh, 1994; Nonaka, 1998) and their application, and, more importantly, how people and the organization functioned to make effective use of the possible faster, yet more accurate means to information as well as to control its flow. At the same time skepticism within organizations developed because information system integration work was mostly not well done. Poor data collection timeliness and its questionable relevance to help people to effectively carry out their jobs added to a growing resistance to change. Management too was dubious because past significant investment in IT had not come up to expectation. As a consequence this stimulated risk aversion to try any new offering, however good they might intrinsically be. And, at the far end of the company spectrum amongst the many SMEs[8] there was little IT and an immaturity in the use of management and control systems. Research work through DARPA in the USA and collaborative industrial research and development projects in Framework III, IV and V in Europe helped to stem this negativism.

A Barrier to Change

Goldman, Nagel and Preiss (1995) state "It is easy to misunderstand the nature of revolutionary change and to suppose that it happens overnight, with one well-defined set of rules applicable on one day and a new set of well-defined rules suddenly applicable on the next day. In fact, the transition is prolonged; turbulent and confused, with some period during which it is not at all clear which rules if any are operative. Misunderstanding the nature of the revolutionary change can cause individuals and societal and corporate leaders, who are searching for stability in the midst of turbulence to make the wrong strategic decisions. Living with uncertainty and striving to understand the emerging pattern of the new status quo are essential elements of all revolutionary change."

New Ways of Supporting the Change

Electronic business emerged in the 1990s as a new force to influence the direction of the change process. E-mail communication became the norm for large company intra-communication and was used increasingly for business to business communication for both ease and speed. Moreover, the Internet gave customers greater access to information and provided the means for on-line shopping and selling and provided imaginative SMEs with new business opportunities. Internet communication for electronic business became a focus for enabling a global, networked business operating from anywhere at any time. New IT companies were formed to support this new form of doing business. Many new business models, it has been claimed, were created overnight to better serve business to customer and business to business. Cisco as a networking equipment manufacturing company, with the necessary backbone infrastructure, was to capitalize on this trend with its company mission, "Shape the future of the Internet by creating unprecedented value and opportunity for our customers, employees, investors and ecosystem partners." It's phenomenal growth in size since becoming a public company in 1990, after its foundation in 1984, has increased from $69M in that year to a market capitalization of $260B in 2000. Cisco is still recognized as one of America's corporate successes, a global market eCommerce leader that holds No. 1 or No. 2 position for every market segment it participates in. But not all companies that formed to take advantage of the new business opportunities faired as well.

Visionary Shortcomings

Many of these companies labeled "dot.com" in the closing days of 2000 had either failed or were cutting back on staff. Many had been set up for on line shopping and electronic retailing (eTailing) and discovered that the economics of their markets was not as advantageous as they first thought. They had naively assumed that to capture some share of the transactions in an industry by acting as a market intermediary, or by supplying a small solution into an unformed problem space was a viable business. Mechanisms were either to charge a small margin for buyers and sellers, or to sell at greatly reduced prices to attract customers and hope to make money from online advertising and content, then watch the revenue pour in. For Business-to-Business, B2B, solutions the problem they targeted was superficial solving only a small part of a comprehensive challenge facing industry at large. The challenge was more than about procurement; it was to do more with integrated and collaborative supply chains, people and organization. Moreover even for electronic procurement, Glenn Ramsdell has commented in a McKinsey report of 2000, "Resistance to change within a company can be a huge obstacle to bringing its purchases online.... lots of people charged with procurement are not technologically sophisticated and have little or no experience in buying online. Some feel threatened by the possibility that they could be replaced by software."

Industrial Reservations to Change Expressed

A survey of 2,016 SMEs, carried out by Institute of Information Systems for the Swiss Government (Hunziker & Sieber, 1999), was designed to discover barriers for taking up the Internet or intensifying its usage and the known benefits. It concluded that the adoption of the Internet is influenced by the perception of the changes taking place in large industrial companies and that a major benefit was seen as company-to-customer image enhancement. It illustrated the difficulties of such surveys because of the general lack of understanding of both the direction and degree of industrial change and their place in it as well as what had to be done and the options available for their survival.

In the summer of 2000 Deloitte and Touche (2000) in conjunction with Cardiff Business School's Lean Enterprise Research Center conducted a study of British industry and their conception of the future of eBusiness to produce a group report. Their key findings were an inherent risk aversion to change because of fear of failure and a lack of understanding of the implications, although it was believed that major benefits could result from closer supply chain cooperation and collaboration. Customers were seen as the driving force for any change and at the same time stakeholders in general also wanted a company commitment to eBusiness. Nevertheless, eBusiness was not appropriately on the strategic agenda per se but was part of a general strategy to improve business. Moreover, technology for eBusiness was not seen as a major barrier but was more to do with people and the wider organization.

These surveys serve to illustrate the degree of uncertainty surrounding the Internet despite its potential to serve change and that this uncertainty is largely to do with people and organization. A quotation, in the Deloitte & Touche survey, from a CEO of one of the automotive companies when responding to a question on return on investment for eBusiness serves to illustrate a dilemma not only facing large companies but also SMEs, "There's a leap of faith, because you have to believe it's going to come in the future. It's frightening. I think it's very scary. Like the Emperor's New Clothes.... The payback is usually in things like knowledge sharing, which will make the organization more efficient, more able to respond to customers, more able to maximize growth opportunities. All these are fine words, but they are very difficult to turn into hard payback."

Importance of Security and Trust

Another challenge in the change process is security and along with this trust. These are big issues and are being addressed by governments and other specialist organizations (CEC Directorate General Information Society). It is too much for this chapter to cover but suffice it to say that solutions may be found in further regulation, biometric solutions for individual identification, and securer forms of data protection.

Strategy for Change

Even so, pressure for change is both overpowering and relentless, and however apprehensive CEOs may be they must address these pressures full on with a level head and a clear strategy for both the short and long term. It is obvious many are finding it tough to adjust to the continual demands. Global competition has hit a number of old established companies and as a consequence they are having a hard time hanging on to their profitability and shareholder value. Factory closures, contracted manufacturing and other services, seeking new alliances, selling off all but core competence and so on are all part of today's industrial scene. Smaller companies too are not unaffected and can no longer rely on former business practices. If they do not take the new opportunities on offer they will fail to realize their full potential. Failure to appreciate the importance of the key and the many varied elements in the value chain with its accompanying risks will prove disastrous. New solutions for both business improvement and an enlarged shareholder value must be found. There is no prescriptive process for this. Nevertheless, solutions will be found in a blend of proper reengineering of business processes between companies, technology, and organization development with an accompanying skill and empowerment development for employees in the supply networks. Those CEOs who are unfit to deal with the challenge appropriately will assuredly fall by the wayside. This will leave others to grasp the complex decisions to be made as well as to ensure continual self-assessment. For there is no doubt that the magnitude of industrial change taking place invokes a clear vision, a capacity for innovation and reformation together with a strong leadership. The winners will be those that create very flexible and highly adaptable and moreover continual learning companies. These will have an entirely new set of values as well as encouraging rewarding relationships with both their customers and suppliers.

TOOLS AND SYSTEMS FOR OPERATIONS AND MARKETS

Software tools and ICT[9] systems are important enablers in the change process and have played a major role in the emerging new ways of doing business.

An Early Parochial Emphasis

During the early 1990s changes were afoot to improve planning scheduling and manufacturing control. They were mainly aimed at parochial solutions, being shop floor or company centric. The shop floor execution systems although responding to the dynamics prevailing were mostly out of sync with an input-driven planning system that had expectations from its outputs. It was essential that better foundations were laid and much research during that time was aimed to create flexible systems built on good models for product flow in a resource-limited environment. Such improvements contributed to the health and vitality of a company, but not all managers understood the essential differences and completeness of the functionality expressed by the three separate parts. Moreover IT service companies had a lack of expertise across the whole supply chain and only had specialist skills that supported a limited functionality.

Limitations of Application Toolbox Approach

Planning systems invariably used out-of-date information with embedded policies that were at variance with the real needs of an enterprise. For example lead times and stock levels were not optimized but invariably used standard settings agreed for a budgetary year or some other fixed period of accounting. This inevitably in turn led to a frustration between the production planning departments and the shop floors and led to disbelief and lack of confidence in the IT system. It created fire fighting as a norm. The cause and effect, however, was heightened or reduced by the current status of demand exceeding capacity or the reverse. Many systems at that time encouraged a deliberate reduction of the effect by having plenty of reserve capacity so that adjustments in the shop floor were made easier. This did not solve the problem but hid it and at further expense to the enterprise by ineffectual use of its resources, which in some industries was at a very significant cost.

Pressures for Change

Outsourcing manufacturing to contract service providers begun before the nineties had continued to increase. And, as a consequence some manufacturing companies were part of a close supply network although not integrated with it. These loose supply networks limited improvements to product lead time, delivery guarantees and waste reduction even though special arrangements between businesses for manufacturing capacity were agreed well ahead of the time that they were required. At the same time relationships with customers were not all that they could be. The knowledge of product demand, used in sales forecasts and planning, was unsatisfactory and resulted in poor delivery promises. Yet in spite of the poor performance customers continued to put pressure on reducing the time from order placement to delivery and wanted more and more customized product. Continued business was secured through reduced product life cycles. Postponement of the final steps of product manufacture enabled speedy customization. As a result this put further pressure on companies to reduce the product to market time that led to a requirement for a tighter control of the planning and control processes.

Aspects for Change

These new pressures to improve product, manufacturing and service supply needed a new approach. This involved not only the whole supply chain but also with the added benefit of integrated company functions of manufacturing, design, sales and marketing and finance. One of the challenges faced was to try not to reduce forecast error but to learn to deal with the impact of errors. The key was to close the gap between "what is planned to do" with respect to "what has to be done" taking proper account of capacity in the whole supply chain. So, it was no longer useful spending further money to improve shop floor control in isolation, as some companies had continued to do, without any advantageous impact on the end customer delivery performance and perhaps even having a deleterious effect on it.

Moreover, a more astute use of all resources was essential to reduce waste in time and material, particularly in industries where low margins were rife because of the prevailing intense global competition. It became essential to market products and services to a wider audience of customers and to provide the ordering process with a vision of the capacity available to ensure well-informed delivery promises.

Early Enablers for Large Companies

Large companies with disparate production activities were under pressure to do something to improve upon their lack of good connectivity between a range of IT systems that served different purposes from administration to production. Enterprise resource planning (ERP) became a focus in the middle 1990s to solve the problem. It was designed to improve the underlying business processes for both discrete manufacturing and process industries with distributed manufacturing. It integrated finance, administration, production and logistics. Many large companies invested in this with commercial solutions from the major vendors such as SAP, J.D. Edwards, Baan, and Peoplesoft. These solutions because of the large investment and commitment required by the user, were not usually applicable to the small company.

ERP though offers limited functionality and is designed to improve efficiency with standardized transactions. It is essentially a transaction system that is able to provide some improvements to planning for a company but the planning systems still relied on aggregate data that remained out of sync with reality making for unrealistic plans. ERP does not have models that are needed to respond rapidly to real time changes in supply, demand, resources, or capacity. Nevertheless ERP brought some rewards although it was nowhere near the total solution for a future need; it is company centric and cannot support a supply chain. At the same time a number of IT providers were offering supply chain management (SCM) software. This software has customized and special algorithms and in-memory processing that allowed flexibility in planning. It generated delivery promises based on actual production capacities. These systems are able to allocate production between different plants for various stages in manufacture, whereby costs of supply; transport, inventory and production are optimized for the whole chain. Among the leaders of these solutions are i2 Technologies and Manugistics. In addition to these supply chain offerings special software for advanced planning and scheduling (APS) became available. Also a fusion of all these technologies became possible through open extensible architectures, frameworks and special middleware. Yet these solutions were aimed mainly at the larger company and still tend to provide a hub company centric view without shared risk and equitable profit throughout the supply network and not least with a lack of true collaboration, or ability for dynamic trade.

New Technology Possibilities for All

Research work in the 1990s originating in both America and Europe provided the next advancements in systems. By 2000 results had not only provided a potential for better concurrent planning and control but were also applicable to an adaptive supply network. They supported a highly collaborative extended enterprise or virtual corporation through appropriate filtered yet shared information. As a result synchronized supply chains will have a major impact on all partners in the network by streamlining the supply route and its options. The conditions to satisfy these new forms of an agile collaborative supply chain are:

- Companies collaborate with supply chain partners and synchronize operations
- Technology and the world wide web are the key enablers
- Supply chain organizations must be restructured and reskilled to achieve these goals.

The next section will deal with collaborative aspects and the organization, whereas here the status of technology accomplishments will be further elaborated.

Information and knowledge sharing to provide good real time visibility is the key. Advances in open technical architectures and communication via the World Wide Web and intelligent agents (Weiss, 1999; Dyck, 2000; Weiss, 1999; IACT open standards, RosettaNet) have made this possible. Moreover, advances in planning and scheduling algorithms and optimization logic that deals with the highly dynamic, distributed and disparate nature of the supply network with its numerous constraints have proceeded at a fast rate (Makatsoris, 1996). They shape end-to-end planning of the entire delivery system from customer to supplier. New planning solutions are created as new incremental commitments are made. This is achieved by selecting or rejecting orders within seconds that is based on both the feasibility and profitability of individual orders, which in turn synchronously drives planning into execution. Also realizable are software applications for assisting decisions. They can deal with various forms of event-driven business situations and processes with 'what if' exploration and an ability to evaluate consequences of decisions before they are taken. Furthermore, advances in product and service visibility via online catalogues and intelligent information searches, customization possibilities, available inventories, and current capabilities enable commercial solutions for not only both rapid order configuration and a high quality online order promising but also opportunistic selling of capacity and inventory (Orion Logic Ltd. 2000). All this is achieved without the excessive bureaucracy that limits speedy delivery in most current systems.

Customer Service

It is now possible for customers to be served better than ever before by providing them with a greater visibility of their orders and a better control of the order process through direct online responses with the supplier. It is also possible for customers to be directly involved in the product design process. But new metrics (Frick & Lill, 2000) are still required that will provide further information to stimulate both customer confidence and loyalty.

Stacie McCullough of Forrester Research has stated, "To survive, supply chains are going to have to work at Internet speed, which will mean turning outward and cooperating with customers and suppliers in a new way. Executives must implement changes to their companies for 'dynamic trade'–the ability to satisfy current demand with customized response–by creating supply chain networks that include dynamic planning, constant communication, and make/move logistics."

Progress Toward Dynamic Trading

Electronic Markets grew quickly at the end of the nineties supported by technology from companies such as Ariba. Ariba and others have solutions that have encouraged market makers to accommodate many types of trading for the benefit of mainly the buyer and partially the seller. Most marketplace architects are committed to open standards but as yet they are to be universally agreed on. Inevitably work on standards is slow and requires considerable effort before they emerge. In the meantime start-ups such as webMethods (2001) have developed the equivalent of translation software to ensure open communication between buyers and sellers as well as between marketplaces. Dynamic pricing and online auctions (Levy, 2000) have provided the necessary flexibility for selling off excess inventory. Yet the scale and scope of emarkets are still to develop. There will be many failures as well as successes (Whiston et al., 2001) before emarkets mature in a form and with network flexibility that forges comprehensive support to the supply chain, incremental supply, and a high quality customer service. To survive supply chain networks have to change to become more nimble with constant meaningful communication at Internet speed between partners. They need to more accurately respond to customer requests and need to deploy technological improvements astutely to assist with new opportunity taking, effective commitments, improved resource utilization and speedy in time delivery. These dynamic trading networks are not only possible for particular supply chains but will be part of a much wider industrial market that can pit supply chain against supply chain.

Technology to support the synchronized collaborative supply chain and dynamic trading markets is available from an increasing range of suppliers (Whiston et al., 2001; Orion Logic Ltd., Extricity Inc., Atlas Commerce Inc.) that covers the whole spectrum of industries and size of company. Alliances between third party service providers, technology providers and management consultants are expected to be a growing force to help support the process of change with a supply of a massive range of speciality solutions with pick and choose propositions for users comprising two or more collaborative partners in business.

DEVELOPING AND CHANGING ORGANIZATION

But ICT alone is almost never a source of sustainable competitive advantage. Rather it is through the use of ICT in support of business strategies focussed on people that an organization can gain a significant advantage.

The Agile Company

During the late 1980s a process began which seriously questioned the way businesses operate. New ideas and concepts began to be formulated for new ways of working. A seminal work on the subject, requested by the US Congress, was published in 1991 by Lehigh University's Iacocca Institute as "21st century manufacturing enterprise strategy; an industrial led view." The report came to a unanimous conclusion by executives from around 200 companies, government agencies and public organizations that supported the work. One of the report's conclusions was that further incremental improvement of the mass production system for manufacturing could not regain competitiveness for US companies and that new ways of working would be the agile enterprise. The vision of the agile enterprise was further developed and elaborated in a book *Agile Competitors and Virtual Organizations* (Goldman et al., 1995).

A quote from the book describes the agile company as, "An agile company is one that has fully assimilated the new understanding of production and the implications of the shift in value toward information and service products. Such a company is thus able to pursue two concurrent marketing and product development strategies: the proactive creation of new customer opportunities, and a rapid reaction to unanticipated opportunities. To implement these strategies, a company must be able to develop new products more quickly, at much lower cost, than has been done historically for its markets; and the products must provide high customer-perceived value through individualization."

Utilization of Teamwork

The change in industrial paradigm meant a significant change from the hierarchical and at the same time inherently high inertia organization to one of a different form and principle. Some companies improved their agility with cross-functional teams focussed on well-defined business scenarios with the resources and new tools to assist them. Their rewards were based on the value solutions they created. More importantly, cross-functional teams began to be organized in the larger companies to serve the supply chain, far more closely than the mass production environment ever did. They work for both suppliers and customers alike to improve operational and market performance. The upshot of this was that people and knowledge have become recognized, as a company's most valuable asset, contributing to both profit and growth. For the smaller company agility can be inherent through its entrepreneurial management structure but even the smaller company needs to become faster acting through encouraging both new people skills and teamwork.

Importance of a Wider Collaboration

There is no prescriptive way to organize but an organization must be flexible enough to use a multiple of concurrent strategies. These strategies should be the most profitable given the variety of customers and suppliers as well as the various changing markets in which a company competes. Closer collaboration is thus an imperative to improve organization and supply chain performance. During the 1990s the virtual corporation, in which companies collaborate to reach well-defined goals was coined to express the nature of this new collaboration. However it is the degree of collaboration, the constellation of companies involved, the duration of the collaboration, the nature of the business processes involved that are not always easy to express or even to define. But to build such virtual corporations, trust and dependability between partners are prerequisites. Inter-company and Inter-organizational relationships have to be both developed and engineered over a period of time before an effective collaboration is possible.

Dynamic Engagement

The dynamic engagement between companies, their organizations and dedicated teams, and the individual will have to change to be more open. Rules in business processes will subtly alter to allow this openness. They will be expressed in greater knowledge and information exchanges. Decision making will change to take more account of the greater whole for the benefit to all parties involved. An old adage expresses the care that is required by making an analogy to driving a car, "Driving along in normal conditions we steer in the direction we wish to go. But when the weather changes and icy or very wet, conditions prevail, there is less friction between the tires and the road and the car may go into a skid. If it skids it is then important for us to steer into the direction the car is moving to get out of the skid. Unfortunately this is not an instinctive reaction as inexperienced drivers or those that are not sensitive to the conditions, knows to their downfall." So, changes in system parameters can create a new set of rules by which to operate the system. For this reason it is no longer good enough for a company to only improve its internal systems; it needs to work hard at improving its actions when interacting with both suppliers and customers. The necessary deeper relationships foreseen will raise both customer satisfaction and improve supply change performance, as well as increase market opportunities.

Company Motives

A Deloitte and Touche report (2000) describes three different forms of company perspectives. First they identify the global company with diverse and globally spread semi-independent companies. Secondly, the multi-customer businesses of varying size and that have many types of service channels (B2B, B2C) and forms. Thirdly, the SMEs that are driven by a strong desire to be integrated into a supply chain. They still have a high level of enthusiasm despite their disillusionment with the poor adaptivity and high cost of ICT and their concerns about the motives of partners and the degree of transparency required. To quote,

- The globally dispersed corporation: "To create a connected corporation, reengineering the organization and the supply chain to offer high performance and flexibility. The outcome of ebusiness is regarded as new business; seamless integration of customers and suppliers, inter-organizational collaboration and learning, twenty-four hour access to competence centers and stabilization of purchasing costs."
- Multi-customer network: "To create an environment for 'unleashing the ability to enter new niches, and to differentiate by offering quick response to consumers and last minute configuration of orders....the pressures of the

market include lead time reduction, increasing the range of products, customization, synchronized replenishments and cost reduction.'"

•   Enthusiastic SMEs: "Faced with uncertainty, many small businesses are engaging in collective efforts and sharing risks by jointly developing electronic marketplaces."

Motives then are dissimilar for different companies as how they see the outcome of the change process and their imposition on others to conform. Large companies are only interested in gaining competitive edge, not in creating a level playing field where actions are taken that deliver the most benefit across the supply chain. On the contrary their action is to cultivate a clique of key trading partners. In any event, behavioral patterns can confine many companies to narrow approaches that may not allow them to reach their strategic goals. Process practices deemed best could even limit a company's ability to truly deal with change.

Allowing Adaptivity

Changes in company organization that over the last decade force individuals to conform to a company norm tend to prevent a new idea for reengineering a business process being accepted, particularly if a 'best practice' is already enshrined in the system with strict disciplines enforced. The current turbulent economic environment needs a strong leadership that creates an atmosphere in which both individuals and organizations can respond to new stimuli with nothing set in concrete. Reinforcing this, the purpose of ICT is to help organizations reach their strategic goals.

Need for Intelligent Use of Information

The use of ERP in recent years has constrained some companies to historical accounting systems, which conceal the ability of an organization to perform a task. Traditional costing systems take little account of the individuality of orders, or the specific consumption of company resources and capacity, and can lead to poor decision making. Although there is no general agreement on how costs should be allocated, an agile company must change its perspectives and methods to ensure good decision making. Time-based costing has been proposed as a methodology (Goldman et al., 1995) but is as yet not generally adopted. It is an example where a company must become more intelligent in its operations and look carefully at its knowledge base, business and inter-business processes.

Use of Knowledge

Conventionally people as experts in "long-term" jobs have acquired knowledge that deals to some extent with the wrinkles of every day company life which assists them in performing their job. This tacit knowledge is likely to be lost if the individual leaves the company. Although these insights, experience and wisdom exist within an individual and are in turn difficult to document, cross-functional team working and collaborative supply chain interactions help to encourage knowledge sharing as well as stimulate a learning process. Eventually this may be expressed as explicit knowledge for use in a reengineered business process that will assist in trust building between organizations. Knowledge is continually gained within the highly dynamic environment of business today and is important to fully use for competitive edge. Mechanisms to express knowledge may be difficult but it is important that company leaders encourage the process of how to do this.

Decision Making

Individuals and teams need to use their full intellect and make total use of their experience and skill. Accordingly, ICT systems must be engineered to support this and provide them with the power of useful tools for information acquisition and assisted decision making to the benefit of the organization and the company stakeholders. It is important that tailored interfaces are used and supplied with easy but rapid access to all relevant up-to-date information from within a dispersed company as well as across the whole supply chain, and that applications allow for assisted informed decision making. This is used in the many situations where automated decision making is not appropriate. Nevertheless, automatic processes should be available for routine normal processes, whereby excessive bureaucracy can be removed to free up valuable time.

Insights in Organizational Theory

Some insights for how change may take place may be found in organizational theory . There are a number of organizational forms (Scott, 1992), and the open system, which is defined as, "organizations are systems of interdependent activities linking shifting coalitions of participants; the systems are embedded independent continuing exchanges with and constituted by–the environment in which they operate," seems most applicable for a virtual corporation. Boulding (1956) described a nine-point classification to describe the notion that types or level of systems vary both in the complexity of their parts and in the nature of the relationships among the parts. Two systems seem particularly useful to discuss in the context of this chapter, the cybernetic system and the open system. Boulding defines these as follows,

- *Cybernetic System*: systems capable of self-regulation in terms of some externally prescribed target or criterion.
- *Open System*: systems capable of self-maintenance based on throughput of resources from its environment.

The Cybernetic System

A general view of a cybernetic system is to emphasize the importance of centers for operations, control and policy and the flows amongst them. The policy center, for example, a hub company in a supply network, sets the goals for the system. This activity occurs in response to demands or preferences from the environment for instance, as customer orders or market demand. Setting goals is based upon information received from the environment and encourages favorable exchanges between the environment and the organization. The policy center transmits the goals and performance standards to the control center, which for an extended or virtual enterprise has additional linked distributed sub-control systems serving the individual competence centers or companies in the network or virtual corporation. The local control centers will have local forms of sub-goals that may be in terms of sub-order starts and outs schedules. The control center also monitors order flow in the distributed value network and compares results with a set of schedules for products, services, quality, quantity and time control windows. Any discrepancies must be dealt with by corrective action reschedules as prescribed by an inherent decision-software program. A second feedback control loop to the hub company is intuitive in a cybernetic system of this kind where outputs of the complete system are viewed and reacted to by external influences such as a new customer expectations and fed to the hub company policy unit. A system of this type may be mapped to one used for automated decision making in a virtual corporation.

An Open System

However most organizations are subjected to a great deal of uncertainty and function at a much higher level of complexity. Open systems are capable of importing energy from their environment. They can acquire inputs of greater complexity than their outputs and are thus able to restore their own energy and repair the organization. So, such systems maintain themselves and even evolve toward an increase in order and complexity. Thus a constellation of partner companies in a collaborative supply network can form temporary virtual corporations by which orders can be incrementally split to access the available capacity in the highly dispersed network and meet delivery and cost requirements.

Organizational Choice and the Change Process

Not all environments place the same demands on organizations or for the IT employed. Scott (1992) has stated, "the best way to organize depends on the nature of the environment to which the organization relates." Lawrence and Lorsch (1967) argued "different environments place differing requirements on organizations: specifically environments characterized by uncertainty and rapid rates of change in which market conditions or technologies present different demands.. involving constraints and opportunities... than do stable environments."

Organization change is driven at a pace that will be governed more by the social and cultural needs as well as economic imperatives than any prescribed form. Their effectiveness may not be so much their adaptation to the environment but their ability to use their full potential and to swiftly learn and reconfigure.

A Methodology for Change and Industrial Cases

According to James P. Womack and Daniel Jones in their book *Lean Thinking* to get the best from any technology, including that of information and communications; you look before you leap, think before you act, and aim to make improvements in three crucial elements of time, money and efficiency–cutting the first, saving the second and increasing the third.

Industrial Paralysis

Fear to adopt new business practices in full is underlying in managers and executives in both North American and European companies. How do you persuade company management to abandon the systems and strategies that have made their companies and them rich and successful? This is not a trivial matter but the lesson for all major industrial change is that the new order has always won in the past. Nevertheless, some believe that different modes of industrial paradigm can live alongside each other. But, this will only happen to a limited extent, as seen from the historical perspective, in which the old order peters out to very niche areas. Nonetheless, business is still reluctant to accept the obvious conclusion, the current state of transition to eBusiness will be resolved by revolution not by evolution.

Management Awareness

Company management must first come to grips with understanding their current state and defining where they need to be in the next year the one after and the one after that and so on into the future, although the next two year horizon will be the most critical. The change is so fast and the technology and applications available to assist are emerging at no less a pace that choice is vast for any action plan. So, how do companies get to grips by focussing on an achicvablc plan?

Early Movers

Leading-edge companies as Dell, Wal-Mart and Coca-Cola have been well reported for their "early-mover" change to tightly controlled value networks with good business and customer benefits. According to the Stern Stewart EVA 1000 database the eight-year period growth from 1988 to 1996 for the three companies exceeded the industry average: 250% for Wal-Mart, 500% for Coca-Cola and 3000% for Dell. Dell, a leading supplier of computer systems, based its business on direct selling and build to order that is tailored to suit individual customers.

Case Studies

The following cases are cherry-picked to provide some insight to some early challenges with respect to the change process as well as organization variations.

Case 1: Furniture Supply and Retail

In 1998 a North American family furniture company and a retail outlet that had recently changed to a younger management got together to discuss the situation of stock and stock turnover. The furniture trade like many others is subject to fashion and cyclic demand, but the demand is very difficult to predict. The historical reordering process was based on irregular order periods due to long lead times and uncertain delivery performance and as a consequence there were missed sales opportunities and much stock at the retail outlet was left unsold. New rules of engagement were looked at throwing out the old constraints as a historical baggage. A new promise by the furniture supplier was a sixteen-day delivery promise, providing orders were placed weekly. These regular orders were to be based upon what was sold the previous week, eliminating any need of forecasts. So, the furniture manufacturer was then able to change the shipping process for goods because of the now regular receipt of orders, and was also able to organize transport routes on a regional basis with a guaranteed shipping price regardless of order size. The retailer was also able to change the pay policies for his sales staff by rewarding for actual billed sales and not bookings. With these new arrangements the sales staff knew the actual stock to sell and as a result the sales went up. The new business arrangements provided a competitive edge. In a short time the salespeople no longer talked about better inventory management but the guaranteed delivery, a very important change in perspective for customer service. As a consequence the now very profitable business grew with a larger variety and range of products that were introduced on the same basis to satisfy an increasing customer demand. The moral of this story is that ICT need not be used to transform a business but more intelligent thinking by intelligently questioning the reasons for all the existing constraints in business, marketing and operations.

Case 2: Microelectronic Chip Supply Network

Traditionally the semiconductor (silicon chip) industry had been limited by the capabilities of process equipment. R&D had driven the process developments for the device manufacturer, and in turn the equipment manufacturers were challenged to rapidly provide reliable and quality tools that were suitable for economic manufacture of microelectronic circuits. In this way the time to market for new products provided a competitive advantage for the chip manufacturer. Within this scenario the "silicon-chip" companies were the driving forces for major industrial change. The turbulent global economic climate of the 1990s was to change all this. Kristine Perham writing in the *Semiconductor Magazine* in September 2000 states, "Although suppliers were at the mercy of their customers, the industry was not truly customer-driven. End consumers based purchase decisions on available products. Today, consumers have many alternatives and often wait for the next version if a product does not have every feature they want. This has led to a (further) shrinking of product life cycles and accelerated product roll out cycles for consumer goods, which puts pressure on the entire supply chain." As a consequence the supply chain companies looked for new solutions to improve efficiency, cut costs and preserve margins to remain competitive.

The supply network for "silicon chips" is highly fragmented with much contracted manufacturing of key process stages. At the beginning of 1996, a three year ESPRIT project X-CITTIC (1997) started with the aim to tackle the end-to-end planning, scheduling and control problem of the microelectronics extended enterprise, with hub company control, from silicon wafers to packaged chip deliveries to customers. The extended enterprise comprised global-based companies involved in the manufacturing and distribution process on a contracted basis. The project's research resulted in a scalable distributed client-server framework; embedded flexible and adaptable models for capacity, cost, and product manufacturing; and object-oriented software modules targeted at online order promising, an optimizing extended enterprise scheduler, and an event-driven reactive control module linked and integrated with a globally distributed information manager that was integrated with local manufacturing site ERP and shop floor systems, or other relevant databases. The distributed and integrated system was designed to fit between the higher level local company planning systems and the lower level local shop floor execution systems. It was an ambitious project for its time but has since resulted through Orion Logic Ltd. (Orion), with a commercial offering 'StarActive Platform' that comprises a series of enterprise assisted collaboration applications and an open distributed computing framework for deployment, suitable for a broad range of B2B eBusiness solutions. Orion's platform and applications help businesses to create their own private collaborative B2B e-commerce and eHub solutions across multiple tiers of suppliers, subcontractors, customers and trading partners. It offers new methods to sell more products and services and cut inventory and resource wastage and as a result achieves very significant cost savings as well as providing the infrastructure and means to develop inter-company collaboration.

Case 3: An Outsourced Manufacturing Service

Such large networks, as the above, which involve companies that are part of other supply chains are tough projects to carry through with great difficulties to predict the return on investment. Challenges on the micro-model rather than the macro-model in the first instance are more rewarding to solve. Such a challenge is for the contracted service provider for one or more manufacturing stages in microelectronics value network. These companies have the standard processes and sell capacity to a large number of hub 'si-chip' manufacturers and specialized design houses.

Taiwan Semiconductor Manufacturing (TSMC) is the world's largest contract manufacturer with revenues in excess of $1.5B. TSMC has the challenge of producing custom-made integrated circuits for over 400 customers around the world, each having unique products, proprietary system infrastructures and different ways of doing business. In 1997 TSMC chose Extricity Alliance software (Extricity, 2000) to drive a major strategic initiative to fundamentally improve the way they interact with their customers. They wanted to improve visibility of order flow to their customers as well as to manage lead time, key for their customer interests. At the same time TSMC was not able to support the "virtual fab" model (as in X-CITTIC). Nevertheless in essence they wanted to appear to their customers as near to an internal manufacturing group as possible. Manual communication processes involving faxes, e-mails and EDI had proved to be error prone and did not reflect the up-to-date picture. Extricity's solutions provided a limited means of B2B information exchange between different forms of local legacy IT systems. By these means, information sharing on forecasts, work in progress tracking, engineering and design and linking order management processes eliminated inefficient manual processes, reduced work-in-progress levels, provided improved capacity planning and resulted in a 25% reduction in lead time. Such gains, although attractive and can be expected by sharing information, go only a little way to collaborative enterprise. Further advances in collaboration will be necessary to deal more effectively with the highly dynamic environment prevailing.

Case 4: Micro-Company Suppliers for Ceramic and Stone Tiles

The construction industry is important to the global marketplace and many SMEs and micro-companies fit within its compass. One such example is the industrial supply of tiles. Supply of tiles is part of the vertical market for the construction industry. Europe has a wealth of micro-companies and SMEs and used to be a market leader for supply with production generally carried out from the Mediterranean countries. The current total turnover is around 15B Euro from 600 companies. But over the last decade China has steadily gained market share and is now recognized as the world market leader. This has challenged the European supply industry to do something to stem market share loss.

Tile suppliers are generally micro-businesses characterized by a small numbers of employees. Tiles are highly fashionable with generally short product life cycles but are also difficult to quality control with respect to color match. Each batch tends to be different. There is also no universal standard for the product identification. The micro-businesses tend to sell to local traders or to foreign wholesalers through use of tile samples to stimulate interest. The form of selling and quality variations tend to result in unsold stock either in finished or in a partially finished state that could be sold if there were new economic opportunities to a wider market through better information flow between the seller and the buyer. In general the micro-companies have a small production capability, no inventory management or policy, a weak commercial structure, poor visibility of the wider market or supply chain and no marketing policy.

But importantly these companies generally belong to trade associations that are set up to help industry through trade fairs as well as to provide technical help. In Italy, which is the largest European producer, there are Industrial Zone Consortia that are regionally set up to serve small local industries. In the Massa Carrara Versillia District the Consorzio per la Zona Industriale Apuana (CZIA) is such a consortium and has 72 stone tile manufactures within its remit. The challenge is how to broaden the vision of CZIA to help the tile industry by setting up an eMarket for the local cluster of companies, their customers as well as a wider global catchment of potential customers where dynamic trading can take place. This will involve finding out what is available through a one-stop-shop, with searching, bidding and online ordering.

A market is now possible through new technology solutions for displaying as accurately as possible products online with good color replication. These are under investigation in 2001. Additionally a standard means of product identification that will allow integration with similar markets to broaden the selling opportunities is now possible at least in Europe. To establish an eMarket to assist the tile producer's intermediaries, such as CZIA, must manage the market and provide affordable interface solutions and support tools to the tile suppliers as well as to extend the scope and scale of the market through an integrated network of smaller markets. The challenge is similar to many of other suppliers in the tile manufacturing sector as well as SMEs in other parts of the construction industry and other industries and regions. The European IST Program (CEC, 1997) is designed to help such companies find both technical and commercial solutions for these markets. In particular project eBip (Zabel, Weber & Steinlechner, 2000) targets the tile industry from tile supply to tile laying and the end customer. The motivation to find a solution is strong. It is obvious however that the business and technological starting point is far removed from the eventual goal of dynamic trade and small steps will have to be made to gain benefit but at the same time be balanced against the ever-eroding market share. The number of European research projects aimed in particular to help SMEs will provide the knowledge leverage that together with an increasing customer motivation for more varied product, change of procurement and delivery will stimulate a more rapid change in trading methods. In the end it will not be technology that will be the limiting factor but the ability of companies to change their business methods, accept new procurement practices and have trust in a new market form.

Constraints to Change

Although case studies may help to visualize certain problem domains, such as sharing information, they are not helpful enough for assisting a migration plan to be formulated to change business operations and its supply chain interactions and take effective part in dynamic trading markets. Indeed each company case or pairing of companies will be different. There will be different technology and organizational entry points and different strategic thrusts and as a result there should be different action roll out stages. So, first the 'as is' situation must be carefully synthesized. Strategic thrusts must then be formulated to cover basic business needs. These will involve particular goals that may involve reduced time to market for new products and services, or near to instantaneous response times to customer requests, or meeting 100% delivery promises, or achieving reduced order lead times, or having a zero waste mentality, or utilize resources and capacity more effectively, or ensuring an increased shareholder value, and so on. Strategic thrusts can be many and varied to improve the business. Knowing the strategic thrust and the entry point the company should then engage in an incremental action plan to realize its new objectives. It will be a fact that leading-edge companies in leading-edge industries will be further up the entry point position than those that are immature or that have had little ICT experience but nonetheless have a strong motivation to change.

Point of Entry

Entry must start with a first stage that is a motivation to change. The next stage will then include, from a company perspective, identification and synthesis of the risks and vulnerabilities and inefficiencies in the supply chain. Examples of shorthand descriptions of other stages in ascending order will probably involve having already a Web presence with some "brochureware"; having already identified and synthesized the degree of collaboration between suppliers and customers in the extended enterprise or value network; already having an architecture and means to share a broad scope of information with customers and suppliers; already having a limited eCommerce for online intelligent ordering; and, possibly last but not least, being part of a collaborative dynamic trading network that wishes to remain competitive. It is no use providing a detailed structure for this analysis, as the boundaries are inevitably fuzzy and difficult to define.

Strategic Thrust

CEOs and their boards will create the vision for the business and create strategic thrusts that are reviewed on a regular basis. These strategies must in turn be conveyed to their workforce and to their partners within the supply chain or in the limit, the whole virtual corporation. An example of such a strategy may be to manage and control the supply of product and services without waste and to make better use of capacity to grow the business, or another may be to tailor ICT for business in relationship to all supply chain and trading networks in which the company takes part to increase profitability and stimulate growth.'

Formulating an Action Plan

Great care needs to be taken in matching any action plan with the strategic goals together with a sound assessment of the current situation or entry point. The actions should be on all fronts of technology, organization and business processes. It will be important to carefully choose ICT supply partners and possibly consultants from the plethora of commercial offerings that can be found through the World Wide Web, through prior knowledge, via consultant recommendation or through a system supplier. The best tools and applications must then be selected to fit with an open infrastructure or framework. Clearly no one vendor will support all the facets required. Each stage of the plan must be clear and specified for implementation, result evaluation and should take no more than a few months to carry through. At the same time the implementation stage must have a well thought out and goal-oriented payback. It will also be important to carefully define and mutually agree requirement with contracted ICT vendors and to stipulate the measures to judge success. Each action stage should flow from the one before it and should include training and education of the workforce to enhance their skills as well as to develop the wider organization.

Expectations from the action plan should always be documented and disclosed to the organization. Moreover, this must result in a clear understanding of what is intended by the action plan and the new communication means for the supply chain.

Leadership

The Internet is a relatively new but fast-growing medium and, it must be emphasized, is for communication and rapid information exchange only. It will be the tools and applications that use it that will require the most technical effort, along with the effort for redefining inter-business processes. At the same time people and the organization will expect care and attention from leadership. Leadership should direct the change process as well as place significant effort on building trust between businesses. By these means stronger inter-company relationships will be achieved and will lead to attainment of strategic goals. It should not be underestimated that the effort required for this is significantly large.

Managing the Changing Organization

For a value chain to reach its common goals or to achieve sustainable and effective dynamic trading, the wider organization will demand continuous rigorous development to manage the direction for business. These actions will not only involve revision of business rules but rules for engagement and new handling methods for explicit knowledge, its acquisition and use.

The enrichment process for people should also be fostered by revision or new provisioning of decision support tools with personalized computer GUIs and possibly proxy information-agents. Performance measures will need to be defined and revised according to changing needs, national legislation or global trading rules. Targets and current achievement with respect to the measures must be available to all suppliers and customers through the shared information system.

ICT TECHNOLOGY WATCH

New technology is continually being developed and commercially produced. So it is important that the suppliers of solutions to support the change to virtual corporations and dynamic trading networks do not take their eyes off the ball. User companies should be aware of these technological changes so that appropriate solutions are selected with sufficient stretch to satisfy their strategies and improvement plans. A few important recent developments are given here.

Information Interchange

The wide use of XML (Extensible Markup Language) as a universal format for structured documents and data on the Web is expanding for all kinds of information exchange. The World Wide Web Consortium (WC3) is broadening its activities across a number of working groups to derive new specification standards (WC3, 1999; Sperberg-McQueen, 2001).

Intelligent Software Agents

A considerable amount of research work in both academic and industrial institutions is taking place targeted at the deployment of intelligent software agents. A long-term vision is for more and more goal-oriented agents to be used for finding, processing, and disseminating information to both people and other agents. Whether agents will become fully accepted for this process, being tagged to a locality is currently uncertain; nevertheless, the developments need to be watched closely for automated processes (Kephart, Hanson & Greenwald, 2000).

N-Tier Architecture

N-tier architecture is set to grow in 2001 as an integrating architecture that embraces the need for highly flexible and adaptive and open distributed computing systems to serve a modern eBusiness. It is able to separate the user interface from application logic and underlying data allowing separate implementation developments, and can deal effectively with the complex system environments for dynamic trading networks or virtual corporations and the orchestration in concert of B2B processes.

Broadband High Speed Network

Optical communication technologies are set to become economically viable to make an impact on the Internet. The new Internet will be a broadband network enabling new and richer application possibilities to drive the dynamic trading networks and virtual corporations through its ultra-high speed optical transmission of voice, video and data. A company to watch is Lucent Technologies with its strong alliance of companies to redefine the way the Internet will develop as a powerhouse for eBusiness.

Applications

It is expected that new tools will become available from 2001 onwards to serve the collaborative aspects of business. Tools for ease, adaptability and reengineering of B2B processes will help with the joined up supply chain. Fast acting constraint-based optimization tools are also expected to deal with the wealth and complexity of shared information for planning, order promising, rescheduling and control-based decision-making.

THE FUTURE

The greatest threat to our prosperity is the complacent assumption that little needs to be done for industrial change.

Skill and Sensitivity Required

Industry has still a lot to learn about collective responsibility and total customer satisfaction for any situation. Mistakes continue to be made but it is essential to analyze them and sort out why they occurred and what to do to put them right. When a number of people from different businesses are involved this is more difficult and will require new skills and sensitivity.

Beware Potential Disasters

An example of how not to do this is the British Rail Network. It was once a relatively successful, although cash-starved monopolistic nationalized company then it was privatized and divided into a large number of separate autonomous companies with their own shareholder interests. The network, ownership and responsibility were fragmented. A unified Web site for information provided little comfort to customers and provided little detail for customers to judge the service provided. Operational functions such as maintenance were contracted out and together with some other operational functions: a lack of common goals between all of the companies involved in the network, a lack of understanding of capacity, poor scheduling precision, all combined to a poor-end customer service and ultimate satisfaction. In turn this was not corrected or pulled together by a good inter-company collaboration or by a strong competent leadership. As a consequence it turned into one of the worst examples of service enterprise for the new millennium and the antithesis of a successful virtual corporation, which was probably originally intended by the then conservative British government, whom administered the breakup, for an improved integrated rail service. The severity of the problems encountered eventually required a new Labor government administration to intervene because of network safety problems and detraction from its much-lauded Integrated Transport Policy. It tried to put some sense into a collapsing system via regulation and strategic direction,[10] but the damage was done and it will take considerable time, expense and effort to recover.

Hope Springs Eternal

Media, consultancy, and technology hype will continue. Panaceas will continue to be offered to solve the challenges. The world economy will be in turbulence. Skill shortages will be manifest. Through all this, agile and influential industrial leaders, enthusiastic entrepreneurs, champions for change and the sheer motivation for company survival will change the industrial landscape.

Opportunities Through New Solutions

Although the future is unknowable, dynamic trading networks and virtual corporations are likely in time to emerge as a normal way for doing business. The effort required will be high but the opportunities will expand exponentially for global business. New biometric solutions for authentication and security will be found through continued technological advances. Applications and tools will continue to improve with aids for revising, or creating, new inter-business processes as well as providing aids for flexible expanding, or contracting, value network configurations. Universal standards will make integration between applications and distributed databases and knowledge bases both easier and cheaper and new telecommunications technology will improve both the speed and the volume of information flow per unit time from anywhere at any time. Intelligent software agents will continue to be developed not only for special information searches but for acting upon information in an intelligent manner, thus allowing better automated eBusiness processes.

Fulfillment

The workforce and end customers will experience a new way of living and fulfillment. The basic novelty of our age is the spirituality of consumerism and voracious appetite for information. How these may be blended with an increasing capacity for sympathy and mutual understanding will inspire both ways of life and collaborative business.

CONCLUSIONS

The changing global economic climate, technology and the current position of a company with respect to the industry leaders will continue to challenge business. It is clear that a number of opportunities exist to advance a business to dynamic trading networks and markets and also to virtual corporations. The future path is cut according to business strategic goals and on the ability to determine the right course of action by a strong capable leadership. Strategy can change at any time to set a company on the right path with respect to its business partners in dynamic supply chains and eMarkets. How customer interests, organization strategies, inter-business processes and choice of technology are handled will be key. There is no prescriptive solution. It will be essential for short-term stepwise actions to ensure company benefits that progress toward a larger landscape for business with an ability to deal with the real dynamic world in synchrony with the supply chain and market need. Ultimately all companies will strive to be part of dynamic trading networks and/or virtual corporations.

ENDNOTES

[1] Consultant with MAPS, project leader for X-CITTIC and non executive director of Orion Logic Ltd. (richards@rmplc.co.uk)
[2] CEO Orion Logic Ltd. (h.Makatsoris@orionlogic.com)
[3] Just-in-time manufacturing
[4] Computer integrated manufacturing
[5] Enterprise resource planning

[6] Flexible manufacturing systems
[7] Customer requirement management
[8] Small and medium enterprises
[9] Information and communications technology
[10] See UK government, the Strategic Rail Authority, and rail regulator Web sites

REFERENCES

Ariba Inc. (2001). Available on the World Wide Web at: http://www.ariba.com.

Arguello, M. (1994). Review of scheduling software. Technology transfer 93091822A-XFER. Sematech: Austin Texas.

Boulding, K. E. (1956). General systems theory–The skeleton of science. *Management Science*, 2.

Commission of the European Communities. (1997). A European initiative in electronic commerce. Communication to the European parliament, May. *COM*, (97)157. Fifth Framework Program–Information Society Technologies (IST) 1998–2002. Available on the World Wide Web at: http://www.cordis.lu/fp5.

Commission of the European Communities. (2000). Developing a coherent policy and regulatory framework for advancing electronic commerce in Europe. *Directorate General Information Society*, January. DGIS-C3-Electronic Commerce.

Deloitte & Touche. (2000). *Manufacturing with a small e: An account of eBusiness in UK and US manufacturers*. Manufacturing Group Report.

Drucker, P. F. (1992). *Managing for the Future*. Oxford, England: Butterworth-Heinemann.

Dyck, T. (2000, December). Refined standards, new concepts taking shape. *eWeek*.

Extricity Inc. (2000). *Extricity Alliance Solution*. Retrieved M D, Y from the World Wide Web: http://www.extricity.com.

Frick, V., and Lill, A. (2000, August). Ten imperatives for e-business success. *Gartner Group*, 4th Report.

Goldman, S. L., Nagel, R. N., and Preiss, K. (1995). *Agile Competitors and Virtual Organizations–Strategies for Enriching the Customer*. Van Nostrand Reinhold.

Goldratt, E. M. (1988). Computerized shop floor scheduling. *International Journal of Production Research, 3, 26*.

Hardwick, M., Spooner D. L., Rando, T., and Morris K. C. (1996, February). Sharing information in virtual enterprises. *Communications of the ACM*, 39(2).

Hunziker, D. and Sieber P. (1999). Turbulence and the dynamics of Internet diffusion [Special issue]. *eJOV*, 1(1).

Hutton, W. (1996). The state we're in. Jonathan Cape 1995, Vintage 1996.

i2 Technologies. (2000). Available on the World Wide Web at: http://www.i2.com.

International Alliance for Compatible Technology open standards. (1998). Available on the World Wide Web: http://pages.cthome.net/iact/connexion/open_standards.html.

Kanet, J. J. (1988). MRP96–Time to rethink manufacturing logistics. *Production and Inventory Management*, 29(2).

Kephart, J. O., Hanson, J. E. and Greenwald, A. R. (2000). Dynamic pricing by software agents. *Computer Networks*.

Lawrence, P. R. and Lorsch, J. W. (1967). Organization and environment–Managing differentiation and integration. Graduate School of Business Administration. Boston: Harvard University.

Leachman, R. C., Benson R. F., Lui, C. and Raar, D. J. (1996). IMPReSS–An automated production-planning and delivery-quotation system at Harris Corporation. Semiconductor Sector, *Interfaces*, 26(1).

Levy, M. (2000, August). Dynamic pricing reaches most industries. *ECMgt.com. Pemiere E-commerce Management Electronic Magazine*. Available on the World Wide Web at: http://www.ecmgt.com.

Lucent Technologies. (2001). Available on the World Wide Web at: http://www.lucent.com.

Macintosh, A. (1994). Corporate knowledge management state of the arty review. *Proceedings of ISMICK (Management of Industrial and Corporate Knowledge) Conference*, October. AIAI Edinburgh University AIAI-TR-151.

Manugistics Inc. (2001). Available on the World Wide Web at: http://www.manugistics.com.

Makatsoris, C. (1996). *Planning, Scheduling and Control for Distributed Manufacturing Systems*. Unpublished doctoral thesis, Imperial College of Science, Technology and Medicine, University of London.

Makatsoris, C. and Besant, C. B. (1995). Production planning and control strategies for cellular manufacturing facilities. *In 11th International Conference on Computer-Aided Production Engineering, IMechE Conference Transactions 1995*. London: MEP.

Mertins, K. (1996). *PULL-Oriented Synchronization of Logistics and Production Flow in Autombile Industries, IT and Manufacturing Partnerships–Delivering the Promise*. IOS Press.

Nonaka, I. (1998). The concept of "Ba." Building a foundation for knowledge creation. [Special Issue] *California Management Review*, 40(3).

Orion Logic Ltd. (2001). Available on the World Wide Web at: http://www.orionlogic.com.

PASSE, ESPRIT Project No 9245. (1995). Planning and scheduling and manufacturing control systems. *Final Report*, October.

Possl, G. W. (1991). *Managing in the new world of manufacturing*. Prentice Hall.

Richards, H. D., Dudenhausen, H. M., Makatsoris C., and Ridder, L. de. (1997, August). Flow of orders through a virtual enterprise–Their proactive planning, scheduling and reactive control. *Computing & Control Engineering Journal*.

Ridder, L. de, Rodriguez B. and Basset, T. (1997). The uroframe initiative–Building a CIM framework for semiconductor manufacturing. *The European Conference on Integration in Manufacturing–IiM.* 01069 Dresden: Selbstverlag der Technischen Universitat.

RosettaNet. (1999, November). *Implementation Framework Specification Version 1.1*, November. Retrieved M D, Y from the World Wide Web: http://www.rosettanet.org.

Scott, R. W. (1992). Organizations. *Rational, Natural and Open Systems*. Prentice Hall.

Sperberg-McQueen, C.M. (2001). *XML-Related Activities at the WC3*. Available on the World Wide Web at: http://www.xml.com/pub/a/2001/01/03/w3c.html.

Taiwan Semiconductor Manufacturing Company. (2001). Available on the World Wide Web at: http://www.tsmc.com.tw.

Warnecke, H. J. (1993). *The Fractal Company–A Revolution in Corporate Culture*. Berlin, Germany: Springer-Verlag.

WebMethods. (2001). Press release. Available on the World Wide Web at: http://www.webmethods.com.

Weiss, G. (1999). *Multiagent systems: A modern approach to distributed AI.,* MIT Press.

Whelan, P. T. (1995). Sematech's CIM application framework–A new paradigm for manufacturing systems. *Proceedings for the International Conference on Improving Manufacturing Performance in a Distributed Enterprise*. ESPRIT working group E9245: Advanced Tools and Systems 1995; Sematech: Computer Integrated manufacturing (CIM) Application Framework Specification 1.3 technology Transfer #93061697F-ENG.

Whiston, A., Barura, A., Shutter, J., Wilson, B., and Pinner, J. (2001, January). *Measuring the Internet Economy*. Cisco Systems and University of Texas. Available on the World Wide Web at: http://www.internetindicators.com.

World Wide Web Consortium. (1999). Available on the World Wide Web at: http://www.w3.org/Consortium/Activities.

X-CITTIC. (1997). CEC Framework IV ESPRIT project No 20544 1996 to 1999.

Zabel, O., Weber, F. and Steinlechner, V. (2000). *Process Reengineering and eBusiness Models for Efficient Bidding and Procurement in the Tile Supply Chain*. ECPPM Lisbon, Portugal. Available on the World Wide Web at: http://www.ebip.net.

Chapter V

The Virtual Web-Based Supply Chain

Ashok Chandrashekar
IBM Corporation, USA

Philip Schary
Oregon State University, USA

The virtual Web-based supply chain is emerging as a new form of industrial organization. This paper discusses the concept as a juncture of three forces: the virtual organization, Web-based communication and the application service provider (ASP). The virtual organization is a familiar concept in many industries, even without electronic connections. Web-based communication provides access and networks with new institutions. The ASP makes rapid change and flexible connections feasible. Together they establish focus, flexibility and rapid response to change in demand and customer requirements. Casting it in a strategic framework of structure, process and organization provides a basis for projecting its future.

INTRODUCTION

The concept of the supply chain is now familiar territory (Houlihan, 1985). Successive stages of closely coordinated product and material flow become a process of long-linked technology (Thompson, 1967). Similarly the virtual organization, even without computer connections, is recognized in practice (Hedberg et al., 1994, Davidow and Malone, 1992). The new elements are the impact of the Internet with the World Wide Web, and the application service provider (ASP). Together they create a new form of business organization with implications for major sectors of the industrial world. This new form promises the ability to supply customer requirements more directly than ever before through focus, flexibility, adaptability and capacity.

The supply chain was enabled through electronic communication and transaction-oriented software, first to link functions within the enterprise, then to customers and suppliers, spanning a process from resources to final customers. The traditional supply chain involves long-term relationships, such as an underlying IT system with direction from a dominant organization. It is an inter-organizational process linking functional activities to serve a common customer (Hammer and Champey, 1993).

This view is now being modified by new developments. Software extends beyond corporate boundaries with faster, high capacity Internet connections, creating new directions for strategy through ease of access, speed, capacity, simplicity and low cost. It changes the rules so dramatically that it reorders business organization and the nature of competition.

Observers project business-to-business (B2B) electronic trading exchanges as the major thrust of the Internet economy, encompassing customers, suppliers, manufacturers and service providers (Radjou, 2000). It is driven by the efficiency and simplicity of electronic transactions, compared to older computer-based legacy systems and manual procedures. The reach of the virtual Web-based supply chain however goes farther. It enables focused systems of supply to appear for a specific need and then disappear until a similar need arises.

This paper emphasizes organization of the virtual chain beyond the exchange process, managing a sequence of activities leading to delivery of products specifically configured for a customer. We begin with the concept of the Web-based supply chain. It is built on the underlying concepts of the virtual organization and the Web with other technologies to organize the process. We then turn to the implications for strategy. The final section projects a future that is almost upon us, with some unresolved issues. The focus is on organizational impacts of technology on management and strategy, not the technology per se.

THE CONCEPT OF THE VIRTUAL WEB-BASED SUPPLY CHAIN

The traditional supply chain emphasizes long-term fixed relationships, with close collaboration for both product creation and delivery. In one sense, relationships are already virtual, because all firms deal with external sources of supply and services to some degree. They rely on proprietary firm-resident software and communications with a limited number of partners. Partners should have visibility extending over the entire span of the chain, share plans and contribute innovation in product and process development. It presupposes an atmosphere of trust and management integration for joint planning, control and sharing data. Integration becomes the basis for specific investments both in IT and operations, and connections through software and EDI connections. This model remains valid for many industries, even allowing for change in information technology (IT).

The Design

The virtual Web-based supply chain (denoted in the this discussion as the virtual chain) departs from this traditional form. It begins as less a linear sequence of activities than a network of possible partners for selection. Essentially, it is a generalizable process without necessarily permanent partners. The Web serves as a communication and coordination system, to coordinate operations and potentially a means to collaborate. The potential scope ranges from the simple to the complex, depending on whether standard components (possibly purchased through B2B business-to-business exchanges) or proprietary designs involving collaboration with supplier and customer are used.

Figure 1 depicts a typical virtual chain with three different exchange sites. A customer negotiates with a lead firm who then initiates the supply chain in the first exchange. The firm and its web of potential providers then form the chain through other exchanges. The network therefore emphasizes flexibility. The information flow may take a different path than the physical flow. The virtual chain is thus completely flexible and does not necessarily involve long-term relationships. The lead firm decides whether to perform operations in-house or to subcontract them to outside vendors. A third-party logistics provider could coordinate inventory and product movement, even absolving the lead firm from operational control

A single organization could utilize both traditional and virtual chains as parallel operations. Traditional supply chains would serve the market for standardized proprietary products and services; virtual chains would supplement it in different situations such as: 1) providing commodity items for the market, 2) additional temporary production or logistics capacity to meet peak demands, or 3) customized items to meet special customer product requirements. The virtual chain thus can either stand alone or provide flexibility to supplement existing arrangements.

Figure 1: The Web-based supply chain

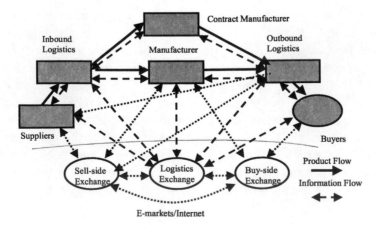

The characteristics of the emerging virtual chain are:
- Orientation to customer requirements
- Operation in response to real-time customer orders
- Flexible response to changes in market requirements
- Organization around tasks rather than organizations
- A process orientation around complementary competencies

THE NEW ELEMENTS

The combination of new developments enables the virtual chain: the virtual organization, the configuration of computers and Web-based communications and the ASP. We discuss each in turn.

Virtual Organizations

The many definitions of virtual organizations include elements in common separate geographically distributed functionally diverse organizational units collaborating as a network in a common purpose, managed by teams in a process orientation (e.g., De Sanctis and Monge, 1999; Moshowitz, 1994, 1997; Pihkala et al., 1999). Their relationships are determined by their complementary activities. Selection depends on a specific need at a particular time. Tenure can be short. Davidow and Malone (1992) describe the network relations as an "ever-varying cluster of common activities in the midst of a vast fabric of relationships" (p.7).

For some authors, the virtual organization is a single enterprise, for others a series of connected enterprises with task specialization, contractual relations and permeable boundaries, as a supply chain. In this mode, the virtual organization is a dynamic organization structure to be reconfigured to match changing conditions. Pihkala et al., 1999) emphasize that "...the virtual organization breaks the rigid assumptions of organizations and their stability in time."

The essential characteristics are dispersed actors, resources and activities serving a global objective. In the resource-based business strategy, the virtual organization (and by implication, the virtual chain) combines resources and capabilities to create unique, complementary competencies, providing flexibility, fast response and adaptation to supply products and services to meet the needs of the market (Wernerfeldt, 1984; Peteraf, 1993).

Moshowitz (1994) abstracts a theoretical base of enabling factors: simplification, combinatorial freedom and switching. Simplification subdivides tasks to allocate among organizational units. Combinatorial freedom assigns tasks and units to meet new requirements. Switching changes connections and resources as needs arise. The ability to change interorganizational structure rapidly becomes the hallmark of the virtual chain.

Management acts as entrepreneur, bringing organizations together for a common goal, serving in the role of both broker and manager (Miles and Snow 1992). Moshowitz divides the virtual organization into a supervising metamanagement and the fulfilling "satisfiers." Management establishes market connections, defines tasks and selects the specific "satisfiers." The selection process can even be automated using pre-selection to establish qualified partners (Hoogewegen, 1999). In later discussion, it will be identified as a Web community" (Franke, 1998).

The critical management role is to provide the "glue" that holds the virtual organization together (Pihkala et al., 1999). Trust between manager and members is essential. Motivation is difficult to maintain. Bonding and loyalty are weak, with potential conflict and a high risk of failure. The importance of a shared vision should not be underrated, related not only to immediate products or customers, but also to potential operations reflecting the collective competencies of members. The critical competence for the manager as broker is a network competence, the ability to organize and supply the guiding vision.

Computers and Communications

By universal recognition, computers and electronic communication have enabled the virtual organization and the virtual chain. Coordination required over transactions can only come through the communication network. This includes software, the Web, standardization of data, and the physical capacity of the network itself.

Software makes the virtual chain possible. The role of software has progressed from functionally-oriented programs such as warehouse management, production scheduling and transportation management functions to firm-oriented enterprise resource planning (ERP) systems with internal transaction management. The functional walls and organizational boundaries are now breached by supply chain management software that connects the lead firm with customers and suppliers. At present, problems of compatibility among software packages from different vendors, act as a further barrier to coordination. Their development is limited in both scope or capabilities such as scheduling production in real-time, but progress makes the goal of interorganizational data visibility and coordination more attainable.

Web-Based Communication

Electronic communication becomes the centerpiece for both transactions and building inter-unit relationships. Transactions can be routinized and automated. Relations however develop from informal communication. Together, they free the organization from both geographic and structural constraints (Ahuja and Carley, 1999). Moshowitz describes the "pillars of virtual organization:" 1) standardizing interactions, 2) treating knowledge separately from the individual, as in programming machine operations, and 3) abstracting information from operations, as in the use of real options, financial instruments, to hedge against operational risks. Together they form a central core of information.

Communication in traditional supply chains relies on a variety of modes, from written documents to telephone and fax. EDI was a major step forward for direct computer-to-computer connections but is limited to prescribed data, messages and file formats. Its advantage lies in the high level of security as a separate communication system. It is costly, with limited access and is inflexible in switching among multiple customers and partners. Installation and training add to this cost and created a lucrative business for EDI service providers.

In contrast, the Internet and the Web have ease of access, low training requirements and low direct costs of installation. Access becomes pivotal in determining the success of the virtual chain (Noumens and Bouwman,1995) The ease of access provides an advantage in the ease of connecting new suppliers and customers, although the problems of user computer system and software remain. The Web portal becomes the gateway and entry point for suppliers and customers and a marketing tool for the customer to make inquiries, place orders and specify product options.

Web communications can include standard EDI messages using EDIFACT and ANSI X.12, but the real contribution lies in its content flexibility. Both data and personal messages can be transmitted in a variety of forms. Groupware promotes collaboration. CAD and other visual images can be exchanged. The Web provides a rich potential for communication

The Web also has disadvantages: the current lack of high-speed service, potential disruption, incompatibility of Web products, and inadequate Web infrastructure. Inadequate capacity and disruption may be partially solved through redundant networks. Security problems are more overshadowing. The ability to penetrate networks makes the entire chain vulnerable to disruption or theft of data. Solutions include establishing firewalls around intranets and extranets to prevent unauthorized entry. Another is to require authentication of transactions through certifying current users and documents.

Standardization of data and product descriptions presents further difficulties. Product codes can be proprietary, promoted for internal efficiency, or oriented to specific industries. Data mapping to identify codes and languages is critical for coordination. The data gap will ultimately be reduced through XML, a meta language to identify and tag data files, with additional code indicators for specific industries, assisted by translation dictionaries such as Rosetta.net.

Bandwidth is the governing constraint on communication. The current shift to fiber-optic cable networks promises a major expansion in capacity (Gilder, 2000). The change opens up new possibilities for collaborative software, complex model images, training modules and personal visual dialog and conferencing. Growth depends less on technology than on organizational context.

Exchanges and Trading Networks

Business-to business (B2B) exchanges are the most publicized element of the virtual chain. They have been the source of both optimism and disappointment. Their essential structure consists of buyers and sellers connected through an e-hub as an electronic marketplace. Most transactions are concerned with prices for clearly described, comparable products sold on specifications in a catalog. This description fits business purchase items, but not with ongoing commitment by both buyers and sellers. Kaplan and Sawhney (2000) note "exchanges are not designed to support systematic or contractual purchasing" (p.101).

Kaplan and Sawhney also distinguish between spot and systematic sourcing on one hand and operations versus manufacturing inputs on the other. Maintenance, repair and operating supplies are sold through catalogs. Manufacturing items are usually purchased under contract except where unanticipated requirements appear, where supplementary transactions can involve exchanges. In the end, however, exchanges have limited capabilities compared to other business transactions.

Horizontal exchange offers wide product ranges across an industry. Vertical exchanges specialize by industry. Competition pushes more exchanges into a vertical focus on narrower product scope.

Exchanges work best when they are equally balanced between buyers and sellers. Too few sellers leads to monopolistic pricing; too many sellers or too few buyers to unprofitable pricing. The result is that both buyers and sellers move to other means of conducting transactions.

Future exchanges however may differ. Using the financial services industry as a prototype, they (Kaplan and Sawhney, 2000) project five different solutions:

- Mega exchanges–the currently conventional model.
- Specialist originators–intermediaries that will assist buyers and sellers to define the product objects to assist them in the transaction.
- E-speculators–risk takers who would take positions in the products they sell in search of profit.
- Solution providers–exchanges with analysis support to aid in purchasing decisions.
- Asset swaps–exchanges that avoid the formal exchange process by exchanging commodities, future positions and production capacity.

The B2B trading network exchange began as auctions, matching price bids and offers, searching only for the lowest price with little role in either pre- or post-matching activities. This role has now expanded beyond price discovery to multiple criteria such as delivery schedules, adding supporting activities. Some exchanges such as Covisint (covisint.com, 2001; Weiss, 2000) offer added services or links to other exchange sites for logistics and other services necessary to complete the transaction as end-to-end services. Three supplementary features to support transactions are: supply chain inventory management, product development and procurement administration. In addition, B2B exchanges now provide transaction control, order tracking, order fulfillment and accounting modules.

Exchanges add unique capabilities to the virtual chain. Suppliers are added or dropped in a dynamic process with changing players for each transaction. A variety of matching mechanisms can be used, including reverse auctions, direct price and delivery quotations. Exchanges become an arena for pricing, scheduling, delivery and financial terms. Future additions may include self-financing, warehousing and brokerage.

Automation can enhance the use of exchanges. When a buyer seeks specific product components, the order message triggers a series of automated actions: searching an electronic product catalog with prespecified supplier selection criteria. The exchange sends RFQs to suppliers and then collates and forwards them to the buyer for automated selection. It then initiates supporting logistics activities: analysis, delivery, transport planning and documentation. These messages, placeholders for action, await responses from other parts of the system. One action has the capability to trigger a chain of automated actions.

Application Service Providers (ASPs)

The application service provider (ASP) enhance the ability to switch partners (Paul 2001; *Fortune*, 2001; Harrington, 2000; *Infoworld*, 2000). ASPs host software for users, in lieu of their own networks. The ASP can take over the client's information system to be available on user demand, investing, installing, managing and upgrading software, and technical problems. Responsibility for software shifts to the ASP, while the user integrates applications and data, makes organizational adjustments and provides training. One potential disadvantage is a loss of competitive advantage with common ASP hosting (Davenport, 1998).

The roles of user and system manager must be well defined. The ASP can become the central node in the supply chain information system, providing access and communication for customers, suppliers and the managing organization. Users access software and receive and supply data for customers and suppliers through predefined extranets. Users are responsible for decisions with their own data. The ASP usually determines the software architecture and dictates the speed of response, flexibility for new requirements and scalability. They also become responsible for system capacity, software upgrading, monitoring, data mapping standards and security.

The structure of ASPs is only emerging now. Some software application remains with the customer and other software with the ASP, requiring compatibility. Three different role models for ASPs are 1) "the pure play," using best-of-breed software, 2) the integrated software provider presenting a single unified product, and 3) a convergence of the ASP and the trading exchange. Some ASPs now specialize. ERP software often requires its own server. Logistics software generates its own set of providers. The ASP can be independent, or hosted internally. As control shifts toward the ASP, the chain manager may also become the host of the ASP.

Some companies with ASPs have gone back to their own systems, largely because of cost, data and software compatibility capacity and security problems. Further they are subject to failing providers and networks, losing their ability to operate.

STRATEGY

The virtual supply chain changes business organization (Moshowitz, 1994, 1997; Tapscott et al., 2000). It starts not like a traditional supply chain with stable relationships, but as a clean slate with new connections. The foundation is the core and outsourcing paradigm (Hamel & Prahalad, 1994; Quinn, 1993). A lead firm organizes a process with other firms to perform activities to deliver a product in response to an identifiable market need. The lead firm maintains control over a strategic core, but contracts for other activities that do not provide unique superiority. It results in two interdependent, complementary networks: information and operations, both supporting the delivery of finished products to match specific customer requirements. In this section we consider the essential elements of strategy for the virtual chain: structure, management and decisions. They are interdependent in that structure sets the management tasks, both leading to strategic choices.

Structure

The virtual chain fits a particular set of conditions. Figure 2 describes supply chains in two dimensions: demand stability and volume. Stable demands involve staple products with predictable forecasts. Volatile demands involve both changes in products and volumes.

With low volume and stable demands, the niche supply chain can be handled with minimal coordination. Traditional supply chains have stable demands with high volume. Low volume operations, as in construction, suggest project management, but volatile demands matched to high volume could become virtual chains. Project-type supply chains can become virtual but may be economically undesirable. These last two also have a common dimension; they only last for the life of the project. In effect, the virtual chain must apply the decision context of project management to a process with higher volume.

Figure 2: Types of supply chains

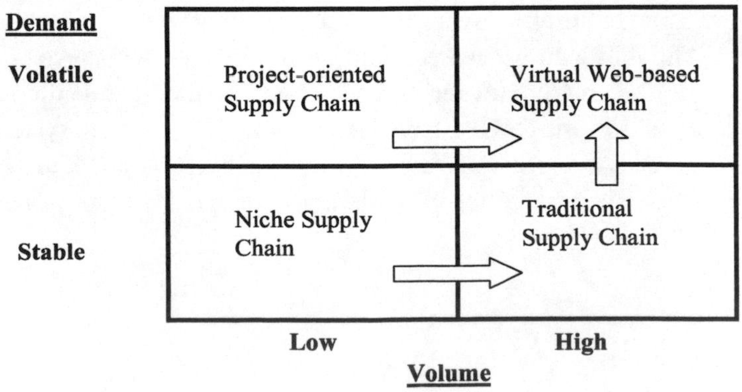

Highly turbulent industries adopt the virtual organization model because of flexible production, real-time order fulfillment, rapid response and short development cycles. Their markets change rapidly, losing stability of product lines and the ability to predict revenues. Small-scale pilot projects become large-scale operations. Stable industries renovate themselves as virtual chains. This points toward a convergence. While all business arrangements are not conducive to virtual chains, the general direction is inescapable.

The most significant element is the ability to switch connections. This flexibility comes at a price. The cost of switching involves enterprise and supply chain software for control over transactions, data, training and connections with partner organizations. Software investment alone may run to several million dollars. Adding the costs of data collection, coding, editing and mapping for compatibility both between software programs and organizations, and the combined costs of coordination and IT management, the total limits the number of competitors.

Costs can be shifted. ASPs can assume the cost and responsibility for software installation, maintenance and upgrading in return for higher monthly or transaction charges. The net effect is to increase the costs of managing volatility. Virtual chains then become not general applications, but relevant to industries such as high technology with high volume and volatility where the payoff from flexibility is high.

Switching partners becomes more common in B2B market exchanges. As an auction, a single seller confronts multiple buyers, or more recognizably as a reverse auction, where a single buyer meets several potential suppliers. The common use lies in price-searching mechanisms. However, exchanges such as Covisint offer other services and links to other exchanges to complete the fulfillment process.

Some lead firms use private B2B exchanges. Prequalified suppliers quote bids on particular standardized items in an electronic catalog, reducing many procurement items and their profit margins to the status of commodities. Vendors are selected by price, delivery dates, or available production capacity. Exchanges simplify transactions and administration, reducing both time and costs.

Short-term relationships do not always prevail. The virtual supply chain also adds value at each stage of the process. Value is embodied in information incorporated within the product and its associated services. The strategic issue is how to capture value for competitive advantage. This may require coordination with suppliers over extended time periods, stabilizing the relationships during the development phase, and possibly into production.

Management

Directing the virtual chain is evolving with a management role not clearly established. At the most basic level, it must balance potential customers and prospective suppliers, matching specific customer requirements with the defining technologies for competitive advantage. The most salient issues for managers include sensing the market, managing relations with the Web community and managing the information system.

The virtual chain alternates between two types of leadership. The organizational structure of virtual chains appears to take two divergent paths, depending on the path of interaction. Ahuja and Carley (1999, p.751-52), note that "overall, we expect that when routine tasks are performed in a highly structured network, and non-routine tasks are performed in a less structured (loose) network, superior performance will result." Supply management tends to be hierarchical, although operating decisions are made where actions are performed. Coordination necessitates joint planning and execution. Routinized boundary-spanning transactions utilize lateral communication but are centralized and hierarchical for control, coordinated by supervisory lead organizations. Communication is largely unidirectional, and negotiation deals with structured problems such as production scheduling and capacity planning.

Collaborative systems for product and process development require freedom for interaction among participants for creativity and innovation with participative decisions. Communication is informal and bidirectional, as in joint product development. Some observers (Franke, 1999) note not permanence, but rotation in response to particular expertise. Leadership becomes decentralized, although the lead firm may coordinate the communication network hierarchically.

Sensing the Market

Sensing the market becomes the primary task, setting direction for the chain. However, the process is not simple. In many cases, the market evolves with the technology. One immediate source of information on product preferences and options comes from direct customer orders entering into the production system. Another is customer collaboration in product design, forecasting and sales planning. Other sources test the market through experimentation (Brown and Eisenhardt, 1998), placing basic products with customers to incorporate their experiences into further development (Moore, 1996). Technologies and markets together define the strategic direction.

Managing the Web Community

The second major task is to forge the organization, managing suppliers, both currently active and latent. Moore (1996) describes the task: "The function of ecosystem (virtual chain) leadership is valued by the community because it enables members to move toward shared visions, to align their investments, and to find mutually supportive roles" (p.26). This requires a sense of present and future direction of the technologies and recruiting firms with relevant expertise. It establishes strategic vision for motivation and profitability.

Relationships take the form of coordination, cooperation or collaboration (Bressler and Grantham, 2000). One objective of leadership is to extend collaboration. The taxonomy of potential partnerships includes:
- Standardized commodity suppliers in market relationships but who must coordinate operations.

- Integrated suppliers sharing process knowledge and participating in joint planning.
- Collaborative suppliers involved in both product and process development.
- Latent collaborators available for future development activities.

They reflect varying degrees of both complexity and creativity (Bressler and Grantham, 2000). Routine procurement is low in both dimensions. Project management and production involves complexity without necessarily creativity. Full collaboration involves both complexity and creativity.

The Web Community itself is a collection of organizations with potential concern with the economic outcome of the virtual chain, including customers and current and potential (latent) suppliers (Franke, 1999). Membership includes pre-qualified members with a potential connection to the virtual chain. Criteria include standardization of operations, computer systems and data for rapid response, trust and a common identification with the overall vision of the virtual chain.

Membership is fluid, depending on orientation of the virtual chain and the projects in which it engages. Suppliers are often encouraged to participate in other chains to develop their own competencies, and reduce their dependence on a single project or virtual chain (Miles & Snow, 1992). The task here is to maintain a fine balance between the needs of the chain and preserving the vigor of its members.

Trust is critical in partner relations. Establishing it is difficult when tenure is short and partners have incomplete assurance of follow-on business. The penalties for failure however are high. Motivation through a common vision becomes the strongest foundation, supplemented by personal contact, reputation and the accumulation of experience. The danger of losing control over exposure of corporate data is central to the trust issue.

Managing Information

The third task of management revolves around the information system. In some cases, the specific responsibility for managing the information system falls to a technical leader, creating a second source of direction. Information requirements place the IT manager in a crucial position, able to define the operating characteristics of the virtual chain (Moshowitz, 2001).

Supply chain operations are data-rich. Their information systems must have standardized formats for coordination between computer systems and organizations. The chain must also be transparent to suppliers, management and customers if possible. They should have access to actual and forecast demand as the data become available.

Collaborative systems are less structured and more open to diverse forms of communication, including voice and visual modes. Collaboration requires the ability to transmit complex imagery and data. It also requires maintaining the community through casual connection. The advent of broadband communication enables proliferation of communication technologies such as video streaming for conferencing and informal contact across time and space.

Strategic Choices

The long-term nature of the virtual chain permits only general targeting: a set of competencies searching for a specific niche within a broader market. The task is to determine what characteristics should match requirements that may be only emerging but not yet fully defined. There is no single strategy, but one that is continually in flux, searching for different partners for new roles or using established partners in new roles.

Supply operations require tight coordination. Forecast demand, actual orders and production schedules should be made selectively available to suppliers on the basis of need. The short tenure of the virtual chain makes the problem of sharing sensitive data difficult because of the need to establish trust between partners. Establishing trust in advance becomes important in building the Web community.

Products and service determine long-term competitive advantage. Product design enters the virtual chain through software such as collaborative product commerce, a set of coordination and design tools for new products. (Hutt & Ross, 2000). Modularity in product design is also important (Baldwin & Clark, 1997). Modular products assembled at the last possible moment reduce response time in online order fulfillment, while also reducing finished product inventory. They also create the flexibility to supply a full range of products and product options. Finally product modularity defines the boundaries of supplier component production.

The tenure of the virtual chain is determined by the project. The chain however may be reconstituted with new partners for other projects, drawing on the community as a pool of suppliers. This provides it with the virtues of agility and avoids retention of activities without a role in a given project configuration.

The agility of the virtual chain is determined in part by the ease and speed of response. Virtual supply chains respond to changes in volume or product by the choice of suppliers (Chandrashekar & Schary, 1999). Agility may always not provide lasting advantage over competitors, although management skills may provide short-term advantage. Lasting advantage comes from unique knowledge-intensive products and services, usually involving partner collaboration. Collaboration involves time. The result is a trade-off in flexibility, determined by the role of the virtual chain in the marketplace–unique products versus shorter time-to-market cycles. The first stresses use of proprietary product development; the second, off-the-shelf components. The first potentially provides a potential barrier against competition; the second depends directly on agility.

Strategy in the end is shaped by competition. The virtual chain is oriented to serve short-term demands and niche markets too small for major competitors (Porter, 1980). Short tenure leads to "hit-and-run" actions that recognize and respond to market needs quickly. Issues of market share do not apply, as virtual chains try to stay ahead of competition. Virtual chains may utilize high levels of competency in product development, but they must be nimble to stay ahead of competition. Ultimately they become vulnerable because of their high transaction costs to competition from later lower cost rivals. Timing of market entry and exit become competitive tools.

THE FUTURE

In one sense, the future has already arrived. Dell Computers and Cisco have demonstrated the ability to operate with minimal production facilities, relying on their suppliers. Automobile companies such as General Motors will soon introduce Web-based customer order systems leading directly into production planning. Taiwan Semiconductor Manufacturing Company now uses a system where customers design their own chips for production.

The future virtual chain will include:
- Close collaboration with customers
- Multiple paths from suppliers to customer
- Management freedom to change both organization and partners
- Flexible networks as a critical element in competition
- Common standards for product components and communication
- Use of automated processes wherever feasible.

Virtual chains will not completely replace traditional supply chains, but their agility will satisfy increasing demands for product variety. At the same time, this flexibility comes through costly software and communication systems, defining their role in medium-sized markets. Small enterprises become virtual without formal supply chain connections. Larger firms only become agile by creating smaller scale units.

Market exchanges would standardize product components, reducing the power to differentiate. Differentiation places pressures to collaborate with suppliers. This will be favored by the developing capabilities of IT, expanding capacity in broadband communications and further development of collaborative software. The trade-off between rapid response and collaborative product development will become an opportunity to differentiate virtual supply chains according to purpose.

The ability to organize and manage virtual chains can become a skill in its own right, a source of advantage that under some conditions may be difficult to counter. The example has already appeared in the Hong Kong-based company (Magretta, 1998). The firm that began as a trading company now creates and manages short-term supply chains for garment retailers, using computer-based planning and communication.

CONCLUSION

The virtual chain developed as the conjunction of the virtual organization, IT and electronic communication. It is both a new paradigm and an extension of an older form of organization. It takes on an expanding role through its ability to connect organizations as an integrated short-term system to supply markets. It brings agility, the power to select markets and match their requirements through high-level competencies. We cannot predict its future evolution except within broad parameters. How far collaborative processes penetrate the virtual chain will be specific to the situation and technology. The virtual chain itself appears to be emerging as an independent vehicle, with its own advantages from organizational skills. The convergence between IT and supply chains will require a combination of management skills that may be difficult to find.

REFERENCES

At Your Service. (2000). *InfoWorld*, October, 36-37.

Baldwin, C. Y., and Clark, K. B. (1997, September-October). Managing in an age of modularity. *Harvard Business Review, 75,* 84-93.

Bressler, S. E. and Grantham, C. E. (2000). *Communities of Commerce*. New York: McGraw-Hill.

Brown, S. L. and Eisenhardt, K. M.(1998). *Competing On The Edge: Strategy As Structured Chaos*. Boston: Harvard Business School Press.

Chandrashekar, A. (2000, November). *Research issues in supplier network management—Future trends*. Paper presented at Decision Sciences Institute Annual Meeting, Orlando, FL.

Chandrashekar, A. and Schary, P. (1999). Toward the virtual supply chain: The convergence of IT and organization. *International Journal of Logistics Management, 10*(2) 27-39.

Covisint. (2001). Retrieved January 22, 2001 from the World Wide Web: http://www.covisint.com/.

Davenport, T. (1998). Putting the enterprise into the enterprise system. *Harvard Business Review*, July-August, 76, 121-29.

Davidow, W. H. and Malone, M. S. (1992). *The Virtual Corporation*. New York: Harper Business.

De Sanctis, G. and Monge P. (1999) Introduction to the special issue: Communication processes for virtual organizations. *Organizational Science*, 10(6), 603-703.

Evans, P. and Wurster, T. S. (year). *Blown to Bits Boston*. Boston: Harvard Business School Press.

Fortune. (2001). *Apps on Tap (Winter Tech Guide)*, 142, 217-220.

Franke, U. (1999). The virtual Web as a new entrepreneurial approach to network organizations. *Entrepreneurship and Regional Development*, 11, 203-229.

Hamel, G. and Prahalad, C. K. (1994). *Competing for the Future*. Boston: Harvard Business School Press.

Hammer, M. and Champy J. (1993) *Reengineering the Corporation*. New York: HarperBusiness.

Harrington, L. (2000). The ABCs of ASPs. *Dot.Com*, November, 15-18.

Hedberg, B., Dahlgren, G., Hansson, J. and Olve, N. G. (1994). *Virtual Organizations and Beyond*. Chichester, England: Wiley.

Hoogeweegen, M. R., Teunissen, W. J., Vervest, P. H. M. and Wagenaar, R. (1999). Modular network design. *Decision Sciences*, 20(4), 1073-1103.

Houlihan, J. B. (1985). International supply chain management. *International*

Journal of Physical Distribution and Materials Management, 15(1), 22-38.

Hutt, K. and Ross, G. (2000). *Collaborative Product Commerce Manufacturing Systems*, December, 18, 64.

Kaplan, S. and Sawhney, M. (2000). E-hubs: The new B2B marketplaces. *Harvard Business Review*, May-June, 78, 97-103.

Magretta, J. (1998). Fast, global and entrepreneurial: Supply chain management, Hong Kong style. *Harvard Business Review*, September-October, 76, 103-114.

Miles, R. E. and Snow, C. (1992). Causes of failure in network organizations. *California Management Review*, Summer, 24, 53-72.

Moore, J. F. (1996). *The Death of Competition*. New York: HarperBusiness.

Mowshowitz, A. (1994). Virtual organization: A vision of management in the information age. *The Information Society*, 10, 267-288.

Mowshowitz, A. (1997). Virtual organization. *Communications of the ACM*, 40(9), 30-37.

Mowshowitz, A. (2001). *Virtual Organization: The New Feudalism Computer*, April, 112-111.

Nouwens, J. and Bouwman, H. (1995). Living apart together in electronic commerce: The use of information and communication technology to create network organizations. *Journal of Computer-Mediated Communication*, 1(3). Retrieved M D, Y from the World Wide Web: http://jcmc.huji.ac.il/vol1/issue3/nouwens.html.

Paul, L. G. (2001). The ASP dilemma. *Electronic Business*, January, 99-102.

Peteraf, M. (1993). The cornerstone of competitive advantage: A resource-based view. *Strategic Management Journal*, 14, 179-191.

Pihkala, T., Varamaki, E. and Vesalainen, J. (1999). Virtual organization and the SMEs: A review and model development. *Entrepreneurship and Regional Development*, 11, 335-349.

Porter, M. E. (1980). *Competitive Strategy*. New York: The Free Press.

Porter, M. E. (2001). Strategy and the Internet. *Harvard Business Review*, March, 79, 63-77.

Quinn, J. (1993). *Intelligent Enterprise*. NewYork: The Free Press.

Radjou, N. (2000). Deconstruction of the supply chain. *Supply Chain Management Review*, November-December, 30.

Schary, P. B. and Skjoett-Larsen, T. (2001). *Managing the Global Supply Chain* (2nd ed.). Copenhagen Business School Press forthcoming.

Schrage, M. E. (1995). *No More Teams!* New York: Currency Doubleday.

Shuga, M. J. and Carley, K. M. (1999). Network structure in virtual organizations. *Decision Science*, 10(6), 741-757.

Tapscott, D., Nicol, D. and Lowy, A. (2000). *Digital Capital*. Boston: Harvard Business School Press.

Thompson, J. D. (1967). *Organizations in Action*. New York: McGraw-Hill.

Weiss, P. (2000). Covisint–Implications for logistics. *Automotive Logistics*,

3(2) 18-23.

Wernerfeldt, B. (1984). A resource-based view of the firm. *Strategic Management Journal*, 5, 171-180.

Wise, R. and Morrison, D. (2000). Beyond the exchange: The future of B2B. *Harvard Business Review*, November-December, 78, 86-96.

Chapter VI

Towards a Framework for Managing the Business-to-Business e-Commerce Chain

Vincent Wade
Trinity College, Ireland

David Lewis
University College, London, UK

Jacques Brook
KPN Research, The Netherlands

William Donnelly
Waterford Institute of Technology, Ireland

The rapid of growth in e-Commerce/e-Business provides new opportunities and challenges for next generation Internet and telecommunication service providers. The collective global e-Commerce activities are estimated to exceed $6 trillion dollars in 2004. However, a key element in successful e-Commerce/e-Business operation is the improved integration and management of the e-Business value chains (i.e., management of business-2-customer (B2C) and business-2-business (B2B) chains. Current e-Business managed solutions, where available, tend to concentrate on only single aspects of the e-Business integration, e.g., outsourced accounting management or virtual private network (VPN) services. This is analogous to first-generation telecommunication management systems which delivered stand-alone management applications for specific management concerns, e.g., performance management and configuration management. However, e-Business organizations of the future will require a more holistic, integrated approach to e-Business management networks. Such e-Business services would support integrated management solutions (e.g., quality of service, accounting, service level agreement, negotiation and management, virtual private network mgmt., etc.) across the B2C and B2B value chain.

This paper proposes a management component framework to support the rapid and flexible construction of an e-Commerce management infrastructure. This management solution is based on a holistic management approach supporting seamless integration of network and application management services (i.e., vertical), as well as integrating management across distinct functional areas (i.e., horizontal). The chapter also presents an analysis of the business model for a provider of such B2B and B2C management and examines the requirements for such management services. It also identifies best practice and state-of-the-art research upon which this framework is based and describes how this research is being developed as part of a large EU telecommunications research project.

DRIVERS FOR INTEGRATED MANAGEMENT OF E-BUSINESS VALUE CHAINS

In the business-to-business value chain, providing "e" services means much more than building Web-front interfaces with fancy features to end customers. An e-Business value chain can be defined as commerce conducted between businesses over an Internet, extranet or intranet (i.e., IP networks). The rapid growth in e-Business is enormous. While organizations in different countries move online at their own pace, their collective e-Commerce activities are estimated by Forrester Research Inc. to reach $6.8 trillion dollars, or 8.6% of the global sales of goods and services, in 2004 (Sanders & Temkin, 2000).

A key aspect in successful e-Business operation is the integration and management of the e-Business value chains (i.e., management of business-to-business chains). Research has consistently identified that a crucial element of successful e-Business operation is the ease and flexibility of *integrating and managing* inter-business interaction. However, in ever-increasing competitive markets, organizations are focusing on their own key market competencies and seeking *outsource managed solutions* for non-core competencies.

Such e-Business requirements provide new opportunities and challenges for next generation Internet and telecommunication service providers. In order to support e-Businesses across their supply/value chains, these next generation Internet and telecommunication providers must offer dynamic managed communication as well as interorganizational application service management.

Thus, in much the same way as organizations have become reliant on third-party managed connectivity services, e-Businesses are beginning to seek managed e-Business networks where the e-Business value chain is managed and supported as an integrated service. Providers of such e-Business management services must provide managed solutions across e-Business value chains (end-to-end management of B2B supply chains).

Current e-Business managed solutions, where available, tend to concentrate on only single aspects of the e-Business integration, e.g., outsourced accounting management or traditional virtual private network services. This is analogous to first-generation telecommunication management systems which delivered stand-alone management applications for specific management concerns, e.g., performance management and configuration management. However, the lessons learned from such "stand-alone" management applications were that management function integration was vital to support increasing customer demands. Such integration was difficult if not impossible, if integration had not been considered from the outset. Thus, rather than developing piecemeal, isolated e-Business management applications, more functionally integrated solutions are required. Hence, e-Business management services must be constructed rapidly and dynamically across different management functional areas.

An e-Business management provider would:

- Support the seamless extension of a customer organization's internal business processes across existing or new e-Commerce value chains.
- Support an integrated service level agreement for the end customer which should be dynamically negotiable, thus allowing faster service subscription (to the e-Business management services).
- Support automated processes for creation, activation, delivery support, accounting and billing of the end-to-end e-business chain, in order to allow real-time service provisioning.

In this way an e-Business management provider may aim to offer a one-stop-shop for outsourced B2C and B2B management.

In this chapter we first present an analysis of the business model for a provider of such B2B and B2C management and examine the requirements for such management services. Then a component framework is proposed to support the rapid development of e-Business managed solutions. The chapter also illustrates the operation of such a framework in the flexible construction of an integrated VPN-based management service using Internet protocol (IP) quality-of-service guarantees. It identifies best practice and state-of-the-art research upon which this framework is based and describes how this research is being developed as part of a large EU telecommunications research project.

BUSINESS MODEL FOR E-BUSINESS MANAGEMENT PROVIDER

The e-Business management service (e-BMS) provider is a "managed solution provider" offering a range of services, including managed connectivity (advanced VPN), accounting, managed security, and quality of service management of both connectivity service and application services. Figure 1 illustrates a generalized e-BMS provider and its relationship with potential customer(s).

Figure 1: Generalized business model for e-business management service provider

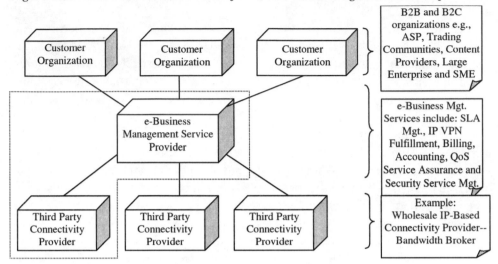

The business model supports several types of potential customer organizations types, namely,

- Customer organization which uses the e-Business management provider to manage its B2B cooperation.
- Customer organization which is a consumer of a third-party service (the access to which is managed by the e-Business management service provider).
- Customer organization which is an application service provider and which uses the e-Business management provider to manage certain parts of the application service (e.g., accounting, quality of service, etc.). Examples of such customers are an ASP providing online IT solutions to businesses, an online trading community mediating any-to-any transactions amongst businesses (auctions, exchanges, aggregation), and an SME and a large enterprise in a selling chain or supply chain.

Figure 1 also illustrates that the e-Business management provider may utilize the communication services of an Internet provider/wholesaler or may be an Internet provider itself. It is also important to note that the e-Business management provider may have business relationships with one or many Internet providers and that customer organizations may exist in one or multiple Internet provider domains.

The generalized business model also identifies two interorganizational interface types, the customer interface (for the managed service) and the interface between the e-Business management provider and the Internet provider.

The Value Added Aspect of E-Business Management

Customer Perspective

The value-added aspect of e-Business management service for customer organizations is that it offers a single service interface providing access to a well-integrated set of customer management services. The provision and operation of these services can be defined within a single service level agreement. Thus enabling the customer, for example, to place management service orders, check the status of existing orders and check the performance of their services against the SLA. An important gain is the ability for customer organizations to speed up their business transactions and to have access to highly managed services at lower cost.

Service Provider Perspective

Competition is driving the customer need for faster service access at lower cost. However service providers need to differentiate themselves by providing more than just basic connectivity services in order to create new revenue streams and increase their overall return. The advantage of e-Business management service in such a context is that it allows the e-BMS provider to provide dedicated solutions to customers, which speed up the provisioning of services and reduce the cost of the integration of different management components. Furthermore e-BMS will enable service providers, in the role of e-BMS providers, to generate new revenue streams by widening the range of customers.

Requirements for e-Business Management Provider

In order to realize such management services, the e-Business management provider must apply flexible software architectures and components to respond rapidly to customer needs. Three important technology requirements can be identified as:
- A flexible software architecture for rapid management system construction;
- Use of off-the-shelf management components to reduce cost and increase reliability; and
- Use of open interfaces and relation to standards needed for inter-domain management interactions.

Requirements for e-Business Management Services

The e-Business management service could comprise management services supporting the e-business needs of dynamic federated organizations that conduct business across intranets, extranets or the Internet. Customer organizations of such E-BMS would be small-to-medium sized enterprises (SMEs) participating in business-to-business e-commerce or application service providers (ASPs) and their customers. The dynamic nature of the customer organizations places stringent service requirements on the design and implementation of the e-Business management service. The main customer requirements are:
- A consistent view of e-business communication/information services (operating across the e-Business value chain).
- A single customizable interface for services operation (across the e-Business value chain).
- Low cost of adding new e-business services (i.e., based on low-overhead new service integration).

- Support for dynamic restructuring of the e-commerce value chain by allowing the rapid introduction and removal of services from the value.
- Capability to dynamically introduce and customize new e-business services.
- Flexibility in choice of service provider.
- Ability to customize service feature from the desktop.
- An integrated service accounting and billing service irrespective of the origin of the service (operating across the e-Business value chain).
- A clear audit trail for service monitoring and performance management.
- The e-business services should be capable of integrating with traditional communications services.

In effect the customers view services not as stand-alone services requiring separate customer service parameters, but rather as service applications of an integrated e-business service. The additional value provided by the e-BMS provider is that the e-BMS system acts as a mediator between the customer and the individual application and value-added service providers' systems.

A COMPONENT-BASED E-BUSINESS MANAGEMENT FRAMEWORK

The pressure to rapidly develop new services to operate over Internet-based networks has left little time for the development of an open architectural framework for management systems in this domain. However, without some common architectural principles to guide the analysis and design of systems that manage these IP-based services, the industry runs the risk of finding it increasingly difficult to provide high quality (and thus high value) services capable of interoperating with peer services and to provide open customer management facilities. More importantly, the cost of developing such services and the lack of an agreed standardized management architecture will deter software vendors from investing in developing low-cost off-the-shelf component for this market.

Thus, a key aim of this work is to try and establish an open development framework to assist in the development of new services and to promote the development of commercial off-the-shelf software component for management systems. The proposed framework consists primarily of the concepts listed below.

Business Roles

Business roles are abstract roles that may be taken by a business organization and which can be used to describe its participation in a business relationship. A business organization can take up any number of business roles at any one time, depending on the business relationships in which it is currently involved. Business roles can also be used for relationships between reconfigurable organizational units within the same enterprise. The framework contains a predefined set of abstract roles to aid analysts to define their particular set of business relationships.

Reference Points

These are used to establish the open interoperable specifications to which the interfaces of management systems may conform either completely, in part or not at all.

The framework proposes the business roles and reference points shown in Figure 2. The model is focussed on an e-BMS provided by an e-BMS provider to a group of e-BMS customers via an e-BMS-customer management reference point. The e-BMS customers may be a group of cooperating peer organizations or an ASP supplying multiple customers utilizing the e-BMS (the AS-CP reference point supports the direct application service provision interactions). The model also identifies a guaranteed quality-of-service internet protocol service (GQIPS) provider role. This may receive DiffServ traffic from a customer (via reference point DS-CP) and forward it to peer role in adjacent ISPs (via DS-PP). The GQIPS-PP reference point allows QoS management provision and charging settlement between ISPs performing the GQIPS role. The e-BMS may be provided either directly using the GQIPS, in which case the two roles interact via the GQIPS-PM reference point. Alternatively the e-BMS service may be layered over a VPN service (VPNS), which in turn uses the GQIPS. In this case the e-BMS provider role interacts with the VPNS via the VPNS-PM. The VPNS provides end-to-end management of guaranteed QoS communications and security over multiple domains including the customer's CPE (via VPNS-CM), adjoining ISPs (via VPN-GQIP-PP) and the GQIPS provider role in its own domain if present (via GQIPS-PM).

Additional concepts related to the analysis and design of management systems within the framework are as follows.

Business Processes

Business processes describe areas of activity in the operation of an organization and the interactions that take place between those activities. The TeleManagement forum telecoms operations map (TMF, 1998) represents a commonly used model of management business processes and has been adopted for this part of the framework. This model is being gradually refined by the TM Forum and thus may need to be modified in a future version of the framework.

Building Blocks

Building blocks are the main reusable structural element in the framework. The most comprehensive definition of management-related building blocks currently available is being worked on in the TM Forum's Application Component Team (ACT). This is based on the requirements established by Telcordia (formerly Bellcore) in their extensive OSCA/INA analysis. This has already seen some application in the use of INA principles in the work of TINA-C (Telecommunication Information Network Architecture Consortium). The ACT, however, has further refined and condensed the OSCA/INA work in TMF TIM (1998). The concept of building blocks used here has been adopted for the framework. The ACT work forms

Figure 2: Logical business roles and reference points

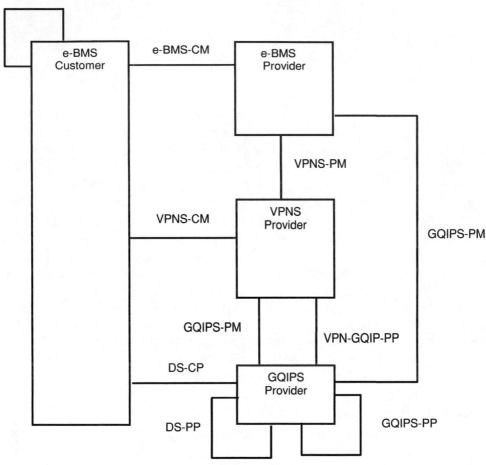

the basis of the next generation OSS initiative currently being conducted in the TMF. It is anticipated that the implementation work associated with the framework defined here will provide valuable input to the TMF NGOSS work.

The ACT work identifies a "building block" as a deployable unit of interoperating software. In line with contemporary software architectures, building blocks are described as being in one of three computing tiers:

- **Enterprise Information Tier (EIT):** This tier is concerned with the storage and maintenance of enterprise data, i.e., data used by multiple business processes.
- **Process Automation Tier (PAT):** This tier is concerned with business operations and management.
- **Human Interaction Tier (HIT):** This tier is concerned with issues related to human/computer interaction.

Building blocks are an abstract concept used in the analysis and design of systems. Their actual implementation as software involves the mapping of building blocks to technology-specific concepts such as component assemblies from the OMG's CORBA component model or jar files from Sun Microsystem's enterprise java beans.

Building Block Contracts

The interfaces of a building block are termed contracts, and a building block may have multiple contracts. Contracts may be designed to conform to specifications of reference points. Management system interfaces may therefore be defined in terms of aggregation of contract specifications.

CASE STUDY: AN INTEGRATED, MANAGED E-BUSINESS NETWORK BASED ON THE COMPONENT FRAMEWORK

Figure 3 provides an example of how the concepts may be applied for an organization playing the roles of e-BMS provider (e-business management service provider), VPNS provider (virtual private network service provider) and GQIPS provider (guaranteed quality-of-IP service provider). The figure focuses on business processes related to the fulfillment of the e-BMS service. This involves order handling within the e-BMS provider role, VPN configuration, outsourcing, and security management and customer reporting within the GQIPS provider role. Customer service management and customer premises management processes are also identified in the e-BMS customer domain. Within each of these business processes, initial identification of building blocks within the different computing tiers have been identified, as well as their binding via contracts and the mapping of those bindings to reference points.

Relationship With Other Work

The framework presented is based on best practice in component-based system design and construction as well as incorporating state-of-the-art technology. A framework can be thought of as a reusable design of part of a system that may be extended or customized by an application developer (Johnson, 1997) and thus is a generic semi-complete solution designed to solve a set of similar problems in a number of customizable or configurable ways (Johnson & Foote, 1988). Based on Fayad and Schmidt's (1997) classification of frameworks, the framework presented in this paper represents an enterprise application framework aimed at enabling the rapid development and deployment of management services.

The description of the framework components is specified using UML v1.3, employing use case, object and class models and collaboration diagrams (Rumbaugh, Jacobson & Booch, 1999). The components also use several well-established design patterns (Gamma, Helm, Johnson & Vlissides, 1994), e.g., factory, façade, etc.

Figure 3: Application of framework focusing on VPN and GQIP management processes

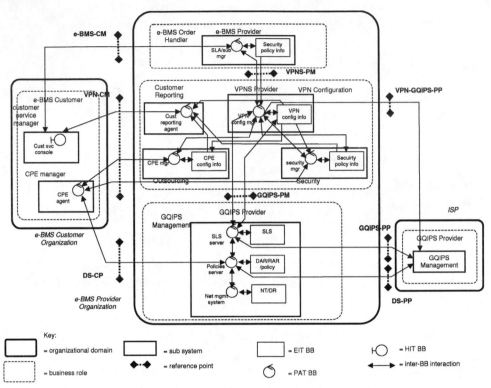

As described in section 3, the most comprehensive definition of management-related building blocks currently available is being worked on in the TM Forum's ACT. One of the primary motivations for the proposed framework endorsing the TMF building block approach is the need for service providers to seamlessly integrate their service with the minimum of overhead. With the presented framework, a building block is considered an atomic unit for the purpose of deployment, management, distribution security and interoperability.

In addition to the separation of concerns according to the three-tiered architecture as described in section 3, the issue of the relationship between building blocks and business processes also needs to be addressed. An important consideration is the mapping between the specification of building blocks and its relationship to the business processes as defined in the TMF business process model (BPM). An important aspect of the work is to provide guidance on the construction of sets of building blocks to support fulfillment, assurance and billing business processes. The level of granularity of the building block in relation to the service management business processes as defined by the TMF BPM is a key framework consideration.

The VPN technology considered for this framework is the IP VPN based on Multi Protocol Label Switching (MLPS) that is an emerging IETF standard. The advantage of MPLS comparing to other VPN technologies (IP tunneling based on IPSec, for example) is that it allows a large-scale VPN provisioning with simpler configuration and management for both provider and CPE sites. It provides a high degree of flexibility, enabling any-to-any IP VPN connectivity across switched or routed networks. In combination with Diffserv, MPLS allows fined-grained QoS for different traffic types (data, voice, video) over the same network infrastructure. Security is supported through a combination of border gateway protocol (BGP), IP address resolution and optional IPSec encryption.

Furthermore, various VPN access scenarios are considered, enabling end users to access quickly and easily corporate VPN sites independently from their locations through access services integrating different existing access technologies, including dial (analogue or ISDN), cable, ADSL and wireless (mobile IP).

CONCLUSIONS AND FURTHER PLANS

This paper has presented an analysis of the business model for a provider of e-Business management services and examined the requirements for such management services. Further, a management component framework to support the rapid and flexible construction of e-Commerce management infrastructure has been presented. The framework is based on a holistic management approach supporting seamless integration of network and application management services (i.e., vertical), as well as integrating management across distinct functional areas (i.e., horizontal). Such a framework concept for e-Business management is very important as it is one of the very few ways in which flexible, rapid development and one-stop-shopping e-business management can be achieved.

Future work consists of further elaboration of the framework, which is an ongoing activity as part of a large European telecommunication project called FORM (http://www.uhc.dk/form). This project will also trail the implementation of an e-Business management system, supporting the features of the management component framework presented in this paper. Also, close liaison with industry standards bodies will be considered as well as contribution to the development of an integrated management framework for the management of a dynamic e-business environment.

ACKNOWLEDGMENT

This work was conducted under the partial funding of the EU through the IST project FORM (contract IST-1999-103571). The views expressed in this document do not necessarily reflect those of these consortia.

REFERENCES

Fayad, M., and Schmidt, D. (1997, October). Object-oriented applications frameworks. *Communications of the ACM*, *40*(10), 32-38.

Gamma, E., Helm, E., Johnson, R. R., and Vlissides, J. (1994). Design patterns: Languages. *Pattern Languages of Program Design*. Reading, MA: Addison-Wesley.

Johnson, R. (1997). Frameworks = Components + patterns. *Communications of the ACM*, October, 40(10), 39-42.

Johnson, R. E., and Foote, B. (1988). Designing reusable classes. *Journal of Object Oriented Programming*, July, 1(2), 22-25.

Rumbaugh, J., Jacobson, I., and Booch, G. (1999). *The Unified Modeling Language Reference Manual*. Reading, MA: Addison-Wesley.

Sanders, M., and Temkin, B. (2000, April). Global e-commerce approaches hypergrowth. *Forrester Report*. Retrieved M D, Y from the World Wide Web: http://www.forrester.com.

TMF. (1998). TMF telecoms operation map: A high-level view of end-to-end service fulfillment, service assurance and billing. *TeleManagement Forum*. NMF, Morristown. Available on the World Wide Web at: http://www.tmforum.org.

TMF TIM. (1998). SMART TMN technology integration map. GB 909, Issues 1.1, *TeleManagement Forum*, October. Available on the World Wide Web at: http://www.tmforum.org.

Chapter VII

Value Webs: Cases, Features, and Success Factors

Dorian Selz
Namics Ag, Switzerland

Stefan Klein
University of Muenster, Germany

The new information infrastructure redefines the roles and relationships between buyer, seller, and middleman, allowing new ways of accessing and tapping information and price arrangements. Most importantly information about a product or service may be separated from the product or service itself. The chapter scrutinizes how companies are using these opportunities to establish networked retail businesses and generate customer value in innovative ways. We have tried to reconstruct a widespread interorganizational arrangement for product and service retailing on the Web, its antecedents, its challenges and its economic logic.

INTRODUCTION

"That all this is in some sense true, as it is in some sense false."

Augustine

One of the most profound consequences of the ongoing information revolution is its influence on how economic value is created and extracted. Within a brief span of time the silicon chip altered the course of world, and the consequences of this are just being felt in even the most secluded parts of our societies. The lifeline of our world today is no longer ships bridging the seas, railroads or interstate highways crisscrossing continents, or airliners spanning the globe, but networks linking these little, tiny bits of electrified silicon. A standard car today musters more computing power than the Apollo mission to the moon some 30 years ago. Moore's Law of ever cheaper and more powerful computing and Metcalfe's Law (cf. Downes & Mui, 1998) on the exponential increase of the utility of an expanding network, currently best represented by the Internet and the World Wide Web, suggest that we are only at the start of this revolution.

This chapter scrutinizes how companies have responded to opportunities that the Web has provided to establish networked retail businesses and to generate customer value in new ways. In economic terms, the new information infrastructure redefines the roles and relationships between buyer, seller, and middleman, allowing new ways of accessing and tapping information and price arrangements. Most importantly, information about a product or service may be separated from the product or service itself.

This chapter attempts to combine the results of research which is looking for patterns of organization and management advice on how to reap the benefits of the Web. We have tried to reconstruct what has become one (not the) dominant form of interorganizational arrangements for product and service retailing on the Web, its antecedents, its challenges and its economic logic.

Value Webs are emerging forms of fluid and flexible organizations. Deconstructed firms focus on a subset of the value-adding process and rely on coordinated relationships with other firms to provide the remainder of the value chain activities needed for a market offering. Value is rarely created with information itself. Value Webs, on the contrary, excel at creating new values with information by coordinating the complex relationships of independent companies. Often of transitory character, such Value Webs are organized around a specific market opportunity, lasting only for the length of that opportunity.

While management science has been primarily concerned with the alignment of strategy and organization or strategy and structure (Schewe, 1998), information systems science has extended this question and has included information technology, thus looking into a triangular relationship of alignment between IT, strategy and organization (Frank & Klein, 1992) or strategy, process and IT (Österle, 1995). The notion of value Webs not only aligns but integrates the three concepts in a unique and intricate way: Value Webs are organizational arrangements which at the same time represent (strategic) business models within a particular technical environment, the Web. The World Wide Web, which incorporates a basic set of (inter-)organizational roles and linkages, is structurally mirrored by the value Webs. While virtual organizations have been primarily characterized in dimensions like market interaction, competence leverage and work configuration (Venkatraman & Henderson, 1996), i.e., innovative ways of organizing distributed operations, value Webs focus on innovative value propositions and customer service. They systematically integrate (end) customers, which have access to basically the same infrastructure and similar services, into the network of Web-enabled relations.

This chapter tries to reconstruct underlying design patterns of interorganizational arrangements and gives a stylized description of their features. This leads to the question why and in which way the Web makes a difference for the design of networked enterprises and how we can explain the economic logic of value Webs.

VIGNETTES

Four vignettes of successful Web businesses have been selected which represent extremes of product and service retailing. Brief and stylized descriptions introduce the core ideas, contingencies and destructive power of value Webs as far as established industry structures are concerned: The respective industries have undergone a profound transformation since the Web has started to have an impact on business.

Vignette 1–The Picture of Automotive Distribution

Cars are sold nowadays typically through a plethora of dealerships around the country. Most dealerships offer the standard models of the manufacturer they represent and have a limited geographical reach. In contrast, Web sites like Autoweb or AutobyTel, so called cybermediaries, offer an abundance of car-related information, including side-by-side comparisons of different brands, reviews of trade magazines, links to dealers and the option of a price quote. Cybermediaries are changing the marketplace thoroughly: About a quarter of all automotive purchases are influenced by information found on the Web. A core element of their strategy is cherry-picking: They provide a service that bundles together the products and services of car dealers, car manufacturers, financial and insurance services, consumer reports, and more. Each of these products and services was previously part of an existing value system that the cybermediary picked clean to combine them into a new value proposition for the consumer. The recent sharp downturn of Internet ventures also affected the car platforms. However, studies indicate that by offering competitive prices online vendors succeed to attract buyers.

Vignette 2–The Democratization of Capital

For a long time access to the financial markets was limited to large financial institutions. Individuals had to go through these often very pricey intermediaries to do their trades. When independent stockbrokers such as E*Trade went online, the large banks initially were unimpressed. That has changed. Charles Schwab, E*Trade, and many other online brokers changed the way many Americans, Europeans and Asians handle their financial assets. Today, these sites offer the private investor everything one needs to properly assess the markets and build up an investment portfolio. The private punters are on equal terms with their cousins from the large banks. The retail branch of the financial services industry performs an intermediary role based on privileged access to financial information. Emerging Value Web brokers, such as E*Trade, are leveraging the effects of the Internet in opening up previously closed systems, establishing themselves as trusted intermediaries and pulling together the best of category offerings to create a custom-tailored financial solution. The recent downturn of financial markets has drastically reduced the transaction volume of the online brokers, which, because of their specialization, are particularly vulnerable.

Vignette 3–Birth of a Salesman: The Digital Retailer

Most books are sold in bookstores across the country, and most of them have quite a few books in stock but need to order special books from the wholesaler. The online bookstore Amazon changed the marketplace by creating a virtual bookstore, holding more than 2.5 million titles, about 10 times as many as even the biggest physical bookstore. But once someone has shown the way, it is easy for competitors to set up their own database and start selling books. To maintain a competitive advantage, Amazon relies on customer loyalty that goes beyond the thrill of finding the best bargain in the market. It offers its readers a service: information on books. The company collects reviews from various sources: Authors submit their own interviews, reviews from literature magazines are added, and readers are invited to contribute their own reviews. The more books the reader buys and the more reviews the reader contributes, the better the collaborative filtering mechanism will be at suggesting books that the reader might like. Amazon has created a loyal customer base, resulting in a at times mind-boggling stock valuation, and a profound impact on the distribution channel of books.

A core element of Amazon's strategy is to be close to the customer and to mobilize customers to become a part of the firm's value-adding process. By establishing a close relationship with the customer, Value Web brokers, like Dell or Amazon, have turned the consumer into a producer-consumer or prosumer. The relationship results in products and services that better match the expectations of the prosumers. Amazon successfully established itself as a leading online retailer; however, the firm has not yet shown how to generate profits.

Vignette 4–A Travel Odyssey: The Distribution of Tourism Products

In an industry which is fragmented and still characterized by numerous mom-and-pop outlets, Travelocity.com has leveraged the combined power of computer reservation systems or global distribution systems (CRS/GDS) and the Web. Travelocity has built the equivalent of an online travel supermarket with access to a huge breadth and depth of touristic offerings and (destination) information on the one side and low prices and efficient transactions on the other side.

A packaged holiday typically consists of (air) travel arrangement and local accommodation. Value Web brokers, such as Travelocity or Airtours, specialize in selling travel products. Alliances between travel and tourism principals, on the one hand, and tour operators or CRS/GDS, on the other hand, shift the financial risk from the principals to the operators or CRS/GDS, allowing the operator or CRS/GDS to assemble a comprehensive holiday package guaranteeing a steady stream of commission-based revenue, and guarantee the consumers lower prices because of the bargaining power of the operators.

THE VALUE WEB MODEL

In these examples, winning firms are taking full advantage of the emerging online marketspace with varying degrees of physical scope of the core product they offer. Precisely what made these online ventures so successful and how did they extract economic value in this open electronic network called the Internet?

We describe the main characteristics we have found: cherry-picking from existing value systems, a Value Web broker that acts as central coordinator, an endeavor to gain proximity to the final consumer, and an integration of upstream activities. This integration is either coordinated with market platforms or with hierarchical mechanisms.

The Value Web Model: Four Building Blocks

"Relationships are one of the most valuable resources that a company possesses" (Hakansson, 1987, p. 10).

The sine qua non of a Value Web is the ability of Value Web brokers to attack and successfully cherry-pick existing value systems. The Value Web broker plays a central role in the model. The broker's primary aim is to create a highly attractive value proposition for the customer and he aims to move as close to the customer as possible. As sketched out before, a Value Web broker will rely extensively on component suppliers to build the product or deliver the service precisely as the customer wishes.

New entrants are able to challenge the business of historically dominant firms. The incumbents have pursued pricing, product and service policies that, although presumably highly effective, make them now attractive targets for aggressive new entrants (Clemons & Croson, 1996). The newcomers' strategies rely on new (IT) technologies, alternative, more direct marketing channels, lower operating and overhead costs, and interfirm cooperation to contest specific segments of the market. The Value Web model (cf. Figure 1) comprises the key notions and the actors, their roles, activities, and resources. It is primarily interested in two viewpoints: first and foremost, the viewpoint of the Value Web broker. His viewpoint is primarily determined by the relationship with consumers, the second viewpoint.

Step 1: Cherry-Picking of Existing Value Systems

Industries have traditionally been structured into vertically integrated value systems. Often the asset structure, operating culture, policies, and processes have all been designed without explicitly focusing on customer value.

Creative new entrants will emerge that focus on specific niches. They will differ from the old value systems in two ways: First, they will focus on selected high-profit, high-growth niches. Second, they will not own all or even most of the assets

Figure 1: The value Web model

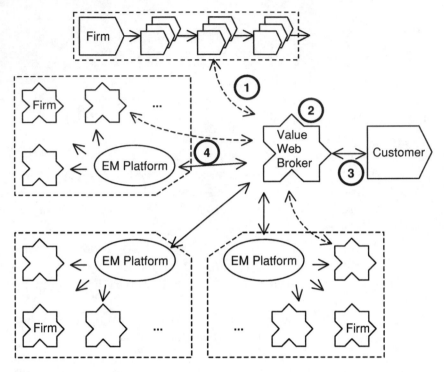

in the value system and thus show some traits of a virtual organization. Rather the value Webs will cherry-pick and configure only those value-adding activities that are meaningful for a targeted customer segment. In essence, these firms will have created what is termed in this study a Value Web (cf. Figure 2).

In a Value Web, one firm–the Value Web broker–exploits the strengths of each supplier and coordinates production and delivery across the network. The Value Web broker coordinates the activities of other companies in the Web, choosing and assembling capabilities according to the product or service specified by customers.

The kernel of a Value Web is a tight network of communication and coordination relations among all players, whether currently active or in for future cooperation. The Value Web broker leverages the disaggregated business units by coordinating the new players, each of which possesses highly distinctive, yet complementary, operating and process-based competencies to deliver new levels of customer value. Specific competencies are sourced from within an extended network (Anderson & Hakansson, 1994; Rayport & Sviokla, 1995; Sarkar et al., 1998).

Step 2: An Intermediary of Value–The Value Web Broker

Central to the Value Web is an intermediary acting as coordinator, integrator, and interface–the Value Web broker. An intermediary in an electronic market

Figure 2: Cherry-picking of existing value chains

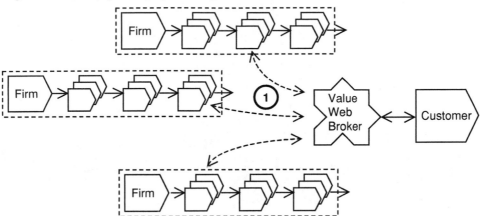

provides very little value associated with the traditional roles of intermediaries. Then how do they add value is the logical question? Bailey (1997), referring to Resnick et al. (1995) and Malone et al. (1987), identifies five roles that intermediaries, i.e., Value Web brokers, provide (cf. Table 1; Figure 3).

Bailey explored these roles in 13 case studies covering a number of industries. His findings suggest that for electronic brokers facilitation and aggregation are reduced in importance inasmuch as matching, trust and marketing increased in importance.

The Value Web broker acts as market maker and covers three roles: (1) the broker acts as intermediary between suppliers of inputs and consumers of final goods, (2) he undertakes directly or applies control to a variety of activities in the Value Web to sustain it, e.g., a certain price or quality level, and (3) he deals with competitive threats (Carter et al., 1998).

Step 3: Close to the Customer

The Value Web, especially the broker as the interface to the customer, will try to move towards the final position in a value system (cf. Figure 4) to establish a direct and loyal link with customers. Four phases are of importance (Bradley, 1995; cf. Table 2).

The social processes of interaction still have to mature in the electronic domain. The Web is made for customer services of a new dimension, because the Internet offers a whole new way of establishing relationships with customers. Both the customer and the Value Web can interact at any time with the other party. Order status information; specific account information, for example, in the case of a customer; special promotions and new product announcements are information that can be pulled or pushed precisely when and where necessary. Famous examples of companies achieving on this account are Cisco, FedEx, and Dell (Sterne, 1996).

Table 1: Intermediaries' roles

Intermediaries' roles	Explanation
Facilitation of inarticulable knowledge and information	Although there is a powerful drive towards standardization, much product and service related information and knowledge, especially for customer-specific production, cannot be standardized. The broker helps to coordinate the flow of information by coordinating and translating the information that is exchanged between supplier and consumer.
Aggregation of demand and supply	Instead of a single firm or an individual negotiating a contract, by aggregating the preferences the broker will notch up better conditions. The potential gains include reduced transaction costs, economies of scale, and, eventually, scope.
Matching suppliers and customers by creating the space for the match	Manifold reasons exist why a broker is better at matching. Facilitation and communication relate to points already raised. Bailey (1997) further identifies limiting of the search space and providing a filtering mechanism as reasons why an intermediary is better at matchmaking than supplier and consumer alone in a disintermediated market.
Trust is essential in electronic transactions	A well-established broker with a good reputation will ensure that both sides of the contract will live up to their obligations. Since the broker is compensated only for a successful transaction, this creates an incentive for the intermediary to do the maximum to ensure a successful transaction. Furthermore, the intermediary will have a disincentive for fraud because this would damage his reputation and trust relation with all parties involved and lead to bankruptcy over the long haul.
Marketing information of the aggregated supplier and consumer base is a source of value	The broker is best placed to understand the communities which develop. Because of this information, a broker can deliver superior matching services, which translate into a competitive advantage when compared to the disintermediated situation. Hagel and Rayport (1997) call this type of broker an *infomediary*.

Figure 3: The Value Web broker

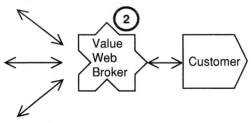

Why is this position preferable to a traditional position in a value system? The digital economy offers new entrants the same possibilities, i.e., the ability to process large amounts of data, independent of space and time. Moreover, the position is as open to the multinational automotive corporation with all its organizational muscle as it is to small and nimble newcomers selling cars on the Internet. Informational advantages will quickly be competed away. Thus, the Value Web will compete on utility not on power. As outlined before with the modularization argument, standardization and commoditization of many product and service categories is occurring. To be successful the Value Web must adhere to these open standards although this is a self-limiting strategy. To add value, the Value Web will focus on the unique utility provided–a combination of superior product, price, convenience, and velocity.

Table 2: Four phases of establishing a key position towards customers

Phases	Explanation
Thinking value for markets, customers and competitors	Each firm must decide in which market it should compete. In dealing with products and services offered, the value web will distinguish between different levels of aggregation (product class, type, and brand). The value web will further need to distinguish the relative positions of its competitors and the structure of supplier and component markets.
Organizing value for customers	A product defined as *"the need satisfying offering of a firm"* (McCarthy & Perreault, 1996) has four dimensions: (1) the customer perceives the product is of an appropriate appearance and quality, (2) packaging and promotion convey information about the product, (3) the way a company communicates the benefits associated with the product, and (4) the image of a product in a market. In the electronic realm the latter two characteristics are especially important to compensate for the lack of the touch-and-feel sensation of a physical product in a store. The value web must unceasingly develop product enhancements or new products all together. The value of new products is unambiguous. They help add value to the product portfolio of the firm (Bradley, 1995). Pricing decisions must be transparent to customers, so they can easily compare with competing value webs.
Communicating value to customers	The company must communicate with its customers to ensure that they know about the value provided by the firm. In exchange, the firms may learn about their needs and preferences. The value web preferably wants to become the sole entry gate for certain product and service categories, monopolizing these areas. This is achieved by maximizing the sophistication of the value the web delivers, while minimizing the sophistication of the technology consumed.
Delivering value to customers	*"Marketing channels perform the function of accumulating products and services into assortments required by customers, and ensuring that this assortment is delivered to the location desired at the time required and in the quantities demanded"* (Bradley 1995, 750). The value web broker being close to the customer in the first three phases of a market transaction must closely cooperate with the unit that delivers the logistics solution for the products sold.

Figure 4: The Value Web broker: Close to the customer

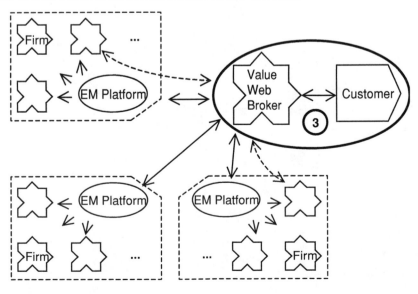

Step 4: Alliances With Partners

The Value Web broker is seldom able to provide the entire value proposition himself and resorts to third-party component suppliers (cf. Figure 5). The key to capturing value within a relational form is ownership of an asset that is needed to make the value creation possible and which is not readily available elsewhere (Day & Wendler, 1988). Smaller units are better incubators for the flourishing of knowledge. The linchpin then becomes the sharing of knowledge across the Value Web. One of the main forces holding together the relations in a Value Web is the possibility of spreading risk, increasing flexibility, enhancing an industry's innovation capability, and reducing complexity for individual participants across the cluster of companies that collaborate in a particular Value Web (Hagel, 1996).

> In one sense, the new coordination technologies allow us to return to the preindustrial organizational model of tiny, autonomous businesses. ... But there's one crucial difference: Electronic networks enable these microbusinesses to tap into the global reservoirs of information, exper-tise, and financing that used to be available only to large companies. (Malone & Laubacher, 1998, p. 148)

Picot et al. (1996) refer to this as bringing the firm to the market and the market to the firm. In this ambiguous, complex and fluid configuration of firms that constitute a Value Web, in which relations between firms have such an importance, the firms will develop network identities. Following the analysis of Snow et al. (1992) some divergent Value Web patterns can be identified. The more efficiency-oriented and stable value systems will become the dominant organizational form in

Figure 5: Alliances with partners–securing backward integration

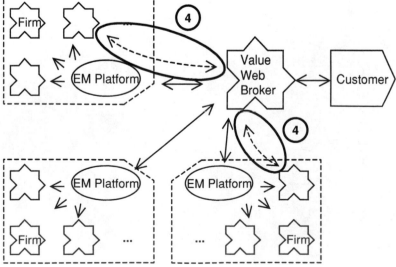

mature and healthy industries. Dynamic value Webs will appear on the fringes of mature industries. The ability of networks to generate new products with lower levels of investment will help to rejuvenate these industry segments. Large organizations may try to adopt internal value Webs to contain the inflexibility associated with rigidly organized structures.

Differences and Analogies With Other Models for Configuring Value

The notions of modularization of business, the disintegration and reconfiguration of value systems, and the network-centric firm have been around for some time. What is different about the Value Web model, what elements are the same, and where does the proposed model make its mark?

Comparison to Value Shops

The value shop is an organizational form that relies on intensive technology deployment to resolve customer problems. The selection, combination, and application of third-party resources and activities varies according to the requirements of the problem to be solved. Examples include architecture, consulting, and law firms. Stabell and Fjeldstad (1998) single out information asymmetry as the most important attribute of an intensive technology-linked value shop. This is in sharp contrast to a Value Web. The Internet in combination with software agent technologies and specialized intermediaries will diminish the information asymmetry to a minimum and put the customer on equal terms with the Value Web broker. Besides the value shop model is more adapted to deal with unique cases. The Value Web model is applicable for products and services that come with some degree of standardization and mass production to secure economies of scale and scope. Both models are similar with respect to information acquisition activities, a significant amount of sequential and reciprocal interdependence between activities, and the linking of additional capabilities and resources.

Comparison to Value Networks

Value networks (Stabell & Fjeldstad, 1998) rely on mediating technology to link customers; examples are the postal system, retail banks and telephone companies. Whereas the value network describes how value can be generated out of distributed infrastructures such as the postal system, the Value Web model applies the notion of value-generating networks to much more divers (in the infrastructure and services) and flexible arrangements which are suited for a newly set up intermediary. The underlying difference is comparable to the differences of the Internet as a flexible, packed-switched infrastructure and the phone system, which has been built for circuit-switch voice transmission (Steinberg, 1996). This is especially true when that new intermediary considers both the networking service provided to customers and the jigsaw-puzzle-like assemblage of the final product and service. A large organization might have a cost advantage in providing the networking services. A nimbler newcomer will have a cost advantage on the assembly side, as a green-site start-up, and in bringing partners together on short notice and for a limited period of time.

Comparison to Business Webs

Tapscott et al. (2000) have developed the notion of the business Web, which is characterized by nine features: Internet infrastructure, value proposition innovation, multienterprise capability machine, five classes of participants, co-opetition, customer-centricity, context reigns, rules and standards, bathed in knowledge. The concept of business Webs has numerous similarities to the notion of the value Webs, which might be taken as support for the underlying idea. However, there is a significant difference in the sense that value Webs are constituted and defined by the role of the broker while business Webs are characterized by more open and flexible exchange relations.

Comparison to Virtual Organizations

The dissemination of open electronic networks amplifies the effects that made virtual organizations possible. A virtual organization is built around a common goal to exploit a specific opportunity. It is constituted by a pool of potential partners and a smaller, project-specific group, which is assembled out of the pool and will diminish as soon as the project has been concluded. The best of each participating firm is mixed and matched to extend the resource base available to a single firm. Central to a virtual organization is trust among the partners, equal rights and stakes in the venture (Business Week, 1993; Sieber, 1998). The organizational form of a Value Web is not necessarily one of trust and equal rights. The Value Web broker plays a central role and can establish and terminate relationships as business requires and reputation allows. However, all parties involved have an interest evolving along the lines of virtual organizations as outlined by Sieber. The main difference then is one of relationship: It is the Value Web broker that organizes this particular community and therefore enjoys more rights than the other parties concerned and might products resorts rather to a market mechanism, which offers better value than a fix alliance with a supplier, for the provision of some components.

Overall, virtual organization is an older and much broader concept, which might even incorporate value Webs as a particular instance, with the specific scope that we have outlined.

Value Webs: A Temporary or Lasting Organizational Form?

Although organizational adaptation is a complex and dynamic process, Miles and Snow (1978) state that it can be broadly conceptualized as a cycle of adjustment requiring the simultaneous solution of three interrelated problems: (1) entrepreneurial (domain definition), (2) engineering (technology), and (3) administrative (structure). When patterns of behavior within a single industry are observed, four organizational types begin to emerge: (1) defenders are organizations with a narrow product market and devote their primary attention to improving the efficiency of their existing operations, (2) prospectors continually search for market opportunities and experiment with change and uncertainty but are, therefore, often not completely efficient, (3) analyzers operate in two product markets, one relatively stable, the other changing, and transfer the innovations of the latter rapidly into the first, and lastly (4) reactors may perceive change and uncertainty but are unable to respond effectively.

A Value Web is naturally a prospector as it continually looks for ways to propose unique assortments of value to the customer. The broker is distinguished by a high willingness to continually adapt to a frequently changing environment. The Value Web under the stewardship of the broker is a combination of actors with varying types of relations among each other and to the broker and resembles an umbrella design (Malone & Laubacher, 1998). This leaves open the issue of what type of organization each component unit is to the Value Web itself. The Value Web in its entirety is driven by the competitive pressure emanating from the marketplace to optimize system-wide. Constituents have basically a shared interest in such an optimum but depending on their respective competitive position may swing out and pursue a path of their own. The whole system will suffer only incrementally.

The proposed model resembles a biological model of organization similar to a cell tissue (Economist, 1993). The nervous system–the broker–coordinates the functions of the cells. There is a natural rate of replenishment of inefficient cells for new ones and the possibility of constructing cells for a specific purpose (e.g., white blood cells). However, as the underlying technology is changing at a fast pace, it is difficult to predict whether value Webs will prove to be a sustainable model as the metaphor suggests.

ANALYSIS

In their book on virtual organizations, Hedberg et al. (1997) present a phrase they prefer: imaginary organizations. In their view "imaginary organization" is a "powerful perspective on business," a possible way to look at interorganizational relations and the potential they yield. In this sense, the theme of the final section is whether the inquiry into an elusive phenomenon will yield elusive conclusions.

Analysis of the Vignettes and the Initial Assumptions

An essential similarity of all vignettes is the decoupling of the product from information about the product, combined with universal access to this information. The vignettes focus, in turn, on each of the four essential parts of the Value Web model. Table 3 provides a synopsis of the main findings and their implications for a Value Web.

Table 3: Vignettes' main findings

Vignettes	Main findings	Implications for the value web
Automotive	• *Cherry picking* of existing value systems by new entrants. • New entrants often not related to the industry (e.g., Microsoft in automotive retail). • New and enhanced value propositions.	• Most existing value systems are vulnerable to attack. • In defense, incumbents must be willing to sacrifice (parts of) their marketing channel.
Finance	• New entrants successfully established *value web broker* positions. • Offer best-of-category products. • Often not tied to anyone product or service supplier.	• A consumer is no specialist in finance. For efficiency reasons he will turn to a trusted value web broker, this being the rational for the emergence of such brokers.
Retail	• *Close relationships with customers* are beneficial for all parties. • Customers receive a custom-tailored product or service. • More efficient production.	• Value web brokers must aim at close relationships with customers to create lock-in situations. • Long-term loyalty will translate into higher returns for the broker.
Travel	• A *network of suppliers* is key to provide efficiently and effectively a customer-specific product. • Value web broker manages this Web of suppliers to provide the final product or service. • Main drivers are reasons of efficiency and capability.	• Healthy alliances are key to a successful value Web. • Careful attention must be given to alliances and their structure (e.g., position of suppliers). • The system-wide performance is the determining factor–not individual performance.

In each of the four industries–automotive, finance, retail, and travel–the existing value system and associated marketing channels are under pressure by new entrants or incumbents, who have already redefined their role in that system. There is a significant shift away from a sequential process of value creation towards a simultaneous or parallel process with a corresponding organizational structure that resembles a Web.

The four vignettes paint a mixed picture of success factors. The message they convey is one of change, next to some constant variables. The major force of change is IT. The change produces a new variant in organizational format, which we term Value Web. The variables displaying a penchant for perseverance are the traditional determinants of success in business: a superior product or service at an attractive price that truly fulfills the needs and wants of a consumer, backed up by a collection of individuals forming a company that delivers superior performance on every account. In that respect there is nothing to add to Drucker's (1995) analysis of the corporation as a human effort.

Success Factors and Risks of the Model

As the Value Web model is centered around the product or value broker, the success of the model very much depends on the management of relations and finally the competence of the broker.

Managing Relations

For the analysis of network relations, the description of Cook and Emerson (1978, p. 725) that a network is a "set of two or more connected exchange relations" and Hakansson's (1987) classification of actors, activities and resources as basic classes of variables are useful. The Value Web relies on a network structure as described by Hakansson (1987) for its (internal) organization: It is a special embossment of a network organization. In that sense this organizational form might look in many aspects similar to other network organizations, but in one respect it differs: The Value Web is a boundary-less organization. Relational and behavioral patterns that are today constrained by a firm's vertical, horizontal, external, and geographical boundaries are freed and superseded by patterns of free movement across those boundaries. The focus of the Value Web is how to quickly move ideas, information, decisions, talent, rewards, and actions to where they are most effective. Competition will shift to some extent from within the Value Web into a contest between different Value Webs providing similar products and services. The added flexibility within a Value Web translates into better value for the customer and increased competition between alliances of networks. However, all players must be ready at any moment to forge new alliances, to abandon old ones, to question their entire business model, to cannibalize existing revenue streams, and above all to focus on their core capabilities. The key to becoming a successful participant in this game is a talent to handle change.

Given the contradicting forces in the Value Web, the question is whether the forces tying together the various units of a Value Web are strong enough to contain the centrifugal forces that permanently erode its shoreline. If too much formal control has to be established, the arrangement will lose part of its attractiveness; if too little control is maintained, effective and efficient coordination can become impossible and again the appeal of the model is diminished. As exchange relations will be often based on flexible pricing, price negotiations and the division of network profits can become cumbersome.

The Broker Role

A successful Value Web broker will possess and maintain superior knowledge of both its suppliers and customers. The broker will try to maintain lasting relationships with customers. Being more knowledgeable enables the broker to intermediate between other market participants and to capture a share of the gains of trade. The broker will apply controls to a variety of activities. These include assembling of component products, physical distribution through the wholesale and retail network, determination and control of prices, monitoring and controlling inventories, disseminating information through advertising, and organizing sales and promotional activities. A process-oriented view of the broker role has been developed by Bach and Österle (2000) in the concept of a process portal, which integrates suppliers and links providers of e-services via a standardized business bus. Activities also include monitoring and assuring quality in order to sustain a level of prices and quality by all Value Web participants agreeing to certain criteria. This requires the Value Web broker to share the management of these contexts with his partners and it actually calls for an augmented set of management techniques (Faucheux, 1997).

The risks associated with the position of a Value Web broker include opportunism, relation-specific investments, small-numbers bargaining, and a loss of resource control (Clemons & Reddi, 1993). As the broker cannot resort to an established power base, (1) maintaining the balance between the advantages and incentives of the flexible arrangement and (2) securing the necessary commitment of the participants are major challenges.

Challenges and Future Avenues for Research

Thinking about value Webs has opened many more questions and issues than it has solved. We would like to highlight a few in order to indicate research issues that have emerged or been highlighted by our work.

Technology Lever

Value Webs illustrate again that technology can be a strong lever for creative construction of established business models. The analysis suggests that transmission mechanisms are a complex combination of relative cost advantages (information and transaction costs can be significantly reduced) in combination with network effects, which are working on several levels at the same time: enabling closer relationships to customers and to actual or potential cooperation partners. However, our understanding of the changes, let alone the potential effects these changes have and how they are enacted, is still very limited.

The Winner Takes It All

The vignettes highlight that competition on the Web has become a the-winner-takes-it-all game; i.e., cost reduction potentials can only be achieved if a significant scale of business can be built. Otherwise, costs of building and maintaining increasingly complex Web systems, which reflect a better understanding of customer needs as well as technology potentials, are eating any cost advantages electronic commerce might provide. Furthermore, being successful puts companies into a very attractive broker position where many other successful players, even competing incumbents, become eager to cooperate. The dynamics (dialectics) of becoming successful and vulnerable at the same time are not yet fully understood.

Success May Be Dangerous

There is some indication that in the online world a first-mover advantage exists. However, it remains to be seen whether a first mover reaps superior returns relative to competitors that are late entrants. The flip side of being successful and attractive is that Value Web brokers become perfectly visible targets for incumbents, which might–after studying the sources of success–be tempted to fight back and use their power and resources. Incumbents may not be the quickest to adopt new (marketing) ideas, but they have some inherent advantages like financial resources and, after all, control over the core product (Lieberman & Montgomery, 1988).

Empirical Evidence and Industry Contingencies

This study would greatly benefit from a broadened case study base. The vignettes paint a mixed picture of the validity and applicability of the Value Web model. The–temporary–success of the cases provides anecdotal evidence from diverse settings, it is not a proof of success factors of value Webs. Given the dynamics of the electronic marketspace, even monitoring and understanding what is happening has become an almost impossible task.

Each industry is worthy of a broadened set of case studies to work out industry-specific contingencies key features of change inflicted by digitalization, and the properties of successful and less successful emerging value Webs. The insights gained would allow scholars to derive a set of recommendations. Intra-industry comparisons would increase the validity of these recommendations further.

REFERENCES

Airtours Group. (2000). Retrieved M D, Y from the World Wide Web: http://www.airtours.com.

Amazon.com. (2001). Available on the World Wide Web at: http://www.amazon.com.

Anderson, J. C., and Hakansson, H. (1994, October). Dyadic business relationships within a business network context. *Journal of Marketing*, *58*(4), 1-16.

Autobytel.com. (2001). Available on the World Wide Web at: http://www.autobytel.com.

Autoweb.com. (2001). Available on the World Wide Web at: http://www.autoweb.com.

Bach, V. and Österle, H. (Eds.). (2000). *Customer Relationship Management in der Praxis*. Berlin, Germany: Springer.

Bailey, J. P. (1997). The emergence of electronic market intermediaries. *Proceedings of the 18th ICIS Conference, Atlanta*, vol, 391-399.

Bradley, F. (1995). *Marketing Management*. London: Prentice Hall.

Carter, M., Casson, M. C. and Suneja, V. (Eds.). (1998). *Critical Writings in Economics–The Economics of Marketing*. Cheltenham, England: Edward Elgar.

Casson, M. C. (1987). *The Firm and the Market: Studies in Multinational Enterprise and the Scope of the Firm*. Cambridge, MA: Press. (Reprinted in Casson M.C. (Ed.). (1996). *Critical Writings in Economics–The Theory of the Firm*, 72, Cheltenham, England: Edward Elgar).

Clemons, E. K. and Croson, D. C. (1996). Market dominance as a precursor of a firm's failure. *Journal of Management Information Systems*, Fall, 13(2), 59-86.

Clemons, E. K. and Reddi, S. P. (1993). The impact of information technology on the organization of economic activity: "The move to the middle" hypothesis. *Journal of Management Information Systems*, Fall, 10(2), 9-36.

Cook, K. S. and Emerson, R. M. (1978). Power, equity and commitment in exchange networks. *American Sociological Review*, October, 43, 721-739.

Day, J. D. and Wendler, J. C. (1988). The new economics of organization. *McKinsey Quarterly*, (1), 5-25.

Dell Computer. (2001). Available on the World Wide Web at: http://www.dell.com.

Downes, L. and Mui, C. (1998). *Unleashing the Killer App: Digital Strategies for Market Dominance*. Boston: Harvard Business School Press.

Drucker, P. F. (1995). *Concept of the Corporation* (1st ed.). New York: John Day. Reprinted in 1946. London: Transaction.

E*Trade. (2001). Available on the World Wide Web at: http://www.etrade.com.

Evo-economics–Biology meets the dismal science. (1993). *The Economist*, December, 91-93.

Faucheux, C. (1997). How virtual organizing is transforming management science. *Communications of the ACM*, September, 40(9), 50-55.

Frank, U. and Klein, S. (1992). Unternehmensmodelle als Basis und Bestandteil integrierter betrieblicher Informationssysteme. Arbeitspapiere der GMD, Nr. 629, St. Augustin.

Hagel, J. (1996). Spider versus spider. *McKinsey Quarterly*, (1), 4-18.

Hagel, J. and Armstrong, A. G. (1997). *Net Gain: Expanding Markets through Virtual Communities*. Boston: Harvard Business School Press.

Hagel, J. and Rayport, J. F. (1997). The new Infomediaries. *McKinsey Quarterly*, 4, 54-70.

Hakansson, H. (Ed.). (1987). *Industrial Technological Development*. London: Routledge.

Hedberg, B., Dahlgren, G., Hansson, J. and Olve, N. (1997). *Virtual Organization and Beyond–Discover Imaginary Systems*. Chichester et al.: Wiley.

Holland, C. P. (1995). Cooperative supply chain management: The impact of interorganizational systems. *Journal of Strategic Information Systems*, 4(2), 117-133.

Jeuland, A. P. and Shugan, S. M. (1996). Managing channel profits. *Marketing Science*, Summer, 2, 239-272. (Cited in Lusch R.F. and Brown J.R. (1996). Interdependency, contracting, and relational behavior. In *Marketing Channels. Journal of Marketing*, October, 60, 19-38.)

Lieberman, M. B. and Montgomery, D. B. (1988). First-mover advantages. *Strategic Management Journal*, 9, 41-58.

Lusch, R. F. and Brown, J. R. (1996). Interdependency, contracting, and relational behavior in marketing channels. *Journal of Marketing*, October, 60, 19-38.

Malone, T. W. and Laubacher, R. J. (1998). The dawn of the e-lance economy. *Harvard Business Review*, September-October, 145-152.

Malone, T. W., Yates, J. and Benjamin R. I. (1987). Electronic markets and electronic hierarchies: Effects of information technology on market structure and corporate strategies. *Communications of the ACM*, 30(6), 484-497.

McCarthy, E. J. and Perreault, W. D. (1996). *Basic Marketing–A Global Managerial Approach* (12th ed.). Chicago: Irwin.

Miles, R. E. and Snow, C. C. (1978). *Organizational Strategy, Structure and Process*. London: McGraw-Hill.

Moore, J. (1996). *The Death of Competition*. New York: Harper.

Österle, H. (1995). *Business Engineering–Prozess- und Systementwicklung*. Berlin, Germany: Springer.

Picot, A., Ripperger, T. and Wolff, B.(1996). The fading boundaries of the firm: The role of information and communication technology. *Journal of Institutional and Theoretical Economics*, 152(1), 65-79.

Rayport, J. F. and Sviokla, J. R. (1995). Exploiting the virtual value chain. *Harvard Business Review*, November-December, 21-36.

Resnick, P., Zeckhauser, R. and Avery, C. (1995). Roles for electronic brokers. In G. W. Brock (Ed.), *Toward a Competitive Telecommunications Industry: Selected Papers from the 1994 Telecommunications Policy Research Conference* (pp. 289-306). Mahwah, NJ: Lawrence Erlbaum.

Sarkar, M., Butler, B. and Steinfield, C. (1998). Cybermediaries in electronic marketspace: Towards theory building. *Journal of Business Research*, 41(3), 215-221.

Schewe, G. (1998). *Strategie und Struktur*. Tübingen: Mohr Siebeck.

Schwab.com. (2001). Available on the World Wide Web at: http://www.schwab.com.

Sieber, P. (1998). *Virtuelle Unternehmen in der IT-Branche*. Bern: Verlag Haupt.

Snow, C. C., Miles, R. E. and Coleman, H. J. (1992). Managing the 21st century network organization. *Organizational Dynamics*, Winter, 21(1), 5-20.

Stabell, C. B. and Fjeldstad, O. D. (1998). Configuring value for competitive advantage: On chains, shops, and networks. *Strategic Management Journal*, 19, 413-437.

Steinberg, S. G. (1996). Netheads vs. bellheads. *Wired*, October, 4(10).

Sterne, J. (1996). *Customer Service on the Internet–Building Relationships increasing Loyalty and Staying Competitive*. New York: John Wiley & Sons.

Tapscott, D., Ticoll, D. and Lowy, A. (2000). *Digital Capital–Harnessing the Power of Business Webs*. Boston: Harvard Business School Press.

The Virtual Corporation. (1993). *Business Week*, February, 1.

Travelocity.com. (2001). Available on the World Wide Web at: http://www.travelocity.com.

Venkatraman, N., and Henderson, J. C. (1996, October). *The Architecture of Virtual Organizing: Leveraging Three Independent Vectors*. Discussion paper, Boston University.

Chapter VIII

Web Organizations in the Professional Services Sector

Hugo Meijers
Contraview, The Netherlands

This chapter covers a specific type of Web organization in the professional service sector. Due to the knowledge-intensive, project-based and service-centric characteristics, it acts as a prime example of possible new organization models. A general overview of all system elements is based on theoretical and practical experience out of three cases. Theoretical systemic models, academic literature and personal involvement as business architect in Web formation form the basis of this chapter. Many challenges lie ahead in developing the described Web organization form. Its limitations are not yet clear. The first signs are hopeful; its application in other sectors may well turn out to be limited.

INTRODUCTION

The new millennium brings many opportunities as well as new challenges. In this hypercompetitive market, bottom and top lines are driven by new solutions, shortening cycles, reduction in time-to-market, speed of response, as well as customer and employee retention. In response, organizations are changing faster and becoming more customer-specific, service-focused, community-centric, knowledge-intensive, responsively adaptive and project-based. As answer to the market changes, many new business models have emerged, but few new ways of organizing have been tried out. Traditional organization design principles are still being applied, having been deeply rooted and anchored in our thinking about organizing. Nevertheless, some new and exiting organization models are emerging.

The foundation of business in the 21st century is talent, information and innovation. A move is ongoing from an economy of hands to one of heads (Hamel, 2000). This implies that companies, struggling for survival and sustainability, will

Figure 1: Key paradoxes

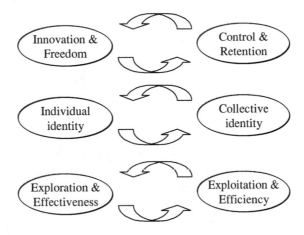

have to become more people- and knowledge-focused. Management will increasingly become a high-wire balancing act of handling paradoxes (see Figure 1). Giving talents the space to explore by embracing change and unpredictability and letting them thrive on instability and dynamics force companies to search for alternative organization forms. With 75% of Western business being classified as service-oriented; guidance, motivation and inspiration for new organization models can come from one direction: the professional services sector. It consists of strong peer-to-peer relationships, highly educated and professional knowledge workers and project-based work with a fair degree of creativity and (ad)venturing. The sector is an excellent breeding ground for Web concept building with many practical examples. This chapter zooms in on professional service webs (PSWs), which might well turn out to be the disruptive technology (Christensen, 1997) of traditional organization principles.

This chapter consists of two main sections. The first is descriptive and conceptual; the second contains three practical cases. The first section starts with the applied worldview and theoretical background of this chapter. Using the embedded system model in conjunction with a simple Web-classification model, five different types of PSW are presented. One type of PSWs, called the Web organization (WO), is described in more detail. The first section ends with some of the key issues and challenges for forming a WO, ending in a brief conclusion. The second section starts with the Web-positioning model used to distinguish the three cases, after which each case is described.

THE LOOKING GLASS

Applied Worldview

We appear to be caught in a dualistic worldview. Descartes' mind and matter are closely linked with brain and muscle power. Whether we uphold the existentialistic view of two separate things or a more symbiotic systemic view of an inseparable whole, mind and matter are elementary components of organizations. Knowledge and physical labor are key factors in organizations. A gradual shift from physical to knowledge work is taking place, as well as from atoms to bits. This does not rule out one of these factors or make one dominant over the other. This absolute worldview would be naïve. It does mean that the role of knowledge work is getting a more prominent place in organizations and that organizations are becoming more dependent on this factor. Bearing this in mind, are companies properly organized for knowledge work? Does organizing knowledge work not imply a different approach from organizing physical labor? Are different design principles not applicable or more appropriate? The answer is simple; different principles do apply.

Military and machine metaphors are dominant views in industrial age thinking. Machine thinking is mechanical, linear, analytical, controllable, stable and predictable. McMaster (1996) states: "In our mechanistic world people have been reduced to automatons that must have goals to function effectively". Traditionally organizations are designed according to this belief. Bak (1996) makes a case of humanity's preferential status from an evolutionary point of view. He states that our view of nature being in balance is not the only way. Nature is perpetually out of balance, but organized in a poised or critical state. In this state anything within boundaries can happen. A set of simple properties applies to complex aspects of our world. The Greeks have indoctrinated us in seeking truths in the stable, regular and consistent instead of the unstable, irregular and inconsistent. Truth is in both. PSWs should be viewed from both viewpoints.

Military thinking implies that business is war; a company has to capture the market, beat the competition, and make a killing. This leaves the impression that war is organized and predictable. However, both in war and in combat conditions are chaotic. In battle it comes down to managing chaos. This is done on professional instinct, sincerely upheld values and norms, and rule-based behavior. In battle, the power to improvise in combination with the will to survive is what gets people through life-threatening situations. There is nothing predictable in a battle zone; the situation is far too chaotic and complex. In this chapter the military is also viewed as nimble, flexible, purposeful and cohesive micro-organizations working in a highly resourceful, innovative and improvising manner. As remarked by Marcel Proust the real voyage of discovery consists not in seeking new lands but seeing with new eyes. Understanding the way PSWs work implies seeing through different eyes. Many aspects of PSWs are traditional; in fact, most are. Subtle differences make them unique and unorthodox.

Theoretical Foundation

Web organization theory as applied in this chapter has its roots in interorganizational network theory. Trist (1983) was one of the first to highlight the key features of interorganizational networks. He emphasized a network where members are loosely coupled, control is a mutual responsibility and all members are equal. These features are to some extent applicable to specific types of PSWs. However not all types of PSWs have as primary function to enhance collaboration. For most PSWs this is a means to a more commercial or innovation-oriented end. The same is true for the degree of coupling. Some PSWs are loosely coupled (e.g., individuals in self-employment using a collaboration platform), where others are tightly coupled (e.g., under one legal entity, usually a holding). Some PSWs have central coordination and control; others do not. This will be explained in more detail further on.

System thinking can help in understanding organizations (Ackoff, 1999). A system is defined as a bounded whole consisting of definable parts and the interrelationships between those parts. A system is a whole that cannot be divided into independent parts without the loss of the properties or functions it possesses as a whole. If it is disassembled it becomes something else. Organizations do not possess the property of the whole being represented in each of its parts. For this reason each layer in the ESM must be placed into a context when it is described. Each layer can be viewed as a system in a larger context (synthesis), viewed autonomously, or decomposed into elements (analysis). In order to gain a better understanding of the different types of PSWs, an Embedded system model (ESM) with six layers is used, as shown in Figure 2. Embedded means either to be relationally associated with or forming part of another system layer. The model is a hierarchical construction from the perspective of a professional. The professional can be perceived as an autonomous system–usually referred to as a free agent, elancer, self-employed or virtual agent–or can belong to a cell. A cell can be autonomous or be part of an entity consisting of a group of cells. Multiple entities make up a Web system, which will usually have a separate (legal) status. In this respect, Web structures do not differ from traditional organizations. A Web is a collection of professionals and can consist of two or more layers. Layers are identities binding

Figure 2: Embedded system model

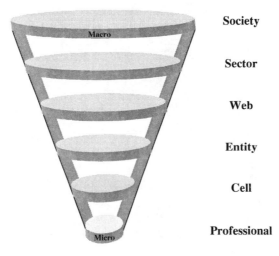

professionals, either structurally or opportunistically. The boundaries in the layers are two-way filters of information. They are there to enhance self-organization by filtering information in order to prevent disruption and dysfunction. No boundary leads to chaos; strong boundaries to rigidity and tenacious inertia. A system layer as such does not interact. People have relationships and interact with people, not with cells, entities or Webs. Peer-to-peer relationships drive Web formation and form the lifeblood of a Web. People can act on behalf of a layer, fulfilling an accepted or assigned role.

Instead of using a standard model to describe organizations–consisting of stakeholders, products, processes and resources–a systemic model is used as shown in Figure 3. The purpose of the system includes its environmental image or function and its identity for agents within the system. Structure includes infrastructure or technology, as well as formal and informal patterns within the system. Rules include procedures and policies, both enabling and constraining. Behaviors include governance, decision making, roles, relationships and processes. This model is used to explain the functioning of Web organizations. Important to bear in mind is the fact that virtual organizations are not a universal alternative for traditional organizations with hierarchical coordination mechanisms (Chesborough & Teece, 1996). Many advocates of the new economy have raised theories in favor of market mechanisms, governance and coordination (Miles & Snow, 1993). In this chapter, PSWs are viewed from a different coordination mechanism, one of initiative and competence.

Complexity science shows that when agents interact and affect one another new things will emerge. What emerges cannot be predicted; it can be small or large (Holland, 1998). Behavior of agents in a system is governed by simple rules. Richer patterns will emerge when diversity of agents increases. When the level of interaction is too low, the result will be inertia; when too high, it results in chaos. Filtering of relevance based on affinity instead of managerial preference brings order into

Figure 3: System decomposition model

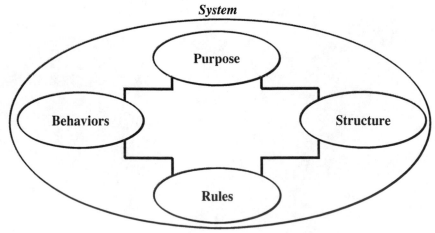

chaos. Economist Adam Smith suggested centuries ago that if individuals were left free to pursue their own selfish interest, patterns of economic activity would emerge. Complex systems grow without central coordination, but with rule-based purpose. Key is finding the simple rules, which result in large and complex configurations.

PSW TYPES

PSWs are social networks of interacting professionals. They are modular organizations; i.e., a Web decomposes into relatively small, autonomous, temporary units without hierarchical coordination mechanisms as basis (Wigand et al., 1997). Central in PSWs are relationships and the exchange of information through interaction. Depending on the context, interaction may vary in intensity, frequency, duration, range and multiplicity.

Different types of PSWs are emerging. To position and understand the variation in PSWs, the model containing a PSW typology is used (see Figure 4). In this model the depth of the Web hierarchy, the degree of coupling, the degree of heterogeneity of the system layers and the purpose of collaboration are left as variables. The vertical axis contains the accessibility on a scale from fully open (no entry barriers or preconditions) to completely closed (controlled access). The horizontal axis contains the approach to service providence (net-broker or not). Collaboration platforms usually consist of single autonomous (self-employed) agents, for example, the numerous community groups. The provision of access to the platform itself is not seen as a brokered service. Professional exchanges offer a platform on which services are brokered. These predominantly individual-oriented models pave the way towards intra-organizational adoption of open collaborative exchanges on corporate intranets. Closed models are mostly found in Webs where large and small companies have agreed to form alliances or partnerships with formalized mutual expectations. They are often non-brokered although one partner in the Web might

Figure 4: PSW types

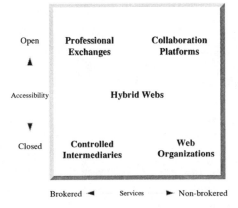

exploit the collaboration platform. A brokered example is the franchising construction of Cap Gemini Ernst & Young Management Associates. They link independent interim managers with the net-broker in exchange of access to knowledge, standards and norms. CGEY acts as broker for contract transactions.

This chapter focuses on Web organizations–also referred to as network organizations, Web firms, business ecosystems or economic Webs–with multiple legal entities. As closed and non-brokered models, they represent a unique group of Webs that are changing the rules of corporate gaming. Specific focus is on Web organizations that are organic, nonlinear, synthetic and unpredictable systems. The key principles upheld are: markets cannot be shaped or made, talents cannot be caged or tamed, customers cannot be retained or locked-in and companies cannot be sustained indefinitely. Instead of focusing on shareholder value, the focus is on optimizing customer and employee satisfaction. These Webs act like a franchising umbrella to evoke a higher-level purpose that enables professionals to conceive of and do things they cannot conceive of or do independently. These Webs are multi-purposeful, allowing simple and effective clustering of individuals. If no sense is seen in an initiative, no clustering takes place. In these Webs social structure is more important than technical. Critical is the free and uncontrolled flow of information as lifeblood between the entities. Web organizations are very similar to adhocracies. Toffler (1970) first introduced this term for organic ad hoc formation of projects and workgroups. Adhocracies are temporary structures to solve specific problems. They are highly result-oriented and were originally viewed as a way to create unique solutions for client-specific problems. People in such a throwaway organization do not have a fixed function or place. At the end of a project a new role must be found. Often people are involved in multiple projects.

ISSUES AND CHALLENGES IN WEB ORGANIZATIONS

Purpose

Traditional organizations consolidate purpose in strategic intents and mission statements. All activities and decisions are related with these and are centrally controlled and exercised by the power hierarchy. In Web organizations, this is generally not the case. Purpose can vary greatly between individual professionals and the Web as a whole. The diversity in purpose is what creates inspiration, attraction and flexibility. It allows for anyone or any group to connect to the Web on his or her own terms. The degree of coupling also plays an important role. Tighter coupling normally implies aligning largely with the purpose of the Web. If purpose is lost or not explicit enough, Web formation and connection will quickly destabilize. The reason for this is the looser or more informal basis on which Web is formed. Purpose gives coherence to a Web in the same manner as it does to traditional organizations.

To better understand the variety of purpose found in Web organizations the SCCI model, as shown in Figure 5, is used. The model consists of four categories of connection criteria. Infrastructure usually implies sharing facilities and technology. The main drivers are cost reduction, risk sharing and development speed. Customer-related criteria for Web formation are easier acquisition by lead and relationship sharing, geographic spread, new market development and improvement of competitive positioning. Service criteria have to do with full service or solution delivery and cost sharing in service development. The category competence implies joint development of methods and models, talent development through cross-pollination, and broader career perspectives, which should lead to employee retention.

Purpose gives meaning to a system. Rules and behavior give identity. Perhaps even more important than purpose is identity. Besides the four business reasons in the SCCI model, most Web organizations are formed due to social capital and the will to collaborate. Key in Web formation is believing that coalescence creates more value than remaining autonomous. The relative uniqueness, freedom and flexibility create a form of solidarity, of being different. The desire of wanting to work in a control- and supervision-free environment where entrepreneurship is expected is a potent incentive attracting high potentials. How long this attraction will last depends partly on the rate of adoption of this form of organization.

Structure

The new economy is often associated with organizing without hierarchy. Hierarchy is taken to be synonymous with power. New theories about shifting from power-over to power-to principles still assume the existence of power structures. Web organizations may have flatter power hierarchies but primarily

Figure 5: SCCI model

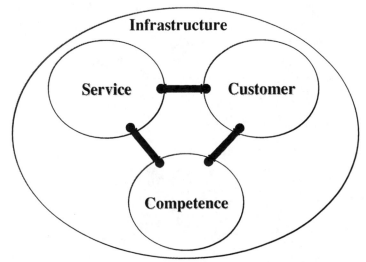

differentiate from traditional organizations in their rules and behavior. The reason is a need for minimal level of order in the entrepreneurial chaos. There are also market and regulatory reasons for formalizing structure. However there are multiple forms of hierarchy. One such form is a hierarchy of competency (meaning knowledge, skills and practical experience). Structure should not be fixed but context-specific. Competency is not absolute but relative to the initiative taken. Desired result dictates the type of competency required. Each initiative requires a different structure to achieve optimal results. One of the main challenges in Web organizations is not to take control of the initiatives, especially when business is taking a downturn.

Design of organizations up to now has been predetermined. According to Drucker (1994), structure does not grow by intuition but needs careful design and systemic approach. This certainly applies to the formal structure of Web organizations. However, organic development and evolutionary design give rise to natural or informal structure that continuously changes. The natural structure is more dominant in Web organizations. In Table 1, the main differences in design principles are highlighted. The emerging design principles apply to the way clusters are formed within a formal structure.

When interaction complexity becomes too large, human networks or social systems tend to break down naturally in small-world networks (Kauffman, 1995). Loose-ordered structures emerge as seen in user groups and community spaces. These structures are transient with ordering principles based on affinity and relevance. Project teams are by nature transient with skills phasing in and out. The clear separation between operational line and transient projects is fading. Maintaining a clear matrix view across organizational boundaries is no longer possible. Organization boundaries are determined by projects. Structure follows opportunity and initiative. The result is multiform and dissipative structures of collaboration. The structure has autopoietic properties like self-bounded, self-perpetuating and self-generating.

It is a general misperception that secondary functions like ICT, HR and finance are cost centers. Primary, secondary and tertiary process thinking are misguiding and clouding other possible designs. A business is an integral system of highly interconnected functions. All functions are important for the purpose and behavior of the system. From a systemic point of view, these functions can easily be set up as profit centers providing value for the Web. A precondition is that Web participants

Table 1: Organization design principles

Traditional Design Principles	Evolutionary Design Principles
Predictability	Possibility
Standardization	Differentiation
Specialization	Generalization
Static	Dynamic
Inequality	Equality
Retrospective	Prospective

and network partners are viewed as customers and pay a fee for the fixed costs and a commercial price for variable costs. Many examples exist of commercial exploitation of these functions normally regarded as overhead. In this light, diminishing transaction costs based on classic Coasian economics are less relevant than transaction revenue and increasing returns. On engagements involving the hiring of competence from a Web partner, it is normal for the contract holder to take a percentage of the earnings. This automatically leads to direct sales being more lucrative than indirect, same as in other sectors. It also leads to diminishing collaboration and undesired interdependency, which is dysfunctional to Web formation. Some Webs have therefore evolved beyond the mutual exploitation of partners and share relations openly.

The size of the Web as a whole as well as of the individual nodes will have an impact on the behavior of the Web. The larger nodes in some cases try to get a larger say in the shared interests of the Web. In this sense the Web acts like the European Union, where the larger participating countries have more votes. Another aspect of imbalance in the Web is the diversity in interdependency. If smaller nodes disproportionately depend on the larger, this might lead to power abuse. Dominance behavior is normally addressed in the rules and should be regarded as (mis)behavior that needs continuous attention. When the growth gradient is steep, maintaining the integrity of the social structure is one of the main challenges. This is certainly the case when growth is through alliances. The level of maturity in the joining organization, the gap between social structures, the level of interdependency and the willingness to collaborate will predominantly determine the success of coupling to the Web. Compatibility of culture and behavior is critical for maintaining balance. Successful Web growth is easier through autonomous growth from within the Web to assure the right mind-set.

Web organizations strive to make boundaries between the nodes nonexistent. Free movement of talents, initiatives and knowledge is a crucial factor for maintaining the integrity of the Web. To some extent this also applies to the boundaries between the Web and the environment. This is kept fuzzy to allow maximum collaboration with customers and partners outside the Web. An issue is always the level of fuzziness of the boundary. Boundary-less organizations do not exist. Walls exist, whether permeable or semipermeable. They act as filters and insulators on information, both creating comfort and discomfort. They are crucial for coherence.

The core of a Web organization is its technical infrastructure or common platform. Entry barriers to join such a platform, albeit temporary, need to be low. The longer a company is attached to such a platform, the more it shares information and the more dependent it will become on the platform. Often vital information is exchanged on products and markets, locking potential partners in. Exit barriers are raised and form a serious adoption issue for such a concept. Intellectual property rights need to be addressed at the start to prevent dissonance later on. To enable an individual-based, open and transparent playing field, a social infrastructure to facilitate this playing is needed. Critical in the success of such a playing field is homogeneity in interests and behavior and heterogeneity in thinking. This can only be reached with a common frame of reference, a mutually shared language to guide initiatives. McMaster (1996) emphasizes the importance of a common frame of reference for effective collaboration. Collaboration platforms on the Internet are creating such frames technically but not semantically.

Rules

Complex behavior is based on simple rules. One of the most complex behaviors in organizations is the interaction between people. This type of flocking, as described by Kelly (1994), follows simple rules. People flock when there is something new, when others jump on it (herd mentality) and when there is something to be gained. Resnick (1997) observes that people have a strong centralized way of thinking. Someone or something must be creating and orchestrating patterns. However, self-organizing systems do not need centralized authority to manage. Through interaction, bucket brigades emerge without intervention or preplanned models (Eisenstein, 1997). Exploration is usually not something done solo. Team formation is therefore crucial. Interdependency between the right individuals is based on complementary competency and interests. This natural process must be facilitated by the rules in the Web.

When playing a game, rules are inevitable. However, rules are directly and inversely related to trust. Bureaucratic organizations are heavily rule-based and low on trust; they are overregulated, leaving little to chance or choice. Web organizations apply simple rules and rely heavily on trust. A list of 10 of the main playing rules as found in Web organizations is listed in Table 2. These rules should be enabling and facilitating the purpose of the Web as a whole. An issue with rules is compliance. Normally this is a managerial task. In Webs, compliance is based on social control. Escalation and arbitration are handled democratically.

People cannot act on things they do not know. Participation comes with transparency, equality and respect. Traditional organizations are weak on all three points. Closed-door meetings, limited accessibility to information and inequality are inherent properties of present management styles and organization theories. On the other hand total transparency can cause dysfunctional behavior due to unrest and information overload. The challenge is finding the optimum which is context-specific. Possibly the most important activity in a Web is ensuring the rules are upheld.

Table 2: Web organization rules

Interact unselfishly
Take initiative and explore
Give unconditional support
Seek advice from those experienced
Learn from mistakes
Respect ideas and relationships
Act in multiple roles
Treat everyone as peers
Be open, honest and transparent
Add tangible value

Fayol (1950) viewed management as a process of visioning, organizing, ordering, coordinating and controlling. This implies that management and leadership are the same, which they are not. Leadership is giving direction, meaning and purpose to a unit. Leadership is focused on change and the future; management on controlling and the present. For Webs to function properly, (initiative) leadership is essential. Managerial behavior is functional when accepted by the team and will depend on the context. Pre-appointing managers will in most cases be dysfunctional, depending on their individual behavior.

Self-management, as described by Emery & Trist (1960), and self-organization are often incorrectly viewed as being synonymous. Self-management implies empowerment of a team by someone with authority and can only apply to power hierarchies. Self-organization comes from autonomous interacting agents within a system. Both autonomy and interaction are essential for self-organization to occur. Web organizations rely more on self-organization than self-management. Teaming is based on volunteering and not assigning. One of the greatest challenges is to create the conditions for employees to feel and act as self-employed.

Behavior

People interact when there is mutual benefit. Traditionally benefit needs to be instantaneous and transparent or interaction will most likely not take place. This is certainly the case in stressful environments within companies that have an operational and short-term focus. The temporal constraint results in enormous dampening of interactions. Faith, trust and patience are new virtues needed to overcome temporal constraints. Web participants need to be unselfish and selfishly committed at the same time. This paradox is hard to uphold especially when trust has been abused. Understanding that trust will be abused (willingly and unwillingly) is critical in maintaining an open information flow. Interaction, certainly when interdependency is low, is not naturally stimulated. It is more efficient not to interact, because an individual will have to invest, than to have faith that someday the favor will be returned. Individuals with a short-term focus or skeptic nature will have great difficulty in coping with this.

Interaction is dependent on context. The extent of dependency is called situatedness (Lissack & Roos, 1999). Situation drives how rules come together. The right setting is a necessary condition for interaction to take place. This is why Web organizations spent tremendous effort in facilitating settings where professionals can interact. Furthermore, interaction has much to do with response. Response has two main properties, speed and dependency. Dependency implies that response will depend on the request or requestor. With e-mail systems causing information and communication overloads, dependency might cause inequality. Principles of locality (who knows who) and fanout (with how many is interaction taking place) are very important issues. Extra attention to these issues is given in Web organizations.

Personality is closely linked with individuality. Individuality is the amount of distinction a person has in terms of skills, knowledge, thinking, talent and behavior. Individuality is the driving force of innovation and serendipity. If the personality of an individual coincides with that of the Web, the individuality decreases to nil. Homogeneity, something that organizations strive for in their socialization processes to build an identity and corporate culture, depletes and crushes personality. An individual cannot develop himself in two opposite directions. Professionals have a lively desire to think and act for themselves and cannot be inclined to think and act as others in the Web (Durkheim, 1947). Standard management practices to enforce solidarity and ensure collective harmony is maintained, along with conformism to corporate policy and guidelines, are dysfunctional to Web behavior. It is a complex balancing act to enforce conformity and leave enough room for personality.

Not everyone can handle the level of freedom described. Taking initiative and showing leadership are unique skills few possess. This is not to say that more introvert and following types of individuals have no place in a Web organization. Some form of reconditioning will have to take place to anchor new patterns of behavior based on the rules in Table 2. All Web participants must be able to handle the level of freedom and uncertainty. Figure 6 shows an example of typical roles in a team. Managers will need to change from span of control to span of support thinking. Professionals will each have to develop a span of collaboration as well as a span of sounding. The latter implies the conscious act to consult experienced colleagues.

Professionals can handle multiple roles in teams or act in multiple teams. One of the core skills critical for quick and effective team formation is the ability to bond fast with new people, to settle in quickly and to easily let go of ties with previous teams. Adaptation and association are key attributes. The risk is that people forming such teams protect themselves by only bonding superficially, undermining the team's efficiency to some extent. Often teams do not work. Some reasons why teams do not work are mismatched needs, unresolved roles, personality conflicts, and insufficient communication (Robbins & Finley, 2000). Ego-driven team mem-

Figure 6: Typical spans and roles in team formation

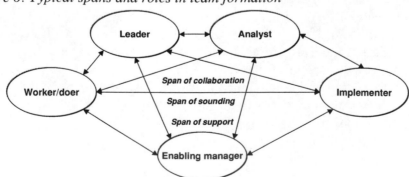

bers must learn to collaborate and appreciate the interdependency of activities. They must accept that the end result is the objective, and that can only be reached by a coordinated, synergetic effort. When organizations depend more on teams, the effort for right team formation must increase.

According to Mintzberg (1973) there are three categories of activities that managers do, namely, interpersonal, informational and decisional. The interpersonal activities are the coordinative, symbolic and representative roles of a manager. These activities encompass the promotion of the unit and the coordination of work by ensuring that interunit relationships are maintained or formed. Informational activities are concerned with the capture, exchange and transfer of information. Decision-making activities are the de-allocation, allocation or reallocation of resources. These activities will change significantly in Web organizations. Decision making is a democratic, collective activity or an individual activity based on self-determination. Informational activities are reduced to a minimum through openness and transparency facilitated by a common technical infrastructure. Interpersonal activity is common to all participants. Management as a traditional autonomous function will fade.

Central in Web organizations is competency. This needs to be made transparent if a Web organization is to function properly. Traditionally the registration is a task for the HR department. Some Webs have evolved beyond this to a self-service model, where individuals market themselves by maintaining their own profiles. Profiles are captured in a structured and centrally accessible form. Matching can be automated using, for example, a (reverse) auction. The level of freedom depends on the empowerment within the Web and can vary per participating node. Important is two-way matching (what is offered versus what is desired by the professional) to ensure that suitable candidates are finally selected. Work environments can be used to execute projects when geographic displacement of the team is large, as will be the case for most multinational corporations. Peer-to-peer appraisal systems are often incorporated.

CONCLUSION

Successful Web organizations focus on the individual. They understand better than traditional organizations that profitability is driven by imagination, creativity and motivation of professionals. Management is creating conditions and context for individuals to explore and experiment. The entrepreneurial spirit can only survive in relative freedom. Unhindered flow of people, money and knowledge to those initiatives where they can add most value is the governing allocation rule. Individuals can perform multiple roles at the same time and should not be forced into a single function. Pluralism will increasingly become a competitive force. The same holds for embracing the complexity of dissipative structures and changing relationships. Whether such structures can survive the complexity of fast-changing environments, cultural differences and general human nature will have to be seen. Many challenges lie ahead in developing the Web organization; its limitations are not yet clear. The first examples are hopeful and inspiring.

CASE STUDIES

The following case studies are discussed:
- A Web structure grown partially autonomously: The Vision Web
- A Web structure transforming from a traditional hierarchy: IBAS group
- A Web structure that imploded and is restructuring: Your Knowledge Network.

To assist in understanding differences in Web structures, a Web-positioning model consisting of five key dimensions is used, as shown in Figure 7. The first dimension is about relative size in revenue of the nodes in the Web, ranging from completely balanced to completely imbalanced. The second dimension is about the way the Web is grown, autonomously or through mergers and acquisition. The third dimension is related to the duration for which the Web or parts of it are set up, ranging from permanent to temporary. The fourth dimension is about single or joint ownership of the Web. The fifth dimension is about the type of products produced by the Web. In this case software products are regarded as tangible, or physical, products.

The applied scale is divided into ranges from 0-100% in 25% increments. A whole axis, e.g., from knowledge to physical products, adds up to 100%. If 75% of the products are knowledge-based, then 25% are physical. Scaling is relative to the Web as a whole.

Figure 7: Web positioning model

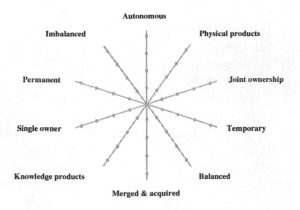

Case 1: The Vision Web

Overview

The Vision Web (see Figure 8) started in early 1996 when the three founders and Web makers set up a unique and daring new organization concept. Central in their concept is flexibility in the customers' best interest. Their unique formula is to focus on individual ambitions and talents instead of traditional corporate structures. The Web has grown to over 500 professional participants in eight separate legal entities. It has an annual profit and turnover increase approaching 50%. The Web has extended geographically to Belgium, Germany Australia and Singapore. The venturing in Spain met heavy resistance to the Web philosophy and the operation was stopped for the time being.

All entities fall under the network and holding company The Vision Web. The common service denominator or portfolio centers on e-business extended enterprises. This ranges from strategic advice to system management and maintenance. The business model centers on a full-service concept in this area. Complimentarily, competence and market experience are what drives the growth and expansion pattern of this Web. The Vision Web does not see itself as a network structure but as the operator of a formula based on continuous change, knowledge infrastructure, virtual communities and participation. Besides the formal structure of the Web the core of the dynamics is centered on business initiatives or projects (BPs as they are called). At present some 60 projects are ongoing. About 20% of the BPs fail.

Web Aspects

Central in the culture is the DNA of The Vision Web. Short and direct lines of communication, an entrepreneurial degree of autonomy and self-determination, free flow of knowledge and the cultivation of intrinsic motivation form the core of this DNA. The dynamics this generates make the network supercritical, thriving on creativity and new business initiatives. Individual drive, ambitions and talents get free

Figure 8: Positioning model of The Vision Web

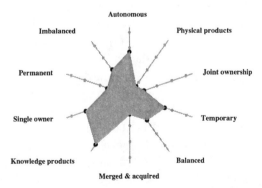

space to blossom within a set of logical and rational rules. Senior Web members and the Web makers (founding partners) are continuously enforcing the DNA. The Web's binding force, besides the DNA, is its mission "enabling e-business". All initiatives fall under this operating banner. As a new economy Web structure it wants to find the structural and cultural synergy between Web and customers. What better way to promote the new economy than to personify it?

People join the Web with their own ideas and drive to create their own little enterprise. In this respect the Web is one enormous incubator, energized to the critical state, where creativity and knowledge flow in abundance. Anchoring the dynamics of spontaneous initiatives is one of the main challenges of the Web. The anchoring takes place in the form of business projects. BPs are predominantly focused on market offerings. Speed and timing are therefore critical, resulting in quick formation of teams and sounding boards. Setting up a BP is like playing a game. It is chaos without rules and compliance. BPs in the start-up phase should not press heavily on the overall Web performance and a sounding board is compulsory. Mutual agreement is needed by the Web makers or colleagues in the legal entity to pursue the initiative. Anyone can start such a project; for this, no formal decision is needed. A business project functions like an autonomous cell. It pursues its own objectives and develops the appropriate services and competencies. Each business project has its own profit and loss. Performance is published openly on a monthly basis. Team members of a BP get part of the profit; how much is up to the team. To get cooperation, support and funding by the Web, team members must apply a logical rational in the division of profit between the Web, the legal entity and the project members.

Proactive initiative is facilitated so participants can explore their talents and potential. The Web provides the conditions for this. It is up to individuals to siege opportunity and take initiative and to start up new projects to which others with the same interest and goals can flock. Within initiatives people divide the roles as they deem fit. No top-down directives or direction are given for this; everyone is an entrepreneur to some degree. Nothing is regarded as permanent, only pertinent to individual development and market needs. Once these have been satisfied business initiatives will naturally die off and new initiatives are undertaken.

Structure is secondary to talent. Squeezing people into predetermined boxes creates passive individuals that wonder what to do and to whom to report. By putting talent and ambitions first they have created a highly dynamic and innovative environment. Of course not everyone can function optimally in such an environment. These individuals either leave the Web for a more stable and traditional organization or are led naturally by those that do take initiative. This natural selection process puts people to the test, especially those that think they can handle the freedom and believe they want to be an entrepreneur. Not everyone has a realistic self-image. Nevertheless the Web has found that surprisingly many do fit the proper profile. Web participants are responsible for their own carrier development. Every Web participant has an own home page where skills, competencies and other things can be displayed. Coaches and counsels are chosen by the individuals themselves.

Free flow of knowledge and initiative is based on the philosophy of give and get instead of give and take. What goes around comes around, giving without expectation. They have discovered that it does work when many apply this rule unconditionally. As social beings we do want to belong and participate and be respected for the added value. Although the Web relies on the common virtual Web-based infrastructure, the core of the interaction within the Web is still people meeting people directly. This can be through telephone contact or face-to-face meetings in their grand cafés (a perfect ambiance to have open discussions).

The common Web infrastructure is the throbbing heart of the knowledge flow. This infrastructure was built by assigning small projects to experts that had some free time available. In this way optimal productivity and utilization was maintained. All information is transparent and fully accessible by everyone. Without this infrastructure there would be little synergy between the Web companies. Everyone understands that all should fill the knowledge base to enrich the free exchange of knowledge. In practice some contribute and some do not.

Treat every stakeholder the same, whether this is a partner, supplier, customer or direct colleague. After all, everyone fills these roles at any specific moment in time depending on the context. This is the reason for a role instead of a function focus. Individuals perform multiple roles throughout the day and should not be caught in the prison of a single function because this is perceived to be more efficient. No fixed functions exist. Roles are dependent on individual drive and talent and other members in the BP team.

Each Web participant is responsible for Web growth. No dedicated HR functionary exists. Personal networks and relationships are used for Web growth. They don't advertise or squander money on expensive headhunters. Potential candidates have a prior affiliation with members of the Web. During the selection process the emphasis is put on commercial drive and fit with the Web philosophy. Personal networks also form the basis for continuity and business. Customer focus teams are set up to obtain detailed understanding of a customer. These teams ensure that the Web or its partners optimally service customers.

One of the issues facing The Vision Web is the evolution of the behavior of the Web. Already the Web is not the same as it was three years ago. Allowing self-organization to take place means letting go of the master design approach. Where units and projects evolve and wither away, there can be no control; the result is unpredictable. This also applies to behavioral changes.

Core Values

The Web DNA is the binding force of all initiatives and participants in these initiatives, both internal and external to the Web. Mutual respect, trust, equality, responsibility, natural entrepreneurship, talent over structure and synergy are the core components of this DNA: the Web formula. Talent and enthusiasm drive every new business initiative. Without these initiatives the Web will not blossom. Natural curiosity, self-consciousness, open-mindedness and mutual interest create synergy in pursuing and exploring these initiatives. Performance and attitude are key factors in the application of the DNA. Individual motivation and affinity are key in the ownership and responsibility taken by the Web participants.

Key Lessons
- Creating an open and free environment does allow individuals to blossom.
- Hierarchies are not needed to control people; playing rules suffice.
- Free flow of information, transparency and equality creates an enormous, dynamical and exciting Web.
- Not every individual has the right profile for a Web culture. Country cultures in parts of Europe have proven not to be ready for this radical approach.
- Initiative-based leadership is crucial for this concept to work; traditional management has no role.

Case 2: IBAS Group

Overview

IBAS (consultancy, interim management and business solutions; see Figure 9) was a privately owned cluster of companies operating in the ICT sector. Unsatisfied with the traditional paradigms, a quest for new identity and form was undertaken. The interior and exterior needed refurbishing. A transformation from traditional organization to Web structure is still ongoing.

The core Web size is approximately 170 people with multiple relationships with free agents and other companies. The mission of the IBAS Web is continuity. The purpose of the Web is to exploit the synergy between competencies. Its unique selling point is client intimacy. This is an extension of the core competence of the Web, namely, the knowledge of how to sustain valuable relationships and make them profitable. To embrace the new economy they felt they had to understand the implications and perceptions of their clients. By doing so they decided on becoming a network organization based on sharing

Figure 9: Positioning model of IBAS group

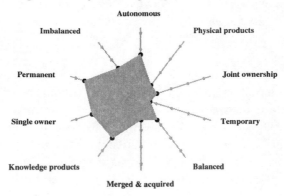

knowledge, people and money. As part of the Web they became an incubator for dot-coms. The Web is in healthy shape with profit and revenue growth between 30-40% annually over the last years.

Web Aspects

Originally IBAS was a hierarchical organization. They underwent a transformation from being a single company and legal entity to a Web with multiple legal entities (called nodes) and interorganizational relationships. The drive to do this was the understanding that the market could not be controlled or made. The changes in the market force companies to adopt more flexible structures to respond. Further reasons for this transformation were transparency, freedom, fun and openness. The desire to better fit with the culture also played a role, as well as having more attention for new economy features and the desire to be different.

Critical for the binding force within the Web is a common identity. The first attempt at transforming to a Web failed, which nearly resulted in the downfall of IBAS. The main reason was lack of direction and understanding what it is to function like a Web. This created such a negative tension within the Web that it became catatonic. Too much freedom, insufficient (infrastructure) conditions and the missing link with the client within the Web structure forced an inward focus. In the brief managerial vacuum, new hierarchies evolved at lower levels in the Web. An intensive reevaluation process was needed to ensure the integrity of the Web could be maintained. The problem facing the Web was slow but certain drifting away of the nodes, creating autonomous islands. The whole concept of the Web and its strengths was in jeopardy. Transition skeptics were separated from transition ambassadors; most of the skeptics left eventually. The key lesson learned in this first failing attempt is that people need guidance and leadership, especially in a more open and flexible environment. The second lesson is the one of identity. When identity becomes vague, people get lost in the wilderness. As social creatures we need to belong to something tangible; this is crucial for continuity.

A second and more gradual evolutionary attempt is still ongoing. The transition is not pre-designed and no elaborate plans are made. A natural and gradual evolutionary change approach through continuous monitoring and experimenting followed. The final design is reflected in Figure 10. Conditions and identity issues have been addressed and have brought fruitful results. Management roles have been changed from directive, control and staff exploitation to support, stimulation, networking, interacting, initiation of innovative projects and the building of relationships. Central in the transformation is an open communication about the change, the choice given to all employees to speak their mind and strong customer relationships. When employees were faced with the transformation question everyone bought into the new concept of the Web structure. With the removal of top-down autocratic decision-making processes, a new managerial concept had to be implemented. New roles and a working model based on more consensus and a collaboration base were forced on management.

Figure 10: Final design of the IBAS Web

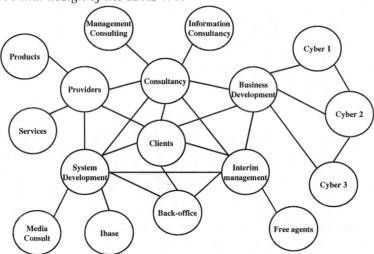

The Web consists of seven major nodes: client, consultancy, interim management, business solutions, back office, business alliances and business development. Unique is the node client which is central in the Web. The founder acts as ambassador and spokesperson for the client and the market. This node ensures Web transparency to the environment. Web boundaries are thus reduced to a minimum. The concept behind this Web structure is free flow of people, money and knowledge. Each node has its own profit and loss. Even the node back office is not considered a cost center but is exploited as a profitable business. This is partly achieved by providing services outside the Web. The traditional perception of back office activities being inferior or tertiary to other business processes was discarded. The node business development acts as an incubator for dot-com initiatives and gives room to the creation and development of new opportunities. Initiatives are commercially exploited and the knowledge is made available to the whole Web. The node business alliances focuses on vendor management and co-makership. Its objective is to enhance and optimize relationships between the Web and alliances. Strong and effective alliances on the buy-side of the Web are better equipped to add value to the client as a central node in the network organization. The seven node managers run the Web jointly.

The main focus during the transformation is on making the new model work. For this 25% of net profit was invested in the first year. All personnel have been formally brought into one of the legal entities. The other Web nodes don't have any personnel on the payroll. In this way transparent and barrier-free flow of people from team role A to B can be facilitated without elaborate control and (re)charging mechanisms.

Core Values

Firing is not a possibility being considered. One of management key competencies is helping people to fit in or relocate, either within or outside the Web. Role fitting individuals' strength and affinity within the Web is the first option. IBAS upholds that change is desirable for high moral, continuous involvement and participation. Principles of self-organization and self-initiative play an important part in keeping the Web energized.

To unleash creative energy the following values are strongly upheld: openness, honesty, mutual respect and trust. Although these sound generic, IBAS has managed to create a unique, open culture based on these values. This culture facilitates the free flow badly needed for prosperity, creativity and innovation. Free flow of knowledge is one of the critical factors in the Web. For this reason knowledge management has been anchored in the management level of the Web. The IBAS Web realizes that the purpose of their Web is to create and share knowledge.

Key Lessons
- Embrace the client; make them part of the structure.
- Evolve slowly from traditional to Web structure, ensuring the right infrastructure, financial risk management, (independent) leadership and identity conditions.
- Keep enforcing the core values; they demand continuous reinforcement by example.
- Emotional and rational commitment of management is critical for success.
- Web organizations act as magnets attracting talent.
- Web organizations allow entering into strategic alliances that would traditionally not be formed.
- Web organizations heighten the sense of freedom through initiative space and condition management.

Case 3: Your Knowledge Network (YKN)

Overview
YKN (see Figure 11) started in early 1999 to create a Web structure of independent but highly collaborating consulting units. The structure was to be built primarily through autonomous growth. Two incubator legal entities–one focusing on consultancy and the other on software engineering–were set up within which multiple independent cells started. In six months, these two entities contained more than 100 employees. On top of this, multiple existing companies wanted to join the Web in various forms and intensity. The expansion put an enormous strain on the relationships and infrastructure. The explosive and uncontrolled growth resulted in chaos. Insufficient detail of the concept, incoherent values and uncertain coordination mechanisms created a loose structure with no footholds. To get some sense of security, people fell back on traditional values and patterns. The Web partially imploded and started to disintegrate, many relationships with existing companies were broken, and the two incubators fell apart. After a period of reconciliation, regrouping and realignment, the Web is making a second start.

Web Aspects

The reason for forming YKN was to build something new and different, an environment based on development of individual talents. It was to be a platform where talents could freely connect with kindred spirits to coalesce, explore, experiment and innovate. YKN strongly believed that, by sharing things opportunistically and by taking initiative, new markets, products and competencies are developed. There is also a strong belief in the logic and fun of Web organizations.

The Web positioned itself as a network of diverse cultures and competencies. Within the Web multiple layers of autonomous systems were formed from individual legal entities to cells within these entities and independently operating professionals. It was designed as a complex hybrid organization structure with multiple coordination points between independent entities and cells with market, service and competency orientations. The diversity was a direct resultant of the multiple small cells being formed, which lacked critical mass to be self-supporting and self-sustaining. Some 15 cells were simultaneously set up, putting an enormous strain on the energy and focus of the Web. Coordination friction, identity claiming and territory fights absorbed much of the badly needed energy for market acquisition. The focus on individual cells instead of interdependent and collaborating units was the main cause of this. During the start-up phase, little incentive came from the market to collaborate, taking away one of the strongest reasons to join forces. Market-driven alliances enforce cohesion in a Web.

Like any commercial Web, YKN needed a value proposition to the market. Despite many discussions a clear differentiator was not agreed upon. Considered were flexible team formation, higher quality service, partnership with equity stake in projects, no-cure-no-pay engagements, pluralism and multidisciplinary approach, volume player and full service provider. The ambiguity in these differentiators was the start of the disintegration of the Web. Lack of a binding force to enforce coherence in the structure had an even stronger effect than expected. The consequence was a lack of clarity of the unique selling proposition and therefore a badly weakened proposition to the market. This is critical in the Web formula where the

Figure 11: Positioning model of YKN

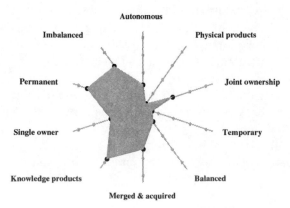
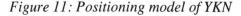

customer is an integral part of the Web boundary. YKN was faced with one of the classic managerial dilemmas of a 21st century organization: too much management and not enough leadership.

The lack of transparency of the Web's identity created little mutual interest and interdependency. This was strengthened by the fact that professionals within the cells had part ownership of their own cell but no share or stake in the Web as a whole. This caused a strong inward instead of outward focus and much time had to be spent on internal alignment and coordination. As with any formation of a Web organization YKN had a Web maker. Where other PSWs often have multiple Web makers with varying competencies complementing each other, in YKN this load was placed on a single individual. In hindsight, due to the inward focus, unorthodoxy, complexity and dynamics of the Web formation, YKN feels that a group of Web makers would have been better equipped to handle the issues at hand.

Figure 12 contains the working model of the Web. The springs have multiple meanings. The length of the spring is the distance between the Web and the entity, depicting the level of coupling to the Web (tight or loose). The frequency shows the amount of interaction. The amplitude shows the intensity of interaction. Although in part being perception, the central coordination and facilitation unit caused friction in adopting the model. Instead of a transparent platform accessible for all, a central unit gave the impression of control and power by this unit.

YKN grew by exploiting personal networks. Friends of friends were contacted and asked to join. In this way the core of YKN was quickly formed in the first 6 months and grew to well over 100 professionals. On top of this, mergers with existing companies were started with multiple due diligence processes running in parallel. The result was a potential Web size of some 500 professionals operating under one Web identity within one year. Despite the fact that there was full understanding of the implication of merging with existing companies and the likely cultural clashes, this

Figure 12: Design of the YKN Web

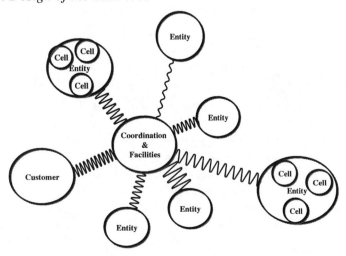

route was still pursued. Instead of pursuing the original plans of autonomous growth, the major part of growth would be through merging. The cultural differences between the new entities and existing companies had a significant effect on the disintegration of the Web. Lack of openness, integration and collaboration caused skepticism towards the feasibility and desirability of a Web concept. Lack of trust caused protectionist behavior and persecution of own interests. This blocked transparent sharing of information and customer relations, both crucial to a successful professional service organization.

The extensive growth rate was one of the main reasons for the Web to implode. Basic procedural and infrastructure elements were not yet in place, while badly needed for Web congruence. Control of utilization, internal developments and customer work required mammoth efforts of a small group of individuals. On top of this, little effort was made in creating a social and technical infrastructure as a backbone for the Web. Playing rules were ill-defined or nonexistent; anarchy ruled.

YKN is made up of professionals in the ICT and consulting sector. In general these people have extensive experience in more traditional organizations. Many cherished the idea of being an entrepreneur and being successful at it; however, few actually fitted the profile. Most had been part of traditional hierarchical organizations that cater for their employees. Clear behavioral rules and guidelines were needed to help the professionals make the transition to a new behavior in line with a Web culture. These rules turned out to be ill-defined and were not enforced enough by senior people in the Web.

Core Values

The core values within the Web were mutual respect, openness, pluralism, professionalism and trust. Sincerity and interaction on equality basis were prophesized to counter hierarchically based behavior. Power exploitation, directives and dictating what professionals ought to do were deemed unacceptable. In the start-up phase these values were upheld and the level of social control was high. Anyone slipping back into old patterns was held accountable for the dysfunctional behavior. With things taking a downward turn, trust and openness were lost. Closed-door meetings became more frequent and information was treated confidentially, resulting in a lack of transparency. This caused unease and inertia. The incubators fell back in traditional roles and structure.

Key Lessons

- A Web organization structure is a hybrid structure requiring complex coordination. The mutual identity and interest need to be reflected in mutual interdependency, not in traditional clustering, for maximum autonomy.
- Creating a Web culture is hard and continuous work. People quickly fall back in traditional patterns of behavior.
- Managers from traditional organizations with control-based management styles are ill-equipped for promoting a Web culture.
- A social and technical infrastructure enforced by simple rules is needed to lower interaction, collaboration and sharing barriers.

REFERENCES

Ackoff, R. L. (1999). *Ackoff's Best: His Classic Writings on Management*. New York: John Wiley & Sons.

Bak P. (1996). *The Science of Self-Organized Criticality*. New York: Springer-Verlag Inc.

Chesborough H. W., and Teece, D. J. (1996, January-February). When is virtual virtuous. *Harvard Business Review*, 65-73

Christensen C. M. (1997). *The Innovator's Dilemma: When New Technologies Cause Great Firms to Fail*. Boston: Harvard Business School Press.

Drucker P. F. (1994). *Management, Tasks, Responsibilities*. Harper & Row.

Durkheim E. (1947). *The Division of Labor in Society*. New York: The Free Press.

Eisenstein D. (1997). *Bucket Brigades: Self-Organizing Work, Embracing Complexity II: Colloquium on the Application of Complex Adaptive Systems to business*, 90-95. Cap Gemini Ernst & Young Center for Business Innovation, Cambridge.

Emery F. E. and Trist E. L. (1960). Socio-technical systems. *Management Science Models and Techniques*, 2. London: Pergamon.

Fayol H. F. (1950). *Administration Industrielle et Générale*. Paris: Dunod.

Hamel G. (2000). *Leading the Revolution*. Boston: Harvard Business School Press.

Holland J. H. (1998). *Emergence From Chaos to Order*. Oxford, England: Oxford University Press.

Kauffman S. A. (1995). *At home in the universe: The Search for the Laws of Self-Organization and Complexity*. New York: Oxford University Press.

Kelly K. (1994). Out of control. *The New Biology of Machines*. London: Addison-Wesley.

Lissack M. and Roos J. (1999). The next common sense. *Mastering Corporate Complexity Through Coherence*. London: Nicolas Brealey.

McMaster M. D. (1996). The intelligence advantage. *Organizing for Complexity*. Newton: Butterworth-Heinemann.

Miles R. E., and Snow C. C. (1993). Het functioneren van netwerk organisaties. *Holland Business Review*, (34).

Mintzberg H. (1973). *The Nature of Managerial Work*. New York: Harper and Row.

Resnick M. (1997). Unlocking the traffic jams in corporate thinking. *Embracing Complexity II: Colloquium on the Application of Complex Adaptive Systems to Business, Cap Gemini Ernst & Young Center for Business Innovation*, 1-6.Cambridge.

Robbins H. and Finley M. (2000). Why teams don't work. *What Went Wrong and How to Make it Right*. Texere.

Toffler A. (1970). *Future Shock*. London: Pan Books.

Trist E. L. (1983). Referent organizations and the development of interorganizational domains. *Human Relations*, *36*(3), 269-284.

Wigand R., Picot A. and Reichwald R. (1997). *Information, Organization and Management: Expanding Markets and Corporate Boundaries*. Chichester, England: John Wiley.

Chapter IX

A Survey of Distributed Information Management Approaches for Virtual Enterprise Infrastructures

César Garita, Hamideh Afsarmanesh and L. O. Hertzberger
University of Amsterdam, The Netherlands

The support of real collaborative virtual enterprise (VE) scenarios sets forward particularly interesting challenges in terms of distributed information management, regarding the proper sharing and exchange of information among preexisting autonomous enterprises. In order to address these challenges, it is necessary to achieve a comprehensive analysis of advanced information management approaches that can be applied in VE platforms. In this context, this chapter provides a representative survey of several VE-related information management standards, technologies, and existing approaches that can be applied to support future VE infrastructures.

INTRODUCTION

The virtual enterprise (VE) concept can be defined in brief as an interoperable network of preexisting enterprises that collaborate by means of specific IT components towards the achievement of a common goal (Camarinha-Matos & Afsarmanesh, 1999). In principle, these enterprises can function together and be regarded as a single organization, for a determined period of time, until the common objective is achieved or until the enterprises decide to dissolve their cooperation. In most cases, the driving force for enterprises to join such collaborations derives from the emergence of a business or market opportunity, whose fulfillment would not be feasible for a single enterprise under normal circumstances. The virtual enterprise goal becomes viable thanks to a global management of activities and coordination of a selected set of resources and services that are made available by individual members of the VE. The VE paradigm is nowadays an active research area, for which many existing technological approaches and tools are required to be applied. In recent years, several significant research efforts and initiatives addressing this field have materialized in the form of international and European research projects and conferences.

Furthermore, currently available information and communications technology (ICT) resources and tools, such as those offered by the Internet environment, enable enterprises to share information and strengthen their interactions with other companies representing partners, clients or suppliers in different collaboration scenarios. Nevertheless, most of the current ICT developments provide solutions to only certain specific technical problems that arise when supporting certain basic interactions among enterprises. There are still many obstacles and open issues that need to be properly addressed when supporting complex collaborations among enterprises involved in VEs. Here, one challenging case for virtual enterprise platforms is the proper sharing and exchange of information among preexisting heterogeneous and autonomous enterprises and their internal systems. In fact, without an adequate support framework for information management, it is impossible for enterprises to collaborate as a single virtual entity. Among the key problems faced in information management approaches supporting the VE domain we can mention:

- Lack of standard definitions of information models and access mechanisms.
- Support for sharing and exchange of distributed information, while maintaining the proper level of autonomy and security for each VE member.
- High degree of heterogeneity encountered at every VE node.
- Wide diversity of information technologies and tools.
- Adequate performance and scalability.

The design and implementation of an information management system aimed at supporting VE infrastructures must address these general challenges, as well as many other specific requirements related to the particular application domain under consideration.

In this context, one of the objectives of this chapter is to present an analysis of several information management techniques and VE support infrastructures that need to be considered when designing and developing an information management system for future virtual enterprise support platforms. Due to the diverse nature and complexity of the requirements described above, the intention of this analysis is to identify a set of potential technological solutions and reference infrastructures that are applicable for addressing the described information management needs. The presented work is also useful for enterprises that are considering to join virtual organizations, since it points out some crucial ICT administration issues that will be faced by these companies in the future.

In order to achieve these objectives, this chapter addresses two main aspects related to the VE information management. First, it provides a survey of related information management technology, including general approaches to manage distributed information, as well as some relevant information management standards and tools. Secondly, it presents a study of information management approaches that have been applied in several actual VE-oriented research and development projects. The study of those approaches reflects the way in which existing VE infrastructures incorporate and adjust some of the standards and tools described in the first point above.

The main focus of this chapter, however, resides on the second point, for which specific relevant research projects in VE support infrastructures are described and compared according to a predefined set of information management characteristics that have been specially introduced in this chapter for their evaluation purposes.

The structure of the chapter is therefore organized as follows. First, a summarized description of VE-related information management technology is provided, including generic approaches for distributed information management, information representation models and standards, and related technologies and tools. Second, a survey and evaluation of existing information management approaches for VE support platforms developed in several research projects are provided. Furthermore, for the evaluation of different approaches, a set of information management criteria is defined, and consequently, a comparison of the different infrastructures is carried out and shown in a tabular form according to this defined set of criteria. Finally, the major conclusions and future directions of this work are summarized.

VE-RELATED INFORMATION MANAGEMENT TECHNIQUES

In order to address the information management requirements described in the previous section, there are many different technologies that can be applied. In this section, three main areas of information management technologies relevant to VE support infrastructures are introduced. The first area refers to the generic approaches for distributed information management, through which a certain level of information sharing and exchange among VE nodes can be achieved. Secondly, several related information representational standards and proposals are analyzed. The third and last related area analyzed in this section addresses several component technologies that definitely play a crucial role in the VE information management support.

Generic Approaches for Distributed Information Management

The need to support the general information sharing and exchange among different organizations is not something particularly new nor exclusively related to the VE domain. For example, different multi-database management approaches have been historically conceived and designed in order to support interoperability and integration among independent databases, based on fundamental principles such as seamless access to distributed data, support for software/hardware heterogeneity, interoperability mechanisms, and node autonomy issues.

In general, the application of heterogeneous distributed database management systems in VE infrastructures seems a natural choice because, in the end, the VE itself can be seen as a network of distributed autonomous nodes that exchange and share particular sets of local information. However, most existing multi-database systems are still research prototypes, and the commercially available DBMSs provide only limited functionalities for the fundamental principles mentioned above (Bouguettaya, Benatallah, & Elmagarmid, 1999). Nevertheless, advanced distributed information management techniques provide a good base that must be studied, evaluated, and eventually tailored to apply it to the VE infrastructure.

A detailed analysis and comparison of particular multi-database approaches are outside the scope of this survey. Some classifications and taxonomies can also be found in Sheth and Larson (1990) and Bouguettaya et al. (1999). However, despite the big diversity of possible classifications and architectures of these systems, after an analysis of the VE application domain to identify the information management requirements, the following approaches seem relevant to be considered in the design of a VE infrastructure support framework: distributed databases, multi-databases, and federated databases (see Figure 1).

In the first approach, the most coupled version of a distributed database management system involves the administration of several databases by one general management system. Usually, the management system and the depending databases have the same data model and provide the same functionality at all levels, and one global schema is kept where every database is represented. The users can submit queries applied to the global schema, and the management system is in charge of the distribution of subqueries between the components and the processing of the individual results to satisfy the global request.

On the other hand, a multi-database system supports the operation of several databases, where each of these components is ruled by a given database management system. The management subsystems for every database may be different and could be either centralized or distributed among several computers. If the management subsystem is the same for all databases, then the multi-database system is

Figure 1: Main distributed information management systems relevant to VEs

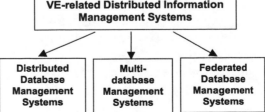

homogeneous; otherwise, it is heterogeneous. The component databases, despite this interaction with a global system, preserve their local autonomy.

Finally, the federated database systems represent a subset of the multi-database systems. In this case, instead of creating a single local schema, every node in the federation maintains local autonomy on the data and defines on it a set of export schemas that are made available to other specific nodes. Also, every node will be able to import schemas from other nodes according to the defined access permissions. As a consequence of this general interaction, this approach allows the cooperation between the nodes in the federation to accomplish a common or global task, while the local autonomy and independence of every node is preserved and reinforced.

An extensive classification and analysis of relevant distributed, multidatabase, and federated database systems are outside the aim and the scope of this chapter. However, the approach of some of these systems is briefly described next, since it is definitely related to the study and design of the information management system for VE infrastructures.

- The PEER system is a federated object-oriented information management system that primarily supports the sharing and exchange of information among cooperating autonomous and heterogeneous nodes (Wiedijk, Afsarmanesh, & Hertzberger, 1996). The PEER architecture inspired the design of the information management system in VE infrastructures such as PRODNET and MASSYVE.
- InfoWeb is a general-purpose information management infrastructure based on interoperable and independent components that are interfaced by specific middleware (Lee & Noah, 1999). The end user has access through a Web browser interface, and all the distributed information that is retrieved from local and remote sources is presented in a uniform and consistent way. The VE-related project EisNet uses InfoWeb to integrate internal and external enterprise information resources.
- InfoSleuth is an agent-based system, aimed at the integration of heterogeneous distributed information sources using common ontologies definitions (Nodine et al., 2000). The InfoSleuth agents collaborate with each other to retrieve and process information distributed in a dynamic Web-based environment. The application of InfoSleuth agent technology has been evaluated in VE environments such as EisNet.

Examples of other related federated and multidatabase management systems that may eventually be applied in VE infrastructures include IRO-DB, UniSQL/M, Pegasus, VHDBS, VODAK and DISCO. Several well-known and widely accepted RDBMS among enterprises in different sectors have also been used by some VE infrastructures to support their internal information management, including Oracle, MS-Access and MS SQL Server.

The actual application of some of the systems described in this section as internal DBMSs in existing VE platforms will be illustrated in further sections of this chapter.

Related Information Representation Models and Standards

Besides the generic distributed information management approaches described in the previous section, there are a number of existing information management models and standards that also need to be carefully considered for the design and implementation of the VE information management platform. The management of information represented in some of these standards can become crucial for the adoption of VE infrastructures for existing enterprises, since they facilitate the integration of internal company information with the information managed by the VE platform. These models and standards include, among others (see Figure 2):

- Electronic Data Interchange (EDI). EDI encompasses a set of standards that basically define a common format for representing and exchanging business data. By adopting the EDI standard, companies have achieved to a certain extent their goal of having a mechanism for business data exchange that is independent of existing applications, communication media and hardware systems at each site.
- Distributed business processes (DBPs). In general, the business process (BP) concept encapsulates a global goal or objective being carried out by an enterprise, such as the manufacturing of a product, provision of a service, delivery of goods, etc. In the context of VEs, the VE goals can be modeled as a distributed business process (DBP) composed of a set of BPs, where each BP can be in turn carried out by a different VE member (Klen, Rabelo, Spinosa, & Ferreira, 1999). The application of DBP models in the context of VEs has proven to be very advantageous in several projects, such as PRODNET, FETISH, and MASSYVE.
- Standard for the Exchange of Product Model Data (STEP). The STEP ISO standard has as its main goal the uniform representation and management of product-related data during the whole life cycle of the product (Schreiber, 1999). In general, the use of STEP applications promotes the sharing of a common product data model in which system independence, data consistency, and interoperability features are fully supported. Several VE research projects have adopted this standard, in particular, VE application fields.
- Ontology models and definitions. In a few words, an ontology can be defined as a shared understanding of some domain of interest (Uschold & Gruninger, 1996). It encompasses a set of concepts and their definition within a given

Figure 2: Main VE-related information representation models and standards

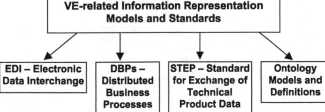

domain, as well as the interrelationships among these concepts. In the case of Virtual Enterprises, ontologies can facilitate the integration of different enterprise information models by providing a common interpretation of their semantics; see, for instance, Gruninger & Fox (1995).

Related Technologies and Tools

In addition to the information representation models such as those described in the previous section, there are many other technologies, standards and tools that are strongly related to the information management aspects of VEs. In order to guarantee the success of the VE application, existing component technologies need to be properly synthesized and integrated into the new VE framework (Camarinha-Matos & Afsarmanesh, 1999). The main component technologies include (see Figure 3):

- Workflow management techniques. Workflow management techniques represent a particular coordination approach that can be conveniently applied in VE support infrastructures at different levels. For example, these techniques have been extensively applied by several VE projects such as PRODNET, VEGA and NIIIP. In all these cases, the reference model defined by the Workflow Management Coalition (WfMC) (WFMC, 1994) has been followed.
- Advanced Web application support mechanisms. Web application standards and technologies obviously play an important role in the support of VE infrastructures. For instance, the development of VE infrastructures based on Internet communication protocols, Java applications, and XML not only allows a high degree of portability, but also opens new possibilities to deal with the associated enterprise heterogeneity problems.
- Distributed object management. Service brokerage and middleware interoperability approaches based on object-oriented technology such as CORBA (Common Object Request Broker Architecture; OMG, 2000) can be applied to integrate external enterprise information sources with the VE platform in a flexible and dynamic way. CORBA has been extensively applied by a number of VE research projects such as NIIIP and VEGA.
- Secure and reliable communication protocols and services. In the design and implementation of any VE platform, the importance of a reliable, secure and efficient communication channel between any two VE members is clearly evident. The application of sophisticated data encryption algorithms, digital

Figure 3: VE-related component technologies and tools

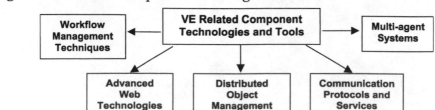

signatures, and other security mechanisms is also essential in this kind of enterprise collaboration.

- Multiagent systems. Multiagent approaches have been successfully applied in the past as a base for the data sharing and exchange mechanisms among autonomous and independent nodes. Moreover, collaborative agent architectures are being proposed as a suitable framework to directly enable VEs (Rabelo, Afsarmanesh, & Camarinha-Matos, 2000; Shen & Norrie, 1999). In addition, mobile agent technology is also being applied to implement certain VE functionalities (Chrysanthis, Znati, Banerjee, & Chang, 1999).

A FRAMEWORK FOR EVALUATION OF VE INFRASTRUCTURES

In the previous section, a set of information management technologies and standards was described, which can be applied by the VE infrastructure in order to cope with some of the challenges identified in the introduction of this chapter. In this section, a framework for evaluation of VE support infrastructures is developed in order to illustrate the way in which existing infrastructures incorporate and adjust some of the technologies described previously. The resulting evaluation framework can be used as a common base for comparison of existing and forthcoming VE information management infrastructures. The evaluation results are represented in a matrix composed of VE information management infrastructures and the identified set of VE information management requirements and criteria used to compare and evaluate different platforms.

Consequently, the proposed approach for evaluation of VE information management infrastructures is described in the following sections in terms of the following points: (1) a classification and description of specific existing VE platforms; (2) a set of required features and criteria for evaluation of VE information management infrastructures; and (3) the set of tables that compare the specific VE infrastructures according to the identified set of features.

Specific VE Information Management Platforms

In this section, a description of several specific VE projects and initiatives is provided. In order to achieve a more comprehensive presentation of the initiatives, they need to be classified according to some criteria. Given the nature and focus of this chapter, the different projects are categorized according to the main technological approach used to manage and integrate the VE-related information that is actually distributed among the VE nodes. Here, the projects are classified according to the following technological approaches for distributed data integration:

- Internet-based integration approaches. In these approaches the distributed VE information is retrieved and integrated by making an extensive use of Internet information technology and resources, e.g., Web browsers, public Web page information, URL identifiers, XML documents.

- Object-model-based integration approaches. In this category, the integration of the VE distributed information mainly relies on the consistent application of object-oriented models and interoperability architectures, such as CORBA-based approaches.
- Federated database integration approaches. This particular approach for distributed information integration is based on the principles of federated/distributed databases, including different levels of schema definitions that ultimately support the integration of distributed data.
- Message-passing approaches. In this case, the VE information is queried, retrieved, and presented to the end user or application through the exchange of specific messages among VE nodes. The messages comply with a pre-defined format and protocol such as e-mail or special service request functions among tools.

Please notice that this general categorization does not mean that a given project, classified under a given approach, does not apply the other kinds of technologies used to characterize the other approaches. In other words, it is possible that, for instance, integration approaches based on object-oriented models or federated database architectures can also take advantage of Internet facilities such as communication services. In the following subsections, several VE projects are classified according to the presented classification approach (see Figure 4).

Internet-Based Integration Approaches

The VE support infrastructures presented in this section are strongly based on the Internet environment and facilities in order to integrate the VE distributed information. These infrastructures include:

- EisNet. The Enterprise Intelligence System Network (EisNet) project has as its main objective the integration of diverse internal and external enterprise information resources in order to make them accessible to users in a consistent and seamless way (Lee & Noah, 1999). These resources include local databases, corporate databases, and external Web sites. The EisNet system platform uses InfoWeb™ to integrate information originating from the sources mentioned above. In this way, the EisNet system can support decision-making

Figure 4: Classification of approaches for integration of VE distributed information

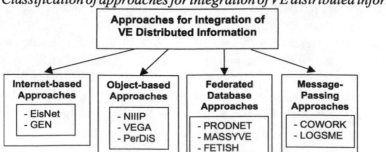

processes by integrating information coming from distributed data sources accessible through Inter/intranet technologies.
* GEN. The Global Engineering Networking (GEN) initiative has been established by a group of European organizations in order to address the cooperation challenges faced when supporting virtual engineering enterprises in the areas of building construction, mechanics and electronics (Radeke, 1999). The architecture of the information management system in GEN is composed of GEN client modules and GEN cooperation layer (server) modules. By using the GEN clients, end users have access to both local and remote data distributed in other enterprises.

Object-Model-Based Integration Approaches

The following approaches are strongly based on object-oriented technology, such as CORBA, in order to represent and manage the VE distributed information:
* NIIIP. The NIIIP (National Industrial Information Infrastructure Protocols) project has as its main objective to develop, demonstrate, and transfer technological solutions to support industrial virtual enterprises (NIIIP, 1998). The NIIIP project is one of the most representative ones in the VE domain. The NIIIP architecture provides a set of standard protocols that will support the sharing and exchange of industrial information among systems in many application areas. The core technologies that support the NIIIP infrastructure are Internet communications, OMG object model, WfMC for task management, and STEP for data modeling and access.
* VEGA. The VEGA project aims at the support of the technical operations and business activities of VEs in the area of large-scale engineering projects (Zarli & Poyet, 1999). The VEGA infrastructure incorporates four main kinds of information management technologies or standards: product data modeling (ISO STEP), middleware technology (CORBA), workflow management (as defined by WfMC), and Web-related standards (HTML, VRML, Java, etc.). The VEGA system integration backbone is embodied by the COAST (CORBA Access to STEP repository) component, which provides transparent access to distributed product data specified in the EXPRESS language.
* PerDiS. The PerDiS system targets the support for cooperative engineering applications in the VE by providing an efficient and secure platform for distributed data sharing called the Persistent Distributed Store (Sandalky, Garcia, Ferreira, & Poyet, 1999). PerDiS is based on a distributed shared-memory store for the VE applications. This means that applications located at different sites can access distributed objects as if they were stored in local memory.

Federated-Database-Based Integration Approaches

In the following projects, the generic federated database approach for information integration has been specifically tailored in order to cope with the specificities of the VE application domain:

- PRODNET. The project PRODNET II (Production Planning and Management in an Extended Enterprise) had as its main objective the development of a reference architecture and a support infrastructure for industrial VEs (Camarinha-Matos & Afsarmanesh, 1999a). In the PRODNET architecture, every enterprise in the network of potential VE members is extended with a PRODNET Cooperation Layer (PCL), which provides the necessary functionalities to support the inter-operation between nodes in the network. The PCL consists of several internal components including the workflow-based Local Coordination Module, the STEP and EDI components, the Communication Interface module, and the Distributed Information Management System (DIMS). The DIMS supports the VE information management requirements and is based on federated/distributed database principles.
- MASSYVE. The MASSYVE (Multiagent Agile Manufacturing Scheduling Systems for Virtual Enterprises) project addresses the application of multi-agent systems in agile scheduling and its extension towards the operation in a virtual enterprise environment (Rabelo et al., 2000). In this project, the HOLOS framework is applied as a base for advanced scheduling. In HOLOS, a given multi-agent scheduling system is composed of a set of distributed nodes with particular capabilities that need to exchange and process information in order to address the global scheduling problem. The information integration approach to support multi-agent systems is based on the PEER federated information management framework, as well as the distributed information management system developed for the PRODNET project.
- FETISH. The main objective of the Federated European Tourism Information System Harmonization (FETISH) project is to build a "federation" of both basic and value-added services in the tourism sector (Afsarmanesh & Camarinha-Matos, 2000). Examples of these tourism services include hotel reservation and booking facilities, car rental, organization of holiday packages, mobile access to travel information, etc. In terms of information management, the requirements being analyzed in the project include the support of: catalogues for common service interface definitions, federated database features, and distributed business process support. The system infrastructure is developed using Java/Jini as core technologies.

Message-Passing Integration Approaches

The following list of projects includes approaches that use some kind of message-passing approach to integrate physically distributed VE-related information:

- COWORK. The COWORK (Concurrent Project Development IT Tools for SMEs Networks) project aims at the development of a software infrastructure to enable small and medium enterprises (SMEs) in the mechanical sector to cooperate in a distributed engineering environment (Alazaga & Martin, 1999). The objective is to promote the systematic application of concurrent engineering and codesign techniques in the target SMEs in order to achieve a significant performance improvement. Network interoperation in COWORK is achieved by means of an Internet-based message passing mechanism.

- LOGSME. The main objective of the LOGSME project is the development of an open platform and appropriate protocols and tools to support VE environments in the area of food supply chain (LOGSME, 1999). The designed platform would provide SMEs in this sector with a set of reliable and low-cost modules to support their operation within several food supply chains. These modules include functionalities such as, for example: monitoring of stock levels and replenishment orders, production planning, advanced forecasting techniques, logical warehouse transactions, supply chain simulation, and access to information located at the local and remote VE partner nodes. Information from other SMEs in the supply chain is exchanged through some form of standard messages that comply with different formats.

Finally, it can be mentioned there are many other relevant projects related to VE support, including X-CITTIC, VIRTEC, PLENT, CALS, FREE, GERAM, MARVEL OUS, and CROSSFLOW.

Table 1: Key characteristics of VE information management systems

Characteristic	Description
General System Information	
Organization	Main developer organization, company, or consortium
Sector	Field of application (e.g. manufacturing, supply chain)
Platform	Computer system platform and/or operating system
Data Management Framework for Information Sharing/Exchange	
Data Models	Standard or proprietary data models applied
Internal DBMS	Use of base underlying DBMS (e.g. Oracle, Sybase, O2)
DB Access Method	Support mechanism for basic data access (e.g. ODBC, JDBC, http, hyperlinks, CGI)
High-Level Functions	Provision of specific high-level information management functions developed on top of basic mechanisms
Transactions Mgmt.	Support for local and/or distributed transaction management
Middleware	Use of some kind of middleware technology (e.g. CORBA)
VE Information Access Rights	Access rights and visibility levels for protected information access among VE members (e.g. user account/password; access rights per VE partner role)
Federated DB Architecture	Explicit use of federated/distributed database concepts (e.g. local/import/export/integrated schemas)
Other Characteristics	
Directory Mgmt.	Directory information management for partners, products, company profiles, etc.
Workflow Mgmt.	Application of workflow techniques to support information management activities
Safe Comm. Techniques	Support for communication techniques to ensure safe and reliable data exchange (e.g. encryption, digital signature)
Internet Data Access	Application of Internet technology and tools to support high-level aspects of VE information management (e.g. use of Internet client interfaces, Internet browsers, XML)
Main Special Features	Provision of specific support for special information management functionalities (e.g. data mining, caching)

Characterization and Comparison of VE infrastructures

Based on the requirements and challenges and the VE related information management techniques identified in previous sections, a basic set of required features and criteria for evaluation of VE information management infrastructures have been defined. In Table 1, this set of characteristics and features are represented as the critical points to be used for evaluation and comparison of information management approaches adopted in different projects.

This criteria has been applied to the projects described before, and the results are reported in several tables. The tables included in this section represent a classification and characterization of several projects based on the criteria defined in the previous section. Tables 2, 3, 4 and 5 depict the main features and capabilities that are commonly provided by VE information management infrastructures.

In particular, Table 2 shows the information and characterization of the projects EisNet and GEN, which represent the Internet-based approaches for integration of VE information according to the proposed classification strategy.

Table 2: Evaluation of Internet-based infrastructures for VE information management

General Information	EisNet	GEN
Organization	TRW (US company)	GEN European Organization
Sector	Intra/Internet Business Information Integration	Engineering Enterprises
Platform	Server on Sun/Solaris	Multiplatform (Java/CORBA-based)
Data Mgmt.		
Data Models	Proprietary organization and model of data sources	Standards such as IEC 61360; own DTDs
Internal DBMS	InfoWeb (Illustra and Oracle also used under InfoWeb)	Any relational DBs can be used through JDBC
DB access method	Clients provide DB access via html, CGI, and Java; InfoWeb also supports ODBC	Via GEN Clients (www interfaces and other data loading tools)
High-level functions	High-level functions for meta-data generation are provided (e.g. filters, classifiers extractors)	GEN clients and services (through URLs)
Transactions Mgmt.	No info. available	No info. available
Middleware	InfoWeb middleware layer considers CORBA, http, ODBC among others	Mainly CORBA
VE Information Access rights	Accounts/passwords are issued for access to local DBs; additional layer of password protection used	Based on account/password; distinction between company-private and VE-public data
Federated DB architecture	None	None
Other characteristics.		
Directory Mgmt.	No info. available	No info. available
Workflow Mgmt.	None	None
Safe Comm. Techniques	Web server firewall	No info. available
Internet Data Access	Netscape browser/client interfaces using html, CGI, Java applets	GEN Client interfaces are WWW based; XML is used
Main special features	InfoWeb provides some meta-data generation services	Flexible integration of distributed info. via Internet

Table 3: Evaluation of object-based infrastructures for VE information management

General Information	NIIIP	VEGA	PerDiS
Organization	US consortium	European ESPRIT	European ESPRIT
Sector	Industrial enterprises	Large Scale Engineering	Cooperative engineering
Platform	Multiplatform (CORBA-based)	Multi-platform (CORBA-based)	Unix / Windows NT
Data Mgmt.			
Data Models	STEP, OMG, others	Mainly STEP data models	C++ object model and text files
Internal DBMS	Implementations can use different DBMSs	No info. available	A local file server is used for data storage
DB Access Method	Different DB access methods (e.g. JDBC, ODMG, SDAI)	COAST-based	API with specific functions
High-Level Functions	High-level services are defined for most NIIIP components	COAST layer defines high-level data functionalities	No info. available
Transactions Mgmt.	Object services also include transactions	Explicit distributed transactions functions	Optimistic / pessimistic models
Middleware	Mainly CORBA	CORBA	Based on TCP/IP comm. approach
VE Information Access Rights	User ids, passwords, roles, and groups are defined for VE info. access	User account /passwords; part of enterprise workflows can be hidden	Groupware-oriented access rights approach based on task/role model
Federated DB Architecture	A kind of federated DB support for the VE Global Schema	None	None
Other Characteristics			
Directory Mgmt.	NIIIP data directory	No info. available	No info. available
Workflow Mgmt.	WfMC models used for VE task mgmt.	WfMC models for VE mgmt. support	None
Safe Comm. Techniques	On-going work for advanced security mechanisms	Mostly based on existing company firewalls	Public/shared key schemes
Internet Data Access	Internet services (e.g. WWW access, client interfaces, public forums, mailing lists)	A web-based presentation layer is provided for end-users	Programmers use URLs to refer to object clusters
Main Special Features	One of the most representative VE initiatives	Strongly based on IT standards (OMG, CORBA, STEP)	Based on persistent, distributed shared-memory approach

Table 3 describes infrastructures in which the distributed information management approach is based on an object-oriented model, including the NIIIP, VEGA, and PerDiS projects. Table 4 characterizes the projects PRODNET, MASSYVE and FETISH, in which University of Amsterdam has been a partner and has developed the VE information management functionalities based on a federated database architecture. Finally, Table 5 includes the characterization of the COWORK and LOGSME projects, which are mostly based on a message-passing approach to integrate the VE information.

Table 4: Evaluation of federated database infrastructures for VE information management

General Information	PRODNET II	MASSYVE	FETISH
Organization	European ESPRIT	European KIT/INCO	European 5FP-IST
Sector	Industrial Manufacturing	Manufacturing Scheduling	Tourism Services
Platform	Windows NT	Windows NT	Multi-platform
Data Mgmt.			
Data Models	EDIFACT, STEP, DBP, others	DBP, other proprietary models	DBP, Tourism Datasets
Internal DBMS	Oracle	Oracle, PEER	Oracle
DB Access Method	Client library of services	Client library	JDBC, client library
High-Level Functions	High-level functions for VE creation and monitoring	Advanced functions for VE scheduling support	Support functions for VE service interface catalogues
Transactions Mgmt.	Local transaction mechanisms are considered	Transactions support the high-level functionalities	Services use local transaction facilities
Middleware	RPC	RPC	Jini
VE Information Access rights	Definitions of fine-grained VE access rights and visibility levels on local info.	Fine-grained access rights at a given node are defined at every other VE member	Access rights on shared VE info. are defined at every node of other VE members
Federated DB architecture	Federated DB architecture approach	Federated DB support secured information access	VE services based on a federated database architecture
Other Characteristics			
Directory Mgmt.	No	No	Catalogues for services definitions
Workflow Mgmt.	Federated query processing modeled as workflow plans	Workflows used to retrieve info. from existing systems	Value-added services are represented as workflow plans
Safe Comm. Techniques	Encryption, digital signature, multi-comm. protocols	Encryption, digital signature, and several comm. protocols	Not defined yet
Internet Data Access	Future extensions	No	Java, Jini , and XML technologies are used
Main special features	Use of a VE-tailored federated DB	Based on multi-agent architecture	Extensive use of Java/Jini

CONCLUSIONS AND FUTURE DIRECTIONS

In this chapter, several information management challenges for the specific field of VE support infrastructure were introduced. In order to harness the involved complexity in this application, a survey of VE-related information management techniques was presented, including distributed information management techniques, related information models and standards, and related technologies and tools. Furthermore, a set of international VE projects was described and classified in terms of the main approach being used for integration of the VE distributed information. The projects were also analyzed against specific criteria for comparison and evaluation of their different features.

The survey of distributed information management approaches for VE infrastructures presented in this chapter is useful, for instance, for managers of enterprises that are considering to join virtual organizations since it not only describes some of the crucial ICT management issues that will be faced by these companies, but also points out how these issues have been addressed by existing, actual VE support platforms in a wide variety of application domains.

In terms of future directions, the following issues need to be further analyzed:

- It is clear that there is still a sensible need for a common reference model for the VE paradigm, encompassing different functionalities along the full VE life cycle. Currently, there are too many independent efforts with distinct points of view, and the definition of a common VE conceptual framework has not been achieved yet.
- In order to facilitate and promote the data exchange among enterprises, there is also a trend towards the establishment of commonly agreed data documents,

Table 5: Evaluation of message-passing infrastructures for VE information management

General Information	COWORK	LOGSME
Organization	European ESPRIT project	European ESPRIT project
Sector	Mechanical Sector	Food supply chain
Platform	Windows NT	Windows
Data Mgmt.		
Data Models	STEP; internal models for product, design process and enterprise competence	EDI and other common message formats are supported
Internal DBMS	Lotus Notes R5 and other DBMSs can be used	Microsoft Access
DB Access Method	Internet, ODBC (for SCM info.)	Gathered data can be accessed via a database view e.g. record set
High-Level Functions	Several predefined search criteria can be applied supported by a search wizard	High-level services for specific VE support including inventory stock, forecast, planning
Transactions Mgmt.	No info. available	No info. available
Middleware	No info. available (TCP/IP and email mechanisms are used)	Based on standards such as CORBA and DCOMM
VE Information Access Rights	No info. available; identified need to protect know-how information	No info. available
Federated DB architecture	None	None
Other Characteristics		
Directory Mgmt.	Competency repository serves as a directory of potential partners	No info. available
Workflow Mgmt.	WfMC models were applied in the process model	None
Safe Comm. Techniques	Encryption is supported by Lotus Notes	Security checks are used for data transmissions
Internet Data Access	Internet clients for competence model	External info. requests submitted via email or http; messages sent via FTP, HTTP, and SMTP
Main Special Features	Support for competency repository and co-design activities in a distributed environment	LOGSME tools are easy, reliable and low-cost modules for SMEs;

based on, for instance, standardized data type definitions (DTDs) in a given application domain. The use of XML may play an important role in this point. Furthermore, the definition of DTDs in relatively new application domains may be better supported in the future by formal ontological methodologies.

- The concept of access rights and visibility levels in VEs is also an issue that needs to be better supported and reinforced by existing VE infrastructures. Most of the analyzed VE information management systems do not support a proper level of granularity and flexibility regarding the definition of access rights on shared information among VE members, although the need to protect internal enterprise information is usually well identified.

As a final remark, given the complexity associated with the VE paradigm and its enabling technologies, it is also foreseen that enterprises will more frequently need to use information management surveys and evaluation frameworks similar to the work presented in this chapter in order to successfully join and adapt to existing and future virtual organizations.

REFERENCES

Afsarmanesh, H., and Camarinha-Matos, L. M. (2000, June). *Future smart-Organizations: A virtual tourism enterprise.* Paper presented at the 1st International Conference on Web Information System Engineering–WISE'2000. Hong Kong, China.

Alazaga, A. and Martin, J. (1999). A design process model to support concurrent project development in networks of SMEs. In L. M. Camarinha-Matos & H. Afsarmanesh (Eds.), *Infrastructures for Virtual Enterprises–Networking Industrial Enterprises* (pp. 307-318). Kluwer Academic.

Bouguettaya, A., Benatallah, B. and Elmagarmid, A. (1999). An overview of multidatabase systems: Past and present. In Elmagarmid, A., Rusinkiewicz, M. and Shet, A. (Eds.), *Management of Heterogeneous and Autonomous Database Systems*, 1-24. San Francisco: Morgan Kaufmann.

Camarinha-Matos, L. M. and Afsarmanesh, H. (1999a). Tendencies and general requirements for virtual enterprises. In Camarinha-Matos, L. M. and Afsarmanesh, H. (Eds.), *Infrastructures for Virtual Enterprises–Networking Industrial Enterprises*, 15-30. Kluwer Academic.

Camarinha-Matos, L. M. and Afsarmanesh, H. (1999b). The virtual enterprise concept. In Camarinha-Matos, L. M. and Afsarmanesh, H. (Eds.), *Infrastructures for Virtual Enterprises–Networking Industrial Enterprises*, 3-14. Kluwer Academic.

Chrysanthis, P., Znati, T., Banerjee, S. and Chang, S. K. (1999, March). Establishing Virtual Enterprises by Means of Mobile Agents. Paper presented at the *9th International Workshop on Research Issues in Data Engineering–Information Technology for Virtual Enterprises–RIDE-VE'99*. Sydney, Australia.

Gruninger, M. and Fox, M. (1995). The logic of enterprise modelling. In Brown, J. and O'Sullivan, D. (Eds.), *Reengineering the Enterprise*, 83-98. Chapman and Hall.

Klen, A., Rabelo, R., Spinosa, M. and Ferreira, A. (1999). Distributed business process management. In Camarinha-Matos, L. M. and Afsarmanesh, H. (Eds.), *Infrastructures for Virtual Enterprises - Networking Industrial Enterprises*, 241-258. Kluwer Academic.

Lee, E. and Noah, W. (1999). An enterprise intelligence system integrating WWW and intranet resources. Paper presented at the *9th International Workshop on Research Issues in Data Engineering–Information Technology for Virtual Enterprises–RIDE-VE'99*, March 23-24. Sydney, Australia.

LOGSME. (1999). *LOGSME Project Summary*. Available on the World Wide Web: http://cimru.ucg.ie.

National Industrial Information Infrastructure Protocols. (1998). *NIIIP Reference Architecture*. Retrieved M D, Y from the World Wide Web: http://www.niiip.org.

Nodine, M., Fowler, J., Ksiezyk, T., Perry, B., Taylor, M. and Unruh, A. (2000). Active information gathering in infosleuth. *International Journal of Cooperative Information Systems (IJCIS)*, 9(1-2), 3-28.

Object Management Group. (2000). *The Object Management Group*. Available on the World Wide Web at: http://www.omg.org.

Rabelo, R., Afsarmanesh, H. and Camarinha-Matos, L. (2000). Federated multi-agent scheduling in virtual enterprises. In Camarinha-Matos, L., Afsarmanesh, H. and Rabelo, R. (Eds.), *E-Business and Virtual Enterprises–Managing Business-to-Business Cooperation*, 145-166. Kluwer Academic.

Radckc, E. (1999). Precisely accessing engineering information on the Web. Paper presented at the *CME-GEN'99 International Conference on Concurrent Multidisciplinary Engineering and Global Engineering Networking*, September 14-15. Bremen, Germany.

Sandalky, F., Garcia, J., Ferreira, P. and Poyet, P. (1999). PerDis: An infrastructure for cooperative engineering in virtual enterprise. In Camarinha-Matos, L. M. and Afsarmanesh, H. (Eds.), *Infrastructures for Virtual Enterprises–Networking Industrial Enterprises*, 319-332. Kluwer Academic.

Schreiber, A. (1999). STEP support for virtual enterprises. In Camarinha-Matos, L. M. and Afsarmanesh, H. (Eds.), *Infrastructures for Virtual Enterprises–Networking Industrial Enterprises*, 209-218. Kluwer Academic.

Shen, W. and Norrie, D. (1999). Implementing Internet-enabled virtual enterprises using collaborative agents. In Camarinha-Matos, L. M. and Afsarmanesh, H. (Eds.), *Infrastructures for Virtual Enterprises–Networking Industrial Enterprises*, 343-352. Kluwer Academic.

Sheth, A. and Larson, J. (1990). Federated database systems for managing distributed, heterogeneous, and autonomous databases. *ACM Computing Surveys*, 22(3), 183-236.

Uschold, M. and Gruninger, M. (1996). Ontologies: Principles, methods and applications. *The Knowledge Engineering Review*, 11(2).

Wiedijk, M., Afsarmanesh, H. and Hertzberger, L. O. (1996, September). Co-working and management of federated information clusters. Paper presented at the *7th International Conference on Database and Expert Systems Applications–DEXA'96*. Zurich, Switzerland.

WorkFlow Management Coalition. (1994). *The Workflow Reference Model* (TC00 - 103, Issue 1.1). Brussels, Belgium: Workflow Management Coalition.

Zarli, A. and Poyet, P. (1999). A framework for distributed information management in the virtual enterprise: The VEGA project. In Camarinha-Matos, L. M. and Afsarmanesh, H. (Eds.), *Infrastructures for Virtual Enterprises–Networking Industrial Enterprises*, 293-306. Kluwer Academic.

Section II

Virtual Web Management Issues: Special Issues and Possible Solutions of Managing Virtual Web Organizations

Chapter X

Global Manufacturing Virtual Network (GMVN): Its Dynamic Position in the Spectrum of Manufacturing Collaborations

Yongjiang Shi and Mike Gregory
University of Cambridge, UK

This paper seeks to understand the relationship between virtual organizations (VOs) and international strategic alliances (ISAs) in the manufacturing industry. Aiming to develop frameworks demonstrating the position and role of the global manufacturing virtual network (GMVN) in the spectrum between VO and ISA, the paper suggests that GMVNs represent a new form of manufacturing system based on Internet interfirm collaborations.

INTRODUCTION

Manufacturing increasingly relies on swift collaboration and on agile re-configuration of its whole supply chain to effectively and efficiently deliver benefits to customers worldwide. Global manufacturing systems are expected to have much more flexible organizational architectures and operational mechanisms to respond to dramatic changes and an accelerated customization in the world market. But responsiveness and resource flexibility are limited by a company's physical and commercial boundaries as well as geography. The concept of manufacturing networks without such limitations–sometimes called virtual networks–is attracting increasing attention. Indeed practical progress has been made in some sectors.

However, as promising as manufacturing globalization and virtualization are, as difficult are they to establish and manage. There are many outstanding questions:

- Why does e-manufacturing develop much slower than e-commerce?
- Why do companies need e-manufacturing or virtual manufacturing networks?
- What are the virtual manufacturing implications for strategic alliances?
- Is there a common framework which could draw together different strands and provide guidance?

This paper seeks to take a first step towards understanding the underlying issues, especially the relationship between virtual organization (VOs) and international strategic alliances (ISAs). It aims to build conceptual frameworks demonstrating the position and role of global manufacturing virtual networks (GMVNs) in VOs and ISAs and to develop a common language among different disciplines. It suggests that GMVNs represent a new form of manufacturing system based on Internet communication and new models of collaborations.

The paper is structured into four sections. The first section reviews the wide range of relevant researches, especially from the perspectives of ISAs, e-business, global manufacturing networks, and virtual aspects including virtual manufacturing, organization and corporations. The second section maps the GMVN in the context of VOs and ISAs to demonstrate the missions, structures and attributes of the GMVN. Then, further research considerations develop the implications of the GMVN and related issues and how these might be tackled. The paper ends by summarizing emerging knowledge about GMVNs and new frameworks for understanding practice and research.

IN SEARCH OF NEW MANUFACTURING SYSTEMS

In an era of globalization, the nature and the intensity of competition have been changed drastically. In the new game, no company can play without partners in either domestic or global markets. ISAs and networks have become one of the most critical vehicles pursuing globally competitive advantages (Hinterhuber & Levin, 1994). If the strategic networks were the dominating forms in the 1990s as Figure 1(a) demonstrates, how will these be influenced by the rapid growth of e-business? In this section, ISAs and VOs are reviewed and contrasted to clarify the characteristics of virtual organizations and explore whether GMVNs can be better designed based on existing knowledge and principles.

What Are International Strategic Alliances (ISAs)?

International strategic alliances are a logical and timely response to intense and rapid changes in economic activity, technology, and globalization, which require

corporations to consider globalization and the changing future environment concurrently (Doz & Hamel, 1998). Some people characterize the alliance relationships by defining them as a cooperation between two or more industrial corporations, belonging to different countries, whereby each partner seeks to add to its competence by combining its resources with those of the other partners (Jain, 1987). More people take a broader view of ISAs as a spectrum including any form of cooperative activity involving two or more companies across borders, although there are some differences between the "strategic degree" (Faulkner, 1995; Lu, 1994; Murray, 1995).

As the Figure 1(b) demonstrates, some people exclude interfirm projects and focus on the idea that an ISA is "a particular mode of interorganizational relationship in which the partners make substantial investments in developing a long-term collaborative effort and common orientation" (Mattsson, 1994).

In ISA literature resource extension, capability capturing, mutual learning, sustainable development and value creation are identified as the main driving forces setting up alliances. Co-option, co-specialization, and learning and internalization are primary purposes of an alliance (Doz & Hamel, 1998). All of these imply that ISAs need a seriously strategic plan, long-term cultivation of the relationship, flexibility to meet changing environments, and learning and evolution within alliances.

ISA research currently focuses on the introduction of this emerging organization form, seeking to change managers' mind-set, style and strategic orientation. Issues of future, latent competence and collaborative "art" have been addressed, but the financial implications, emerging business opportunities, and, particularly, new technology development and its impacts have been largely ignored. This has stimulated research into virtual organizations (VOs).

Figure 1: (a) Evolution of networks (adapted from Hinterhuber & Levin, 1994) and (b) Different understandings about ISAs (adapted from Faulkner, 1995; Terpstra & Simonin, 1993)

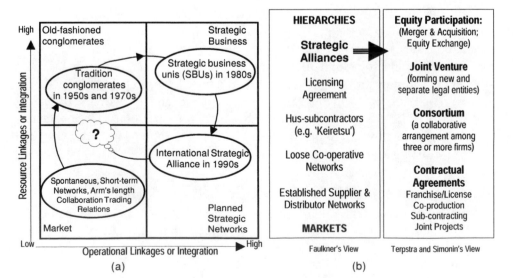

Why Do Virtual Companies Become So Attractive?

"Just as the strategic alliance has become the popular phase to describe the growing interorganization form of the 1990s, so does it seem probable that virtual corporation will fill that role in the first decade of the new millennium" (Faulkner, 1999). Why?

There are at least three main reasons making virtual enterprises or organizations more and more popular in the manufacturing industry. The first reason is market changes. More and more diversified and fragmented demands ask companies to provide more integrated solution-based service than category-based product. Many companies are being pulled out from traditional manufacturer and becoming system integrators. When these system integrators seek to cover more individualized demands and a wider as well as unpredictable scope of businesses to exploit their competence potential and market opportunity, they are surprised to find that their old assets and capacities have little to contribute to their new business and instead are becoming a burden. Except their recognized core competence, continuous waves of outsourcing have been observed in a very wide scope of industries to streamline manufacturing resources and operations and enhance internal efficiency and external effectiveness.

The second reason is partly a consequence of the first reason. Since some companies pursue integrated solutions to their customers and outsource non-core manufacturing business outside, it is emerging a group of companies that provide specialized manufacturing service as their core competence to fill the gap between system integrator and raw material providers. Although these manufacturing service providers maybe have a lower margin than system integrators, but they have a much stronger position to provide professional services to a wider scope of system integrators than the traditional style of internally vertical integration. This configuration change in supply chain marks not only new relationships between companies but also new capabilities of manufacturing systems.

The third reason lies in the substantial opportunities arising from new information and communication technologies (ICT). These opportunities are not only for smaller newcomers to access markets formerly the preserve of global corporations, but also for global corporations themselves to restructure. The transparency of the value chain allows companies to reposition themselves in the chain and dynamically collaborate with companies to optimize their business position. In such an environment, even a small company can operate a large amount of resource based on an alliance network (Hammond, 1996). It is worthy to notice the three reasons incubate an infrastructure in which virtual organizations or enterprises can be functioned to achieve currently more challenging missions–quick responsiveness, high value, consistent quality, global mobility, and sustainable growth.

What Could Be Virtual Organizations (VOs)?

There is no common shared definition of virtual organization. Different people with different experiences or different discipline backgrounds have different views about what a VO should be. A few years ago, virtual manufacturing was just a technological terminology representing virtual reality and its techniques used in the manufacturing engineering area (Banerjee, 1998). Most recently, however, virtual manufacturing has been extended into interfirm relationships to formulate a temporary supply chain (Miscioscia, 2001). Table 1 presents a spectrum of opinions on VOs from a theoretical perspective. This paper argues that a virtual organization can be recognized as a new and interorganizational dynamic network, which works as an integrated supply chain to meet customers' fast-shifting demands, supported by communication technology.

Many researchers have sought to characterize virtual organizations (e.g., Bultje & Wijk,1998; Goldman et al., 1995; Jagers et al., 1998). The following characteristics of VOs are widely accepted:

- A company seeking to form a virtual organization with other companies is basically opportunism-oriented and tries to make use of core competence and to share risk with its partners.
- A virtual organization is a dynamic clustering. It can be a single identity organization from the view of market, although it is made up of a group of independent companies.
- A virtual organization is geographically dispersed; globalization to access worldwide proper resources is its driving force and characteristic.
- A virtual organization may start from a short-term contract, and may or may not become a strategic alliance.
- Partnership reflects partial mission overlap and no hierarchy or formal structure. The boundary of the virtual organization is thus vague and fluid.
- A virtual organization is based on communication tools such as EDI, Internet and intranet, and some intelligent working tools: groupware, organizational memory system (OMS), etc.

Table 1: Different definitions and perspectives on virtual organizations

New or Old Phenomenon	**Old phenomenon** VO is the way of doing business in the form of information opposite to physical (Czerniawska and Potter, 1998).	**New phenomenon** VO is a new form of business in the time of the information era (e.g. Travica, 1997 and most researchers).
Personnel or Organization	**Personnel level** VO as a way of labour organizing or distant work system (Fritz and Manheim, 1998).	**Organization level** VO is an interorganizational network (e.g. Wassenaar, 1998).
Organization or Organizing	**Organization** VO is a new form of organisation (e.g. Loebbecke & Jelassi, 1996; Faulkner 1999).	**Organizing** VO is a strategy--virtual organizing or virtual business (Venkatraman and Henderson, 1998).
Stable or Dynamic	**Stable** VO is the collaboration of corporations with long-term characteristics (Arnold et al., 1995).	**Dynamic** VO is a temporary collaboration relation set up to achieve a task or project (Palmer and Speier, 1997).

- A virtual organization needs high trust between member corporations. To integrate the operation, shared loyalty and shared leadership are needed. The process of operation is also a process of distance teamwork and distance learning.

What Are the Global Manufacturing Networks (GMNs)?

Global manufacturing network research has its roots in production and operations management (POM) and manufacturing engineering (ME). Contrasting to the virtual organization focusing on inter-firm collaboration, the global manufacturing network (GMN) research seeks to extend traditional manufacturing system boundaries from the factory towards globally dispersed and coordinated factory networks, but still mainly limit within one multinational corporation (Ferdows, 1989, 1997; Flaherty, 1986, 1996; Shi & Gregory, 1997, 1998). In multinational corporations, strategic business unit (SBU) or product family based international manufacturing networks can have much stronger power to help companies compete globally, if companies can capture the benefits of a globally coordinated network. The weakness of this research, however, is its focus on single corporations or even smaller SBUs. Inter-firm collaboration is not addressed nor is the impact of emerging technology on manufacturing systems.

Table 2 reviews key characteristics of research on ISAs, VOs and GMNs, highlighting their differences. But, there are many similar characteristics between ISAs and VOs. For example, a longer-term virtual business network and a contractual collaboration can be a same relationship, such as some original equipment manufacturers (OEMs) with their manufacturing contract services (MCSs). If international strategic alliances can be recognized as a spectrum of collaboration, virtual organizations could be at the end of loose control and engaging with arm's-length collaboration, as demonstrated in Figure 1(b).

In summary, from the mainstreams of recent research work on manufacturing systems in Table 2, there appears to be little integrated and systematic research focusing on inter-firm collaboration in manufacturing, supply chain with value-adding orientation, and globalization of manufacturing networks, especially an integration of these three on an IT/cyber platform. The main gaps between industrial requirement and existing academic research are:

- Lack of integrated research on understanding an evolution of the complex system.
- Lack of shared frameworks to enable the accumulation of knowledge and concepts.
- Lack of multidisciplinary cooperation to tackle the virtual manufacturing network.
- Lack of knowledge transfer mechanisms from theory to practice.

CONCEPTUAL FRAMEWORK FOR GMVN

A research field cannot be built cumulatively until there is a framework and some accepted core of theoretical ideas (Teece et al., 1992). This section introduces some conceptual frameworks to position the global manufacturing virtual network in the spectrum of strategic alliances and analyze its new missions and attributes.

Positioning GMVN in a Larger Strategic Environment

A more generic, three-dimensional strategic environment for a manufacturing system design in the future can be represented as in Figure 2, in which four key decisions must be made to design and operate a manufacturing system (Shi & Briggs, 2000; Shi et al., 2001). The four key strategic options include propositioning manufacturing missions and tasks on three main dimensions–supply/demand chain or manufacturing value creation network, geographic development or internationalization process, and collaboration with other partnering companies–and synthesizing these three options into an integrated manufacturing system with a systematic strategy/design process.

According to preliminary understandings of industrial requirements and research on manufacturing, a global manufacturing virtual network (GMVN) could be considered as a synthesized unity with the four basic decisions in Figure 2.

- Value-creation-oriented manufacturing activities and positioning are represented by M on the value and supply chains dimension.
- Global disposition and manufacturing internationalization evolution process are represented by G on the manufacturing internationalization dimension.
- Collaborations with other companies to formulate a strategic alliance or temporary virtual supply-chain are represented by V on the strategic alliance dimension.
- The synthesis process among the above three dimensions is represented by N, including network strategy process, communication platform and operations mechanisms.

Figure 2: The building blocks of a global manufacturing virtual network

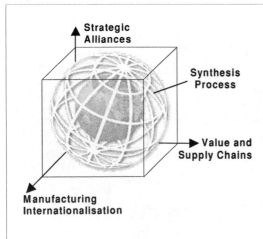

Key Building Blocks of Manufacturing System:
1. Value and Supply Chains – Re-proposition, configuration and optimisation of the chains to create more value and gain more competitive advantages
2. Manufacturing Internationalisation – Not only a geographic expansion or re-position but also system and cultural integration, and new coordination mechanism generation
3. Strategic Alliance – A spectrum of corporation collaboration including intra-firm coordination and inter-firm co-operation. Virtual manufacturing network focuses more on inter-firm co-operations from strategic alliance and dynamic project-based collaboration, to art-length trading relationship
4. Synthesis Process – Not only Cyber Platform and virtualisation infrastructure, but also a contingency roadmap and holistic strategy process for GMVN development

Strategic Alliances

Synthesis Process

Value and Supply Chains

Manufacturing Internationalisation

Table 2: Review of the characteristics of three types of collaborative organizations

Attributes	ISAs	VOs	GMNs
Missions and Purposes	- capability orientation - sustainability push - world and future driven - co-option (collaborating) - co-specialisation (Core) - learning & internalisation	- business opportunity orient. - responsiveness/agility pull - niche/emerging market driv. - scanning and identification - brokering and integration - networking and positioning	- opportunity and capability - coordination & learning - global expansion driven - geographic dispersion - value-adding chain - position - operations coordination

Structures (Architectures)	- seriously strategic planning
	- stable and close relationship
	- four basic forms of ISAs:
	  - contractual collaboration
	  - consortiums
	  - joint ventures
	  - equity collaboration
		- strategic fitness planning
		- order or project based temporary relationship
		- dynamic re-configuration
		- no equity collaboration
		- few stable partners
		- ICT platform and teamwork
			- SBU and Int'l Mfg strategy
			- Product family and globally dispersed factory network
			- owned by one company
			- each factory is a node
			- location and dispersion
			- integration and coordination

Operations (Dynamics)	- longer term co-operations - longer term commitment - sharing strategic resources - seeking synergy from co-op - learning and internalisation - "running-in" and cultivation - adaptation and evolution - int'l cultural synthesis	- temporary co-operations - shorter term business deal - strategic competence fitness - seeking function integration - sharpen core competences - fast engagement & work - responsiveness and flexible - cyber and global sourcing	- Dynamic Response Mechanism: opportunity identification and swift mobility - Product Life Cycle (PLC) and Knowledge sharing and transfer - Operational Mechanisms and ICT network daily co-ordination - Dynamic Capability Adaptation and Network Evolution: learning
Other Characteristics	Like a marriage for longer term commitment and harmony	Like a blind-date, or leisure sport teamwork for competition	Like a personal coordination and capability development

Figure 2 not only demonstrates a static architecture of the GMVN but also illustrates that most current research is still limited to two-dimensional constructions (Harland et al., 1999). The synthesis or integration process has also been largely neglected, which inhibits the development of comprehensive understanding about GMVNs.

As they involve manufacturing systems, GMVNs are not the same as general virtual organizations. The latter could be a pure broker subcontracting anything and everything. But manufacturers, especially global players, have to own some essential processes-based resources, such as technology, facility, equipment, capacity, and even organization. As future development is largely depend on resources, the GMVN mission must sit between that of ISAs and VOs. Therefore, the "virtual" character is very unique in GMVN.

GMVNs Are Emerging in Some Industry Sectors

One of obvious industry development trends is manufacturing outsourcing, driven by strategically focusing on core competences, pursuing higher value proposition in supply chain, radically improving return of assets investments, and providing total solutions to targeted customers. System integrators, original equipment manufacturers (OEMs) and major contractors are becoming a new battle-ground for manufacturing and attracting wide interests, which incubates supply chain management (SCM) like the hottest subject in the management area. But, another very important phenomenon caused by the system integrators' reconfiguration is usually neglected by the research community and is gradually becoming more and more important for the whole manufacturing industry. It is the emergence of professional manufacturing service providers complementing system integrators to integrate a supply chain, especially contract electronics manufacturers (CEMs) or electronic manufacturing service (EMS) providers in electronics and telecommunication industry sectors.

The emerging OEMs and CEMs are restructuring the electronics manufacturing industry. Most of traditional vertical-integrated companies, such as IBM, Motorola, Marconi, Philips, Sony, and Hitachi, are being reconfigured into OEMs focusing more on customer total solution and related R&D, new technology and marketing. Outsourced manufacturing in OEMs fosters a new group of contract electronics manufacturers (CEMs) radically taking care of a wider scope of manufacturing service to OEMs. These CEMs include some key global players like Solectron, Flextronics, Celestica, and SCI Systems, and more than 3,000 other local CEMs. CEMs or EMS providers start from maybe a relatively narrow scope of manufacturing services, such as printed-circuit boarder (PCB) assembly or manufacturing engineering development, but very aggressively get involved in the whole manufacturing chain and even beyond that, towards after-sales service. "EMS providers are working to offer a complete cradle-to-grave manufacturing solution" (Miscioscia, 2001). Nowadays, CEMs can promise to an OEM that "you bring us an idea, we'll manufacture the entire product and ship it directly to your customer" (Labowitz & White, 2001). The traditional relationship between vertical-integrated manufacturers, component suppliers and distributors has been largely broken, and a new network between OEMs, CEMs, component suppliers and distributors is emerging, however, with huge dynamics and complexity.

The EMS providers/CEMs are creating virtual enterprises led by OEMs. The total solution-oriented OEMs are subcontracting more manufacturing tasks to CEMS to gain both flexibility and concentration. In their competition, especially against the newcomers like Cisco and Dell without any manufacturing experiences and resources "burdens," sharpened strategic focuses, higher value creation and responsiveness through external system flexibility are so critical for the game that they cannot afford to keep comprehensive manufacturing resources waiting for potential customer orders. This scenario is exactly like the assumption made for the global manufacturing virtual network, in which a leading company cannot hold comprehensive manufacturing resources because of unpredictable market requirements and it has to depend upon a cooperated resource pool and organize a virtual supply chain to deliver a customer-required solution. In the electronics industry, OEMs and CEMs/EMS providers are actually functioning this competence pool in a specialized and collaborative way and formulating a new generation of manufacturing system–GMVN.

OEMs and CEMs play equally important roles in GMVNs, although CEMs are easily ignored when OEMs generally own more attractive brands and are closer to final consumers. CEMs/EMS providers also can create their strong brand names and even evolve them into an OEM. In a GMVN, each player in the network has similar opportunity to identify business opportunities and integrate the virtual network to deliver a solution to a certain customer. Because everyone has its own core competence in the network, everyone can function the chain. The virtual chain becomes very responsive, flexible and economic. This type of manufacturing system has fundamentally changed the concept of system flexibility and achieves real market agility and global mobility by externalizing flexibility and accessing to the most appropriated resources.

GMVNs: Static and Dynamic Views

If ISAs and VOs are set into a spectrum as Figure 3(a) shows, GMVNs can take quite a wide span in the spectrum. This is mainly because GMVNs should have combined features balancing the virtual organization's business opportunity capturing and the ISA's capability development. This might be a static view about the GMVN's architecture.

A dynamic view of GMVNs is more interesting; see Figure 3(b). It is like a pendulum dynamically moving between VOs and ISAs as well as OEMs and CEMs. It might start from a virtual organization or specialized manufacturing service provider–very vigorous and keen on opportunity hunting. As time goes on, some projects can be gradually "sunk," becoming a serious core business and generating compatible core competences. At this moment, the major company's concern is how to enhance the core competence through a more strategically oriented approach, for example, setting up an alliance network. As the core competences achieve further development, the company is more capable to exploit new market opportunities.

Figure 3: Different views on GMVNs

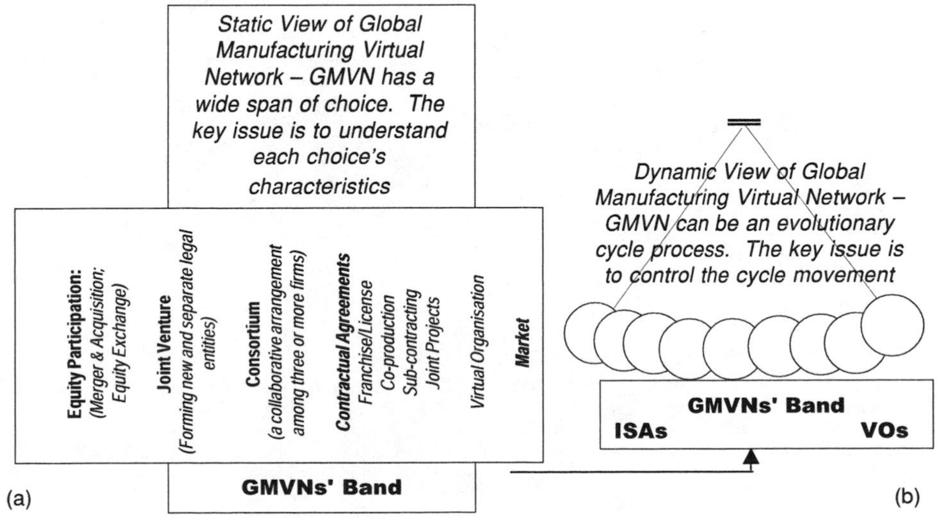

Exploitation of the core competences leads the GMVN to come back to develop its new competence as a new VO. This dynamic model may help managers adopt a more evolutionary vision and avoid competence traps.

LONG WAY TO GO

Although GMVNs have been observed in many industry sectors from electronics to automobile and even aerospace, fully understanding about the virtual networks and how to successfully design and operate them is still a long way off. It is specially important for academic and industrial people to work together.

From a research perspective, some detailed studies on a new GMVN system can include three main strands:
- The GMVN's environmental and industrial sectors, which will clarify the main driving forces for the GMVN emergence.
- The characteristics of the GMVN system, which covers the GMVN's attributes and strategy process for developing an effective GMVN.
- The key new technology identification to building and operating the GMVN, which consists of design techniques for the GMVN community and communication platform and infrastructures.

These three strands of the research can be demonstrated as three layers and six major research modules in Figure 4.

CONCLUSIONS

In the consideration of international strategic alliances and virtual organizations, little attention has been paid to networks devoted to manufacturing and the implication of communication technologies for their structure and operations.

Figure 4: A research framework for global manufacturing virtual network development

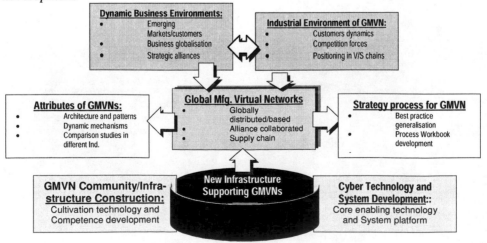

Understanding the nature of manufacturing system operating in the emerging global and electronic commercial and communication environment is fundamental to understanding the implications of e-business for manufacturing worldwide.

A specific class of manufacturing system–the global manufacturing virtual network–has been identified and its characteristics and potential outlined.

The potential of GMVNs to enhance a company's ability to dynamically generate and exploit competence is introduced.

Future work is proposed to better understand GMVNs at three levels–industrial sectors, corporate, and GMVN technology and infrastructures–and to develop more practical-oriented decision tools and strategy processes for GMVN formation and operations.

REFERENCES

Arnold, O., Faisst, W., Hartling, M., and Sieber, P. (1995). The virtual organization as the organization of the future. In *Handbuch de Modernen Datenverarbeitung*, *32*, 8-23.

Banerjee, P. (1998, July). Preface for the special issues of design and manufacturing on virtual manufacturing. *IIE Transactions*, 30(7).

Bultje, R. and van Wijk, J. (1998). Taxonomy of virtual organizations, based on definitions, characteristics and typology. *VoNet*–Newsletter 2, 2(3).

Czerniawska, F., and Potter, G. (1998). *Business in a Virtual World: Exploiting Information for Competitive Advantage*. Basingstoke, England: Macmillan Business.

Doz, Y. and Hamel, G. (1998). *Alliance Advantage: The Art of Creating Value Through Partnering*. Harvard Business School Press.

Faulkner, D. (1995). *International Strategic Alliances: Co-operating to Compete*. McGraw-Hill.

Faulkner, D. (1999). The virtual corporation: The organization of the future?. *Cambridge Research Symposium on International Manufacturing*, Cambridge University, England.

Ferdows, K. (1989). Mapping international factory networks. In K. Ferdows (Ed.), *Managing International Manufacturing*. Amsterdam: Elseview Science.

Ferdows, K. (1997). Making the most of foreign factories. *Harvard Business Review*, March-April.

Flaherty, M. T. (1986). Coordinating international manufacturing and technology. In Porter, M. E. (Ed.), *Competition in Global Industries*. Harvard Business School Press.

Flaherty, M. T. (1996). *Global Operations Management*. New York: McGraw-Hill.

Fritz, M. B., and Manheim M. L. (1998). Managing virtual work: A framework for managerial action. In *Organizational Virtualness, Proceedings of the first*

VoNet, Workshop, Bern, Switzerland.

Goldman, S. L., Nagel R. N. and Preiss, K. (1995). *Agile Competitors and Virtual Organisations: Strategies for Enriching the Customer*. New York, London: Van Nostrand Reinhold.

Hammond, R. (1996). *Digital Business: Surviving and Thriving in an On-line World*. London: Hodder and Stoughton.

Harland, C. M., Lamming, R. C. and Cousins, P. D. (1999). Developing the concept of supply strategy. *International Journal of Operations and Production Management*, 19(7), 650-673.

Hinterhuber and Levin. (1994). *Strategic network: The organization of the future. Long Range of Planning*, 27, 43-53.

Jägers, H., Jansen, W. and Steenbakkers, W. (1998). Characteristics of virtual organizations. In *Organizational Virtualness, Proceedings of the first VoNet*, Workshop, Bern.

Jain, S. C. (1987). Perspectives on international strategic alliances. In S. T. Cavusgi (Ed.), *Advances in International Marketing* (2nd ed.). JAI Press.

Loebbecke, C., and Jelassi, T. (1996). Building the "virtual organization" at Gerling. In Coelho et al. (Eds.), *Proceedings of the 4th European Conference on Information Systems* (pp. 1245-1258). Lisbon, Portugal.

Lu, Y. (1994). *International Strategic Alliances: A Review of Some Literature* (Working paper 1994-1995 No. 32). Judge Institute of Management Studies. Cambridge University.

Mattsson, L. G. (1994). *Interaction Strategies: A Network Approach*, Working Paper, 1988, Quoted from Faulkner, D. *Strategic Alliances*. London: McGraw-Hill.

Miscioscia, L. (2001). EMS evolution has given rise to true virtual OEMs, *EBN*, April 13th.

Murray, E. A., Jr., and Mahon, J. F. (1993). Strategic alliances: Gateway to the new Europe? *Long Range Planning*, 26(4), 102-111.

Murray, J. Y. (1995). Pattern in domestic vs. international strategic alliances: An investigation of US multinational firms. *Multinational Business Review*, Fall.

Nalebuff B. J. and Brandenburger, A. M. (1996). *Co-opetition*. London: HarperBusiness.

Palmer, J., and Speier, C. (1997). *A Typology of Virtual Organization: An Empirical Study*. Retrieved M D, Y from the World Wide Web: http://hsb.baylor.edu/ramsower/ais.ac.97/paper/palm_spe.htm.

Shi, Y. and Briggs, H. (2000). Global manufacturing strategy and network development. In IMNet and CIM (Eds.), *International and Strategic Network Development, The 5th Cambridge International Manufacturing Research Symposium*, Churchill College, September 3-5.

Shi, Y., Briggs, H. and Gregory, M. (2001). Global manufacturing strategy: Content, process, and challenges. In *Proceedings of EurOMA Annual Conference*, Bath, June 3-5.

Shi, Y. and Gregory, M. (1997). International manufacturing networks: New configurations, capabilities and strategic process. In *Proceedings of the Fourth International Conference on Manufacturing Technology,* Hong Kong.

Shi, Y. and Gregory, M. (1998). International manufacturing networks–To develop global competitive capabilities. *Journal of Operations Management*, 16, 195-214.

Sieber, P. and Griese, J. (Eds.). (1999). Organizational virtualness and electronic commerce. *Proceedings of the 2nd International VoNet-Workshop*, Zurich.

Teece, D. J., Pisano, G. and Shuen, A. (1992). *Dynamic Capabilities and Strategic Management.* Working Paper, University of California at Berkeley.

Terpstra, V. and Simonin, B. L. (1993). Strategic alliance in the triad: An exploratory study. *Journal of International Marketing*, 1(1), 4-25.

Travica, B. (1997). The design of the virtual oranization: A research model. In *Proceedings of the Americas Conference on Information System* (pp. 417-419). Indianapolis, IN: AIS.

Upton, D. M. and McAfee, A. (1996). The real virtual factory. *Harvard Business Review*, July-August.

Venkatraman, N. and Henderson, J. C. (1998). Real strategies for virtual organizing. *Sloan Management Review*, 40(1).

Wassenaar, A. et al. (1998). Lessons from managerial theories for improving virtualness in electronic business. In *Organizational Virtualness, Proceedings of the first VoNet–Workshop*.

Chapter XI

Networks of SMEs as Virtual Web Organizations: An Experimental Program Aimed at Supporting SMEs in Depressed Areas of Italy

Roberto Tononi
ENEA, Italy

Gianfrancesco Amorosi
ESCE, Italy

ENEA, the Italian public institution for research on energy, new technologies and environment, is conducting a program aimed at supporting networks of small-medium enterprises (SMEs) in depressed regions of Italy.

The program focuses on the experimentation of a business model for these networks and on the introduction of advanced tools and methods, mostly of concurrent engineering. The business model, developed within the program, has the basic features of a virtual Web organization.

This chapter illustrates the organizational and functional model that has been defined in the framework of a cooperation between ENEA and the SMEs involved in the research program.

INTRODUCTION

In 1998 the Italian Department of Research charged ENEA, one of the Italian major research institutions, with a program aimed at supporting **Small-Medium Enterprises (SMEs)** in depressed regions of Italy. The program is named "Techniques of Cooperative Engineering and Services Provided by Research Consortia to SMEs Through Computer Networks" and has been intended to introduce innovative technologies among those enterprises in order to get around the difficulties posed by the global market, but also to exploit the related opportunities.

Whereas initially the focus of the program was mainly on technologies, very soon it became apparent that some organizational engineering was to be considered, if only to ensure an effective utilization of innovative, but often sophisticated, tools. That turned out to be mandatory when the target of the program shifted from single SMEs to networks of SMEs, in the effort to match a widespread trend of small enterprises and to gain some economy of scale in the utilization of the program results.

Networking is especially sought by small enterprises when they start facing the intrusion of outsider competitors that, often proposing wider product concepts or cutting very low on cost, threaten the traditional client-supplier relationship based mainly on trust. Such contingencies warn about the arrival of the global market, towards which small enterprises find themselves with an inherent lack of resources. A network provides an SME with a chance for offsetting this lack of resources with those of other enterprises, all of which provide specialized and also complementary contributions. Through networking, SMEs can cover all the phases of the product/service life cycle, thereby meeting a widespread requirement in the global market and still focusing on their own core business, i.e., what they are able to do the best, and that turns to the advantage of everyone; in other words, regardless the initial reasons for which it is pursued, networking of SMEs has its own objective merits.

However, if a network has to retain the appreciated features of a typical SME, such as high flexibility, entrepreneurial creativity, high productivity of its employees, low level of internal conflicts, benevolent acceptance by the local community and more, high levels of independence and autonomy, strictly tied to those features, are to be granted to the enterprises that join the network. Hence the classic problem to be faced is well-illustrated by the metaphor of the "orchestra made up of soloists."

The recognition of this problem has strongly influenced the whole strategy of the research program, which has then included the development of an organizational and functional model, specific for networks of SMEs in the perspective of endowing them with tools more powerful than those normally owned by single SMEs and more appropriate to take the challenge of wider and more differentiated markets.

The adopted research method has been that of building, first, a self-consistent framework of criteria and operational procedures, without lingering over details, and of moving, then, to a phase of in-field experimentation with SMEs that are seeking an appropriate form of aggregation, in order to check the soundness of the basic framework and to fill it with proposed solutions for all those detail problems set aside in the first part of the research.

The program is still in progress and well inside the experimentation phase; though not all the facets of the model are consolidated, the whole picture is already available and will be illustrated in the next sections of the chapter.

When compared to other approaches proposed by other researchers and practitioners, the model can be classified as a **virtual Web organization** (Franke 1999), in that it foresees a loose aggregation of SMEs ready to be called to the formation of **virtual corporations** to exploit market opportunities; it also foresees that the management of the virtual Web organization (VWO) be entrusted to a net-broker, a member enterprise which also coordinates the activities of the procurements gained by the network.

The purpose of the chapter is that of illustrating the preliminary result of the research program as a practical example and a case study in which the process of solving the various problems of SME networks has led to the definition of a model that, although developed without making explicit reference to theoretical approaches, has ended up meeting the basic criteria of the VWO concept. This VWO model described in the next sections is just the main result of the experimentation with the SMEs involved in the program and summarizes their proposed solutions for the problems faced by networks of SMEs, as well as practical procedures suggested to cope with the many operational obstacles.

PROBLEMS FACED BY NETWORKS OF SMEs

As soon as the program moved to targeting networks of SMEs, it was recognized that the potential members were confronted with a set of problems, such as in the following.

(1) How to join the network, on the base of reciprocal engagements, and yet maintain one's own independence and autonomy.
(2) How to find the right partners.
(3) How to develop trust in the relationships among partners.
(4) How to get access to endowments of tools that exploit the synergies inherent in a network and increase the opportunities for the member SMEs to conquer wider markets.
(5) Who should coordinate the activities of the network and how.
(6) How to establish a unique interface with the market, meeting a common requirement of procurers that don't want to deal with a multitude of suppliers in a single procurement.
(7) How to gain, for the whole network, an image of dependability in the market.

It was apparent that, though the emphasis of the program was on information technology (IT) tools, these did not grant, on their own, the solutions to the above problems; on the contrary, the large latitudes offered by these tools might act to understate some of the same problems. For instance, the pervasiveness of computer networks might suggest, to more than one researcher, that finding the right partners as no problem in that it could be performed "on the fly," whenever necessary: It would suffice to have a "software agent" navigate the Internet in search of an enterprise that met preestablished criteria. However, a deeper analysis would show that a partner so acquired wouldn't grant the solution of Problem (3). As a matter of fact, trust, to develop, needs time; and time is allowed only if the search for a partner is initiated before it becomes strictly necessary; but this anticipated search may only be undertaken by someone who is in charge of the strategic long-term planning of the network.

Another problem, which can be biased by the dynamic character of IT, is that of coordination; many, especially within the information community, deal loosely with this problem (Camarinha-Mathos & Lima, 1999) and propose to leave the coordination function, in different projects of the network, to different members chosen on the base of various criteria, such as choosing the member that takes the procurement to the network. However, the coordination of networks of SMEs, of that orchestra of soloists, is a very challenging function that would better be entrusted to a member enterprise that has developed the right skills–not readily available in whatever SME has the recognized power to apply the network rules, which it may have contributed to establish–and is always the same in the various projects to prevent confusion among the activated members.

Not always addressed is Problem (7): When an SME network does not base its survival on a relevant main procurer, the problem of gaining an image of dependability is much keener than that faced by monolithic enterprises, in particular, if the network is dynamic. Even though the network resorts to a brand, the market knows that, behind that brand, different enterprises operate, from time to time; in addition, the idea that many different and independent subjects are activated to provide the final product or service may alienate skeptical procurers. Hence the suggestion that SME networks resort to explicit recognitions by third parties about the quality of their organization, such as with ISO 9000 qualification, even without requiring it for each of the member companies.

THE MODEL PROPOSED TO NETWORKS OF SMES

The business model developed within the program has been the result of a screening and development process, performed along with the SMEs involved in the research, of a concept framework proposed by ENEA in the first part of the program.

The basic design criteria of the model are the following:

(1) The levels of autonomy and independence of the member enterprises are to be taken as high as feasible, consistent with the operational needs of the network.

(2) Any single member enterprise is viewed as an autonomous production center: The network asks for a provision of product/service but does not get into the internal processes of the member.

(3) Each member is a featured component for the network, i.e., the member behavior can be anticipated by the network.

(4) The network is a featured entity for the members, i.e., the network activities are conducted according to a set of rules that are accepted by the members when they join the network.

(5) The network is an (intangible) asset owned by all members that must have full control of it through a democratic decision-making process.

(6) Minimum investments in productive tools are required by SMEs which join the network.

The implications of these criteria will be clear in the model illustration that comes next.

Organizational Architecture

As a consequence of Criterion (1), the organizational architecture foreseen for the network is without hierarchy, compliant to the hub-and-spoke schema of Figure 1, in which the featuring of members is provided as a typical example of the manufacturing industry.

All the members are at the same hierarchical level, but for all that concerns the network, refer to a hub which includes two special members: the technical service center and the net-broker. This hub with two members, as opposed to just one, is the result of the verification process of the preliminary conceptual framework (Tononi & Maturano, 1999). As a matter of fact, the initial framework foresaw only one member as the hub; but when the research came up with the functions to be assigned

Figure 1: VWO architecture in ENEA model

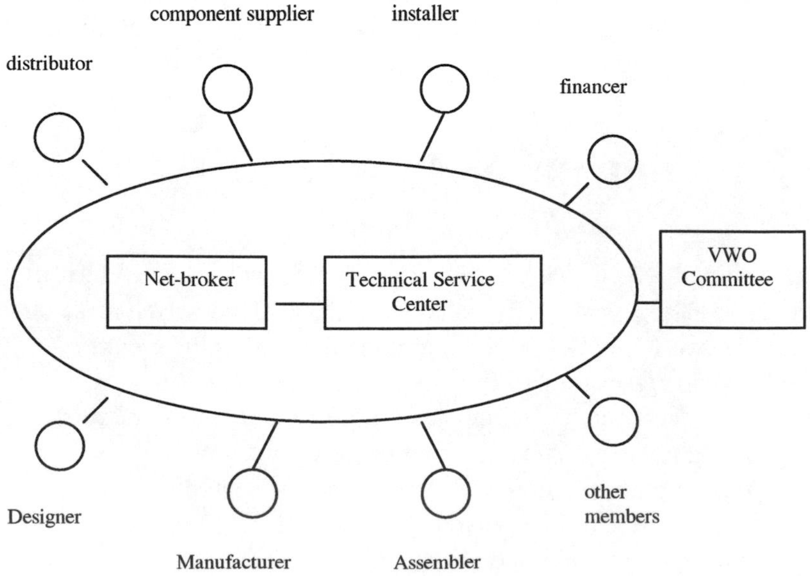

to the hub, it was clear that two were the subjects playing for the game: one devoted to technical matters and the other in charge of organization and management issues.

Ideally, the kinds of members joined into the network should allow the coverage of all the phases of the life cycle of the product/service which embodies the core business of the network; in other words, vertical integration is sought in the network constitution. However, since the network should take the member SMEs towards wider markets, a large reservoir of production capacity should be accumulated joining members of the same kinds; i.e., also horizontal integration should be pursued.

With both vertical and horizontal integration, the network is viewed as a pool of resources, ready to be utilized in order to exploit market opportunities. As already stated, according to some definitions (Franke 1999), this kind of network could be classified as a "virtual Web organization." However, market opportunities do not come on their own; some members in the network should strive to locate and catch them. This requires that there be at least a member at work for the network even when no procurement is in progress; a consequent implication is that the VWO is a stable entity, alive also without current procurements. Stability, to this extent, does not prevent the VWO from being also dynamic: its members, on the whole, will change over time, according to the changes of the market and of the VWO objectives and strategies. In addition, when a market opportunity is caught, the appropriate members will be teamed in order to implement the related product/service provision; on the whole, different members will be activated in the various procurements, depending on the nature of the market opportunity and on the level of the activities already in progress within the VWO. According to some definitions (Franke 1999), the members teamed over a procurement make what can be called a "virtual corporation."

In order to meet the criterion of autonomy, the members are engaged with the VWO only for a fraction of their productive capacity and are allowed to conduct their own business without limitations, even with other VWOs; the partial engagement of each member is also advantageous to the VWO, in that it grants an operational margin to resort to in case of member defaults which may require some other members to increase their contributions beyond what has been already agreed upon.

Network Constitution and Member Behavior

The network set-up process begins when enterprises agree on a set of rules that discipline their mutual relationships and their behavior as to the activities to be performed within the network.

The rules defined in the ENEA experimental program concern the technical service center, net-broker, VWO committee and the other non-special members; this section only illustrates the rules concerning these last ones.

The set of rules each member will be subjected to is included in the contractual agreement between member and network (represented by the net-broker), which the member legal representative formally underwrites at the time of joining the network. The rules apply, on the one hand, to what the member is to provide to the VWO and, on the other hand, to what the member has to expect from the VWO.

What the member is bound to provide is included in an attachment to the contractual agreement called "Registry of Provision" (from the Italian "Anagrafica di Produzione"), which states:

a)   the types of product/service and the related quantities in terms of ranges between minimum and maximum quantity levels;
b)   the maximum lead time granted by the member for each type of provision;
c)   the quality levels granted for each type of provision;
d)   the maximum costs that will be charged to the network for each type of provision.

The Registry of Provision shows the approach of pre-packaging the provision expected by each VWO member in order to meet basic design Criterion (3). This pre-packaging is sought because the VWO has to react quickly to a request for a tender, at least as quickly as a monolithic enterprise can. With the pre-packaging, a provision plan can be concocted automatically with an appropriate software application and without any time-consuming negotiation among members. Whereas the pre-packaging is considered the normal approach to requests for tenders, outstanding opportunities, e.g., those with strategic implications, may be tackled with the more reasoned process that is provided by the **quality function deployment approach** (Akao, 1990). The pre-packaging does not decrease the flexibility of the VWO, in that the terms stated in the Registry of Provision can be renegotiated when it is deemed appropriate either by the member or by the VWO. However, this renegotiation can not occur when a request for supply is already in progress; otherwise, the purpose of the pre-packaging would be vanished.

One limitation of this approach, which has very soon been experienced, is that it tends to favor the internal optimizations of the members and their dependability, whereas it actually limits the optimization range of tenders of the whole VWO; this trade-off is dictated by the need of ensuring an acceptable level of reliability of the VWO operation, which, otherwise, can turn out to be an Achilles heel of the network of independent SMEs. In practice, each member is viewed as a production center, which is asked for predefined services; in addition, each member organizes and manages autonomously its internal operation in order to meet the VWO requests. IT practitioners would recognize here a similarity with the object-oriented approach to software development (Callan, 1994).

Based on the pre-packaging, a provision plan can quickly be developed with procedures proposed by other research projects (Bonfatti et al., 1996).

Members which violate their commitments with the VWO are penalized in terms of downgrading of their levels of involvement in future procurements; other members, which make up for these "failures," are upgraded if they wish so. Both downgrading and upgrading are identified by the net-broker and submitted to the VWO Committee for approval.

In the contractual agreement, the VWO commits to meet the Registry of Provision of each member; however, for the contingencies already mentioned, such as market opportunities of strategic importance or member defaults, the net-broker may ask all or some members to contribute with an outstanding effort beyond the commitments of the Registry of Provision. In case of defaults, negotiations take place between the net-broker and interested members; on its judgment, the net-broker may take the issue of unsatisfactory result of such negotiations to the forum of the VWO committee. In case of opportunities of strategic importance, the net-broker coordinates a meeting of the VWO committee for the application of the Quality Function Deployment.

Of paramount importance is the issue of risk. In the model of ENEA, the reference criterion is that of sharing risk among network participants for accidents not attributable to member negligence. However, whenever this is not the case, faulty members have to pay for the damages caused to other ones.

In the former cases, the risk share of each member, now viewed in the context of the virtual corporation, is equal to its share of the whole cost of the procurement for which a virtual corporation has been set up.

In the latter cases, the amounts to be paid for by faulty members are determined by the net-broker (in the shoes of the virtual corporation manager) that is in charge of the cost control function; those members may appeal to the VWO committee forum to settle disputes. That also applies when the actual production cost of the virtual corporation turns out to be higher than that foreseen in the tender related to the procurement: The virtual corporation manager is in the position to track the member activities and to understand that the increased costs of some members are due to the defaults of other ones, which will be held responsible for the cost increase.

Another very important issue is that of network financing. In addition to financing the operation of the member enterprises, there are two other needs that call for attention. One is due to the risk, faced by each member, that can be perceived at a higher level than that related to the operation outside the network; as a matter of fact, in the virtual corporation, the uncertainties originate not only from the market, but also from the other members' behavior. Although an enterprise accepts this higher risk because of the greater opportunities that the network can offer, it would like to avail of a financial reservoir to decrease the impact of accidents. The other need is that of financing the net-broker activities that are steadily performed beyond the existence of current procurements (see also the section "Net-broker Functions"). As a matter of fact, one of the major functions of the net-broker is that of bringing procurements to the network; this member is, then, at work also when all the other ones are inactive towards the VWO. The model foresees that the members finance the operational expenses of the net-broker, somewhat as a traditional enterprise pays for its management. However, the net-broker returns the financing when paid for its services in occasion of the proceeds from the network procurements.

All these needs require that one of the members be a financial or a banking institution; the involvement of such a subject appears more likely to occur when the VWO has a territorial, regional value and a local institution may decide to join for reasons other than that of pure economic advantage.

Net-Broker Functions

The previous section shows many instances of structured relationships between members and VWO, such as in the negotiation which goes on when a new member joins, or between members and the virtual corporation, like in the definition of a provision plan, or among members, as when defining a network tender with the Quality Function Deployment. All these instances imply an obvious need for a specific member to play the role of the coordinator; the same need arises when the VWO faces potential procurers.

The net-broker is just the member enterprise assigned by the model to meet that need. The following are its basic functions.

(1) Strategic long-term planning. As for monolithic enterprises, a VWO won't go very far without someone devoted to watching the market trends of interest and to defining which markets to target in future time beyond the current activities, which positions to hold in those markets, and which resources to acquire in order for the network to keep those positions. To these purposes, the network needs a member fully devoted to the VWO operation, as opposed to all other members, which may also be engaged in activities other than those of the VWO. In addition, the very nature of its function implies that this member be also active when the network isn't engaged in any production activities, striving for the ultimate result of having procurements assigned to the network. This context shows the net-broker as the strategic marketing planner of the VWO. However, its directions are assumed just as proposals to be submitted to the VWO committee approval. It is up to the net-broker to identify new resources needed for the VWO, in terms both of new SMEs to bring in and of new tools to be acquired. In the former case, the net-broker contributes to solve Problems (2) and (3) previously stated; in that, as the long-term planner, it will anticipate the need of getting new members and will propose them to the VWO for approval, with a time allowance that will favor the development of relationships of trust. In the latter case, the net-broker will identify operational needs that the technical service center will better define as technological tools.

(2) VWO interface with the market. Both public and private procurers want to deal with only one contractor able to supply complete products and services; as a consequence, only one member had better represent the network with the procurers and hide the set of complex relationships among members. That implies, from a legal point of view, the Net-broker is the proxy, towards the market, of the member SMEs joined in the network.

(3) Virtual corporation manager. Whereas the virtual Web organization requires the accomplishment of the long-term planning function, each virtual corporation, established to meet the specifications of a procurement, needs the coordination of the activities related to the procurement, which includes the medium-term planning, i.e., the definition of the network provision plan. The model foresees that the coordination, which is the function of the virtual corporation manager, be also assigned to the net-broker, so that the networked

SMEs always refer to the same member. Hence the net-broker enterprise should include a pool of project managers, each of which will take charge of a procurement. As the virtual corporation manager, the net-broker has the full decision power of a project manager.

(4)　VWO proxy with member SMEs. As already stated, an SME which wants to join the VWO has to go through a negotiation process that ends with a contractual agreement, countersigned by the SME legal representative and by the Net-broker as the VWO proxy. This function of the Net-broker is also accomplished whenever a member faces problems with the VWO (or, more often, with the virtual corporation) in the effort to provide for an accepted solution and so to keep from calling for the VWO committee intervention.

(5)　Implementation of the directives of the VWO committee. Within this function the Net-broker acts with the full power provided by the VWO committee.

Technical Service Center (TSC)

The need for having a member devoted to provide technical services to the SMEs grouped in the network is somewhat similar to that encountered in monolithic enterprises.

However, in the VWO there are a number of specific problems that the technical service center helps solve.

To start with, the TSC allows for a solution of Problem (4) whereas meeting the Criterion (6). As a matter of fact, although it is essential that the SMEs gathered into the network endow themselves with more advanced tools to cooperate effectively and efficiently, it would be very difficult to make entrepreneurs invest in tools that they should share with other enterprises. The solution proposed in the model is that of having one of the members acquire and own all the tools that make up the VWO endowment. On first sight, that appears as a loop around the problem because there is a member, the TSC, which takes on itself all the load of the tool endowment; however, this load is to be viewed as an investment for the TSC that, in the VWO operation, will distribute the utilization of its tools, as a service, to the other members, which, in turn, will pay for this service and so contribute to pay back the tools. Yet one more problem to be solved relates to what kind of enterprise is suitable to play the role of the TSC. The solution proposed by ENEA model is that of the research consortia. These are aggregations of both SMEs and research institutions that, by their very nature, yearn for endowing themselves with advanced tools but need to make a business out of these tools. In addition, these consortia have personnel with high technical skills, so they appear as the natural candidates to the TSC role. The ENEA experimental program has involved four research consortia.

The following is a typical sample of the basic services expected by a TSC.

- Administration of the Cooperative Information System (CIS) of the VWO.
- Provision of **concurrent engineering** (CE) tools to the members.
- Communication network management.
- VWO system quality management.

The provision of concurrent engineering tools originates from the need to join into the network SMEs devoted to different phases of the product life-cycle, i.e., members with differing cultures, languages and approaches to problem solving; in other words, members for which the problem of cooperation and coordination requires some special attention.

Concurrent engineering (Biren, 1996) is proposed as an alternative to the traditional "serial" approach of tackling the phases of the product life-cycle one after the other and which provides an orderly arrangement of the activities to be performed; but the serial approach is prone to highlight problems of the product development process only in its last phases. This feature is a serious inconvenience since, very often, whole phases already completed are to be reprocessed in order to solve the highlighted problems. The concurrent engineering approach implies that the various phases be processed, to some extent, at the same time and that, much more important, the operators, devoted to different phases, cooperate in the development of each phase. The result is that problems are much easier to highlight in the initial phases of the development process, so their solutions are less costly, in terms both of money and time. However, that is much easier said than done because there are inherent difficulties in making operators of different phases dialogue and cooperate with each other. The concurrent engineering tools are just developed with the purpose to create the conditions that spur and ease the above cooperation. A typical CE example is provided by a tool of simulation of a manufacturing facility: When the designer and the manufacturer watch together the virtual implementation of the manufacturing of what has been produced by the designer, they are much more likely to exchange opinions and comments on how to improve either the design or the manufacturing process than if meeting only on abstract concepts.

From the above, it follows that CE tools enable reduction of the time-to-market and the cost of product quality; however, they have a further added value of paramount importance for virtual Web organizations. As a matter of fact, since they ease the cooperation of operators of different phases, as long as these operators are differing members in a VWO, CE tools contribute to lightening the problem of coordination, and this is the reason why they have been chosen as the basic tool endowment of the VWO in ENEA model.

Usually, the high potentials of CE tools go with their cost; in addition, they often imply good technical skills in their operators, hence, the decision to place them as tools to be owned and managed by the TSC, which distributes their utilization to the VWO members.

Many CE tools are available on the market but usually need some refitting to be adapted to the specific use in a network of SMEs; other CE tools, spotted as the facilitators of the core activities of SME networks in particular domains, are not available and need to be developed. Both the refitting and the development are up to the TSC.

Most of the financial resources of the ENEA program are devoted to the development of new, advanced CE tools, believed to take high potentials to networks of SMEs, according to the basic objective of the program.

With regard to system quality management, the TSC builds up the framework of practices and procedures to be followed by the VWO as a whole (Tononi et al., 2000).

In particular, the TSC develops the "Quality Manual" for the VWO, consistent with ISO 10013, and submits it for the approval of the VWO Committee.

The TSC is also in charge of developing the "quality implementation plans" over the whole life cycle of the product/service provided by the virtual corporation, as well as the appropriate "process capability plans."

Likewise, these plans are subjected to the VWO committee approval; following this approval, the TSC supervises their implementations reports to the VWO committee over violations of these plans and proposes corrective actions.

The basic objective of the above system quality management is that of endowing the VWO with ISO 9000 certification, even without requiring that all members be certified; however, the experience gathered within the ENEA program, has shown that this condition can hardly be met, especially if the network deals with public procurements.

The VWO Committee

The VWO committee is equivalent to the board of directors of a real enterprise. It is the forum where all VWO members gather in order to make decisions on issues that have an impact over the future of the VWO. All members must comply with the decisions of the VWO committee.

Basic decisions are to be made on the proposals of the Net-broker and of the TSC. The following is a sample of the major occurrences that require the VWO committee approval:

- Issue of the long-term plan by the net-broker.
- Undertaking of new initiatives by the net-broker, aimed at entering new markets and/or at acquiring new resources for the VWO.
- New SMEs joining the VWO.
- Issue of the Quality Manual and of the quality implementation plan by the TSC.

The adoption of a multiuser videoconferencing tool in the ENEA program has proved to be very useful for the VWO committee meetings.

The committee is expected to meet regularly and to provide a constant control on the operation of the Net-broker; on the other hand, the experience gathered in the ENEA program has shown, with one of the involved SMEs networks, that the committee can become an effective supporter of the net-broker through the activation of a permanent subset of committee members who act as counselors of the net-broker.

THE EXPERIENCE GATHERED WITH THE SMEs INVOLVED IN THE PROGRAM

The VWO model is being experimented within some networks of SMEs in the following application domains:

- Construction, maintenance and restructuring of buildings.
- Production of components for scooters.

- Shipbuilding.
- Production of high-style glass fixtures.

Not all the experimentations in the different domains have the same extent. For instance, in the domain of high-style glass fixtures (the famous glasses of Murano), the program aims at testing the introduction of the above-mentioned design for environment tool since one of the worst problems faced by the glass manufacturers of Murano is the environmental impact on the lagoon of Venice. Likewise, in the shipbuilding domain, the experimentation focuses on the application of concurrent engineering tools, such as the DFMA. Though limited in scope, these experimentations have proved of great utility for tuning the tools to the actual needs of the SMEs that are the target users.

The whole VWO model is being tested with two SME groups in building construction and in the production of components for scooters. The main result of the work already done is the VWO model itself, as presented in this chapter, since the related development process has been conducted along with the SMEs and many of its features are the answers to problems highlighted by the same SMEs.

Many resources have been devoted to information and training activities about tools and methods to be introduced in a virtual Web organization. The experience has shown that these preliminary phases of education are essential since the backgrounds of the various SMEs are often very diverse and, in addition, the various seminars are excellent chances for "developing the sense of network," without which no common project can be successfully implemented.

The program is now in the phase of testing the operational performance of the VWO model in the actual implementation of a procurement. Unexpectedly, a major stumbling block has proved to be the collection of the right data for the Registry of Provision of each SME. As a matter of fact, many SMEs find it difficult to provide all the quantitative information featuring their business, such as, the actual range of their production capacity; on the contrary, some entrepreneur boasts her/his ability to deal with the unexpected. Of course, the problem has been solved but has taken much a longer time than planned.

The lesson learned is that it is illusory to build up out of the blue, a network of SMEs with the features of an industrial modern organization, starting with components, i.e., the potential members, whose working styles are too much of artisans. It is essential, at least when working with SMEs in depressed regions, to have a period of education and information about what is the necessary behavior in a VWO.

Another difficulty which is being faced is that of finding enterprises appropriate to play the role of Net-broker. The solution of creating the net-broker enterprise as a joint venture among member companies is considered to be appropriate and is being tested in one VWO. In another instance, a research consortium is covering both the roles of TSC and of Net-broker; however, this solution is not considered appropriate and its limits are expected to be highlighted over time.

The final results of the whole experimental program are foreseen for the end of 2001.

About future developments, two further projects are expected to be launched in 2001 as applications of the ENEA VWO model: one in the health care sector (Marturano et al., 1998) and the other in an integration between tourism and marketing of typical Italian food (Aronica et al., 2000).

CONCLUSIONS

As already stated the organizational and operational model described in the previous sections includes the indications collected by four networks of SMEs participating in the ENEA experimental program of which the model represents the core result.

Since the program is still ongoing, model changes may be expected in the future, as it's been in the past, especially in the TSC role, for which the involved research consortia keep coming up with new proposals.

Here is a summary of how the problems stated in a previous section are dealt with by the model:

- Problem (1), through a set of preestablished rules that take care of the autonomy of the members.
- Problem (2), through the activity of the net-broker dedicated to the search for the appropriate new members.
- Problem (3), through the timely proposals of new members by the net-broker.
- Problem (4), through the access to precious tools allowed to the members by the TSC.
- Problem (5), through the coordination function of the net-broker.
- Problem (6), through the net-broker function of interface with the market.
- Problem (7), through the ISO 9000 qualification sought by the network of SMEs.

One of the lessons learnt with the program is that, despite the Web usage, SMEs still prefer to network with others of the same geographical area; however, it is not a matter of geography but of culture and of sharing the same problems, such as the market trend for the suppliers of motor-scooter components or the environmental problems of the glass producers of Murano.

Initiatives designed by the local associations or authorities to solve shared problems, have proven to be very good enablers for VWOs of SMEs, as has been the case in the two just mentioned groups of SMEs.

However what has plagued the research program has been the very long time that has taken the creation and the operational start up of the involved networks of SMEs. Within the program, analyses are being conducted to identify which aspects of the model are responsible for this lack of dynamism.

REFERENCES

Akao, Y. (1990). *QFD: Integrating Customer Requirements into Product Design.* Cambridge: Productivity Press.

Aronica, O., Rossi, L., and Tononi, R. (2000). *L'Impresa Virtuale nel ciclo di vita dei Prodotti Tipici: Sinergie tra turismo e tradizione alimentare del territorio, per sfruttare le opportunità del mercato globale.* Paper presented at the International Conference "Sviluppo Economico e Sostenibilità: il Turismo Ambientale e Culturale occasione di nuova occupazione," Anacapri, Italy.

Biren, P. (1996). *Concurrent Engineering Fundamentals.* Upper Saddle River, NJ: Prentice Hall PTR.

Bonfatti, F., Monari, P. D. and Montanari, R. (1996). *Information Flows and Processes in an SME Network.* (Working paper *PLENT* (Planning Small-Medium Enterprise Network) ESPRIT Program Project 20723). Modena, Italy.

Callan, R. E. (1994). *Building Object-oriented Systems.* Boston: Computational Mechanics.

Camarinha-Matos, L. M., and Lima, C. P. (1999). *Coordination and configuration requirements in a virtual enterprise.* Paper presented at The Working Conference on Infrastructures for Virtual Enterprises *(PRO-VE'99)*, Porto, Portugal.

Franke, U. J. (1999). The virtual Web as a new entrepreneurial approach to network organizations. *Entrepreneurship & Regional Development, 11,* 203-229.

Maturano, N., Tononi, R. and Rondinone, A. (1998). *La Sanità come "Impresa Virtuale."* Paper presented at the 10th National Conference on Health Information, Taranto, Italy.

Tononi, R., Amorosi, G. and Federici, G. (2000). *SMEs, research consortia and concurrent engineering–The basic ingredients of the virtual enterprise being experimented by ENEA in southern Italy.* Paper presented at the 6th International Conference on Concurrent Enterprising–ICE 2000. Tolouse, France.

Tononi, R. and Maturano, N. (1999). *A virtual enterprise model as proposed within project ICIV aimed at supporting networked SMEs.* Paper presented at the Working Conference on Infrastructures for Virtual Enterprises -PRO-VE'99, Porto, Portugal.

Chapter XII

Applying a Core Competence Approach in Virtual Enterprise Formation

Carlos Frederico Bremer, Jairo Eduardo Moraes Siqueira and
Luis Fernando Moraes Marques
University of São Paulo, Brazil

The process of core competencies identification has been incorporated by the enterprises within strategic planning. The virtual enterprise, which is a form of cooperation between enterprises, is one of the most benefited with this new process, mainly in its formation stage. The identified core competencies, which are deployed in products, process and technology, may support a more agile gathering of the virtual enterprise partners. This chapter presents a method to identify core competencies, supported by a practical case of successful virtual enterprise formation, where the method was applied and validated.

INTRODUCTION

In recent years, many articles have been written describing an innovative way of organizing enterprises with the objective to exploit business opportunities in a cooperative manner: the virtual enterprises. Many definitions and approaches of virtual enterprise can be found; however, the following characteristics are common in most of the articles:
- Enterprise cooperation
- Distributed control and coordination
- Use of information technology
- Gathering of core competencies

While the three prime characteristics are well known, the latter still lacks concrete definition. Therefore, if the objective in a virtual enterprise is the gathering of core competencies from different enterprises, then it is necessary to know in advance all their existing competencies. However, if the enterprises barely know each other or even do not know at all, there is a prior necessity to expose such competencies to each other.

In fact, a nonexistence of a stable definition about what are competencies and mainly a standard format to represent them is perceived, and can be searched and gathered through other enterprises. The concept of competence is still steady in a strategic level, strongly surrounded by vagueness. Javidan (1998) also states that literature on core competencies does not provide an organizational process for identifying core competence. All steps that an enterprise should take in order to use core competencies effectively are rarely mentioned by the researchers.

The gathering of core competencies is a requirement to achieve an agile virtual enterprise formation, but it is not standardized yet. Therefore, a critical area can be identified as spoiling the success of the virtual enterprise organizational model.

This chapter describes a model to be applied in virtual enterprise formation based on core competencies. It also describes practical results obtained within a virtual organization, a stable network in which the primary aim, according to its established processes, is to facilitate virtual enterprise formation by gathering small and medium enterprises that are already members of a virtual industry cluster.

A method to support virtual enterprise formation is also presented, describing steps to identify potential constituent skills as an explicit representation of core competencies. To validate the method it follows an example of application. Primarily, the process of VE formation is described.

VIRTUAL ENTERPRISE FORMATION

VEs are mainly based on the integration of competencies among independent enterprises providing a product or a service (Sieber, 1997). The proposal of forming VEs shows by itself an advantage because of their capability of quick market response in a saturation environment, changing the manufacturing profile for a customer-focused standard instead of a producer one (Reithofer & Näger, 1997).

Analyzing the context of small and medium enterprises (SMEs), many small high-technology enterprises failed due to the lack of technical as well as management competencies. In general, virtual enterprises (VEs) and their form of organization based on cooperation can be assumed as adequate to fulfil these deficiencies and support the formation of high-technology-based enterprises (Eversheim et al., 1996a).

Few models in the literature represent an adequate virtual enterprise formation process, which is considered just through the abstract view. When practical steps to implement this process are described by models, the responsible entities to perform related tasks are not considered with enough level of detail. Therefore, the model adopted in this chapter is the COSME model because it encompasses different entities responsible through an integrated virtual enterprise formation process.

COSME Model

The framework for Cooperation of Small and Medium Enterprise (COSME) was developed to explain how a global virtual enterprise (GVE) is formed, run and dissolved (Bremer et al., 1999). The GVE can exploit the advantages of being global using local competencies.

This framework (Figure 1) is constituted of three business entities: the virtual enterprise (VE), the virtual industry cluster (VIC) and the virtual enterprise broker (VEB). The VEs are temporary networks of independent enterprises linked by information technology that share competencies, infrastructure and business processes, with the purpose of fulfilling a specific market requirement (Byrne, 1993).

According the COSME model, VEs are formed within virtual organizations (VOs), which are made up of two entities: the potential partners–enterprise members of a virtual industry cluster–and the virtual enterprise broker. Networks are stable or dynamic cooperations whose one aim is the exploitation of market opportunities; therefore, VEs and VOs are candidates to perform an efficient role in the global market.

A VE is formed within a VO. The VIC is an aggregation of enterprises from diverse industries, with well-defined and focused competencies, with the purpose of gaining access to new markets and business opportunities by leveraging their resources. VIC members are elegized by a previous selection among regular enterprises from diverse industries defined commonly as a cluster. A cluster is a group of enterprises located in a determined region with extraordinary success in a specific industry segment (Porter, 1998). However, in the COSME model, this entity is called the virtual industry cluster. It is virtual because of the possibility to be expandable to other enterprises from different clusters. The VEB enables the creation of VEs through the use of services provided by the VICs.

In the framework the VE is created when an opportunity for business can be exploited by the VEB, through the selection of the appropriate competencies from members of a VIC. A VEB will look for business opportunities around the world or will receive requests for specific products/services. In order to satisfy this demand, the VEB will search for partners in VICs for the best combination of competencies that, as a whole, will meet the customer requirements for a product or service. The success of the VE depends on the VEB's abilities to ensure the integration of competencies and the cooperation among partners. Moreover, the VEB has to configure the adequate infrastructures (physical, information, legal and social/cultural) to support the operation/dissolution of the VE. Once a member of a VIC is selected, it becomes a partner of the VE, according to the framework.

It is not necessary that a member of the VIC or the VE partner contribute with a technical, shop floor or design competence. Business competencies, such as

Figure 1: COSME model (adapted from Bremer et al. (1999)

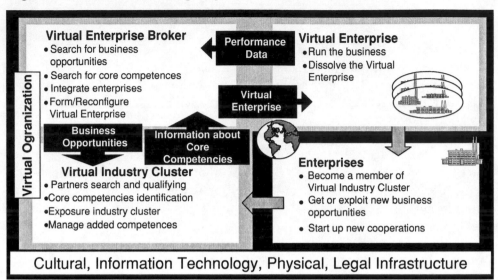

exportation/importation, and infrastructural competencies, such as videoconferencing expertise, are important as well as those mentioned above. In addition to this, the VEB has not necessarily to search for the required competencies only within one VIC, but within other VICs. This denotes, again, flexibility and quick response capability, primary issues for virtual enterprising.

It is important to highlight that the COSME model proposes a profit increase to its members by means of resources, processes and knowledge (skills) leveraging and not by imposing on them the direction to be followed.

Another interesting issue to be considered is that not all the VO or VIC members will join into a VE. Only the necessary competencies will take part in it, and the profit–or losses–distribution will not be equally divided, but they must follow the individual commitment and investment of each partner, in direction to the several interests involved, like profit gain, marketing, knowledge improvement and development.

Now that the process of VE formation has been described, the next section will present a rough conceiving of core competence.

CORE COMPETENCE CONCEIVING

Regarding competencies the literature proposes two strong streamlines: the inherent and incorporated competencies of personnel as individuals based on Nonaka and Takeuchi's work (1995), and the core competence approach covering the strategic level, sustained by Hamel and Prahalad (1990).

Since Hamel and Prahalad (1990) issued an article whose title is "The Core Competence of the Corporation," claiming that the strategic planning process in organizations should be started in an inside-out perspective, many models of viewing competence were published in the last decade by different authors. Based on core competence, whose definition according to Hamel and Prahalad (1990) is "the collective learning in the organization, especially how to coordinate diverse production skills and integrate multiple streams of technologies," the organization has a very important tool to guide business and face external threats and improve internal flexibility.

Terhaag et al. (1996) define core competence as a competence which makes a substantial contribution to the uniqueness of the enterprise and may be developed in two different manners. The first approach is to define strategically important tasks, which guarantee the success or continued existence of the enterprise. The second approach is to analyze the special skills and potentials of the enterprise and then, in a creative process, determine and define promising future tasks.

From the Model for Transforming, Identifying and Optimizing Core Processes (MOTION) Project (Terhaag et. al., 1996) core competence can be characterized following some set criteria, in which it must:
- give potential access to a broad spectrum of markets
- contribute substantially to the advantages of the end product as perceived by the customers
- be difficult for competitors to imitate

Although core competence and its attributes can be defined, it is difficult for managers to include competence-based thinking in their managerial activities (Drejer & Riis, 1999).

A core competence can not be confused with ordinary enterprise capabilities. While capabilities act in the operational level aiming at short-term outputs that do not ensure enterprise development and survival, the core competencies–if correctly constrained to the strategic commitment–may bring success to the enterprise. However, core competence management is very complex (Prahalad, 1998). A major problem is the coherent association between core competence and the ordinary competencies to create new business opportunities

Hamel and Heene (1994) proposed a core competence classification according to strategic streamline in three distinct levels: core meta-competence, core competence and constituent skills. Following that classification Molina and Bremer (1997) deployed the three levels (see Figure 2).
- *Core meta-competence*: is in the highest abstraction level of competence. It contains emotional appeals, which are normally known in an organization. Such level of competence is tightly inserted in customer requirement perception.
- *Core competence*: is constituent-skill aggregation output. This level is a link between core meta-competence and constituent skills. It may not necessarily generate customer requirement perception; however, it can lead the organization to the competitive advantage by internal gains.
- *Constituent skills*: are the basic capabilities that form organization competencies. The product, process and technologies are considered constituent skills.

Figure 2: Core competence model adapted from Molina and Bremer (1997)

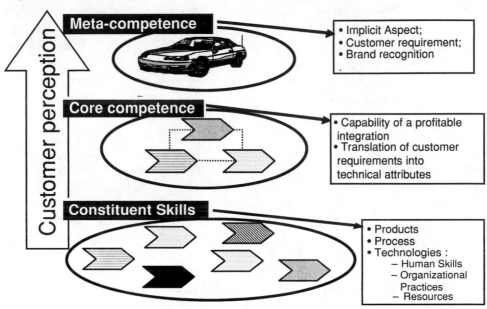

The first two levels of the classification, core meta-competence and core competence, have a high degree of abstraction, and they can not be used to identify what or for what an organization may contribute in a virtual enterprise.

Constituent Skills

The level of constituent skills is the best contributor to the competence's trade-off, due to its role as competence bricks. This level can be used in VE formation because its characteristic are explicitly represented in product, process and technologies.

The constituent skills are classified in:

- *Product*: A product is considered a process output. The adequate representation chosen in this work for product was defined by Eversheim et al. (1996b). The dimensions of a product are the products as a whole and their modules, components and elements.

- *Business process*: is considered a phenomenon that occurs within the enterprises. It contains a set of activities associated with information management, enterprise resources consumption and organizational structure utilization. Business process is a cohesive unit and must be focused on business, generally guided to a specific market/customer and with well-defined suppliers (Rozenfeld, 1996).

- *Technology*: can be defined as "a set of knowledge that is applied in a specific activity" (Ferreira, 1975). Terhaag et al.(1996) deployed technology in three types:

- *Human skills*: involve personal skills to accomplish technical and management tasks and the ability to manipulate various sets of tools.
- *Organizational practices*: represent practices and methods used by the organization or the enterprise in order to execute its projects and process.
- *Resources*: are the equipment used by the enterprise. It includes machines, computers, facilities, etc.

Now that core competence conceiving has been explained, the method developed to identify potential constituent skills, which are primarily used as the brick of core competence, will be presented in summary due to its large volume.

METHOD OF POTENTIAL CONSTITUENT SKILLS IDENTIFICATION

Core competencies are formed by constituent skills in which representation is realized through product, business process and technology. Core competencies are the results of a history of experiences accumulated during application of process and technology in a profitable manner; on the contrary, constituent skills do not represent strategic risk to the enterprises being exposed and offered in the market.

The chief objective of this method is to establish a process to identify core competencies by gathering constituent skills and to provide the appropriate support to the competence match, the next step of virtual enterprise formation. Each type of constituent skill has a specific method developed to assess the regular enterprise before the formation of the virtual enterprise. Due to the wide range of aspects considered in this method, this chapter will just describe the more relevant ones in the analysis of the results.

The method developed for assessing product as a potential constituent skill is divided into three interrelated parts. To cover the enterprise's inside view, its portfolio is identified by product definition and manufacturing typology. The next part collects data from a market perspective of each product, mainly concerning market share and growth. The first two parts are made up of open questions simply elaborated to scan product and its transforming process in detail. To identify product competitiveness, part three uses weight factors to evaluate alternatives of pre-elaborated questions. In this case, the questions were elaborated strictly focusing on dynamic aspects of the product, such as flexibility and innovation, which are critical factors of virtual enterprise success.

Spreadsheets are used to calculate the multiplication of the collected weight factors by product figures considered from different criteria, e.g., Boston Consulting Group (BCG) approach, and percentiles. Analyzing all outputs collectively, a product can be identified as a potential constituent skill.

The assessment of the business process is in accordance with driven criteria with two different perspectives: external (market perspective) and internal (inside view), each of which has qualitative as well as quantitative components. The business processes are chosen from a list of all possible business processes by the respondent, and for each business process analyzed, a weight factor regarding a particular criterion is given. After considering both external and internal perspectives, the final figures are calculated. If the final value represents more than the final average output, the business process can be considered as a potential constituent skill (Figure 3).

As mentioned in the constituent skill description, technology can be classified in three different aspects. Although technology also contains an abstract aspect to be considered, such as human skills, this method encompasses just the assessment of physical resources, e.g., machining equipment, and organizational practices. In order to measure technology evolution, the regular enterprise needs to have the status quo (physical resources and practices) and its respective criticality assessed, and in combination with the assessment of the industrial segment technology average the tool (spreadsheet calculator) can identify technologies as potential constituent skills. The final result is depicted in a spiderweb chart to facilitate visualization and comprehension. Indeed, all the technologies assessed will have at least a null value; therefore, some criteria are required to refine potential constituent skill identification. It can be seen in Figure 4 where a circle was drawn excluding technologies with value less than 4.

The method can identify only core competencies regarding the strategic streamline. The individual knowledge of the employees is not considered, although it is very important to consider in strategic planning.

To validate the method, a project of a Brazilian virtual organization was developed. The next section describes historic and practical results.

Figure 3: Assessment of processes as potential constituent skills

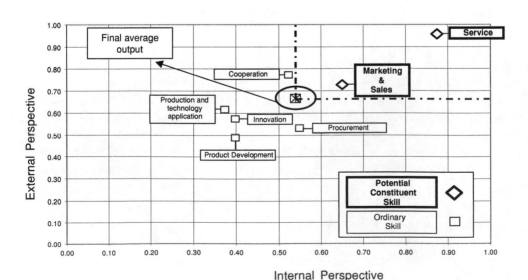

Figure 4: Assessment of technologies as potential constituent skills

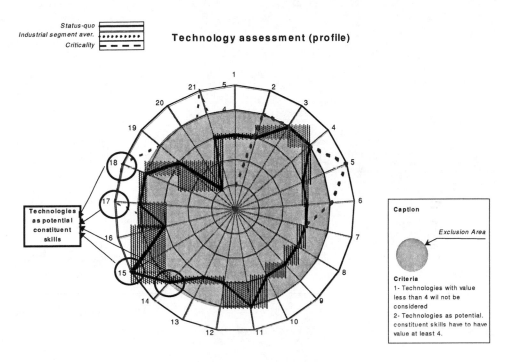

PRACTICAL RESULTS

All methods were developed while researchers catalyzed the first Brazilian virtual organization among small and medium enterprises to become virtual enterprise formation feasible. The research project (scientifically performed using action research method) and a tool for competence matching are described in the next section.

VIRTEC Project Description

The Virtual Organization Technology (VIRTEC) project started up at NUMA–Nucleus of Advanced Manufacturing (Núcleo de Manufatura Avançada), which is located inside the Engineering School of the São Carlos campus, University of São Paulo–as the pioneer project of the first Brazilian VO.

The city of São Carlos has a very particular characteristic within the Brazilian academic environment due to the two technical universities (University of São Paulo and Federal University of São Carlos) and one agricultural research institute (EMBRAPA) recognized for their level of excellence in teaching and research. This characteristic allowed the creation of a wide range of high-technology small and medium enterprises.

The selected members act in different industry segments, promoting products with completely different features of each other. See the profile of the members in Table 1.

Table 1: Profile of the VO members

OV Members	Products	Number of Employees
A	Recycled material	3
B	Special alloy casting	32
C	Automation	123
D	Special polymeric material development	34
E	Hydraulic devices	20
F	Assembly and maintenance process	70
G	Machines and mechatronics	29
H	Measure systems and software	31
I	Dentistry equipment and special furnace	40

Due to the participation of members from different industry segments, instability within the new VO occurred during the beginning of the project. In order to attenuate possible harmful effects in the trust consolidation process, interventions were necessary by the researchers. The interventions–allowed procedure in actionresearch method–obtained a high degree of success as the VO members were incorporating cooperative concepts.

After application of the methods of potential constituent skill identification in members of the VIC, VE formation needs to proceed rapidly in order to exploit any new business opportunities. Whereas at the first moment, cooperation had been supported mainly by an intensification of trust among members, a detailed map of core competencies was built to enhance running performance. The core competence map was obtained combining potential constituent skills and was in accordance with the opinions of the all VIC members.

A tool was designed to display core competencies from all VIC members. It was called a matrix of competencies.

Matrix of Competencies Tool

The importance of the perception of processes and technology as competencies lies on the fact that it ensures the necessary flexibility the VEs require. Moreover, once the members have the capability of realizing their technology and business processes as competencies that can be integrated, products with a high level of differentiation may be conceived and developed, as a result of competencies sharing.

Within the COSME model, the search for new products has a complementary sense, in order to act as enabler of further VEs, which may create or attend business opportunities. A problem in conceiving and developing products is to provide clear and accessible basic information concerning the members' competencies. The importance of this is giving a sense of "what can I do" and "what should I be able to do" within the VO (Terhaag et al., 1996).

In the specific case of VIRTEC, there are enterprises of different industry segments, which to a certain degree may act as a barrier of communication. Therefore, the key issue was finding out the potential cooperation that could be performed, by means of combining the competencies, and sharing ideas.

Primarily, an obstacle is how to put the idea on paper and make it clear for all the members. In the VIRTEC case, the adopted solution was a matrix of competencies (Figure 5). This matrix is a 9x9 one, where in the rows and columns are listed the VIRTEC enterprises and the identified core competencies.

By means of interviews with the industry members, performed individually and in meetings, the potential new products that could be developed and produced by VIRTEC were mapped. All the possibilities of cooperation were considered, involving the three levels of competence (product, business process and technology). After that, each industry member received a copy of the fulfilled matrix to refine the already achieved results. Another copy of the matrix was left with the specialists of NUMA as "free blackboard" to collect opinions and allow the detection of failures in the conception and feasibility of the new products.

As a result of such intensive work, several new products were conceived from the matrix of competencies.

It is important to notice that the matrix acts as a tool which enables VIRTEC enterprises a better understanding of how to set up a VE with different competencies. However, if the number of enterprises increases, the visualization of the competencies as a whole also becomes increasingly worse. Nor does the matrix represent an information system, which specifically deals with and matches competencies.

Figure 5: Matrix of competencies tool

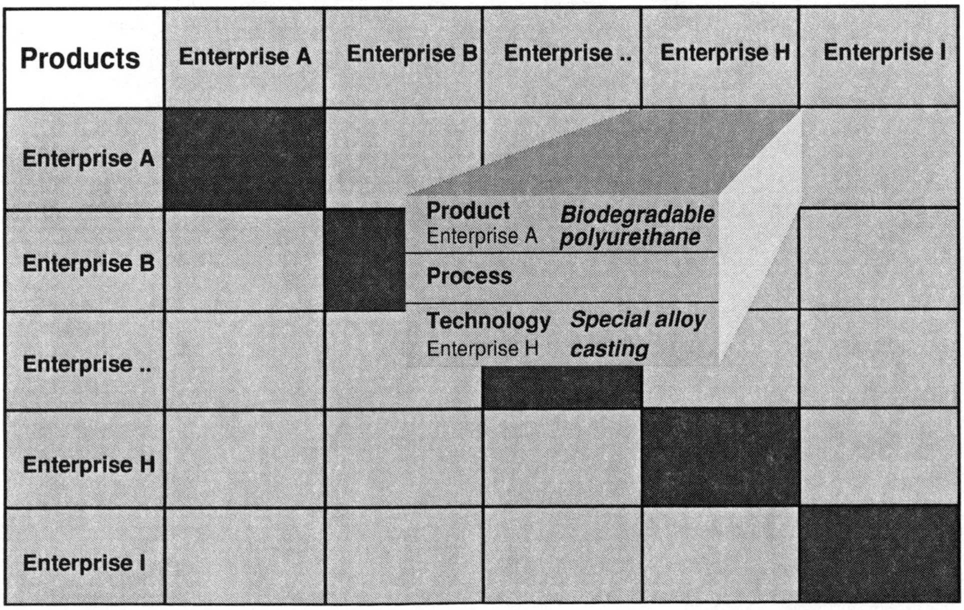

Products	Enterprise A	Enterprise B	Enterprise ..	Enterprise H	Enterprise I
Enterprise A					
Enterprise B			Product Biodegradable Enterprise A polyurethane Process		
Enterprise ..			Technology Special alloy Enterprise H casting		
Enterprise H					
Enterprise I					

Aiming to store data of core competencies, an Internet-based system was implemented in VIRTEC named VISHOF–Virtual Shop Floor (Eversheim et al., 1996a). It was conceived to provide information about the availability of shop floor resources within VIRTEC.

Through VISHOF, the members of VIRTEC provide mutual assistance by selling nonused hours of their shop floor resources, like milling, grinding, and lather. This system can retrieve core competence information of the VIC members and support competence matching; therefore, it may increase the odds of successful product conceptions in the most potential business opportunities.

After discussions based on a combination of specifications extracted from the matrix of competencies, two products were identified as potential business opportunities.

Products Derived From the Matrix of Competencies

- The recyclable polyurethane hammer: One of the VIRTEC members (Enterprise D) has competence on polymeric rubbers and foams, specifically on biodegradable ones. As a result of several years of self-sponsored research, a type of vegetal polyurethane rubber was developed. This rubber has several applications, like in mechanical assembling, finishing of goods, medical diagnosis, and so forth. Because of the characteristics of this material, it is possible to obtain several degrees of rigidity for the rubber, depending on the use. Considering this potential, the enterprise tried to develop a hammer (Figure 6) totally made of vegetal polyurethane rubber. However, the associated costs of the production of the handle and its non-satisfactory life cycle were determinant in searching for new solutions. Enterprise A looked for help within VIRTEC–where it found Enterprise B, a make-to-order producer of pieces in special stainless steel alloys–in order to develop a cheap, lightweight and recyclable handle for the hammer. As a result of this cooperation, the developed handle is cheaper and lighter and has a longer life cycle. Today, this hammer is being sold to the European Community and the United States.
- The rubber damper for a clothing dryer: Another member of VIRTEC, Enterprise F, was searching for an efficient type of damper to be used on the electrical motor's shaft of a new clothing dryer. The problem was that Enterprise F wanted a customized solution for its problem, and there was no solution in the market able to fulfil the requirements. Via VIRTEC, as a consequence of sharing ideas and knowledge, Enterprise F and Enterprise D joined in order to develop a new damper made of vegetal polyurethane rubber. However, there was a lack of knowledge on vibration absorption, a primary issue to develop the damper. To solve this, a specialist from the Department of Mechanical Engineering of the Engineering School of São Carlos was contacted. The damper is on its testing/approval phase.

Figure 6: Successful hammer manufacturered by a VE

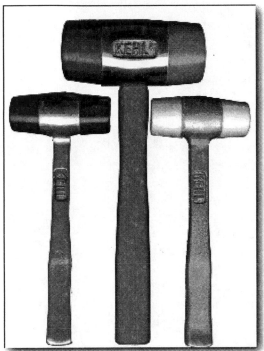

TOWARDS VE FORMATION: BENEFITS AND ISSUES OF THE METHOD

According to definition, a virtual enterprise is a network of enterprises willing to exploit business opportunities by means of cooperation as long as each partner contributes with a specific core competence. To handle core competencies matters adequately would require from the scientific community a set of identification processes to ground managers in their strategic actions. However, a major difficulty to achieve this is the lack of consistent methods with practical relevance. Thus, the method presented in this chapter fits that gap, focusing on identification of core competencies with a normative representation supported by practical cases of business exploitation.

An important aspect to consider is how such a method could help virtual enterprise formation. The method is a way to identify core competencies of the enterprises that are candidates to enter in the virtual industry cluster. Showing the best they can do, the broker entity can choose more rapidly the partners to form the virtual enterprise in order to exploit new businesses. Time reducing of the virtual enterprise formation and configuration and efficiency improvement of the business exploitation, so that it may achieve outcomes in a shorter time span, are benefits that the method may help bring about.

Concerning practical aspects of the VIRTEC project it was possible to point out critical success factors for this method. Some of the critical success factors are listed below:

- Rapid application together with available enterprise information
- Correct explanation of the concept adopted by this method to the respondents
- Participation of key persons from the assessed organization
- When possible the participation of clients and suppliers to validate results
- Desirable knowledge from the respondents regarding the industry segment (trends, innovation degree, market, etc)
- Desirable knowledge from the respondents regarding the enterprise (products, process and technology)

On the other hand, some issues related to the method were identified during its conception and application.

Although the virtual enterprise is a competitive way to exploit business, such a form of cooperation is not much employed by the enterprises to a large extent. Despite the successful cases found in the VIRTEC project, virtual enterprises could be formed more frequently to help in the method validation. Regarding core competencies there is a difficulty in establishing a clear boundary between them and the capabilities of the enterprise. Another issue concerning the method application is the high dependency on the supposed accurate degree of knowledge from the respondents.

CONCLUSION

The identification of potential constituent skills for core competence definition and its consequent use may bring competitive advantage to the virtual enterprise formation process. The method can identify core competencies which belong to the enterprise partners in the virtual enterprise and in this manner gain flexibility and agility to be used in business opportunities. Not only a virtual enterprise is able to obtain gains from this method, but a traditional enterprise can use it in more elaborated strategic planning by being more familiar with its formation. An efficient combination of the potential constituent skills identified by the proposed method may outline core competencies in a VE member.

In order to complement those methods, a matrix of competencies was practically developed to support decision making in product conception process as an early stage of virtual enterprise formation. Indeed, in VIRTEC the use of a matrix of competencies as well as the VISHOF system database facilitated virtual enterprise formation, resulting in eight successful products.

As the matrix of competencies contains core competencies combinations, it makes partially possible the gathering of core competencies.

The method presented in this chapter can be considered an innovative attempt to identify core competence; however, it requires improvement. For this, the method needs to be validated through more practical cases. The criteria used by the method require improvement to attend more effectively a wide range of aspects with reference to product, process and technology.

The formation process is another topic of research that continues to be studied due to a considerable lack of consistent knowledge.

REFERENCES

Bremer, C., Walz, M., Molina, A., and Eversheim, W. (1999). Global virtual business: A systematic approach for exploiting business opportunities in dynamic markets. *International Journal of Agilé Manufacturing*, 2, 1.

Byrne, J. A. (1993, February). The virtual corporation. *Business Week*, 98-103.

Drejer, A. and Riis, J. O. (1999). Competence development and technology: How learning and technology can be meaningfully integrated. *Technovation*, 19, 631-644.

Eversheim, W., Bremer, C. F. and Kampmeyer, J. (1996a). Requirements for virtual enterprise management in developing countries. *International Conference on Engineering and Technology Management*, 84-88. Vancouver, Managing Virtual Enterprises.

Eversheim, W., Graessler, R., Kölscheid, A. and Schulten, I. (1996b). Information management within a concurrent engineering environment. *Report WZL RWTH-Aachen*.

Ferreira, A. B. H. (1975). Dicionário da Língua Portuguesa. Ed. Campus.

Hamel, G. and Heene, A. (1994).*Competence Based Competition*. Chichester, England: John Wiley & Sons.

Hamel, G., and Prahalad, C. K. (1990). The core competence of the corporation. *Harvard Business Review*, May-June, 79-91.

Javidan, M. (1998). Core competence: What does it mean in practice? *Long Range Planning*, 31(1), 60-71.

Molina, A. G. and Bremer, C. F. (1997). *Information Model to Represent the Core Competencies of Virtual Industry Clusters*. Final Report Rheinisch-Westfäliche Technische Hochschule - Werkzeugmaschinenlabor.

Nonaka, I. and Takeuchi, H. (1995). *The Knowledge-Creating Company:How Japanese Companies Create the Dynamics of Innovation*. Oxford, England: Oxford University Press.

Porter, M. E. (1998). Clusters and the new economics of competition. *Harvard Business Review*, November-December.

Prahalad, C. K. (1998). Managing discontinuities: The emerging challenges. *Research-Technology Management*, May-June, 41(3).

Prahalad, C. K. and Hamel, G. (1994). *Competing for the Future*. Boston: Harvard Business School Press.

Reithöfer, W., & Näger, G. (1997). Bottom-up planning approaches in enterprise modeling–The need and the state of the art. *Computers in Industry*, 33, 223-235.

Rozenfeld, H. (1996). Reflexões sobre a manufatura integrada por computador. workshop manufatura classe mundial. *Mitos & Realidade*, 25-38.

Sieber, P. (1997). Virtuelle unternehmen: Eine zusammenfassung. *Workshop Virtualität als Wettbewerbsfaktor*, Universität Bern.

Terhaag, O., Dresse, S., Kölscheid, W. and Nieder, A. (1996). *Model for Transforming, Identifying and Optimizing Core Processes (MOTION)*. Rheinisch-Westfäliche Technische Hochschule–Werkzeugmaschinenlabor, Final Report.

Chapter XIII

Managing Dynamic Virtual Enterprises Using FIPA Agents

Vaggelis Ouzounis
Electronic Commerce Center of Competence
GMD-FOKUS, Germany

Virtual enterprises (VEs) enable the deployment of distributed business processes among different partners in order to shorten development and manufacturing cycles, reduce time to market and operational costs, increase customer satisfaction, and operate on global scale and reach. Dynamic virtual enterprises are an emerging category of VE where the different partners are being selected dynamically during business process execution based on market-driven criteria and negotiation. In this chapter, we present an agent-based platform for the management of dynamic VEs. The main contributions of this approach are the distributed, autonomous agent-based business process management, the XML-based business process definition language, the flexible ontologies, and the dynamic negotiation and selection of partners based on virtual marketplaces. The presented platform has been fully developed using emerging agent and Internet standards like FIPA, MASIF, and XML.

INTRODUCTION

In a global marketplace, companies are continuously seeking for new ways to address competitive pressure. Recognizing the need to shorten development and manufacturing cycles, reduce time to market and operational costs, increase customer satisfaction, operate on global scale and reach, and adapt rapidly to new market changes has historically led companies to automation, collaboration and distribution (Applegate, Holsapple, Kalakota, Radermacher & Whinston, 1996; Malone & Rockhart, 1991; Ouzounis & Tschammer, 2001a). As a result, the information systems in many of today's mid- to large-size companies reflect tremendous diversity.

The original goals for virtual enterprise business systems were to enable deployment of distributed business processes among different partners, to increase the efficiency of existing provided services, to decrease the cost for these services, and to adapt to new market changes (Stricker, Kradolfer & Taylor, 2000). As companies introduced electronic business systems, they started to see new possibilities enabled by those systems. By more closely coordinating the work of suppliers and manufacturers, businesses see dramatic productivity and efficiency increases in manufacturing processes. As communication barriers and costs drop, businesses are able to engage in many more kinds of relationships. These new relationships open additional possibilities for distribution and supply partners, for participation in virtual trading communities or dynamic virtual organizations, and for extending classic value chains to value networks (Doz & Hamel 1998).

Virtual enterprises are not a new concept in management studies (Camarinha-Matos & Afsarmanesh 1999; Ouzounis & Tschammer, 1999). Some of the big manufacturing companies, and especially car manufacturers, already have business relationships with their suppliers and customers. These "virtual" business relationships enable the sharing of business processes and resources among them. However, the level of integration and the information and communication technologies (ICT) used for enabling virtual enterprise concepts is varying. Most of the activities are still performed manually, adhoc, and in a complex way, while the cost to implement and integrate these solutions and the time required to deploy them are high (Lin, 1996; Reichert, Hensinger & Dadam, 1998).

The paradigm of virtual enterprise represents a prominent area of research and technological development for today's progressive industries. The research area is a growing and multidisciplinary one that still lacks a precise definition of the concepts and an agreement on the used terminology (Bolcer & Kaiser, 1999; Camarinha-Matos & Afsarmanesh, 1999). So far, there is no unified definition for this paradigm and a number of terms are even competing in the literature while referring to different aspects and scopes of virtual enterprise (Filos & Ouzounis, 2000). For instance, the NIIP project defines that "a VE is temporary consortium or alliance of companies formed to share costs and skills and exploit fast-changing market opportunities" (NIIP 1996). Byrne says that "a VE is a temporary network of independent companies–suppliers, customers, even rivals–linked by information technology to share costs, skills, and access to one another's hierarchy."

The wide variety of different networked organizations and the emergence of new production and provisioning paradigms have led to the generation of a number of related terms such as the extended enterprise, virtual organization, networked organization, supply chain management, or cluster of enterprises (Ouzounis &

Tschammer, 2001b). Some authors use some of these terms indistinctly to denote virtual enterprises although there are differences between their detailed meanings.

In the context of this chapter the following definition is adopted (Ouzounis, 1998a; Ouzounis & Tschammer, 1999): "a VE is a network of different administrative business domains that cooperate by sharing business processes and resources to provide a value-added service to the customer. Each partner of the virtual enterprise will contribute primarily what it regards as its core competencies, i.e., business processes and resources. There is a time limit on the existence of the virtual enterprise caused by fulfillment of its business purpose. From the viewpoint of an external observer, i.e., a customer, the virtual enterprise appears as a unitary enterprise."

In this chapter we present an agent-based platform for the management of dynamic virtual enterprises using FIPA agents. More specifically, section two analyses and compares the two main categories of virtual enterprises, namely, the static and dynamic VEs. Section three presents a comprehensive state of the art of the proposed technologies in the area of VEs. This analysis includes the comparison of Electronic Document Interchange (EDI), distributed component-based systems (DCBS), workflow management systems (WFMS), messaging systems (MS), intelligent mobile agents (IMA), and virtual marketplaces and negotiation (VMP). Section four introduces the overall framework and specifies the main entities of the proposed management platform and the key administrative domains while section five specifies the reference architecture of the proposed architecture and the key components. Furthermore, section six analyses and specifies the key virtual marketplace services, while section seven discusses issues concerning the business process specification. Finally, section eight describes the business process management issues concerning the management platform, section nine discusses the implementation and validation of the concept and the proposed system, and section ten outlines the set of conclusions drawn and the future plans for the continuation and improvement of the platform.

DYNAMIC VIRTUAL ENTERPRISES

Based on the above common features that VEs have, two well-defined categories can been identified (Georgakopoulos, 1998; Gibon, Clavier & Loison, 1999), namely, the static virtual enterprises (SVEs) and the dynamic virtual enterprises (DVEs).

In static virtual enterprises a set of business partners is linked together in a static and fixed way, i.e., the shared business processes are tightly integrated. The business relationships among the partners, i.e., the process interfaces, are predefined, tightly coupled, fixed, and well integrated and customized among the partners. The number of the network is fixed and predetermined and thus the structure of the VE is static and predetermined.

In dynamic virtual enterprises a set of business partners is linked dynamically, on demand, and according to the requirements of the customers by deploying a virtual marketplace (Wognum, Thoben & Pawar, 1999). The business domains do not have fixed business relationships, and thus the VE is not static and might change continuously based on market-driven criteria. The virtual marketplace provides services for the registration of business process offerings based on some generic, well-known, globally specified process templates. Business domains that want to form VE relationships can register offers on the marketplace in relation to the process templates. Whenever a business domain wants to use a particular process, it searches the marketplace and locates all the potential partners that can provide the process. As soon as the list of VE candidate partners has been found, the partner selection process starts. The partner selection process between the domains is usually performed through negotiation. The negotiation process might be manual or automatic, while the result of it is usually a contract that regulates the business relationship that has been established (Geppert, Kradolfer & Tombros, 1998).

By deploying virtual marketplaces, there are no explicit static business relationships among the partners and thus no integration among the processes of the partners is required (McCaffer & Garas, 1999; Nwana, Ndumu, Lee & Collis, 1999). Marketplaces are usually organized around certain globally specified service or product templates that can be offered by the different vendors. The marketplace is a matchmaking mechanism that brings potential process providers together with potential users of these processes. Organizations may participate in the marketplace only briefly or they may be long-term members. Relationships between process users and process providers tend to be short-term. The number of partners can easily change and thus the structure of the VE can also change from one service provision to another according to the specifics of the customers and the current needs of the partners. This is a significant evolution mechanism that takes advantage of the demand and supply, i.e., the process offerings by the individual domains (Schuldt, Schek & Alonso, 1999).

The dynamic VE model improves significantly on the static one and takes full advantage of the open global opportunities offered by the Internet and the global economy. DVEs feature very short lifetimes, while SVEs feature longer ones. In the former case, the relationships are static and well-integrated, and thus not flexible enough for alterations, modifications and evolution (McCaffer & Garas, 1999). Tightly coupled SVEs, that function essentially as a single virtual organization, exhibit high process integration between partners, while loosely coupled DVEs are at the far end of the spectrum and demonstrate very low process integration between the partners. Additionally, in SVEs, the number of partners participating in the VE is static and predetermined due to the specialized integration activities required, while in DVEs the number can change dynamically, upon demand and supply, and based on the requirements of the individual members of the marketplace (Doz & Hamel, 1998).

Due to the open mechanisms of the Internet economy, dynamic VEs that take advantage of the market conditions are preferred. Although from a business point of view DVEs are the most promising business model, from technical point of view the required technical solutions and systems are more complex, sophisticated and distributed. However, the advent of Internet and open communication protocols, like TCP/IP and HTTP (Berners-Lee et al., 1994), distributed object-oriented middleware systems, like CORBA-IIOP (OMG) and Java-RMI, and extensible meta-languages, like eXtenible Markup Language (XML), provides the basic building blocks for the development of management platforms that will realise the concept of DVEs.

TECHNOLOGIES FOR VIRTUAL ENTERPRISES

Several technologies can be used for the development of dynamic virtual enterprise concepts, including those supporting the exchange of information in loosely coupled interorganizational environments (Redlich et al., 1998), the cooperation of automated business components (Orfali, 1996), the control of work processes across organizational boundaries (Georgakopoulos, 1998; Grefen et al., 1999), and the dynamic mediation of business process providers and users (Stricker et al., 2000).

Systems supporting the information exchange between the loosely coupled systems of dynamic virtual enterprises must enable asynchronous transactions across organizational boundaries, support application domain-specific types and formats of information, and allow for autonomous behavior of the communicating and cooperating business processes. Given the requirements for asynchronous and loosely coupled communication among the different cooperating partners, solutions based on messaging techniques are in favor (Ouzounis & Tschammer, 2001a). Such technologies include EDI, Web Interface Definition Language, Common Business Library, EbXML, BizTalk Framework, and Commerce XML. Most of these technologies are industry-driven standard formats for exchanging business data and not business process execution and management. Although such transactions are performed asynchronously, the currently provided format of the messages is static and cannot be easily extended for dynamic virtual enterprises. The scope and context of such documents is limited and rather impossible to change. Therefore, it is difficult to use such standards as the basis for general-purpose inter-domain business process execution and management (Tombros & Geppert, 2000).

Systems supporting the cooperation of automated business components must enable distribution, intelligent behavior and high degree of automation. Several technologies have been proposed such as object-oriented components, like enterprise java beans, and intelligent mobile agents (McCaffer & Garas, 1999; Orfali, 1996). Object-Oriented Components (OOC) are widely used as a framework for distributed computing and information processing due to the ease of integration and deployment, high degree of distribution, and standard underlying distributed protocols, like CORBA-IIOP and RMI. In these technologies, back-end systems and clients integrate themselves with the distributed framework using the application programming interfaces (APIs) and object models exposed by the underlying levels of the architecture. While clients are insulated from the APIs of the back-end systems, they are tightly bound to the APIs provided by the framework. This design choice has two implications. First, by using object binding as the interaction technique, as opposed to document exchange used in EDI, OOC applications must be adopted at once by all participants in the cross-organization relationship. Upgrades to back-end systems, the component framework, and the business application must be coordinated across all participants. Second, because of the tight binding, security issues are a major factor. For communication and cooperation, objects in different business domains must adopt the same object model. This poses a significant barrier to inter-working in cross-organizational environments. Additionally, the OOC frameworks do not provide a complete solution, but instead serve as the starting point for developers to build applications. These choices make the OOC frameworks most appropriate for deployment inside a single company that needs to link multiple distributed divisions or sites (Doz & Hamel, 1998; Martesson et al., 1998).

Intelligent mobile agents combine many of the benefits offered by messaging systems and OOCs. Agent systems are loosely coupled and communicate asynchronously. Messages exchanged are well defined through the FIPA agent communication language standard (Krause& Magedanz, 1996; Magedanz, 1999). Agents realize the concept of ontologies, which makes them more flexible and autonomous, and agent systems are deployed within a distributed object-oriented framework, like CORBA or Java, and thus can access any type of standard business component. Through these combined benefits, agent systems support autonomy and flexibility, scalability, and adaptability. Flexibility is supported by the distinct communication and cooperation models which have been developed for agent-based systems, scalability comes from the migration capabilities of agents, and adaptability relies on the inherent intelligence of agents. Although agent technology is a very good candidate for the support of virtual enterprises, it has some problems as well. One of the key issues currently is the requirement for a mobile agent platform for the provision of agent life cycle and migration management services. Several mobile intelligent agent platforms have been developed so far, which, however, are mostly incompatible between each other. Agents sitting on different platforms have difficulties in communication and cooperation. Therefore, several standardization activities have emerged, like OMG-MASIF and FIPA, which deal with these problems (Ouzounis et al., 2001a).

In the area of control of business processes across organizational boundaries, workflow management systems are used to specify, execute, manage, and streamline business processes (Lee & Billington, 1993; Reichert et al., 1998). Workflow management systems in general provide several useful functions to be used for business process execution and control across the organizational boundaries which exist within a virtual enterprise (Geppert et al., 1998; Schuldt et al., 1999). However, conventional workflow management systems have certain drawbacks in relation to the virtual enterprise concept. One of the main problems is their limited autonomy and flexibility. So far there are no extensions to the existing business process specification languages towards the support of cross-organizational business processes (Nwana et al., 1999). Furthermore, remote invocation of business processes provided by different business domains should be preceded by access control, authorization, and contract checks. Finally, in current workflow systems, shared business processes are structured inflexibly with respect to subprocesses that have to be executed remotely, i.e., the virtual enterprise partners which are to provide those processes are specified statically (Lin, 1996).

In dynamic virtual enterprises a workflow management system must deal with the fact that, for the same business process specification, different instances can exist. For every instance, a set of different partners may be selected according to the needs and requirements of the process. Standards, currently proposed, are not directly dealing with market-based cross-organizational business process execution and management (Wognum et al., 1999). Critical open issues, like inter-domain workflow execution and management, business process specification languages for inter-domain business processes, and dynamic selection of workflow providers during process execution are not effectively discussed.

Agent-based workflow management systems are to solve several of these problems (Ouzounis et al., 1999; Ouzounis et al., 2001a). For example, control of business processes shared between multiple business domains can be assigned to agents which are either deployed directly in each of the domains involved or can migrate from domain to domain as required by the processes structure (Bellifernine, Rimassa & Poggi, 1999). However, most of the issues related to such agent-based workflow management systems, cross-organizational business process execution, and dynamic selection of partners are still under investigation, and stable, well-defined solutions and concepts are missing (Breugst, Hagen & Magedanz, 1998).

Finally, virtual marketplaces are central parts of dynamic virtual enterprises (Tombros et al., 2000). They increase flexibility and scalability through their search and mediation functions and support the selection of business partners during the establishment and reconfiguration of dynamic virtual enterprises. A marketplace can administer offerings for business processes made by potential providers and can perform searches for partners satisfying required quality attributes. The search and matchmaking services can be further complemented by advanced services, like automated negotiation and electronic contracting. Intelligent mobile agents can be a profitable technical implementation of such functionality due to their inherent autonomy, adaptability, and learning characteristics (Choy, Breugst & Magedanz, 1999). However, most current implementations of agent-based virtual marketplaces do not consider emerging agent standards, like FIPA ACL and FIPA protocols (Finin, Labrou & Mayfield, 1995; FIPA, 1998). Furthermore, most of the negotiation approaches, techniques, and models have basically concentrated on the area of business-to-consumer and consumer-to-consumer electronic commerce and are not addressing the needs of business-to-business marketplaces and the needs of dynamic virtual enterprises in particular. Although some of the above techniques can be extended for the dynamic selection of partners in virtual enterprises based on service templates, this area is considered new, and further research is needed.

MANAGEMENT OF DYNAMIC VIRTUAL ENTERPRISES

In general, a lifecycle model usually describes the key phases and activities required during the existent of an entity. According to ISO (1991), a life cycle can be defined as "the finite steps a system may go through over its entire life history. The different life cycle phases define types of activities which are pertinent during the life cycle of the entity." In our case, the VE lifecycle model consists of two key phases that should be followed for the establishment and management of a VE. These phases are the business process specification and registration phase and the business process management phase.

During the business process specification and registration phase, a VE candidate partner specifies his local and remote business processes. The specification of local business processes is done using the business process definition language (BPDL). For every business process, the input parameters, the output parameters, the subprocesses, and the tasks and the conditions among the subprocesses, and the tasks are being specified. Additionally, every subprocess is specified as a local or remote process. Local process are the processes that can be fully provided by this domain while remote processes are the processes that can be provided only by remote domains. Furthermore, for every specified task, the associated business objects that will be deployed are also specified. The task agents related to specific business objects are called resource provider agents (RPAs). In this way, autonomous agents can easily deploy legacy services provided by existing distributed objects that are physically located in different network locations within the domain. In the following figure the key entities of the business process definition language are presented. The business process has been specified in XML while the key entities of the language and the relationships among these entities are depicted in Figure 1.

In the sequel, every administrative domain that would like to participate in dynamic VE relationships registers its processes in the virtual marketplace. The business process registration is performed by using existing service types provided by the marketplace. If there is no associated service type for a particular process, a new one is being created by possibly inheriting existing service types. This process can be done either automatically or manually through the virtual marketplace administrator. During the registration process, certain values for certain attributes related to the service type, like location, quantity, etc., are provided. These attributes are usually related to the provision of the process to remote administrative domains. In addition to the service-provision-related attributes, a set of attributes that will influence the negotiation process are also specified, e.g., price. These attributes might include the low price that can be negotiated upon, the maximum quantity that can be offered, the best and worst delivery dates, etc.

During the business process management phase, a VE partner provides business processes to customers or other VE partners by deploying the dynamic model of the virtual marketplace. Initially, when a customer requests a business process by a VE representative, a process instance is being created; i.e., the process description for this process is retrieved and interpreted, and the execution of the process is started. The initial request of the customer for a business process execution is served from the personal user agent (PUA). This agent is responsible for managing the requests of the customers and forwarding them to the internal agent-based business process management system. The instantiation, interpretation, and execution of the business process are done by a set of autonomous agents that cooperate to provide the requested business process called workflow provider agents (WPAs). The coordination among the WPAs and RPAs during the execution of the business process is performed by deploying the intra-domain ontology. The intra-domain ontology is the set of messages that the WPA and RPA exchange during the execution and management of local business processes. If one of the subprocesses of the main process has been specified as remote, then the WPA creates a specialized negotiation agent, called requestor negotiation agent (RNA), and sends him to the virtual marketplace in order to locate potential VE candidate partners for the required remote subprocess. Upon request, the virtual marketplace informs the RNA about all the registered domains that can provide the process, i.e., all the potential VE candidate partners. In the sequel, the RNA starts the negotiation process by conducting the specialized negotiation agents located in each individual VE candidate partner. These agents are called provider negotiation agents (PNAs). The negotiation process is performed among the RNA and PNAs by using a

Figure 1: Business process definition language model

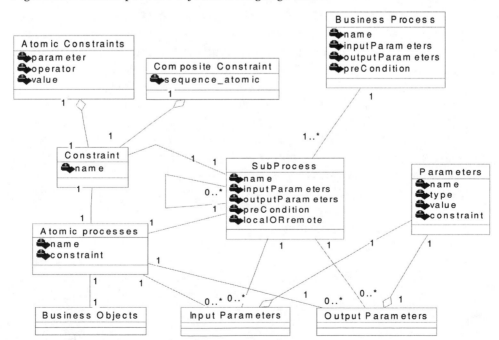

negotiation protocol and a negotiation ontology. The negotiation protocol used is the FIPA Contract-Net protocol, based on a modified version of the original Contract Net protocol. The result of this negotiation process is the selection of the best VE candidate domain that satisfies certain classification criteria. This agreement is being described in terms of a contract that regulates the agreement.

As soon as a VE partner has been selected for a particular remote process, the PNA returns back to his original physical location and informs the corresponding WPA agent about the selected VE partner. Then, the WPA conducts the selected VE partner domain and requests the execution of the business process by referring to the contract id that has been signed during the negotiation process. The VE partner domain checks the list of existing contracts and starts the execution of the requested process if a legitimate contract has been found. The autonomous agent responsible for the access control and authorization is called a domain representative (DR) agent.

During the execution of the main process, the customer can manage the execution of the main business process. The main operations that can be performed are suspension, resumption, or termination of the execution of the process. Every request of the customer is served initially by the VE representative domain. All the WPAs and RPAs, related to the execution of this business process instance, are suspended, resumed, or terminated accordingly. In addition to that, all the remote processes that have been previously requested should also be suspended, resumed, or terminated. Therefore, similar requests are issued and sent from the VE representative to the corresponding VE partners. Whenever the DR agent of a VE partner gets a request to suspend, resume or terminate an existing local business process, it always checks the contract id and serves accordingly the request by requesting the related internal WPA and RPA to resume, suspend or terminate. In that way, unauthorized requests for process suspension, resumption, or termination are not served. The coordination among the different autonomous agents during the execution of remote business processes is performed by deploying the inter-domain ontology. The inter-domain ontology is actually the set of messages that the agents exchange during the execution and management of remote business processes. Additionally, the customer can always ask about the current status of the business process. In a similar way, the VE representative requests from all involved autonomous agents associated with this process, local or remote, to declare their current status. When a process finally completes its operation, the DR agent of the VE representative partner is informed. In the sequel, the DR agent informs the customer by posting to him the output results of the process and other statistical information like the time of completion. Furthermore, if during the execution of a process a fatal problem occurs, then the corresponding WPA, responsible for this process instance, informs the DR agent that the execution of this process can not be continued and thus the WPA needs to abort himself. The DR agent informs ondemand either the customer or the associated VE partner about this event and stops the execution of the business process.

From the above description and definitions, it is obvious that different administrative domains participate in the execution and management of dynamic VE services. These domains are the:

- **customer domain**. This is the domain of the user that deploys the services of the VE. The user can start a service, suspend, resume, or terminate it. When the service is completed the results of the service are returned to the customer.
- **VE representative domain**. This is the domain that the customer logs on and requests certain services. This domain represents the VE to the external world and manages the execution of the VE services by conducting the marketplace, locating candidate partners, negotiating with them, and selecting the best one for the execution of the remote processes.
- **VE candidate/partner domain**. This is the domain that offers a set of business processes to the marketplace community and registers certain offers related to specific service templates for potential cooperation with other domains. If this domain is finally selected after a negotiation process, it becomes the VE partner domain that will provide the agreed processes to other domains.
- **virtual marketplace domain**. This is a third-party domain that provides the service templates that the VE candidate partners use to register their offers. This domain manages the service templates and the offers registered by the VE candidate domains and provides retrieval services for the selection of VE candidate partners. This domain does not actively participate in the VE and thus does not provide any type of business process management services.

The logical relationships among these domains are depicted in Figure 2.

Figure 2: Business model and relationships

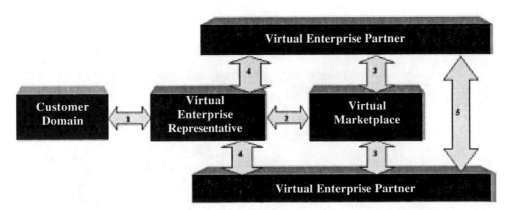

OVERALL ARCHITECTURE

In general, the architecture expresses a fundamental structure of the system under analysis and design. The architecture defines a set of functional components, subsystems or modules described in terms of their behavior and interfaces into which the system is divided. It defines also how these components interact or interconnect to fulfil the goals of the system. In principle, the term component includes functional components that can be either distributed objects or autonomous agents. Taking these definitions into account, the architecture is described, according to the UML approach, with interfaces, operations, use case diagrams, and sequence diagrams. The interfaces can be defined either in Java programming language or in XML. The layered architecture of the agent-based platform for the management of dynamic virtual enterprises consists of three respective layers. These are:

- **Distributed processing environment (DPE)** that supports the key operations for object lifecycle management and distributed services, access to persistent repositories, and deployment of existing legacy systems, and enabling services. The distributed processing environment consists of Java Framework with CORBA middleware services in order to enable interoperable access to distributed objects and components.

- **Mobile agent platform (MAP)** and **supporting services** that provide the basic agent lifecycle services, migration services, messaging services, and access to services provided by the underlying distributed processing environment like XML parsers, JESS expert system, and OMG-Trader. The agent platform deployed is the Grasshopper jointly developed by GMD-FOKUS and IKV++. Grasshopper supports both the OMG-MASIF and FIPA standards.

- **Agent-based business process specification, registration and management system** and **agent-based virtual marketplace system** that provide the basic operations for the specification of inter-domain business processes, the registration of them in the virtual marketplace, the selection and negotiation of partners, the access control and authorization of process requests, and the execution and management of business processes.

Figure 3: Overall system architecture

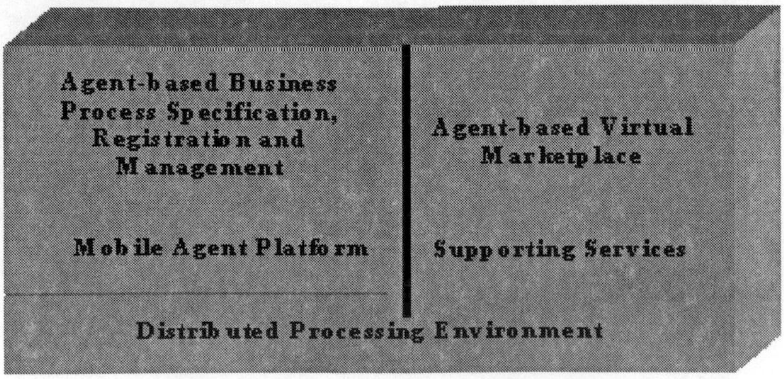

This architecture is presented in Figure 3.

Every administrative domain deploys this architecture in a rather different way. More specifically, the virtual marketplace domain uses only the agent-based virtual marketplace sub-layer, the VE representative and candidate/partner domains use the business process specification, registration and management, while the customer domain deploys only a standard Web browser for accessing the business processes. In both cases the two lowest layers deployed are the same, i.e., the distributed processing environment and the mobile agent platform and supporting services.

VIRTUAL MARKETPLACE SERVICES

A virtual marketplace is a third-party administrative domain that provides matchmaking services to the VE partners. The virtual marketplace enables VE candidate partners to register and administer service offers in relation to certain service types and VE representatives to search for potential partners that can provide particular business processes associated with existing service types.

Every business process registered in the virtual marketplace is associated with a service type. In general, service types describe in a consistent way the interface of business processes. For every service type, the name of the process and a set of named properties are specified. The name of the service type is the name of the business process, while the input and output parameters of the process are named properties of the service type. Additionally, extra properties, related with the negotiation process, are also included into the service type. For every property a (name, value) pair is associated. Service types are mainly managed by the virtual marketplace administrator. The service type management includes creation, deletion, modification and retrieval of service types.

VE candidate partners that want to register their process offerings in the marketplace should always create a service offer in association with an existing service type and register it to the virtual marketplace. A service offer is actually an instance of a service type where certain properties have given certain values. Service offers are managed individually by each domain in a private manner. This means that every domain can manage only its own service offers. The management of service offers includes the registration, withdrawal, listing and modification of offers.

Finally, VE representatives or partners that want to find suitable partners that can provide a particular process retrieve from the marketplace all the registered offers that satisfy certain constraints. The service offer retrieval management process actually includes the retrieval of offers that satisfy certain constraints. Therefore, the basic services provided by the marketplace are service type management, service offer management, and service offer retrieval management. Each one of these services are provided by individual FIPA-compliant agents, namely:

- **Service type agent (STA)** is responsible for the management of service types and more specifically for the addition, removal, listing, and modification of service types.

- **Service offer agent (SOA)** is responsible for the management of service offers and more specifically for the registration, withdrawal, description, and modification of service offers.
- **Service offer retrieval agent (SOR)** is responsible for the retrieval of offers associated with a service type based on some constraints.

These three agents are FIPA-compliant agents, i.e., they communicate with other agents by exchanging standard FIPA ACL/XML messages. The content of these messages is described in XML and it follows the **virtual marketplace ontology**. The virtual marketplace ontology describes the set of input and output messages that the marketplace agents can exchange with other agents. Agents that want to communicate with the STA, SOA, or SOR agents should formulate and understand messages based on this ontology. The key concepts of the virtual marketplaces are very close to the ODP and OMG-Trader. For that reason, a standard OMG-Trader, as a basis for the development and testing of the virtual marketplaces has been deployed. However, the OMG-Trader is a CORBA object and cannot be used directly by the different FIPA-compliant agents in an autonomous and message-based way, and thus the specialized STA, SOA, and SOR FIPA agents, as well as the virtual marketplace ontology, have been specified and developed. These agents are actually offering the basic functionality of the OMG-Trader in a FIPA-compliant way.

In general, VE candidate partners that want to create or administer new service types in the marketplace should always refer to the appropriate service type name. In that case, an instance of the provider negotiation agent (PNA) migrates to the virtual marketplace, composes a FIPA ACL/XML request, and sends it to the STA. The communication protocol among the PNAs and STAs is based on the standard FIPA-Request-Response protocol. The STA receives the request, parses it from the ACL and XML parser, checks the type of the request and decides which action is required. In the sequel, the STA performs the request by deploying the service type repository, generates an ACL/XML inform message and sends it to the PNA. The PNA, upon receipt of the message, parses it first from the ACL and XML parser, checks the response and migrates back to the VE candidate domain to inform its domain.

In a similar way, VE candidate partners willing to register new service offers in the marketplace or administer them should always refer to the appropriate service type name. In that case, in a similar manner like the STA, an instance of the PNA migrates to the marketplace, composes a FIPA ACL/XML request and sends it to the SOA. In the sequel, the SOA receives the message, parses it from the ACL and XML parser, checks the type of the request and decides which action is required. Afterwards, the SOA performs the request by deploying the service offer repository, composes an ACL/XML inform message and sends it back to the PNA. The PNA receives the message, parses it first from the ACL and XML parser, checks the reply of the SOA and migrates back to the VE candidate partner to inform its domain.

BUSINESS PROCESS SPECIFICATION

The business process specification phase is a semi-manual process performed by the business process analyst of each individual administrative domain with the help of an autonomous intelligent agent called the provider negotiation agent (PNA). The main responsibilities of the business process analyst (BPA) in this phase are specification, modification, and deletion of certain terms and conditions related to the registration and negotiation of local and remote business processes to potential partners. These terms and conditions will be used by this domain during the negotiation process with potential VE partners. The business process registration phase includes the following steps for every local process:

- The business process analyst specifies in the offer repository the local and remote processes, including the input and output parameters that can be provided to potential VE partners. For that reason, reuse of the existing business process specifications stored in the business process repository (BPR) can be done. Additionally, the business process analyst specifies the constraints related to the negotiation parameters. These constraints specify the lower and upper bounds of the accepted values and will, in general, drive and determine the negotiation process,

- The provider negotiation agent (PNA) agent retrieves from the offer repository all the local processes and the corresponding input, output, and negotiation parameters and migrates to the virtual marketplace, where it checks for every local process the existence of a corresponding service type. For every local process a generic service type should exist. This service type should have as properties the input and output parameters of the local process and some extra properties related to the negotiation process, e.g., price, delivery day, payment method, payment due, etc. (see the next section). If there is no existing service type available on the marketplace for a given local business, the PNA creates a new one. In the sequel, the PNA registers every local process in the marketplace in relation to an existing compatible service type. For that reason, the PNA interacts with the service offer agent (SOA) in the virtual marketplace. After the successful registration of local business processes, potential VE partners can search the virtual marketplace and locate this domain as a potential VE candidate partner. This is the initial step for the beginning of the negotiation process among the domains that will be described in the next sections.

The offer repository (OR) stores information regarding all the local and remote processes that can be provided to potential VE partners. For every local and remote process, the name of the process and the input, output, and negotiation parameters are stored. All the different types of parameters have a name associated to them, a type, e.g., a string, a value, and a constraint. In addition to that, the negotiation parameters have two classification modes, namely, public and private. The values of the negotiation parameters that have public mode can be revealed into the different agents of other domains and the virtual marketplace. On the contrary, values of negotiation parameters that have private mode should not be revealed into the public agents and virtual marketplace and are the ones that are used for determining the negotiation process. The constraints are simple binary logical expressions related to parameters and values. For example, if one potential negotiation parameter is price, then the following constraint can be assigned: ("price"<="32").

BUSINESS PROCESS MANAGEMENT

Business process management is related with the execution and management of shared business processes across different administrative domains. The management of business processes is performed in a autonomous and distributed way and is fully performed by autonomous intelligent mobile agents without human intervention. The execution of a shared business process starts by the enduser of the VE. The main operations that this role performs are log into the Web site of the VE representative that provides the shared business processes by using a standard Web browser, execute a shared business process and monitor of the status of the running process, and manage a shared business process, i.e., suspension, resumption, or termination of a running business process.

The execution and management of shared business processes in the context of dynamic VEs are performed by the following autonomous FIPA-compliant agents:

- **Personal user agent (PUA)** is responsible for managing the requests of the endusers coming from the standard Web browsers. This agent is located on the VE representative domain. Every user request is checked for authorization and then is forwarded to the domain representative agent (DR).
- **Domain representative (DR)** is responsible for managing the requests of the PUA, if the domain plays the role of the VE representative, and the requests of the remote domains, if the domain plays the role of the VE partner. In both cases, the DR authenticates the requests by conducting the contract repository. If the request is an authorized one and is related to the instantiation of a new process, the DR creates a workflow provider agent (WPA) that will serve the request; otherwise, the corresponding existing WPA is located and the request is forwarded to him.
- **Workflow provider agent (WPA)** is responsible for executing and managing an instance of a process or subprocess. The WPA replies to requests coming from the DR or informs the DR about the status of the process that it executes. Additionally, the WPA cooperates in an autonomous way with other WPAs during the execution of the business processes. Finally, the WPA controls the execution of atomic processes involved the business process by invoking, requesting, or informing different resource provider agents (RPAs).
- **Resource provider agent (RPA)** is responsible for carrying out one specific atomic process of the business process. One atomic process is a simple

elementary processing unit that can be included into one or more business processes. An RPA always deploys existing resources or business objects provided by the domain in a distributed and interoperable way.

- **Requestor negotiation agent (RNA)** is responsible for managing the partner search, negotiation, and selection process. When a WPA realizes that a remote process is required for the continuation of the currently executed business process, it automatically creates a RNA. This agent migrates to the virtual marketplace, selects the potential VE candidate partners, based on some constraints, and starts a negotiation process with them. The result of the negotiation is an electronic contract that regulates this agreement.
- **Provider negotiation agent (PNA)** represents a VE candidate domain during the negotiation process and is responsible for the automated negotiations with other RNAs. Additionally, PNAs manage the business process registration to the virtual marketplace and update the contract repository when a negotiation process has been successfully ended, i.e., a contract has been agreed upon.

For every running business process a process instance is instantiated. This means that different instances of the same process can be executed and managed. Every instance of a process has a unique process id that differentiates it from the others. Although all of these instances are instantiated based on the definition of the business process, they are different due to the different input values that the users have provided for them. Therefore, a process instance is, in a similar way to object-oriented systems, an object while a business process definition is the class specification. Process instances are executed and managed by autonomous, intelligent FIPA-compliant agents. In particular, a process or subprocess is managed and executed by a workflow provider agent (WPA), while an atomic process is managed and executed by a resource provider agent (RPA). This means that the execution and management of shared process instances is provided by a set of WPAs and RPAs that cooperate autonomously to accomplish the completion of the process.

The communication between WPAs and RPAs is performed by the exchange of FIPA-compliant ACL/XML messages while the communication protocol used is the FIPA Request-Response protocol. The content of the messages is specified based on the inter- and intra-domain ontology. The intra- and inter-domain ontology specifies all the messages that the autonomous agents can exchange during the execution and management of a business process. If the agents belong in the same administrative domain, then the intra-domain ontology is used. If the agents belong to different domains, then the inter-domain ontology is used.

IMPLEMENTATION AND VALIDATION ISSUES

The agent-based platform for the management of dynamic virtual enterprises has been fully implemented and tested. The implementation of the platform has been done following the overall architecture, specifications and designs provided in the previous sections. In general, the development of the platform and the different agents has been done using open, interoperable and standard technologies.

The development of the different agents that support the main operations of the platform has been performed in Java programming language. The underlying agent platform deployed was the Grasshopper agent platform with extra OMG-MASIF and FIPA-compliant services. In principle, FIPA-compliant agents should be in position to send and receive ACL/XML messages. For that reason, when a message has been sent to an agent, the agent must first parse the incoming ACL/XML message by deploying a standard ACL parser. For that reason a FIPA ACL parser is provided by the Grasshopper platform. The parser gets as input an ACL/XML message string, parses it and produces a query object called FIPAACLMessage. In general, the ACLMessage class provides operations for getting and setting the type of message, sender, receiver, content, etc. As soon as the incoming messages have been parsed from the ACL parser, the content of the message, which is described in XML, should also be parsed. For that reason, three specialized XML parsers have been developed. These XML parsers correspond to the three ontologies, namely the inter/intra-domain ontology, the virtual marketplace ontology and the negotiation ontology. The XML parser provides all the necessary operations for interpreting and retrieving information from XML content.

Additionally, when an agent wants to send an ACL/XML message to another agent he should always compose a legitimate ACL/XML message. In general, the responsibility of the message composer is to produce a legitimate ACL/XML string based on the corresponding ontology. For that reason, three message composers have been developed and used corresponding to the inter/intra-domain ontology, the virtual marketplace ontology and the negotiation ontology. Using these message composers, the different agents of the platform can easily create legitimate ACL/XML messages following the specified ontologies.

Furthermore, the communication of agents obeys certain FIPA-compliant protocols. In the context of this thesis, three FIPA-compliant protocols have been specified and developed. These are the FIPA-compliant Request-Response, Request-Query and Contract-Net. Additionally, the status of the agents and the internal synchronization of the provided operations are managed and controlled by the Decision Manager module. The Decision Manager is a specialized module tailored to the functionality of each agent that manages and controls the requests and responses of the agent with the agents. It is actually the entity that synchronizes the internal operations and entities of an agent in order to respond to different requests. In the class diagram in Figure 4, the main classes involved in the development of a standard FIPA agent are provided.

Additionally, the virtual marketplace agents deploy and integrate directly a standard OMG-Trader. In that case, the three agents have the appropriate access to the corresponding CORBA objects of the OMG-Trader. More specifically, whenever an agent deploys an object provided by the OMG-Trader, the agent gets a reference to the corresponding object by using the interoperable

Figure 4: Generic FIPA-compliant agent class diagram

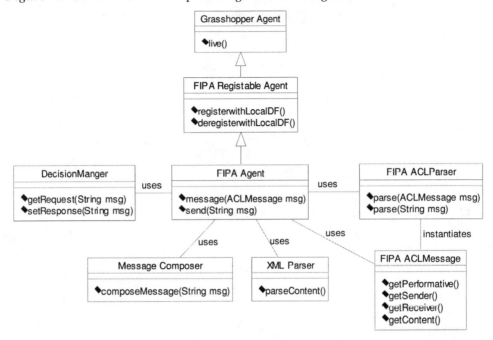

object reference (IOR) and, using the CORBA IIOP protocol, accesses the different methods provided by the object. This interaction is a typical case of using CORBA objects. The OMG-Trader objects deployed by the virtual marketplace agents are the service type repository, the service offer repository and the OMG constraint language parser objects.

Furthermore, for the persistent storage of local and remote business process offers, contracts, and business process specifications, certain XML-based storage modules have been developed. The offer, contract, and business process repository are XML-based persistent modules. In all cases, the different entities of the repositories, i.e. the offers, contracts and business processes, are stored as separate ASCII files with XML content in conventional file systems. For every persistent storage module, a configuration file with references to the individual files of the entities is maintained and configured.

Finally, the execution and management of the VE business process by the user is done through the Web. For that reason, special mechanisms based on TCP/IP and HTTP protocols and the standard Java servlets technology have been developed. More specifically, the interface for the management of the business processes is Web-based. This means that the user needs only to have a standard Web browser. Every request by the user initiates the corresponding Java servlet at the Web server of the VE representative domain. A Java servlet is actually a normal Java object that formulates the appropriate XML request, connects to the TCP/IP server of the PUA agent, and sends the request to the agent. When the request of the user has been fulfilled, the PUA, through the TCP/IP server, informs the Java servlet, which, in the sequel, informs the user by generating a dynamic HTML Web page.

Figure 5: Business process instantiation and execution

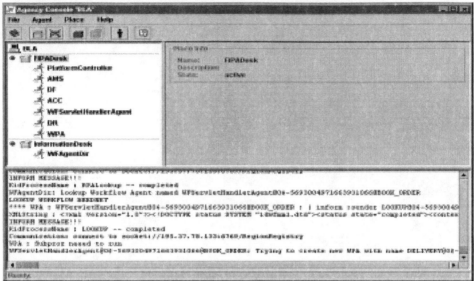

In Figure 5, a screen shot of the business process execution and management system is provided. This figure depicts the main FIPA agents (AMS, DF and ACC) and the agents of the platform, i.e., the domain representative (DR), the workflow provider agent (WPA) and the PUA.

The validation of the proposed system has been done by the development of a characteristic scenario that demonstrates the features of the system. The validation scenario has been done in the context of the ACTS/MIAMI project (1998-2000). More specifically, this validation scenario is a dynamic network management solution. In that case, a third-party network provider called the Active Virtual Pipe plays the role of the VE representative and provides network management services to potential corporations. The Active Virtual Pipe can establish network connections from one physical location to another with certain quality of service (QoS) characteristics. In principle, the Active Virtual Pipe deploys the capabilities of different connectivity providers (CP) to establish physical network connections from A to B. When a user requests a network connection, the Active Virtual Pipe conducts the virtual marketplace and negotiates with different connectivity providers about the potential connection. When a suitable connectivity provider has been selected, the network connection will be established dynamically. During the business process provision, the Active Virtual Pipe monitors the established network connection by querying the status of the process, i.e., the network connection. When a problem occurs, like network fault or performance degradation, i.e., the process aborts, the Active Virtual Pipe conducts the virtual marketplace, negotiates with other potential connectivity providers and finally selects another suitable connectivity provider. Based on this scenario, the Active Virtual Pipe is the VE representative while the connectivity providers are the different VE partners. The VE partners provide physical connections from one physical location to another with some QoS properties. The provision of the network management services to the user from the Active Virtual Pipe is the VE business process while the network connections from A to B locations are local processes of the different connectivity providers. The provision of network connections through the deployment of different connectivity providers is totally transparent to the user.

CONCLUSIONS

Based on the development, testing, and validation of the agent-based platform for the management of dynamic virtual enterprises, the following important characteristics and features have been identified:

- **openness**. This is achieved due to the deployment of the flexible XML-based ontologies for the management of shared business processes and the negotiation process. Additionally, the usage of open, interoperable, standard technologies like XML, FIPA, FIPA ACL, and Java also increases the openness of the system.
- **dynamicity, flexibility and evolution**. This is achieved due to the dynamic selection of VE partners and the automated negotiation during business process execution and management. The usage of the virtual marketplaces, the registration of local business processes, and the negotiation and dynamic selection of VE partners are special mechanisms that enable and support evolution and flexibility. These concepts in conjunction with the generic communication mechanisms offered by FIPA ACL increase the levels of flexibility.
- **asynchronous and loosely coupled communication**. This is achieved due to communication mechanisms supported by the FIPA platform. In general, the intelligent agents communicate in an asynchronous and loosely coupled manner by message exchanges through the FIPA ACC.
- **distribution and scalability**. This is achieved due to the autonomous and distributed execution and management of shared business processes. In principle, the execution and management of business processes are performed by different intelligent, autonomous agents located in different administrative domains. The agents are located in different physical nodes and communicate with message exchanges. Finally, scalability is another feature of the platform. This is achieved due to the autonomous execution of the processes. For every subprocess a specialized agent is created to execute and manage the subprocess. Therefore, as the business process instances running on the system increase, the number of WPAs and RPAs for serving them increases. This concept improves the scalability of the system in the sense that specialized agents are being dynamically created for serving the business processes.
- **autonomy**. This is achieved due to the asynchronous and loosely coupled communication of agents during the execution and management of business processes. Autonomy and decentralization are key requirements for the

management of dynamic VEs. In the context of this thesis, the agents are autonomous and communicate by exchanging messages specified in FIPA ACL, while the content of the requests and responses is specified by the inter-domain, negotiation and virtual marketplace ontologies. The autonomy of the system is also improved by the deployment of the FIPA-compliant protocols.

- **intelligence**. This is achieved due to the deployment of artificial intelligence techniques during the business process execution and management. For that reason, special mechanisms have been developed and tested for the integration of rule engines, like the JESS rule engine, for the assertion of conditions related to the flow of control in business processes. Additionally, for that reason, two generic interfaces have been specified and developed, namely the External Condition Checker Interface (ECCI) and the Strategy Manager Interface (SMI). The ECCI enables the generic integration of third-party condition checkers like JESS while the SMI enables the easy integration of selection and negotiation algorithms during the negotiation process. This means that the intelligence of the different agents can be improved by using the interfaces to incorporate third-party intelligent modules.

- **generality and applicability in various applications areas**. This is achieved due to the generality of the different entities of the platform. In principle, the business process definition language (BPDL) and the service type are generic concepts for describing and specifying processes and process templates. Additionally, the three inter-domain ontologies are generic and can be used in different business sectors or application domains. Finally, deployment of XML as a meta-language for ontology description enables the easy customization and extension of the different entities. The generality and applicability of the proposed approach are proved by the fact that different validation scenarios from different business sectors and application domains have been developed, tested and demonstrated successfully.

In addition to the previously described benefits, one key drawback has been identified. This drawback is performance and it is related to certain entities of the platform. The main reasons for the performance limitations are:

- **parsing of the messages**. The format of the messages exchanged among agents is specified in FIPA-compliant ACL/XML format. Therefore, for every incoming message, parsing of the ACL envelope and parsing of the XML content are required. However, the usage of ACL/XML messages enables the autonomous and loosely coupled communication of agents and thus the performance problem introduced is unavoidable.

- **asynchronous message transportation**. The transportation of messages exchanged among agents is done in an asynchronous way through the FIPA Agent Communication Channel (ACC). Every message sent from one agent to another is forwarded initially to the ACC, which checks whether the destination agent is local or remote to the platform and forwards the message to him. The involvement of the ACC in every agent-agent communication decreases the performance of the system. However, the ACC is a standard entity specified by the FIPA standardization committee and the one that guarantees the asynchronous delivery of messages. Therefore, the performance degradation is also unavoidable in that case too.

- **migration of agents**. The migration of agents from one physical location to another also decreases the performance of the platform. The performance problem is introduced when the migrating agent is rather big enough in terms of bytes. However, when the message exchanges with the remote agent increase, then the migration technique can be profitable. In the context of this work, mobility of agents has been used in a reduced way and only when the circumstances require it.
- **agent platform and third-party module overhead**. The agent-based platform for the management of dynamic virtual enterprises is based on a standard mobile agent platform with FIPA and OMG-MASIF support. All the agent lifecycle management services, mobility services and FIPA-compliant services introduce delays and complexity, which is inherited into the platform. However, this is also unavoidable due to the fact that the platform is based on emerging agent standards.

Although the presented work tried to provide a coherent solution for the management of dynamic VEs, certain issues are subject to further improvements and research. These are:

- **negotiation strategy algorithms**. The automated negotiation was one of the key requirements for the selection of VE partners. The contribution provided the basic infrastructure–i.e., protocol, ontology and standard, open interfaces– for the automated negotiation and selection of partners and the integration of negotiation mechanisms with the process execution and management. In principle, different negotiation strategies can be developed and adopted during the negotiation processes. Therefore, a potential improvement would have been the integration and experimentation of different negotiation strategies for the selection of VE partners. The specification of the Strategy Manager Interface enables the easy and flexible integration of negotiation manager modules.
- **fault tolerance and exception handling**. During the execution of business processes, certain unpleasant situations might arise. In any case, when the execution of a running business process cannot continue anymore, the process should abort. In the current specification and implementation, unpleasant situations are managed with specific exception handling processes specified during the business process specification. When a process aborts, then the exception handling process starts automatically to bring the system in a stable state. However, this approach solves the problem only in intra-domain process execution but not in inter-domain processes. Therefore, a potential improvement of the platform would have been the provision of fault tolerance and exception handling features for the inter-domain processes.
- **secure inter-domain communication**. In general, the execution and management of inter-domain business processes are performed using the native

security features of the underlying platform, i.e., the Grasshopper. The provided solution addressed the problem of access control and authorization to local business processes from remote domains and users. In principle, the Grasshopper security services can be used only for distributed inter-domain multi-agent systems developed in the Grasshopper agent platform. However, when different agent platforms are involved, the FIPA ACL as an interoperability mechanism for agent communication should be used. In that case, the FIPA recommendations do not address explicitly how secure inter-domain communication among agents can be done. Therefore, a potential improvement would have been the introduction of security mechanisms for inter-domain agent communication. However, this is a feature mostly related with the underlying agent platform and not directly with the proposed result.

- **mobility and inter-domain business process execution**. The execution and management of inter-domain business processes are performed in an asynchronous and loosely coupled way by the exchange of messages. The migration of WPAs from one domain to another has been avoided due to the fact that the performance of the system is worsening. The main reason is that the size of the WPAs is bigger in comparison to the string-based ACL/XML messages. This means that it takes less time and resources to send a string message than to send a whole agent. As the performance of migration services provided by the mobile agent platforms might be improved in the future, migration of agents to different domains for the coordination and management of business processes would have been an alternative option and thus an issue for further research and investigation.

REFERENCES

Applegate, L. M., Holsapple, C. W., Kalakota, R., Radermacher, F. J., and Whinston, A. B. (1996). Electronic commerce: Building blocks of new business opportunity. *Journal of Organizational Computing and Electronic Commerce,* 6(1), 1-10.

Bellifernine, F., Rimassa G. and Poggi A. (1999). JADE: A FIPA compliant agent framework. *Proceedings of Fourth International Conference and Exhibition on the Practical Applications of Intelligent Agents and Multi-Agent Systems (PAAM 99)*, London.

Berners-Lee, T., Cailliau, R., Luotonen, A., Nielsen, H. F. and Secret, A. (1994). The World Wide Web. *Communications of the ACM*, 37(8), 76-82.

Bolcer, G. A. and Kaiser, G. (1999, January-February). SWAP: Leveraging the Web to manage workflow. *IEEE Internet Computing*.

Breugst, M., Hagen, L. and Magedanz; T. (1998). Impacts of mobile agent technology on mobile communication system evolution. *IEEE Personal Communications Magazine*, 5(4), 56-69.

Camarinha-Matos, L. M. and Afsarmanesh, H. (Eds.). (1999). Infrastructures for virtual enterprises. Networking industrial enterprises. *IFIP TC5 WG5.3/ PRODNET Working Conference for Virtual Enterprises (PRO-VE'99)*, Boston: Kluwer Academic.

Choy, S., Breugst, M. and Magedanz, T. (1999). Beyond mobile agents with CORBA–Towards mobile CORBA objects. *6th ACTS Conference on Intelligence in Services and Networks (IS&N)*, 168-180, H. Zuidweg et.al (Eds.), IS&N 99, LNCS 1597, Springer-Verlag.

Doz, Y. L. and Hamel, G. (1998). *Alliance Advantage: The Art of Creating Value through Partnering*. Boston: Harvard Business School Press.

Filos, E. and Ouzounis, V. (2000). Virtual organizations: Technologies, trends, standards and the contribution of the European RTD program. *International Journal of Computer Applications in Technology, Special Issue: "Applications in Industry of Product and Process Modeling Using Standards" Virtualorganisation.net, "Newsletter"*, 1(3-4).

Finin, F., Labrou, Y. and Mayfield, J. (1995). KQML as an agent communication language. In J. Bradshaw (Ed.), *Software Agents*. Cambridge, MA: MIT Press.

FIPA. (1998). Retrieved M D, Y from the World Wide Web: http://www.fipa.org/spec/FIPA98.html.

Georgakopoulos, D. (1998, May). *Collaboration management infrastructure for comprehensive process and service management*. Paper presented at the International Symposium on Advanced Database Support for Workflow Management, Enschede, The Netherlands.

Geppert, A., Kradolfer, M. and Tombros, D. (1998). Market-based workflow management. *International IFIP Conf. on Distributed Systems for Electronic Commerce*, Hamburg, Germany, June.

Gestner, R. *Using Objects for Workflow Enabling of Standard Application Software*. Retrieved M D, Y from the World Wide Web: http://laser.cs.umass.edu/workflow/gestner.html.

Gibon, P., Clavier, J. F. and Loison, S. (1999). Support for electronic data interchange. In *Infrastructures for Virtual Enterprises: Networking Industrial Enterprises. IFIP TC5 WG5.3 / PRODNET Working Conference for Virtual Enterprises (PRO-VE'99)*, 187-208. Porto, Portugal, October 27-28. Boston.

Grefen, J., Pernini, B. and Sanchez G. (Eds.). (1999). *Database Support for Workflow Management: The WIDE Project*. Kluwer Academic.

ISO/IEC. (1991). 9596, Information Technology, Open Systems Interconnection, Common Management Information Protocol (CMIP) – Part 1: Specification, Geneva, Switzerland.

Jacobson, et al. (1994). *The Object Advantage, Business Process Re-engineering With Object Technology*.

Krause, S. and Magedanz, T. (1996). Mobile service agents enabling intelligence on demand in telecommunications. *IEEE Global Telecommunications Confer-*

ence (Globecom 1996), 78-85, IEEE Catalog No.96CH35942, IEEE Press.

Lee, H. L. and Billington, C. (1993). Material management in decentralized supply chains. *Operations Research*, 41(5), 835-847.

Lin, F. (1996). *Reengineering the Order Fulfillment Process in Supply Chain Networks: A Multiagent Information Systems Approach*. Unpublished doctor thesis, University of Illinois at Urbana-Champaign.

Magedanz, T. (Ed.). (1999). Special issue on mobile agents in intelligent networks and mobile communication systems. *Computer Networks Journal*, July, 31(10). The Netherlands: ELSEVIER.

Malone, T. W. and Rockart, J. F. (1991). Computers, networks, and the corporation. *Scientific American,* 265(3), 128-136.

Martesson, N., Mackay, R. and Björgvinsson, S. (Eds.). (1998). Changing the ways we work: Shaping the ICT-solutions for the next century. *Proceedings of the Conference on Integration in Manufacturing*, Göteborg, Sweden, October 6-8. Amsterdam: IOS Press.

McCaffer, R. and Garas, F. (Eds.). (1999). eLSEwise: European large scale engineering wide integration support effort, engineering construction and architectural management. *Special Issue*, 6(1).

MIAMI project. (1998-2000). Available on the World Wide Web at: http://www.fokus.gmd.de/cc/ecco/.

NIIP. (1996). *The NIIP Reference Architecture*. Available on the World Wide Web at: http://www.niip.org.

Nwana, H., Ndumu, D., Lee, L. and Collis, J. (1999). ZEUS: A toolkit for building distributed multi-agent systems. *Applied Artifical Intelligence Journal*, 13(1). Available on the World Wide Web at: http://www.labs.bt.com/projects/agents/index.htm.

Ouzounis, V. (1998a). *Electronic Commerce Commercial Scenarios, Business Models and Technologies for SME's*. Invited paper, European Multimedia, Microprocessor Systems and Electronic Commerce Conference and Exposition (EMMSEC 98), Bordeaux, France, September 28-30.

Ouzounis, V. (1998b). *Electronic Commerce and New Ways of Work–An R&D RoadMap*. European Commission–Directoral General III.

Ouzounis, V. and Tschammer V. (1999). A framework for virtual enterprise support services. *32nd International Conference on Systems and Sciences (HICSS32)* Maoui Hawaii, January 3-5.

Ouzounis, V. and Tschammer, V. (2001a). An agent-based life cycle management of for dynamic virtual enterprises. To appear in the *Sixth International Conference on CSCW in Design*, July 12-14. London, Ontario, Canada.

Ouzounis, V. and Tschammer, V. (2001b). Towards dynamic virtual enterprises. To appear in the *First IFIP Conference on E-Business, E-Commerce and E-Government*. October 4-5. Zurich, Switzerland.

Orfali, R. (1996). *The Essential Distributed Objects Survival Guide*. John Wiley & Sons.

Redlich, J. P., Suzuki, M. and Weinstein, S. (1998). Distributed object technology for networking. *IEEE Communications Magazine*, October, 36(10), 100–111.

Reichert, M., Hensinger, C. and Dadam, P. (1998). Supporting adaptive workflows in advanced application environments. *Proceedings of the EDBT Workshop on Workflow Management Systems*, Valencia, March, 100-109.

Schuldt, H., Schek H. J., and Alonso, G. (1999). Transactional coordination agents for composite systems. *Proceedings of the International Database Engineering and Applications Symposium (IDEAS'99)*. Montreal, Canada, August.

Stricker, C., Riboni, S., Kradolfer, M. and Taylor, J. (2000). Market-based workflow management for supply chains of services. In *Proceedings of the 33rd Hawaii Int'l Conference on System Sciences (HICSS-33)*, Maui, Hawaii, January.

Tombros, D. and Geppert, A. (2000). Building extensible workflow systems using an event-based infrastructure. *Proceedings of the 12th Conference on Advanced Information Systems Engineering*, Stockholm, Sweden, June.

Wognum, N., Thoben, K. D. and Pawar, K. S. (1999). *Proceedings of ICE'99, International Conference on Concurrent Enterprising,* The Hague, The Netherlands, March 15-17. Nottingham, England: University of Nottingham.

Chapter XIV

A Planning and Scheduling Methodology for the Virtual Enterprise

Florent Frederix
Alcatel Microelectronics, Belgium

Virtual enterprises consisting of geographically dispersed, independent units are a reality in the global economy. These units concentrate on core technologies and create partner networks for the design, manufacturing and sale of their products. This chapter documents a methodology, more flexible and efficient than the more traditional techniques, to schedule activities in virtual enterprises and enterprise networks. The presented technique that stepwise searches for improved activity schedules has the advantage that in any stage of the iteration process a resource-feasible schedule is available. Investing in network and computation capacity will result in more efficient schedules. The virtual enterprise unit will view the platform as a time-phased capacity trading marketplace.

INTRODUCTION

Few firms are so large and few products so simple that one organization can manage the entire provision of the goods. Rather, most supply chains require the coordination of independently managed units who seek to maximize their own profits.

The basic responsibilities of the virtual enterprise planning and production control system described in this chapter are to provide customers with realistic due dates and to provide units, part of the core enterprise, and subcontractors with realistic plans. The goal is to schedule work such that all customer orders are met on time with low inventory and short lead times and at the lowest production cost.

There are several good reasons for keeping inventory low and lead times short:

- Both allow a VE[1] to stay agile and respond quickly to changes in demand or in the production environment.
- Low inventory of finished products, raw materials and intermediate products will reduce "capital binding" and losses due to "product aging."
- Furthermore, shorter lead times will limit the time between a defect taking place and the discovery of the issue (the moment of discovery will trigger corrective actions; all production since the occurrence of the defect can be scrapped).
- Another strategy in customer support is possible. We do not need to anticipate the demand anymore (using more or less sophisticated forecasting techniques) but we can produce on request of the customer.

Material Flow Dynamics in the Virtual Enterprise

The concept of a virtual enterprise consisting of separately owned, individual units and independent subcontractors creates more agility and increases efficiency. This concept resulted already in tremendous changes all over the industry.[2] Large conglomerates have been split into independent units and new global competing groups have been formed in a few years.[3]

Changes that are the result of market, customer and material flow dynamics make it often necessary to rapidly reconfigure a virtual enterprise and also to swiftly renegotiate with partners (including subcontractors) in the enterprise to manage any critical disruptions to the planning in order to protect delivery precision.

Implications for the Traditional Planning and Control Hierarchy

The flexibility that these virtual enterprises need also changes the traditional product planning and control hierarchy shown in Figure 1:

- *On the strategic level*: Not only a "capacity plan" and "personnel plan" will be created for the core enterprise entities but also a "subcontract plan" that identifies products and volumes subject for subcontracting and preferred subcontractors.
- *On the tactical level*: The "sequencing and scheduling" module has the responsibility to build a schedule not only for one shop floor but for the different virtual enterprise units. Part of the "sequencing and scheduling" task is the selection of subcontractors and service providers that are required to realize the plan. It is worthwhile to mention that this subcontracting gives the tactical level the option to extend or reduce production capacity, in the past the sole responsibility of the strategic level.
- *On the control level*: This level consists of several units, some of them part of the core enterprise and others consisting of subcontracting units and service providers. Every subcontractor partner in the virtual enterprise can behave cooperatively or self-interestedly and this results in an optimization exercise with limited information and concurrent goal optimization.

The ideal system is one in which the virtual enterprise planning manager can combine the planning exercise with the make or buy decision flexibility that he wants. If a feasible schedule is obtained, the system will report it; otherwise, it would identify subcontractors and the additional schedules.

Thus, the goal is to devise, analyze and implement a VE production planning and scheduling methodology that performs the necessary operations needed at the core of such a decision support system.

To do this, it must (1) generate good finite capacity production schedules for the "virtual enterprise" and (2) detect scheduling infeasibilities, and if the instance has no feasible schedule, it should (3) suggest the subcontracting activities to make the schedule feasible.

This goal presents a number of challenges:

* *Generate nearly optimal finite capacity production schedules.* Feasible schedules consider capacity explicitly and provide start and end times of the tasks at

Figure 1: Product planning and control hierarchy for pull systems

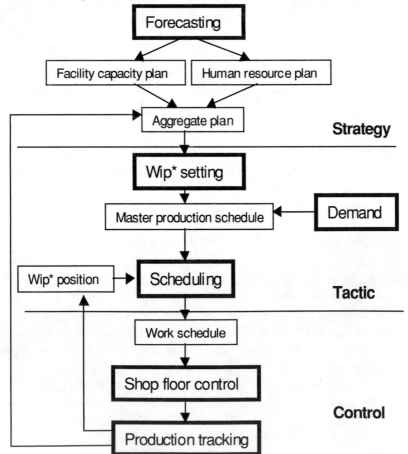

* Wip = work in progress

the different resources. The explicit timing of job arrival and departure does allow an extension of the system to schedule linked resources.

- *Suggest subcontracting activities.* The system provides useful diagnostics on how the schedule can be improved by subcontracting work when some due dates (deadlines) could not be met.
- *Concurrent goal optimization.* Because virtual enterprises consist of core enterprise units and subcontractors or service providers not part of the core enterprise, the used methodology and system should allow direct participation of these partners in the decision process.

The virtual enterprise adds new dimensions. Systems and algorithms must cater with a large number of owned and subcontracted enterprise units and a dynamic configuration and reconfiguration of the virtual enterprise network. The product planning and control hierarchy shown in Figure 1 is transformed in the new architecture shown in Figure 2.

The VE units (including subcontractors) have a decision autonomy that they do not want to delegate to an external system or company. They optimize their own internal schedule and can participate simultaneously in several virtual enterprise networks.

The independent VE unit owner of the information will control access to its data, especially in regard to competitors in the network.

State of the Art

The VE planning and scheduling methodology described in this chapter has several optional starting points. First, (1) it can use time-bucket-based techniques on which the popular MRP technique and its derivatives are based.

Figure 2: Product planning and control hierarchy for the VE

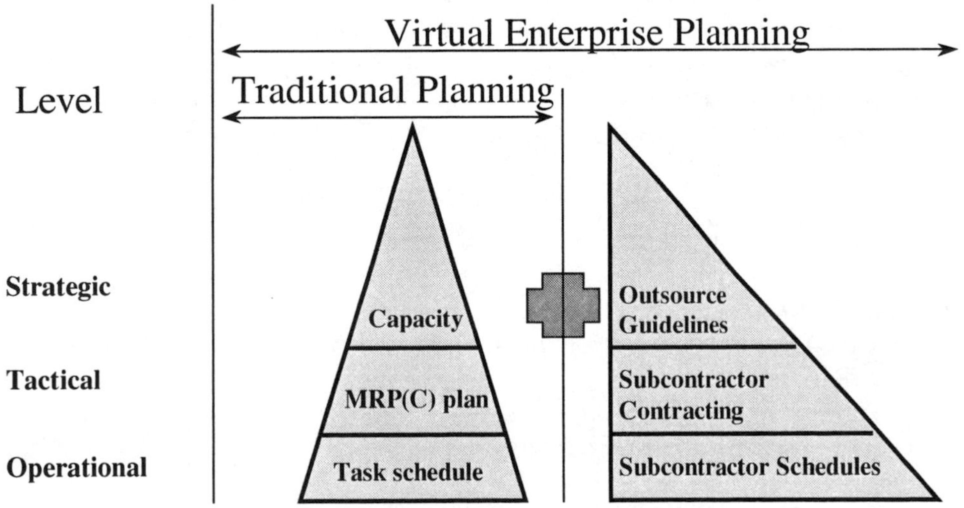

These older techniques (MRP/CRP) are often found as an engine in currently available ERP packages. Recently Valerie Tardif (Tardif, 1995) has published an advanced MRP-C technique. Another option (2) is to use continuous-time-based techniques. These have the advantage that they can incorporate scheduling events and obtain a more precise or even exact schedule. This option however is very computation-intensive and designing the model is complex. The third (3) way to model virtual enterprises and supply chains found in the literature is using statistical or stochastic models (Cohen, Eliashberg, & Ho, 1996). These are fast computational techniques that can be used in steady state mass-production environments. Kaihara (1999) more recently (4) introduced an extension on the Cobb-Douglas microeconomic theory to predict the equilibrium in resource loading and order distribution in the extended enterprise.

In the past most researchers on production planning and scheduling suggested also (5) hierarchical approaches for solving the problem, due to its high level of complexity (Hadavi & Voigt, 1987; Leachman & Ciriani , 1993).

The author also suggests the paper of Beamon (1998) for a more traditional view on supply chain modeling.

Despite the efforts made, these techniques did not receive broad acceptance in industry with the exception of MRP, and none of these techniques or methods integrates the make or buy process. The conclusion is that agile virtual enterprises and enterprise networks enabled by the widespread use of the Internet have need for a new methodology.

THE STEPWISE OPTIMIZATION METHODOLOGY

The methodology (illustrated in Figure 3) creates in the first step (1) a "rough feasible plan" and calculates the rough optimum (2). It can be quickly generated and consists of a set of first routings of the orders in the VE with order due dates for the different enterprise units and a total cost of the schedule. This "rough feasible plan" can be used to answer questions about the feasibility to deliver products to customers at prespecified due dates. (The rough plan can be MRP based, based on dynamic scheduling heuristics or on the combination of local VE unit schedules). The planner can accept this solution that will be feasible but not at an optimal cost or reject it and ask for a better solution. When he asks for a better solution or when the methodology is used to create a fine optimized schedule, sets of "rough feasible plans" will be generated.

If a "rough plan" part of this set is "promising," the methodology will search for a (3) local optimum in the neighborhood of this "rough" solution, using the "fine optimizer" of the methodology.

The "fine optimizer" works on the whole virtual enterprise and looks at the available free slack in the orders at any point in the process routes and will in this way be able to improve the given rough schedule.

The typical rough and fine planning cycle found in discrete manufacturing industries is replaced by one stepwise planning optimizer that can generate fast a feasible plan (rough planner) and then stepwise refines this solution to a detailed fine plan (fine planner) including all VE units.

"Incremental rescheduling" is an additional advantage of the methodology.

The rough planner takes the new orders and plans them into the existing schedule. However if the planner wants a better schedule or if it is not possible to schedule the new orders, the optimizer will start to consider more and more jobs and orders for rescheduling.

The optimizer steps from plan to plan and memorizes a trail of intermediate solutions. To avoid that those schedules that have been modified several times by short rough planner runs deviate too much from a nearly optimal schedule, it is required to run a fine plan at regular intervals.

Figure 4 illustrates how the methodology first schedules new orders on top of the existing plan and, when required, reschedules orders that still have "enough" slack and, if this is not sufficient, reschedules all "nonfrozen" orders. The next step is rescheduling all orders. In real life it will probably be impossible to execute this last (re-) planning stage due to order subcontracting limitations.

When a "fine plan" that includes all orders uses subcontracting, the methodology will search in the next step if a solution can be found that uses less subcontracting without violation of order due dates. An intelligent branch and bound algorithm that captures the specifics of the "make or buy" decision process in the semiconductor industry is used in this step.

The moment a routing, using subcontracting is accepted in a plan, a "supply chain construct" is defined. A plan constructed in this way will consist of a set of "supply chain constructs" that can differ from each other depending on the selected subcontracting entities for the orders.

Figure 3: The stepwise optimization methodology

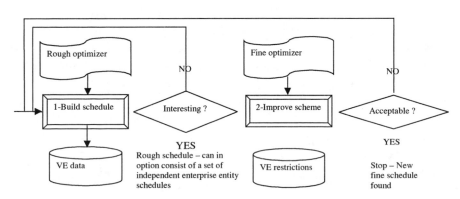

Figure 4: Incremental rescheduling with "frozen" orders

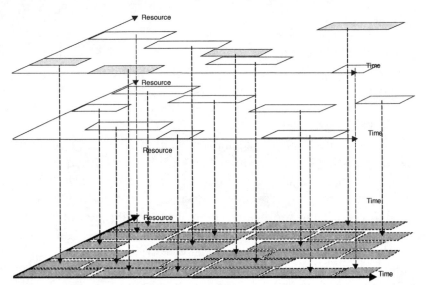

Benchmarking the Two-Stage, Stepwise Optimization Methodology

Sixty-four typical data sets of Makatsoris (1997), Fisher and Thompson (1963), Adams, Balas and Zawack (1988), Applegate and Cook (1991), Lawrence (1984), Storer, Wu and Vaccari (1992) and Yamada and Nakano (1992) with fixed sets of constraints have been used to benchmark the methodology. This larger set of benchmark exercises, some of them known for the issues that arise when you try to solve them, has been selected to tune the fine optimizer algorithm and to benchmark the results of the methodology with some of the best methods.

In a first exercise, scheduling results have been obtained using "dynamic dispatching" rules referenced in recent literature (Sabuncuoglu, 1998; Tipi & Bennett , 1999). A set of 7 different dynamic dispatching rules have been used to schedule the exercise: first in first out (fifo); last in first out (lifo); shortest operation processing time first (sopt); select job with most remaining work first (mrw); select job with least remaining work first (lrw); select operation with smallest ratio of the operation processing time to the total remaining processing time (odt); and select the operation with the smallest ratio obtained by multiplying the operation processing time by the total processing time (omt).

These results have been compared with the schedules generated by the fine optimizer, starting from a randomly generated start sequence for the jobs. The included graph (Graph 1) shows the sum of the obtained solution rankings, based on the makespan value, for every dispatching method applied to the set of exercises. It

Graph 1: Ranking methodology against dynamic dispatching heuristics

Ranking of Schedule approach

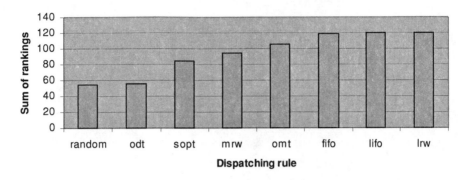

illustrates that the fine optimizer, starting from randomly generated start sequences (random), outperforms the best performing rule (odt). However the remark has to be made that the dynamic dispatching rule that performs best strongly depends on the selected set of exercises, and this is much less the case for the fine optimizer that does a global optimization based on the free slack[4] in the virtual enterprise construct.

Including the Network Enterprise Perspective in VE Planning

The optimization methodology is not only applicable for one virtual enterprise (VE) architecture but offers options for exploitation in the emerging network economy. Let's look at the e-marketplace concept to find the similarities.

Current Web marketplaces mimic real markets behavior as illustrated in Phase 1 (Figure 5). At t^0 (the current time) the market contains products that have been delivered by suppliers and can be bought by customers. If a customer is another enterprise and the product is an "intermediate product," we already have the virtual enterprise structure and the supplier can be seen as an (optional) subcontractor in the model. If the supplier also provides information about products that will be available on the marketplace at different instances in the future (t^0, t^1, ..., t^i, ... , t^n) and the customer expresses his needs at time instances in the future, the actors on the market can synchronize work based on the ATP (available to promise) information at the marketplace. When the marketplace uses resource capacity models and work in progress combined with products-in-inventory information, the two stage optimization methodology that will be described in this chapter can also be applied on this e-marketplace.

Every partner at the marketplace is a VE unit who has its local production optimization needs, and the core VE will use the information at the dynamic Web marketplace to run a global optimization pass. The described model supports VE units that deliver (1) a complete dynamic model with resources, process routes and work in progress; and the other VE units–commonly known as subcontractors–(2) who

Figure 5: The Web marketplace–an exploitation enabler

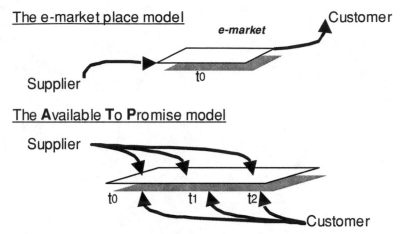

The e-market place model

Customer

e-market

t0

Supplier

The Available To Promise model

Supplier

t0   t1   t2

Customer

Supplier provides list of available products today (t0), next week (t1),...
and **Customer** can order for delivery today (t0), next week (t1),.....

limit visibility on the available information (product lead time, global production capacity).

Often the VE product is only a part (intermediate product) used in other virtual enterprise(s). This is the so-called multitier architecture found in the automotive and other industries. The described methodology also offers the option to combine the information available in this type of multitier virtual enterprise and removes some the disadvantages of traditional supply chains as described in Lee's (Lee, Padmanabhan & Whang ,1997) paper "Information Distortion in a Supply Chain: The Bullwhip Effect."

Figure 6 illustrates that one VE unit can be part of more than one virtual enterprise. These virtual enterprise units will optimize their local schedules first. The methodology can then use the collection of different local VE unit schedules to build a rough plan and the fine-pass optimizer can start from different rough solutions to build the fine virtual-enterprise-wide plan.

CONCLUSIONS

The methodology briefly described in this chapter succeeds to combine the flexibility requested by the industry with an optimization exercise that can work with replaceable constraint sets (so-called supply chain constructs).

The chosen concept is capable to: (1) do finite capacity planning; (2) integrate the rules defined by the planner and leave room for human guidance in the optimization process; (3) use the same consistent and synchronized model for the rough and fine planning cycle; and (4) respect in the optimization steps the commitments made to subcontractors by limiting rescheduling to nonfrozen jobs,

Figure 6: The dynamic n–Virtual enterprise Web marketplace

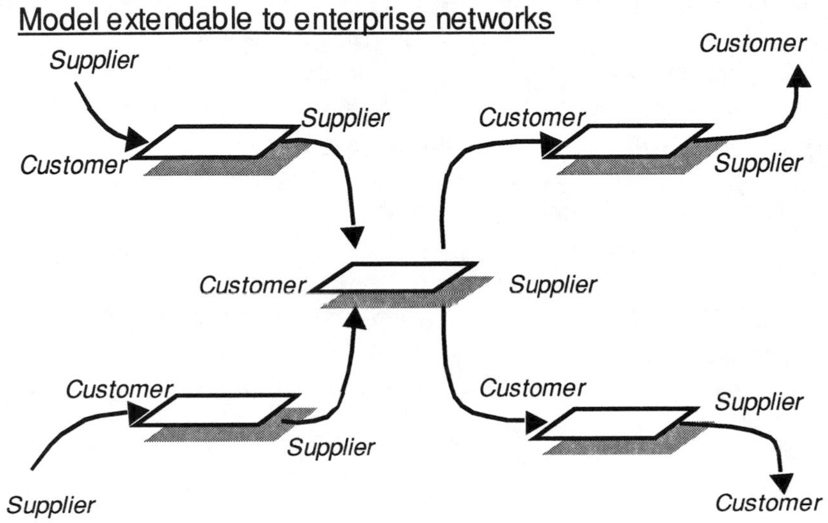

starting from the real work in progress.

ACKNOWLEDGEMENTS

The Imperial College of Science, Technology and Medicine, University of London, has supported this work. The encouraging results obtained so far have initiated enough momentum to start a new project (www.co-operate.org) that will produce a prototype of distributed, but cooperatively interoperating, business processes of a dynamic network of companies.

New collaboration rules and processes that will be developed in the Co-operate project[1] will combine cooperation in the network with the independence and flexibility of the individual virtual enterprise unit. This project shall provide more knowledge with respect to (1) what cooperation models are possible in the virtual enterprise environments and (2) exploring the advantages that can be obtained by linking several customer-subcontractor tiers over a larger part of the value chain.

APPENDIX: THE VIRTUAL ENTERPRISE DEFINED

The global availability of products is influencing the behavior of the customers and stimulating individual customer demands. As a consequence, the producing sector has to respond by an ever-broader product range, while the service sector must offer a more customized service profile. Markets for individualized products or services are small and quickly saturated, so that product life-cycles are shortened and service providers are forced to expand their service range continuously. In the shortest possible time, the producing sector develops new products with more sophisticated and extended functions in order to tap new markets. Cost leadership or a strategy to distinguish oneself from competitors must lead to new market shares to justify the increase in expenditure. Enterprises with the will to survive in spite of changing market requirements must excel their rivals in innovative power, quick learning capability and adaptability. Using global resources for development activities, purchased parts and components, as well as production and logistics has become a common strategy among manufacturers.

Due to the "uneasy triangle" (i.e., simultaneous shortening of product life-cycles, expansion of development and design cycles, and the explosion of preparation costs), enterprises find themselves caught in a "time trap." To escape from it they need to build cooperation and recombine their core competencies.

Possible forms of cooperation are groups, joint ventures, syndicates and strategic alliances. The first three types operate as corporated or incorporated firms, whereas strategic alliances usually enter into long-term cooperation agreements in a specific business area. A virtual enterprise, by contrast, combines various companies while maintaining the greatest flexibility and business independence. A crucial feature of a virtual enterprise is that it appears as a single company in the market though actually consisting of several enterprises. Thus, its internal relations resemble a decentralized enterprise.

Options for the intensity of enterprise cooperation:

1. Some writers specify the VE by the length and intensity of cooperation between different, possibly independent, enterprises. The cooperation between partners can (a) consist of short or long partnership; (b) cover only part of the VE units' available capacity or absorb all the available capacity; (c) have a less or more demanding core VE (a VE with large market potential and product knowledge can demand more from its cooperating units than a core VE with limited scope in time and size). Figure E-1 illustrates these possible scenarios and when it is called a VE (virtual enterprise).

2. Others specify as the most important characteristic of a virtual enterprise the unique face to the customer[5].

3. More often today's publications differentiate the virtual enterprise from the real enterprise by its focus on core competence and the management of the knowledge chain instead of the physical chain found in traditional enterprises. These papers stress that alliances, brand identity, product knowledge, market knowledge, market strategy, problem solving, and joint research and development are elements found in the virtual enterprise and that other elements (human resources, inventory, manufacturing, materials, offices, storefronts) become optional or disappear altogether.

The virtual enterprise definition in (3) is adopted in this chapter.

Boundaries of the Used Virtual Enterprise Concept

If the collaboration is of a short duration and low, in literature specified as the "conventional approach" and not as a "virtual organization," auctioning and competitive bidding can be used to acquire material and components. For VEs found in the semiconductor, microelectronics and automotive sectors, relationships are typical long lasting because the final product is a result of close cooperation, joint engineering and a long product qualification process. However the VE concept used in this chapter does not exclude the use of competitive bidding for capacity and the ability of a partner in the network to supply services at different production and/or supply chains.

While the used model is self-contained, it deals with a subset of a larger problem. The used VE model fits into a category that you can characterize as a traditional supply chain with stable partners. It manages capacity over several stages, multitiering, where the partners have been preselected. If these sub-manufacturers have autonomy, then the scheduling might require negotiation, particularly if the supplier is also dealing with other customers. The chapter recognizes the problem in discussing the multiple stages of supply of the automobile industry. However, it does not incorporate the uncertainties of negotiation directly into the model, but the methodology creates the flexibility for a VE entity to co-ordinate efficiently its work in several supply chains concurrently.

ENDNOTES

[1] See the appendix, *The Virtual Enterprise Defined.*
[2] Large groups (e.g., IBM) have been split in units (e.g., Lexmark) that now have to compete with other not owned subcontractors (e.g., Canon).
[3] Cisco, a merger of network companies, competes against established giants in the telecom market.
[4] For the sake of brevity, algorithmic details have not been included. However the methodology on its own merits should work well with any set of complementary rough- and fine-optimizer algorithms.
[5] Fifth framework Research and Technology Development project 2000-2002 with Alcatel Microelectronics (B), Imperial College (UK), Siemens Automotive (G), MEMC (Italy) and INESC (P).

REFERENCES

Adams, J., Balas, E., and Zawack, D. (1988). The shifting bottleneck procedure for job shop scheduling. *Management Science, 34*, 391-401.

Applegate, D. and Cook, W. (1991). A computational study of the job-shop scheduling instance. *ORSA Journal on Computing*, 3, 149-156.

Beamon, B. M. (1998). Supply chain design and analysis: Models and methods. *International Journal of Production Economics*, 55, 281-294.

Cohen, M. A., Eliashberg, J. and Ho, T. H. (1996). New product development: The performance and time-to-market tradeoff. *Management Science*, 42 (2).

Fisher, H. and Thompson, G. L. (1963). Probabilistic learning combinations of local job-shop scheduling rules. In J. F. Muth & G. L. Thompson (Eds.), *Industrial Scheduling* (pp. 225-251). Upper Saddle, NJ: Prentice Hall.

Hadavi, K. and Voigt. (1987). An integrated planning and scheduling environment. In *Proceedings of the Simulation and Artificial Intelligence in Manufacturing Conference*. Long Beach, CA: Society of Manufacturing Engineers.

Kaihara, T. (1999). Supply chain management with multi-agent paradigm. *Proceedings of the 8th International RO-MAN Conference*, Pisa, Italy, vol, 394-399.

Lawrence, S. (1984). *Resource Constrained Project Scheduling: An Experimental Investigation of Heuristic Scheduling Techniques*. Graduate School of Industrial Administration, Carnegie-Mellon University, Pittsburgh, PA.

Leachman, R. C. and Ciriani, T. A. (1993). *Optimization in Industry:* Modeling techniques for automated production planning in the semiconductor industry. New York: John Wiley & Sons.

Lee, H. L. and Billington, C. (1995, September-October). The evolution of supply-chain-management models and practice at Hewlett-Packard. *Interfaces,* 42-63.

Lee, H. L., Padmanabhan, V. and Whang, S. (1997). Information distortion in a supply chain: The bullwhip effect. *Management Science*, 43, 546-558.

Makatsoris, C. (1997). *Planning, Scheduling and Control for Distributed Manufacturing Systems*. Unpublished doctoral dissertation, Imperial College of Science, Technology and Medicine, London.

Sabuncuoglu, I. (1998). A study of scheduling rules of flexible manufacturing systems: A simulation approach. *International Journal of Production Research*, 36(2), 527-546.

Storer, R. H., Wu, S. D. and Vaccari, R. (1992). New search spaces for sequencing instances with application to job shop scheduling. *Management Science*, 38, 1495-1509.

Tardif, V. (1995). *Detecting Scheduling Infeasibilities in Multi-Stage, Finite Capacity, Production Environments*. Doctoral Dissertation, Northwestern University.

Tipi, N. S. and Bennett, S. (1999). Dispatching rules for scheduling and feedback control in a virtual enterprise–A simulation approach. *Proceedings of the FAIM99 Conference* on CD.

Yamada, T. and Nakano, R. (1992). A genetic algorithm applicable to large-scale job-shop instances. In Manner, R. and Manderick, B. (Eds.), *Parallel Instance Solving From Nature 2*, 281-290. North-Holland, Amsterdam.

Wu, D. S., Byeon, E., and Storer, R. H. (1999). A graph-theoretic decomposition of the job shop scheduling problem to achieve scheduling robustness. *Management Science*, 47(1).

Chapter XV

A Basic Approach Towards Cost Accounting for Virtual Web Organizations

Tim Veil and Thomas Hess
Georg-August-Universität Göttingen, Germany

INTRODUCTION

Virtual corporations (VCs) may be defined as a specific form of inter-company networks. Whereas vertically integrated strategic networks primarily appear in the automobile industry, VCs are frequently found in the software industry or the consulting sector. In the last years, VCs have been subject to different research activities, e.g., the relevance of IT infrastructure for VCs or the economical reasons for their appearance. Today, questions of how to manage VCs arise more and more often. Nevertheless, until today issues concerning planning and control have rarely been discussed. One traditional and major element of a planning and control system is the cost accounting system. As will be shown, multiple questions regarding cost accounting for virtual Web organizations come up theoretically as well as in practice.

Since VCs compete with other forms of coordination in markets, their products and services need to be competitive. Cost accounting in virtual Web organizations may provide important information for the decision making of an intercompany network-management. In order to assure a competitive output of a certain cooperation, costs need to be measured and prices for the marketed goods need to be calculated. Principally, only those partner companies join a VC that, besides certain quality requirements, meet the customers' target price. In addition, with the partner companies transferring products during the cooperation, transfer prices need to be established. Given that costs of coordinating the shared performance may display a significant share of the total costs of a VC, another issue to be discussed in the following is how standardized coordination-cost rates may be reviewed in VCs. In order to generate appropriate information, a cost accounting system for virtual Webs has to bridge the individual cost accounting systems of each partner of a virtual Web, taking into account the general autonomy of the members of a virtual Web organization. Different classifications of costs and variant methods of cost allocation are just two examples demonstrating the need for a flexible cost accounting system for virtual Web organizations.

The following three sections of this paper develop a first solution of how a cost accounting system for virtual Web organizations may be designed in order to support the life cycle of a VC. In section 2 we present the context of a cost accounting system for virtual Web organizations. Therefore, we give a brief overview of the traditional purposes of cost accounting, the state of the art of cost accounting as well as the specific requirements of virtual Web organizations. Section 3 describes the conceptual framework of a cost accounting system for virtual Web organizations. We discuss the typical information needs of the management and submit the basic structure of such a cost accounting system. In section 4, we examine three specific tools of a cost accounting system for virtual Web organizations: transfer pricing, total order pricing and coordination-cost rate analysis. To also refer to the concepts of cost accounting in the practice of virtual Web organizations, empirical experiences will be given throughout the sections. Finally, section 5 summarizes the results of the essay and presents an outlook on future research activities in the field of cost accounting for virtual Web organizations.

CONTEXT

Purposes of Cost Accounting

Cost accounting methods are the result of information requirements of management and their derived cost accounting purposes (Horngren, Foster, & Datar, 2000). Providing cost information to management is entirely purposive. As a dominating part of a firm's internal information system, cost accounting's traditional objective is to map and record the production of goods and services. Since World War II cost accounting developed to a system for decision making and control. The purposes of cost accounting today emphasize planning and control. Nowadays, a central objective of cost accounting is to prepare various kinds of managerial decisions such as production, pricing and capital budgeting decisions by providing knowledge for management (Zimmerman, 1997, pp. 4-5). When decision rights are decentralized to organization units of a firm (e.g., divisions or profit centers), cost information serves to influence the units' decisions and to coordinate the activities of these units. Today, the cost accounting theory as well as the cost accounting practice present multiple purposes of cost accounting (e.g., Horngren et al., 2000, chap. 2; Schweitzer & Küpper, 1998, pp. 38-49):

- to map and record,
- to plan and control and
- to motivate.

The use of a cost accounting system for purposes of mapping and recording displays the goal of evaluating realized, actual usage of resources (or input) for production processes. The calculated actual costs are accumulated and are after-wards assigned directly or indirectly to defined cost objects (Zimmerman, 1997, p. 307). The mapped and documented cost data are the sources for performance evaluations, cost estimations and budgeting. Therefore the purpose of mapping and documenting production processes lies in close connection with the other men-tioned purposes above. Planning and control purposes deal with providing cost information for managerial decisions. Estimated future costs reveal the effects of planning alternatives as well as deriving a goal confirmation planning alternative. Evaluating performance provides information on the efficiency of production processes and shall influence future managerial decisions. Furthermore, cost information may motivate employees to maximize the firm's profits when given monetary or nonmonetary incentives such as bonuses or advancement promises (Zimmerman, 1997, p. 144).

State of the Art in Cost Accounting

Cost accounting is not only a traditional field of research within business administration. Cost accounting has even dominated research activities in business administration for a long period of time (Dorn, 1993). Thus, theoretically based and empirically validated cost accounting tools exist. The traditional concept of cost accounting in general provides accounting methods for two basic stages: cost accumulation and cost assignment. The German cost accounting theory and practice offer three different major sections of cost accounting for the above-mentioned stages: cost classification accounting, cost center accounting and cost object accounting (see Figure 1). The cost classification accounting assigns costs to certain cost classes for purposes of cost accumulation. It answers the question of what kind of costs (e.g., material, personnel, or administration costs) evolved during a certain period of time. The cost location accounting pools indirect costs related to divisions or departments in order to allocate indirect costs to cost objects. It answers the question where the costs appeared in the firm (e.g., supply, administrative or sales division) during a certain period of time. Finally, the cost object accounting answers the question for which cost object (e.g., order, product, activity or customer) direct and indirect costs evolved (Gleich & Pfohl, 2000).

Modern cost accounting systems that are being discussed in theory and practice include target costing, activity-based costing or life-cycle costing (e.g., Fischer, 2000). They adapt the traditional tools of cost accounting in order to improve pricing decisions, product profitability decisions and strategic cost management (Hansen & Mowen, 2000). Until now, traditional and modern cost accounting systems have focused their view mainly on single companies. Whereas multiple challenges of

Figure 1: The basic structure of German cost accounting

Major Cost Accounting Sections		
Cost Classification Accounting What kind of costs evolved?	**Cost Center Accounting** Where did costs appear?	**Cost Object Accounting** For which cost objects do costs evolve?

today's companies have led to these modern cost accounting systems, only a few attempts have been made to put them under a cooperation perspective and to create a cost accounting system for intercompany networks such as VCs (e.g., Scholz 1995). As shall be shown in the following, multiple questions regarding cost accounting for virtual Web organizations arise theoretically as well as in practice.

Specific Requirements of Virtual Corporations

VCs may be defined as one specific variant of intercompany networks. In intercompany networks at least three, but usually 10 or more, legally independent companies participate. The involved companies coordinate their operational functions within the network without merging them into a joint venture. The cooperation's objective is to realize a market opportunity, a so-called order, together. However, the cooperation is not limited to the time of a single order or project. Virtual Web organizations exist on a long-term basis. Therefore, participating companies find agreements, for example, on the goals, the internal rules of transferring goods and services or the marketing issues of a cooperation. On the basis of these agreements, VCs as temporary operational teams are configured for each type of order. Normally, only a few members of the virtual Web are involved in such a team. Figure 2 demonstrates the fundamental idea of VCs graphically. It has to be mentioned, in addition, that the companies' competencies in such a pool typically overlap. Moreover, companies may resign from the pool as well as new members may join the virtual Web quickly.

The key challenge from a planning and control perspective derives from the unstable and polycentric structure of a VC (Hess & Schumann, 2000), whereas a strategic network is a stable form of intercompany network and is usually dominated by one company or a small group of companies. Only the dominating part of the network has access to the market and makes the strategic decisions concerning the

Figure 2: The idea of a VC

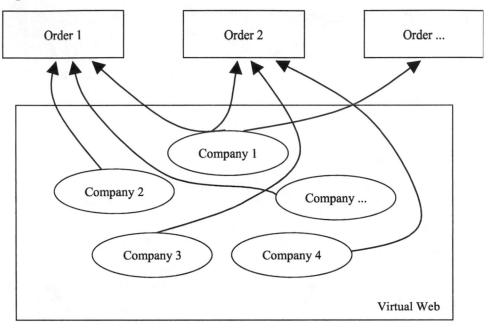

cooperation. Consider a strategic network in the automobile industry where a new automobile product line is produced under the guidance of one company without changing the team of suppliers. In contrary, VCs are configured for every new order. Since there does not exist a dominant partner within a virtual Web organization, every company has equal rights and may influence the cooperation's strategic decisions. VCs are frequently found in the software industry or the consulting sector but also in the manufacturing sector (Veil & Hess, 1998).

A cost accounting system for a virtual Web organization needs to take into account specific requirements. They may be described as follows:

- **Distributed, shared performance**: VCs do not possess any own resources. For any market order, the most competent companies have to be selected from the pool of partners to perform a suborder with their own resources. The interfaces evolving between the performing partners gain major importance.
- **Flexible, process-oriented configuration**: In contrary to traditional organizations, tasks are not necessarily assigned to a partner but are allocated for every type of order. In consequence, the process to be performed to fulfil an order is the main planning and control object.
- **Autonomy of the partners**: In decentralized organizations, the organizations' units (e.g., profit centers) act autonomic to a certain extent. Still, their actions are restricted by the overall management's right to instruct the unit. Consider a management holding that decides which markets are going to be accessed and what product lines are going to be produced by the affiliated group. From a formal point of view, such a right to instruct does not exist in a VC.

Nevertheless, due to actual dependencies, a dominating partner in a strategic network may be in a position to instruct a supplier.

As a result of these specific requirements, a cost accounting system for virtual Web organizations has to deal with the organizational restrictions that derive from this form of coordination. First, such an accounting system needs to cover a high number of partners, in some cases exceeding 10 companies or more, all with their own, individualized accounting system. Secondly, such an accounting system has to be flexible so that it may follow the fast configuration of a project team and show its added value. At the same time, planning and control systems need to be efficient. Their economic value depends on the dynamics of the organization that uses them. Hence, standards and regulations within the inter-company network will be discussed.

CONCEPTUAL FRAMEWORK OF COST ACCOUNTING FOR VIRTUAL WEB ORGANIZATIONS

The Management's Information Needs

As already pointed out above, cost accounting methods are the result of management information requirements. In order to demonstrate the need for cost information of the network-management, we refer to the net-broker tasks in the following. The tasks of the network-management in order to coordinate the performance of a virtual Web organization may be divided into such tasks carried out for each market order and those tasks executed for a set of market orders. The first mentioned tasks shall be discussed under the synonym of "order-related" tasks. The latter shall be called "above-order" tasks. Since the major usage of cost accounting tools can be seen for operative reasons in general, an emphasis shall be laid on the information needed for order-tasks. During the life cycle of an operational team, the net-broker should decide on the acceptance of an order, allocate suborders, price an order, plan and control the realization of an order and allocate operating income or losses. Table 1 displays the attributes of the required cost data for order-tasks.

In order to decide whether an order should be performed and an auction of suborders should be organized, the network-management needs to estimate the profit of an order or the operating income respectively. Because of the autonomy of the members of a VC, each partner may have his own objective or goal concerning his participation in the network. To avoid inefficient coordination, rules for such a decision concerning a set of orders may be defined. Normally, such a rule will induce a positive decision when the order's revenues exceed the total order costs and an operating income can be forecasted.

Table 1: Attributes of required information for order-tasks

Management Task	Required Information	Cost Object
Decide to Perform an Order	▪ Operating income ▪ Contribution Margin	Total Order
Allocate Sub-Orders	▪ Prices ▪ Costs ▪ Operating income	Sub-Order
Price Total Order	▪ Prices	Total Order
Plan and Control the Order	▪ Prices ▪ Costs	Sub-Order; Total Order
Allocate Operating Income or Loss	▪ Operating Income ▪ Operating Loss	Total Order

The allocation of suborders should be based on a comparison of calculated suborder costs or suborder prices, including a margin. After a competitive bidding has taken place in the virtual Web (e.g., Veil & Hess, 1998) and suborders have been priced by the potential members of an operational team, the net-broker needs to evaluate the partners' offers. As a benchmark for allocation decisions, the suborder prices should meet a certain target price (e.g., Horngren et al., 2000, p. 436). Such a target order price is a price that either is demanded by the customer of the virtual company already or has to be estimated by the net-broker himself. Target prices, costs or operating income per suborder may be derived from a total target order price. Usually, those partners will be chosen to perform a suborder that provide the lowest price for a suborder performance with consideration of a certain quality level. In contrary to the information need for the first task discussed, the network-management requires cost accounting data concerning suborders.

Further cost information needs to be derived from the fact that an order price has to be stated. The net-broker may be seen as an intermediary between the market or a customer and the partners of a VC. Therefore a net-broker may negotiate an order price with a customer. The net-broker's basic information object is an aggregated total order price. Due to variable capacity utilization or bargaining processes between the net-broker and the customer, a total order price might need to be decreased and calculated on the basis of partial costs (e.g., variable costs only). As will be shown later, pricing an order based on intertwined performance processes in VCs requires a specific aggregation method.

After an order price is stated and a team is configured, the realization of an order has to be planned and controlled. The shared performance accounts for real coordinated as well as formal objectives. Transfer prices are one popular method for coordinating decentralized units (e.g., profit centers) in a formal way. Their usage in VCs shall be discussed in detail later. Whether the cost data in order to plan and control the realization of an order should be provided in detail, for example, on the basis of cost classes such as material or personnel costs of suborders or if simply the total order price shall be the planning and control object can not be generally stated. As can be seen in some cases of VCs, detailed cost data is presented to the net-broker or even all members of the network for purposes of planning and control. In the practice of VCs, the provided specific, detailed cost data have also an effect of reducing opportunism risk (Veil & Hess, 1998).

Exceptionally, the management of the VC might need to allocate operating income or loss within the network after an order has been performed. Two general cases may occur: first, when partners of a VC base their suborder prices on costs only or, secondly, when the realized revenues exceed or drop below the calculated revenues of an order. In the first case, the management requires the total order's operating income or loss as the difference between the total order revenues and the total order costs. In the latter, it requires the operating income surplus or loss as the residual of the total order revenues and the aggregated suborder prices including a pre-calculated margin.

In addition, above-order tasks cause cost accounting information needs (see Table 2). In contrary to order-tasks, these net-broker tasks are not performed in a sequence.

The most traditional performance measures include revenues as well as operating income. They may be determined to evaluate the success of the virtual Web organization, its members and its fields of cooperation. Another above-order task may be to control implemented standard-cost rates for services like the coordination of orders, network-wide marketing or educational services.

Basic Structure

In this section, the basic structure of a cost accounting system for virtual Web organizations shall be demonstrated. First, answers concerning the following basic questions shall be given:

1. What are the main instruments of cost accounting for virtual Web organizations?
2. What objects does cost accounting in virtual Web organizations refer to?
3. How is cost accounting in virtual Web organizations organized, and who executes the accounting processes?
4. What do the accounting processes refer to in means of numbers of orders and periodicity?

Figure 3 gives an overview of the basic structure of cost accounting for virtual Web organizations.

Table 2: Attributes of required information for above-order tasks

Management Task	Required Information	Cost Object
Evaluate the Virtual Web Organization's Success	• Revenues • Operating Income	Virtual Web Organization
Structure the Virtual Web	• Revenues • Operating Income	Partner
Evaluate Fields of Cooperation	• Revenues • Operating Income	Field of Cooperation
Control Standard-Cost Rates	• Costs	Indirect Services

Figure 3: The basic structure of cost accounting for virtual Web organizations

Selected Cost Accounting Instruments	Order Pricing, Indirect-Cost Rate Analysis	Revenues Analysis	Operating Income Analysis
Accounting Measures	Costs	Revenues	Operating income
Accounting Objects	Sub-order, total order	Virtual corporation, partner, field of co-operation, total order	Virtual corporation, partner, field of co-operation, total order
Accounting Executive	Partner, virtual corporation	Virtual corporation	Virtual corporation
Reference and Periodicity	Single order, non-periodic	Multiple orders, periodic	Multiple orders, periodic

As discussed earlier, the cost accounting system needs to fulfil diverse purposes and information requirements. Thus, several cost accounting instruments have to be implemented and multiple cost accounting objects need to be referred to (see Figure 3). In view of the fact that VCs are configured for the time an order is performed, the general cost object applies to the order. Since orders are not linked to a specific period of time, order-related cost data is non-periodic. Nevertheless, a revenue and operating income analysis concerning the performance of the virtual Web organization is typically carried out for a set of orders. When cost data is derived in order to analyze the performance over multiple orders, these are usually related to a period of time, for instance, one year.

Furthermore, two cost accounting executives have to be differentiated: the partners of the VC and the virtual Web organization itself. Due to the partners' general autonomy to price suborders, they provide the input data for the total order pricing process. The partners' suborder prices are aggregated to a total order price. The aggregation is carried out through a separate, specific accounting process realized by the VC and will be demonstrated later under the synonym of total order pricing. Cost classification accounting as well as cost location accounting (see Figure 1) are executed by the partners exclusively in order to price suborders. These sections with their multiple cost allocation processes are not performed by the VC but the partners. The partners' cost allocation tools and processes are used indirectly by the VC to price total orders.

In addition, the cost-rate analysis presented here discusses the indirect service of coordinating the shared, distributed performance of an order. Given that this service is performed by the management of a VC, it will be analyzed by the cost accounting systems of the coordinating partners (e.g., the net-broker) themselves.

Cost data for purposes of performance measurement analysis are usually generated through accounting processes of the virtual Web organization. The order cost data is accumulated in a central cost database (e.g., by the net-broker) and may then be analyzed. Only on the source of accumulated order revenues and order costs, the periodic revenues and operating income may be analyzed.

In the following section, three key applications in order to provide order-related cost accounting information for the management of a virtual Web organization shall be presented and discussed: transfer pricing, total order pricing and coordination-cost rate analysis. These three applications are chosen since they cover a major part of the management's information needs.

KEY INSTRUMENTS OF A COST ACCOUNTING SYSTEM FOR VIRTUAL WEB ORGANIZATIONS

Transfer Pricing

The distributed, shared performance in VCs has the effect that goods and services need to be transferred from one partner to an other. Prices for suborders concerning intermediate goods and services within an organization are usually denoted as transfer prices. In decentralized organizations (e.g., profit center organizations, affiliated groups), the main function of transfer prices is to coordinate the units' decisions so that the prices meet the overall organization's goal. Market-based, cost-based and negotiated transfer prices are the most frequently discussed transfer-pricing methods in decentralized organizations (e.g., Coenenberg, 1999; Horngren et al., 2000, chap. 22).

Transferring goods and services at market-based prices is considered to lead to the best coordination in means of overall goal congruence. Still, market-based transfer prices are only suitable in conditions of a perfectly competitive market for intermediate products and when a marketprice is available (Ewert & Wagenhofer, 1997). Very often, these conditions do not exist in reality. Market-based transfer prices are therefore rarely employed. It needs to be mentioned, in addition, that market-based transfer prices shift the risk upon the providing unit. Even if market prices are available, their use may not lead to a perfect coordination right away. More important, integration advantages are not taken into account when establishing this method of transfer pricing.

Cost-based transfer prices are usually established when market prices are not available or are hard to obtain. This may be the case when the intermediate product or service is specialized or unique. Basic parameters of cost-based transfer prices include the time reference of the cost data, the cost volume and the enclosure of a margin (see Ewert & Wagenhofer, 1997). When actual costs are considered, an exact coverage of the included costs is theoretically assured. In practice, transfer prices based on actual costs are not suitable because such costs may only be computed after the intermediate product or service has been produced or provided. Due to this fact, transfer prices are usually based on standardized or negotiated costs. They might be determined in advance of the transfer. In this case, the selling unit has an interest not to exceed standardized or negotiated costs. The opportunism risk is reduced.

Concerning the volume of the implied costs, full-cost and variable cost bases can be differentiated. Traditionally, variable cost bases were considered as the optimum solution to achieve goal congruence when establishing cost-based transfer prices. Given that decentralized selling units act on their own behalf and the buying unit as well as the overall management may not validate the cost function due to lack of knowledge, the optimum assuring transfer price might not be determinable (e.g., Küpper, 1997, chap. III, p.4). Yet, if a variable-cost-based transfer price is calculated, the coverage of fixed costs still needs to be discussed. Only in the short run, when additional or unutilized capacities are offered on an internal market and the price for these products is stable, fixed costs do not need to be re-earned by the selling unit. In any other case, fixed costs need to be financed by the overhead unit (e.g., the holding unit) or by the buying unit. Such solutions meanwhile are discussed under the synonym of two-step-pricing methods in cost accounting theory and practice. For example, they suggest a fixed cost budget provided to the selling unit (Coenenberg, 1999). Nevertheless, when pricing services, variable cost bases are inappropriate due to the limited share of variable costs.

Full costs are often used in practice to assure relevant cost information for long-run decisions. Since fixed costs of the selling unit become variable costs of the buying unit, wrong decisions from the point of the overall management are also likely to occur when full costs are calculated. However, full-cost-based transfer prices are frequently established in practice and very often contain a margin. So-called full-cost-plus-margin transfer prices approximate market prices for intermediate products or services. Problems arise when an adequate margin should be defined. For example, calculating a margin as a percentage of the total costs or as a rate of interest referring to the invested capital are discussed as solutions.

No matter what pricing method for cost-based transfer prices is chosen, cost-based transfer prices require a detailed insight into the cost structures of the transferring units. Regularly, standardized cost catalogues are used in specific sections. For example, government contracting officers take advantage of these catalogues in the case of competitive bidding for an official order (Coenenberg, 1999).

Reviewing the presented methods, market-based transfer prices should be implemented as long as they are obtainable. If not so, full-cost-plus-margin prices should be chosen. Empirical studies reveal that both kinds of prices occur in practice (see Ewert & Wagenhofer, 1997, p. 572). Finally, the application of these concepts in VCs shall be discussed.

Transfer prices in a VC are primarily used for purposes of pricing suborders as well as of allocating suborders within the pool of the VC (see Hess, 2000, for details). Like in traditional decentralized organizations, market-based transfer prices should be the paradigm in VCs. In the case that partners of a VC offer their core competencies that they normally use to market their products on an external market,

market-based transfer prices will be obtainable. However, especially when indirect services such as the coordination of an offer or the assumption of risk shall be calculated, market-based transfer pricing will not be a useful solution. Therefore the question arises, how may cost-based pricing as a second-best solution be handled in VCs. Thus, the three basic parameters shall be discussed in the following.

To base transfer prices on actual costs is not useful in VCs. The incentive to perform a suborder efficiently would be too little and the advantages of autonomous acting partners within the VC could not be realized. As far as possible, negotiated or standardized costs should be called on instead. Standardized transfer prices may be observed in the practice of VCs already. Two general types of standardization must be differentiated:

- Standardizing quantities or values: Pricing decisions of VCs in the service sector are often based on standardized service cost rates (see Hess & Veil, 1999). Furthermore, supply chains employ standard cost rates for transported units within the inter-company network.
- Standardizing indirect service rates: Costs of acquisition and coordination services are computed by using a standardized percentage rate of the total order volume including costs and a margin.

Cost rates for indirect services may lead to inefficiencies and wrong pricing decisions themselves. These rates should therefore be analyzed regularly as will be shown in the Coordination-Cost Rate Analysis section.

An important decision is whether standardized transfer prices should relate to market prices (M) or costs ($C_{1..n}$) of n possible performing partners. In order to calculate standardized transfer prices (S) in VCs, we can differentiate three cases:

- $M < \min(C_1...C_n)$: In this case, the VC is not competitive. The VC needs to adapt to the requirements of the market in the long-run.
- $\min(C_1...C_n) < M < \max(C_1...C_n)$: To assure the competitiveness of the VC in the short and the long run and at the same time to maximize the profits of a large share of partners, S needs to equal M.
- $M > \max(C_1...C_n)$: In this case, the profit of each partner can be maximized. S equals $\max(C_1...C_n)$.

Is M likely to be reduced, S should be minimized early on. Only then it may be assured that the VC is competitive in the long run. This solution settles the coordinating function of transfer prices.

For those cost classes which may not be standardized, price comparisons should be organized in order to reduce the risk of opportunism. Comparing prices may relate to the components of the calculation. When the buying unit or the net-broker has perfect knowledge, he is in a position to question opportunistic behavior of a selling partner. By analogy to pricing procedures in affiliated groups, harmonized VC-wide calculation schemes may be established. In addition, suborder prices may be compared with prices of external suppliers or with an obtainable market price. As already mentioned above, specific cost data is often provided to the net-broker due to his limited knowledge of the performing processes. This procedure may assure fair pricing in VCs.

When transfer prices are freely negotiated, it has to be considered that the bargaining processes between the members of a VC are restricted to the limits of so-called "allowable costs" or "allowable prices." They should be derived from a total order price when the VC's aim is to market competitive products or services.

The second parameter concerns the different cost bases. Since variable-cost-based transfer prices ask for a distinct knowledge of the cost structure (the cost function as well as the utilization of capacity) and each partner knows his cost structure best, there is a small incentive to supply such information correctly. Even if the exact information could be provided, the cost of information itself needs to be considered. Furthermore, the question of allocating fixed costs has to be answered as long as not only spare capacities are utilized. The use of variable-cost-based transfer prices in VCs is very restricted. Thus, full-cost-based transfer prices are the paradigm.

Regarding the enclosure of margins, the concrete goals of the partners have to be taken into consideration. Regularly, partners will add a margin to their prices in order to assure their existence and long-term investment objectives. Only in the short term may a partner resign from calculating a margin.

Figure 4 gives an overview of transfer pricing solutions in VCs.

Principally, the presented solutions are relevant for both external and internal orders. In addition, the spatially distributed performance needs to be considered. To assure pricing, planning and control processes, the cost data should be obtained within a decentralized, network-wide IT-based cost accounting system.

Total Order Pricing

As already mentioned above, the net-broker may negotiate an order price with a customer. The net-broker's basic information object is an aggregated total order price. As will be shown here, in addition, pricing an order based on intertwined performance processes in VCs requires a specific aggregation method.

First, it needs to be decided which costs shall be taken into account when pricing an order in a VC. Beside the direct costs of an order, costs related to above-order tasks and services (e.g., costs of marketing or of IT infrastructure) occur in a VC. Since the costs of the above-order coordination are indirect costs in a general

Figure 4: General transfer pricing solutions in VCs

Time Reference of Cost Data	Actual costs	Negotiated costs	Standardized costs
Cost Volume	Full-cost		Variable cost
Enclosure of Operating Income	Not included		Included

sense, the exact cost volume is difficult to determine. Typically, the costs of the above-order coordination are budgeted for a period of one year and are equally shared by the partners of a VC: For example, the partners of "The Virtual Company" in Switzerland pay an annual fee of 800 Swiss francs to finance above-order tasks (Hess & Veil, 1999, p. 449). Thus, budgeted above-order costs are allocated by the partners themselves and are typically included in the suborder prices indirectly. To avoid double allocating above-order costs, these should not be taken into account when pricing a total order in a VC.

Beside the indirect costs of above-order tasks and services, also order-related coordinating tasks induce costs of indirect service activities. In practice, these costs are assigned to the total order as suborder prices by the VC. Usually, standardized indirect service rates are established to allocate the costs of order-related coordinating activities.

Another specific requirement of order pricing in VCs derives from the fact that suborder prices calculated by the partners should include a margin already. Otherwise, the operating income of an order needs to be allocated. The margin enclosed in the suborder prices may be considered explicitly or implicitly in a calculating scheme (see Figure 5). Figure 5 demonstrates the pricing of a total order in a VC in the software industry. In the presented case, standardized, daily cost rates are used to calculate the activities. A margin is included in these cost rates.

Characteristically, the total order price is determined by simply summing up the suborder prices, including the price for indirect services such as the acquisition and coordination of an order or the taking of risk. Thus, order pricing in a VC might be described as a summing-up calculation method.

Specific calculation requirements may derive from the fact that products may need to be exchanged between the partners when performing an order. This is usually the fact in vertically integrated VCs in the manufacturing industry. Due to intertwined performance processes in VCs, a specific aggregation method is required in order to avoid double calculating costs and to map the structure of the costs correctly. To illustrate this problem, an example shall be given. Consider a VC manufacturing truck-driver cabins. Partner A is supplied with the empty cabin from an external company. Partner A then mounts a cockpit and supplies Partner B with the cabin including the cockpit. Partner B then installs electronic devices and afterwards delivers it to the customer, a truck manufacturer. The price for the empty cabin is $10,000 and is included in the variable costs of Partner A. Another $10,000 variable costs arise for direct material and direct manufacturing labor. In addition, Partner A calculates a fixed manufacturing overhead of $3,000 and a margin of $1,000. Partner B's variable costs account for $24,000 for the cabin, including the cockpit delivered by Partner A, plus $10,000 costs of direct material and direct manufacturing labor. The fixed costs of Partner B are $5,000 and the margin is $2,000. Figure 6 demonstrates this example including the relevant cost data.

As the column presenting the total order cost data reveals, simply summing up the suborder cost figures leads to a false total order price of $65,000 (see Figure 6). To solve this problem, the cost data needs to be consolidated (see Veil & Hess, 2000,

Figure 5: Example for an order-pricing scheme of a VC in the software industry

(in $)	Technical specification	Technical realization	Implementation and training
Setup activity costs incl. margin	51*1,000 = 51,000	65*1,000 = 65,000	20*1,000 = 20,000
Expenses	18,000	3,000	4,000
Specific Hard- and Software	0	3,000	0
Total sub-order price	**69,000**	**71,000**	**24,000**

	164,000
Acquisition, coordinating activity costs, risk costs, margin (4% * 164,000) +	6,560
Total order price =	**170,560**

for details). Consolidating cost data is typically practiced in cost accounting for affiliated groups. The total order price should only include those costs that occur in connection with the organization's environment. Internally evoked costs or revenues, e.g., costs or revenues induced by an exchange of products between two units of an organization, need to be eliminated. Concerning the given example, the costs and the margin for the cockpit are double calculated, because they are already included in the variable costs of Partner B. The variable costs as well as the total order price need to be reduced by the suborder price for the cockpit. The consolidated, correct variable costs sum up to $30,000 ($54,000 minus $24,000), the consolidated total order price is $41,000 ($65,000 minus $24,000). Figure 7 shows an example for a consolidated total order pricing in a VC.

Figure 6: Example for a false pricing of a total order

(in $)	Cockpit (Partner A)	Electronic devices (Partner B)	Total order cost data
Variable costs	20,000 →	34,000	54,000
Fixed costs	3,000	5,000	8,000
Margin	1,000	2,000	3,000
Total price	24,000	41,000	65,000

Figure 7: Example for a consolidated pricing of a total order

(in $)	Cockpit (Partner A)	Electronic devices (Partner B)	Cost data adjustment	Consolidated costs
Variable costs	20,000 →	34,000	./. 24,000	30,000
Fixed costs	3,000	5,000		8,000
Margin	1,000	2,000		3,000
Total price	24,000	41,000	./. 24,000	41,000

As the example in Figure 6 shows, not only the total order price may be miscalculated but also the cost data structure might be falsified. The fixed costs of the selling unit (Partner A) become variable costs of the buying unit (Partner B). The total variable costs of the truck driver cabin from the perspective of the VC are $30,000 instead of $54,000. In order to reveal and map the correct cost data structure of the VC, only the so-called primary costs of the VC need to be calculated and the secondary costs of the VC must be eliminated. Primary costs are defined as those costs of an organization that are the result of transactions with individuals or companies that do not belong to the organization itself (see Veil & Hess, 2000, for details). For example, costs of materials supplied by external companies are primary costs as are costs of labor too. In contrary, costs induced by internal exchanges are defined as secondary costs of an organization. Figure 8 demonstrates an example for calculating primary costs in a VC.

Especially when pricing orders on a variable cost-base, the correct, relevant cost data may only be assured when calculating primary costs. For example, calculating primary costs may be necessary when the VC's capacities are not fully utilized and the net-broker requires the lowest possible price in order to negotiate the total order price with a customer.

Since the secondary costs of Partner B ($24,000) correspond with the costs to be consolidated ($24,000), the accumulated primary costs equal the consolidated costs of the total order. Thus, pricing an order in a VC should be based on either accumulated primary costs or consolidated total order costs. Although both pricing methods induce specific calculating efforts, they are necessary when relevant and correct costs shall be determined in a VC.

Coordination-Cost Rate Analysis

Virtual Web organizations may only be competitive in the long run when not only the direct order costs but also the costs of indirect services are re-earned. As already mentioned in the previous section, costs of coordinating orders are taken into account when pricing a VC's total order. In the practice of VCs, these costs are often determined as a percentage of the total order volume. In three out of five cases, we have observed VCs that have implemented a standardized coordination-cost rate: The net-broker of the "Virtuelle Fabrik Nordwestschweiz" in Switzerland receives 3% of the total order volume for his coordinating activities; the net-broker of the "The Virtual Company" in Switzerland charges 10% of the price of each performed suborder; and for coordinating projects, marketing activities and other above-order tasks, the network-management of the "BUS-network" in Germany calculates 30% of the total order volume (Veil & Hess, 2001).

Figure 8: Example for a primary cost calculation

(in $)	Primary costs Partner A	Primary costs Partner B	Accumulated primary costs
Variable costs	20,000 ⟶	10,000 ⟶	30,000
Fixed costs	3,000 ⟶	5,000 ⟶	8,000
Margin	1,000 ⟶	2,000 ⟶	3,000

The risk of cost distortion and therefore misguiding cost data may be reduced when the exact costs of coordinating activities are computed once in a while. In this section, a method shall be presented that allows the VC to determine costs of coordinating activities in a more detailed way of accounting and to verify the standardized costs of coordinating activities.

Due to inaccurate traditional methods of allocating common costs (e.g., on the basis of direct labor), more precise allocation methods were developed and are discussed under the synonym of activity-based costing or process costing for several years now (e.g., Cooper & Kaplan, 1988; Miller & Vollmann, 1985). Assuming that costs of coordinating orders are not driven by the volume of total order costs but by the coordinating activities, a method relating to activity-based costing (ABC) shall be presented.

Determining and analyzing costs of coordinating activities in VCs follow four major steps:

- identifying coordinating activities,
- identifying activity cost drivers,
- assigning costs to coordinating activities, and
- analyzing costs of coordinating activities.

To identify activities, interviews with the responsible performing individuals or an analysis of the relevant documents are proposed (e.g., Haselgruber & Sure, 1999, p. 41). In the following, already presented order-related tasks performed by the net-broker shall be the basis for defining detailed order coordinating activities. Figure 9 shows the possible result of identifying order coordinating activities in a VC.

Whether it is useful or necessary to define more detailed activities depends on the desired degree of preciseness of the analysis. As will be shown next, a more detailed identification of activities may be needed to assure an accurate cost driver definition (Schweitzer & Küpper, 1998, p. 329).

Activity cost drivers should picture the correct resource absorption. Often it is assumed that cost drivers are identical with the cost magnitude of influence or the output of an activity (e.g., the number of customer orders processed). Concerning management activities, it may be difficult to identify such cost drivers that relate to only one cost magnitude of influence. Management activities are often complex activities so that several magnitudes of influence may be differentiated. For example, the activity of synchronizing capacities and know-how for the performance of a customer order may be influenced by the required resources as well as the number of partners in the virtual Web: For how much different know-how does a specific order ask and for how many partners in the virtual Web should capacities and know-how be synchronized?

In view of this fact, cost drivers for coordinating activities should relate to the input absorbed by the different processes and not to the output of the processes. Thus, the costs of coordinating activities shall be determined by evaluating the quantified resource input (see Cooper, 1990, p. 277). When analyzing the resources of coordinating activities, primarily costs of personnel and inevitably costs of

Figure 9: Examples for coordinating activities

Management's order-tasks	Examples for coordinating activities
Decide to perform an order	• Synchronize capacities and know-how • Estimate total order costs and revenues
Allocate sub-orders	• Analyze order objectives and tasks • Advertise sub-orders • Evaluate alternative bids
Price the total order	• Aggregate sub-order prices
Plan and control the order	• Determine monetary and non-monetary defaults • Control monetary and non-monetary defaults • Determine variances
Allocate operating income	• Determine the operating income of an order

infrastructure such as office rental, electricity costs and IT costs (e.g., costs of software and hardware) occur. Assuming that the costs of personnel dominate the costs of infrastructure it seems appropriate to identify the hours of coordinating an order as the relevant cost driver.

In order to assign the costs to the coordinating activities, an activity rate needs to be computed (Hansen & Mowen, 2000, chap. 12). To also take account of the costs of infrastructure, a cost pool for coordinating activities should be calculated that consists of personnel costs as well as costs of infrastructure. By dividing the pooled actual costs associated with the consumed resources by the total hours of coordinating spent, a rate providing a more exact allocation may be determined:

$$Rate\ per\ hour\ of\ coordination = \frac{Accumulated\ actual\ costs}{Accumulated\ hours\ spent}.$$

Supposing that all the performed orders nearly absorb the same resources, a convenient way of computing the above rate is to accumulate actual costs and hours spent on an annual basis. Difficulties may arise from the fact that more than just one partner of the VC is involved in the coordination of orders. Thus, either each coordinating partner should determine his own rate or a common rate needs to be calculated. Conflicts may occur when the rates or the costs of coordinating resources vary between the partners.

Finally, by multiplying the determined rate with the numbers of coordinating hours spent, the actual costs of coordinating a specific order may be computed:

*Costs of coordinating an order = Rate per hour of coordination * hours of coordinating.*

Figure 10 gives an example for a scheme for calculating order-related costs of coordinating.

Finally, the actual costs of coordinating activities should be compared with the standardized coordination costs. In order to determine the cost distortion possibly evoked by the volume-oriented standard-cost rate, the actual costs of coordinating activities have to be subtracted from the standardized costs:

Cost variance= Standardized costs of coordination ./. Actual costs of coordination .

Figure 10: Example for calulating costs of coordinating activities

Coordinating Activities Order 1	Required Hours
Synchronize capacities and know-how	6 h
Estimate total order costs and revenues	4,5 h
Analyze order objectives and tasks	7 h
Advertise sub-orders	2,5 h
Evaluate alternative bids	5 h
Aggregate sub-order prices	2 h
Determine monetary and non-monetary defaults	3 h
Control monetary and non-monetary defaults	12 h
Determine variances	4 h
Determine the operating income	1,5 h
Accumulated hours	47,5 h
Coordination-cost rate	$70
Costs of coordinating activities	$3,325

The computed cost variance may be analyzed more precisely when, e.g., matching cost variances concerning several orders. How often costs of coordinating activities should be calculated based on ABC can not be generally stated. Due to a rising number of cost variances, suggestions concerning a more precise standard-cost rate may be given. However, coordination costs may vary strongly because of the complex nature of the underlying activities. To determine numerous cost variances would only be suitable when the share of coordination costs in the total cost volume is significant (e.g., more than 5%). Only then may coordination cost distortions lead to wrong pricing decisions that may have a severe impact on the virtual Web organization's competitiveness in the long run.

CONCLUSIONS

As we have shown above, the management of a virtual Web organization calls for multiple cost accounting data in order to coordinate the shared performance and to assure the competitiveness of the organization: Transfer prices need to be established, total order prices must be computed and the costs of coordination may be reviewed. Parallel to the cost accounting tools of the partners of a virtual Web organization that submit suborder-related cost information, specific cost accounting instruments need to be implemented to provide order-related cost data. In view of this fact, we have presented first solutions of how a cost accounting system for virtual Web organizations may be designed and applied. Nevertheless, cost accounting in virtual Web organizations requires additional research activities.

First of all, the presented cost accounting methods need to be proved in the practice. On the conceptual side, standards and regulations of cost accounting should explicitly be discussed as these are usually established in affiliated groups and other decentralized organizations. Moreover, an accounting system for virtual Web organizations should also consider nonmonetary performance measures to manage the cooperation effectively. Thus, the implementation of modern methods of performance measurement as the balanced scorecard should be investigated.

REFERENCES

Coenenberg, A. G. (1999). *Kostenrechnung und Kostenanalyse*. (4th Rev. ed.). Landsberg/Lech, Germany: Verlag Moderne Industrie.

Cooper, R. (1990). Activity-Based Costing–Wann brauche ich ein Activity-Based Cost-System und welche Kostentreiber sind notwendig? *Kostenrechnungspraxis*, 271-279.

Cooper, R., and Kaplan, R. S. (1988). Measure costs right: Make the right decisions. *Harvard Business Review*, *66*, 96-103.

Dorn, G. (1993). Geschichte der Kostenrechnung. In K. Chmielewicz & M. Schweitzer (Eds.), *Handwörterbuch des Rechnungswesens* (3rd Rev. ed., columns 722-729). Stuttgart, Germany: Schäffer-Poeschel.

Ewert, R. and Wagenhofer, A. (1997). *Interne Unternehmensrechnung*, 3rd Rev. ed., Berlin, Germany, Heidelberg, Germany, New York, Barcelona, Spain, Hong Kong, China, London, Milan, Paris, Singapure, Tokyo: Springer.

Fischer, T. M. (2000). *Kosten-Controlling: Neue Methoden und Inhalte*. Stuttgart, Germany: Schäffer-Poeschel.

Gleich, R. and Pfohl, M. (2000). Voll- und Teilkostenrechnungssysteme. In Fischer, T. M. (Ed.), *Kosten-Controlling: Neue Methoden und Inhalte*, 167-205. Stuttgart, Germany: Schäffer-Poeschel.

Hansen, D. R. and Mowen, M. M. (2000). *Cost Management: Accounting and Control*. 3rd ed. Cincinnati, OH: South-Western College.

Haselgruber, B. and Sure, M. (1999). Activity-Based Costing: Kostenrechnung nach dem verursacherprinzip. *Io Management*, 68, 40-43.

Hess, T. (2000). *Instrumente und DV-gestützte Werkzeuge für das Controlling in Unternehmensnetzwerken*. Göttingen, Germany.

Hess, T. and Schumann, M. (2000). Auftragscontrolling in Unternehmensnetzwerken. *Zeitschrift für Planung*, 11, 411-432.

Hess, T. and Veil, T. (1999). Controlling in Unternehmensnetzwerken–erste Erfahrungen der Praxis. *Controller Magazin*, 24, 446-449.

Horngren, C. T., Foster, G. and Datar, S. M. (2000). *Cost Accounting: A Managerial Emphasis*. 10th ed. Upper Saddle River, NJ: Prentice Hall.

Küpper, H. U. (1997). *Controlling*. 2nd Rev. ed. Stuttgart, Germany: Schäffer-Poeschel.

Miller, J. G. and Vollmann, T. E. (1985). The hidden factory. *Harvard Business Review*, 63, 142-150.

Scholz, C. (1995). Controlling im Virtuellen Unternehmen. In Scheer, A. W. (Ed.), *Rechnungswesen und EDV. 16. Saarbrücker Arbeitstagung 1995. Aus Turbulenzen zum gestärkten Konzept?* 171-192. Heidelberg, Germany: Physica-Verlag.

Schweitzer, M. and Küpper, H. U. (1998). *Systeme der Kosten und Erlösrechnung*. 7th Rev. ed. München, Germany: Franz Vahlen.

Veil, T. and Hess, T. (1998). Fallstudien zum Controlling von Unternehmensnetzwerken, Arbeitsbericht Nr. 3/1998 der Abteilung Wirtschaftsinformatik II der Universität Göttingen, Göttingen, Germany.

Veil, T. and Hess, T. (2000). Kalkulation in Unternehmensnetzwerken, Arbeitsbericht Nr. 3/ der Abteilung Wirtschaftsinformatik II der Universität Göttingen, Göttingen, Germany.

Veil, T. and Hess, T. (2001). Langzeitstudie zum Controlling von Unternehmensnetzwerken, Arbeitsbericht Nr. 1/ der Abteilung Wirtschaftsinformatik II der Universität Göttingen, Göttingen, Germany.

Zimmerman, J. L. (1997). *Accounting for Decision Making and Control*. 2nd ed. Boston, Burr Ridge, IL, Dubuque, IA, Madison, WI, New York, San Francisco, St. Louis, MO: Irwin McGraw-Hill.

Chapter XVI

Evaluating the Success of Virtual Corporations With CONECT: Basic Procedural Indications and Practical Application

Oliver Wohlgemuth and Thomas Hess
Georg-August-Universität Göttingen, Germany

A fundamental condition precedent to strategic decisions of virtual corporations and their partners is a profound knowledge of the cooperation's success. This paper discusses different evaluation methods and elaborates a specific technique for multidimensional appraisals of success. It reports the first outcomes and implications of its practical use at a consultancy network.

INTRODUCTION

Virtual corporations (VCs), as a means of a company's strategic reorientation, have received a growing attention in both theory and practice since the beginning of the 1980s. The concept of the VCs features a specific variety of cooperations, in which at least three companies cooperate with the purpose of achieving mutual objectives, without giving up their own legal independence (e.g., Miles & Snow, 1986, pp. 64-65).

On the basis of a long-term partnership, these companies undertake projects in different assemblies. In practice, VCs appear in various sectors. For a long time, virtual Web organizations were considered as prototypical in the car delivery industry. At the beginning of the 1990s, especially in the IT-services sector, the "virtual company" was introduced as a new type of VC. Recently, the supply chain network in trade and logistics has particularly enjoyed popularity. Apart from these popular examples there are a number of sectors in which virtual Web structures for cooperations have been used for a long time. The building industries can be referenced as an example.

The more intensively the partner company involves itself in the value-added chain of a network, the greater becomes its dependence from the cooperation. In extreme cases the survival of a participating company can even depend upon the economic success of the cooperation. This results almost inevitably in the necessity for the success of the cooperation to be measured.

The aim of the following is to show practical possibilities for measuring the success of a cooperation. For this purpose, in section 2, applicable procedures will be introduced and their possibilities of appliance in VCs will be evaluated. On that basis, section 3 is based upon a specific procedure which is approved for networks–the so-called CONECT-method (Collective Network Efficiency Control Tool). Section 4 describes the application of the method, using an example from the consulting sector, in order to test its practical suitability. The article ends in part 5 with an overview of the results and further research needs.

APPROACHES TO A METHODICAL EVALUATION OF SUCCESS

An Overview of Established Evaluation Methods

The structure of an evaluation procedure is closely related to the understanding of the term "cooperation success." The perception has generally been accepted that this term refers to the results of continuous cooperative work and not to a single, communal, processed assignment. Therewith evaluation of success belongs to the strategic level of management and controlling activities in VCs, which spans over single assignments. Apart from this commonness, the conceivabilities of the material "scope" of the term are very different. According to the number of success figures covered, a difference between unidimensional (pure quantitative) and multidimensional (mixed quantitative-qualitative) success definitions can be made.

Unidimensional approaches rest upon a single economic objective. However, there exist a number of different views in the literature with regard to the underlying time spread of the objective analysis: The classic approaches are oriented upon conventional, short-term measurements of success. From a narrow point of view, the characteristic "costs" are dealt with. Often these costs are interpreted in terms of cost savings, that is, the difference between savings and costs that have been encountered by the cooperation. Further concepts also take the operating income into account. The success of the cooperation is then defined either as the long-term profit maximization or as the additional profit in comparison to the previous, isolated activities. In contrast, neoclassical approaches build their definitions upon the consideration that the participation of a cooperation can only be understood as a specific investment project of a company and therefore can only be judged on a long-term basis. As a measurement of the cooperation's success, the long-term, positive surplus is suggested. It results from the comparison between all realized and expected expenses and revenues of the cooperation. These basic concepts are also partly modified so that the present value of future surpluses is also suitable as a measurement of success.

Instead of a single economic top key figure, **multidimensional approaches** use a broader evaluation basis, which takes the quantitative and also the qualitative aspects of the success of the cooperation into account. The concepts are established from a behavior-oriented point of view derived from the incentive-contribution theory. Accordingly the voluntary amalgamation and the maintenance of the cooperation will only last if every partner company is offered incentives through the cooperation that are greater than their corresponding contributions to the cooperation. Thus, the investigation of the success of the VC is based upon a comparison between advantages and disadvantages of the cooperation. Its results are interpreted as preliminary indicators to the monetary success of the cooperation. However, it should be remembered that the success of the cooperation is not clearly determined, as it is dependent upon the subjective evaluation of the incentives and contributions, which is based on individual motives. Accordingly, the success of the cooperation can be defined (a) as realized or planned degree of satisfaction of the objectives a company pursues with the partnership, (b) as positive contributions of the cooperation to the objectives of the company as a whole or (c) as a higher objective level compared with an individual strategy. The resulting measures of success are labeled as benefit or value of benefit by the authors.

These different conceptions find their correspondence in three alternative methods that can principally be used to measure the success of the cooperation.

(1) The typical business economics procedure of defining success is the **calculation** in terms of a period-related account of the operating income. The specific corresponding investigation and analysis accounts on the intercompany level have recently been placed under the term "network operating income analysis" (Veil & Hess, 2000). The initial consideration of the evaluation is that VCs are portrayed as being similarly structured to holdings. Therefore the consolidation of the costs and revenues must follow similar principles. As types of operating income analysis, it has to be differentiated between gross and net operating income analysis. The result of the net operating income analysis, in the simplest way, is the aggregation of the individual assignment results (Variant A). Alternatively, the investigation of the net operating income can result from a

separate expense and revenue consolidation (Variant B). Therefore, the revenue is the result of the price of the total performance that had been agreed with a customer or a buyer outside of the VC. In order to investigate the costs, a disclosure of calculations of every partner is a prerequisite. To avoid double counts, especially during aggregation, the intertwining of production between partner companies must be taken into account. From the expenses of the recipient, therefore, the costs of internal deliveries and other activities have got to be taken away. They will comply with the turnover of the delivering partner. Figure 1 shows a simple example in which a transfer of products from Partner A to Partner B occurs. On the basis of such investigated results, different measurements of success (e.g., for a certain cooperation field or the whole VC) can be calculated depending on the reference period and form of the aggregation.

The implementation of the operating income calculation in the sense of the relative single cost calculations of Riebel (1994) requires a different allocation of the indirect cost-structure of the VC. Here, the success of the cooperation can be interpreted as an excess of the operating income over the direct costs, which depend on different typical network reference objects (e.g., an order, an order group or the whole VC). For the determination of these, however, the order-related costs by the effects of internal production intertwining at this variant have also to be rectified.

(2)   A new concept, discussed in the context of strategic alliances, is the **appreciation analysis**, which is built upon Rappaport's (1998) concept of "shareholder value analysis," originally developed for a standard company (e.g., Michel,

Figure 1: Calculation of an operating income in VCs

Level of the partner company

Single Calculations:

Partner A (production):

	Operating Income	14,000
./.	Variable Costs	10,000
./.	Fixed Costs	3,000
=	Result	1,000

Partner B (production/sales):

	Operating Income	31,000
./.	Variable Costs	24,000
./.	Fixed Costs	5,000
=	Result	2,000

Level of the VC

Net Operating Income Analysis:

Variant A:

	Result A	1,000
+	Result B	2,000
=	Total Result	3,000

Variant B:

	Operating Income	31,000
./.	Variable Costs*	20,000
./.	Fixed Costs**	8,000
=	Total Result	3,000

*:   = 10,000 + (24,000 - 14,000)
**: = 3,000 + 5,000

1996). As before, the procedure is based on the capital valuation method, through which a defined cash-flow row is discounted with a weighted capital-costs-rate (see Figure 2).

The basic idea behind specific extensions consists of the quantification and monitoring of all of the cooperation's strategies and measures with respect to an appreciation. From that it can be taken that between performance-related, structural and anticompetitive effects of the cooperative work (the so-called potential sources of an increase in value) on the one hand and the determinants of cash flow and capital costs (the so-called value generators) on the other hand, there exist systematic, qualitative and describable connections (see Figure 3). They should fund the prognoses and supervision of the value generators. In order for this to succeed, there are milestones (inclusive measurements) to define for these projects and with hindsight to evaluate their influence upon the potential sources of an increase in value. Because of this relation, a theoretical connection between the progress of the project and the value generators can be produced in accordance with the following logic: every project of the cooperation consists of the impacts of certain sources of potentialities, which result in changes of the value generators and finally of the shareholder value level. In this manner, the success of the cooperation–expressed through the variation of the realized to the planned shareholder value–should be explained at least qualitatively with the resulting success of strategic projects.

(3)   The third approach is the **benefit value analysis**. This was originally developed by Zangemeister (1976) for a multidimensional evaluation of construction alternatives in system technology. At the beginning of the 1980s it was carried forward with regards to the question of cooperative success

Figure 2: Calculation of the shareholder value

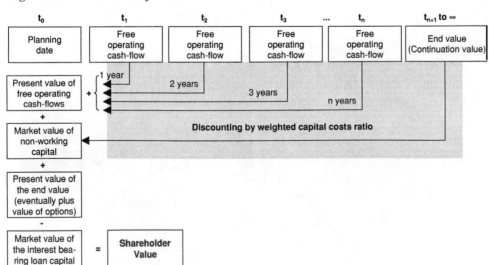

Figure 3: Systemization of appreciation for strategic alliances

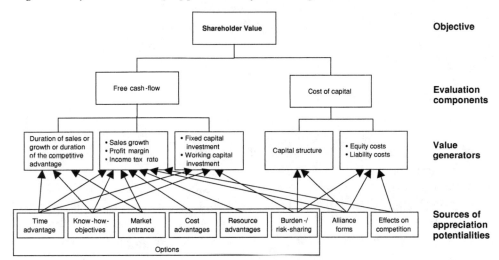

evaluations. For that its application is merely modified so that different (cooperation) alternatives are not assessed at the same time, but the development of the same cooperation is compared at different points in time. The modified approach is developed from the point of view of a single company and is differentiated between six single steps (see Figure 4). The result–the sum of weighted degrees of objective fulfillment– is interpreted as an indicator for the success of the cooperation.

A Critical Analysis of Established Evaluation Methods

With regards to their use in VCs, an investigation into the expediency of the methods introduced a difference between the specific demands of the level of the partner company and those of the cooperation level has to be made. For the latter

Figure 4: Calculation of the benefit value

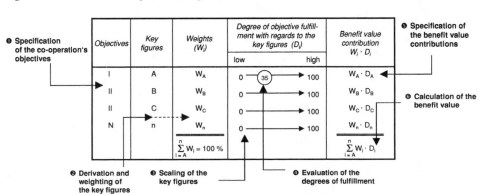

it is mainly the organizational characteristics of the VCs that have to be considered. In comparison to a single company, the low system stability through the entry and exit of partners has central influence because it causes a more frequent structural change to the evaluation objects. Looking at this in an instrumental way, it justifies the demand for a procedure that can flexibly and for a short-term period adapt to such variations, so that the usage of the methods can be kept as economical as possible by minimizing the costs that are caused by necessary changes. Certainly this can only be a rough estimate, as up until now the business economics cannot identify any instrumental way with whose help the efficiency, especially the effects of the success from management instruments, can be evaluated exactly.

Also to be taken into account is the emerging coordination expenditure created during the cooperative work, which has got to be kept low in order to maintain the necessary flexibility of the VC. The use of management instruments, like the success evaluation, creates (additional) coordination expenditure, whether it is through the provision of data or required adjustment of procedures within the corporation. The expenditure connected with this becomes, from the partners' point of view, a specific investment because the realized results can only be restricted or generally not transferred. Because of this, in the earlier stages of the cooperative work the partners strive to limit the height of "investments in instruments." Hence for an evaluation of the success of a VC, above all such methods come into question that distinguish themselves through low installation and procedural expenditure.

As measured by these prerequisites, the usage of the appreciation analysis on the inter-company level is only conditionally possible. Its input on the one hand stands in contrast to the high formal requirements. So the cash-flow calculation requires the existence of a built-up cost accounting system, from which balance or success parameters for the cooperation area of the company can be taken. The consolidation to overall values presuppose comparable accounts, which under circumstances must firstly be lavishly established by the partners. On the other hand, the appreciation analysis produces a forecast of the possible effects on the cooperation of the total duration of the cooperative work. A high continuity in configuration and a processed product-market combination, which is required for a longer forecast, are typically lacking in VCs. As a further difficulty it has to be considered that the actual connections between the activities of the cooperation and the resulting cash flow can barely be declared through the appreciation analysis in a specific case (e.g., Anderson, 1990). The built-up "systematics" deliver only coarse hints with regards to the possible effects. Ambiguities also make a quantification difficult so that the causes of the success scale of an "increase in value" remain difficult to interpret and barely propose any concrete management recommendations.

Also the possibilities of using a net operating income analysis are clearly restricted in VCs. With the judgement criterion "profit" it delivers a familiar measurement of success. But the information to be processed is based on the calculations of the partners and with that on their cost classification and cost center accounting. The specific rules of the individual cost accounting systems (e.g., regarding definitions and demarcations of expenses and performances or the methods and procedures of calculation or in view of different bases of valuation and fictions of consumption sequences) have an effect on the results of the calculation and with that on their comparability within the VC. Therefore a "correct" result delivers the consolidation on the cooperation level if, and only if, the individual calculations follow the same calculation regulations. Typically, for this, extensive adjustments of existing or the establishing of additional accounts are necessary. Whether the companies in the VC are interested in such a standardization with respect to their own economical independence is doubtful. In particular, provisions with which far-reaching interventions into the decision autonomy are connected, such as the guidelines of the amount stated for the calculative cost classes or the calculative profit, are barely enforceable.

The benefit value analysis works best in this comparison. It can be installed and used very flexibly and with comparably low expenditure. Conceptionally it allows a differentiated view of the success potential etc. weak points of the cooperative work. These advantages are only limited through the abstractness of the measurement of success "economic value" and the subjective influence on the evaluation. Referring to this, the benefit value analysis is incurred not to generally (unconsciously) exclude manipulations with regards to the selection of the objective criteria, the transformation of the preferences and the fixing of the objective achievement for the qualitative criteria. Altogether it delivers less "objective" results than the "pay-based" procedures of capital budgeting or cost accounting. Evaluation mistakes, for example, can appear if, during the evaluation, persons have different levels of information or behave strategically in the evaluation process. Such manipulation possibilities also exist with regards to the appreciation analysis and the net operating income analysis, e.g., at the determination of the forecast data or the coding of costs.

On the level of the partner company, it should be questioned as to whether the used success indicator is a suitable indicator for the actual motives of the cooperative work. Periodical profit accounts and appreciation analysis align themselves on a single monetary "top key figure." Their usage therefore only leads in those (special) cases to conclusive results, in which the individual pertinence of nonmonetary cooperation objectives is very low. In connection with VCs, however, always a plurality of predominantly nonmonetary cooperation objectives are always mentioned in both theory and in practice (e.g., Child & Faulkner, 1998). Therefore the individual success of the cooperation might altogether be more realistically recorded with a multidimensional evaluation on the basis of benefit value analysis than with single quantitative or financial measures. When interpreting the measurements of success, "economic value" has got to be taken into consideration, that is, that the method provides an accumulated conjunction of the partial benefits. The synthesis of value therefore equalizes out like an average; that is, bad objective realization can be compensated through the favorable value of another aim.

In summary it can be stated that the benefit value analysis at best meets the demands on the VC and partner levels. Therefore it shall be used to serve as a methodical fundament in the further investigation, upon which the necessary modifications for networks can be placed. The developed procedure shall be described in the following as the **Collective Network Efficiency Control Tool**, or simply **CONECT**.

THE EVALUATION METHOD CONECT

Overview

During the implementation of a success evaluation the CONECT-method discriminates between two main stages (see Figure 5): It is the aim of the first stage to build up a standardized "measurement system" for processing the actual evaluation information. For that, on the one hand, all network-related objectives as well as their relative meaning–their "weight"–must be determined and arranged for each partner. On the other hand, key figures have to be stipulated, with which the degree of importance of the aims can be described simply and exactly. The subject matter of the second stage is to determine and analyze the success of the cooperation at the level of the partner and the VC. The main exercises here consist of the ascertainment of the degrees of importance according to the key figure as well as the transfer of these results to interpretable success measures. Whatever steps are necessary in detail will be portrayed in the following. As a basis for clarity, both of the main stages will be looked at separately.

Stage 1: Construction of the Evaluation Framework

Altogether, the first main stage consists of five steps. The objective of the **first step** is to identify the VC-related objectives of the partner companies. As they reflect the individual intentions and motives of the companies involved, universal standards for the stipulation of their form and content cannot be given. Their compilation is rather a creative process, for whose implementation two basic approaches exist: First, the objectives of the cooperation can be gathered intuitively through the partners. Creativity techniques such as brainstorming can support this search.

Second, the partners can also derive their VC-related objectives from existing objective catalogues, which can be found in the literature of cooperations in a more or less structured way. A comprehensive approach has been suggested by Ebert

Figure 5: The main stages of CONECT

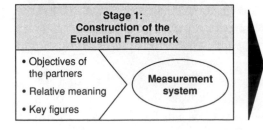
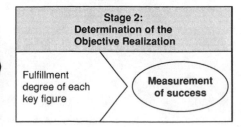

(1998), who originally referred to the systemization of objectives at mergers. As the objectives of mergers and cooperations do not differ widely from each other, the considerations of Ebert can roughly be transferred to cooperations and therefore to VCs. Ebert assumes the synergy realization as the main objective and differentiates between economies of scale and economies of scope as company-related synergy areas, as well as the improvement of the market position and the improvement of the integration possibilities as market-related synergy areas. In connection with a second dimension oriented upon the process of production, which differentiates input-, process- and output-synergies. Thus, 12 main categories of acquisition objectives can be identified (see Figure 6).

Independent of the chosen procedure, the identified objectives have got to be aggregated in the **second step** in order to generate a mutual objective catalogue on the network level. On the one hand, the aim of this process is to avoid redundancies through the removal of multiple evaluations. However, by using a systematic objective-catalogue, from which the partners can choose single objectives relevant to them, this necessity is frequently not applicable. The task is more relevant in connection with intuitive determination of objectives. At first, a terminological specification of the description of the objectives is necessary to fully clear up possible insecurities about their interpretation between the partners. In this way a

Figure 6: Synergy objectives at mergers (Ebert, 1998, p. 66)

Synergy area	Input-synergy	Process-synergy	Output-synergy
Synergies through economies of scale	• Synergy related economies of scale in the preliminary stages of production, e.g. saving of costs during purchasing	• Synergy related operative economies of scale in production, e.g., due to the reduction of the average unit cost	• Synergy related economies of scale during processing and covering of the market. e.g., due to more efficient advertising budgeting
Synergies through economies of scope	• Know-how-transfer in the preliminary stages of the production process	• Operative and technological know-how-transfer	• Know-how-transfer in the processing and covering of the market
Synergies through better market positioning	• Synergy related improvement of the situation of the competition in the market place	• Synergy related market-entry barriers through operative advantages, e.g., due to a higher quantity of production	• Market power or reaching the critical mass
Synergies through better integration	• Improved synergy and input related control through integration, e.g., due to the involvement of suppliers	• Synergy related vertical cost advantages, e.g., through the integration of production stages up- and downstream	• Synergy related improvement of the output related market control, e.g., due to the improvement of the vertical distribution

large proportion of textual overlappings is revealed. For a more detailed examination it is necessary that all network-related objectives are enrolled in lines and columns of a matrix and then compared to one another line by line. The overlapping can be judged, for example, with the help of evaluation figures from a predefined value table, which will be filled into the corresponding place in the matrix. If the evaluation reaches a threshold value, then the according objectives must be removed from the list except one or must be described in more detail. The latter procedure can lead to a multilevel objective system. As a result, however, the comparability of objectives between the partners is ensured, which is a requirement for a consolidation on the level of the VC.

On the other hand, an analysis of consistency must be carried out in order to guarantee the reciprocal compatibility of the individual objectives. In this way, a contradiction-free objective catalogue ought to be built, which is a prerequisite for an interpretable measurement of success on the level of the VC. Such an analysis of consistency can again be supported through a listing in a matrix. In this matrix, all objectives of the cooperation along with the identifiers of the corresponding partners are filled into the lines and columns. Then they are analyzed as to whether they are compatible, neutral, or incompatible with each other (e.g., see Figure 7).

Figure 7: An example of a consistency analysis in VCs

Partner	Objectives of the co-operation	Shortening of the development time	Building up new customer contacts	Broadening of the performance program	Raising of the capacity utilization	Use of the resource X	Know-how-transfer on area Y	Maintenance of the individual flexibility	No co-operation with direct competitors	Compliance to applicable law
A, D	Shortening of the development time		o	o	o	o	o	o	o	o
B, D	Building up new customer contacts			o	+	o	o	o	(-)	o
C, D	Broadening of the performance program				(+)	o	o	o	o	o
C, D	Raising of the capacity utilization					o	o	o	(-)	o
A	Use of the resource X						o	(+)	o	o
C, D	Know-how-transfer on area Y							o	o	o
A-D	Maintenance of the individual flexibility								-	o
C	No co-operation with direct competitors									o
A-D	Compliance to applicable law									

Relationship:
+ :   complementary
(+):   conditionally complementary
o: indifferent
(-):   conditionally competing
-:   competing

Neutral and complementary objective relations are uncritical. In the case of contradictions, it has got to be determined, in the **third step**, whether possibilities of an adaptation of the VC-related objectives do exist. Thereby, it can be differentiated between contradictions which take effect only under certain circumstances and those which are directly based upon oppositions. The latter should be strictly removed. This implies joint negotiations of the partners, in which one party must be prompted to abandon its cooperation objective (e.g., "no intake of competitors into the VC"). In order to realize a coordination of interests, the affected partners can also be given specific advantages (e.g., in the form of a guarantee to participate in orders). In this case the results of the consensus represent a distribution problem, whose theoretical solution is the Pareto-optimum. Through that, a state is described in which no partner can improve his condition without worsening the status of the other. However, in practice such an ideal solution is only conditionally achieved. On the one hand, possibilities for compensations often lack and are respectively very limited. On the other hand, the extent of the concession depends on the structure of power within the VC. For example, a single partner can enforce his interests against the majority of other partners if he holds a key position within the value chain. This virtually means a discrimination against other partners, which is however accepted as long as other, from their point of view, higher-rated cooperation motives remain within the objective system.

After the removal of the overlappings and inner contradictions in the common objective catalogue, weighting factors and key figures have got to be assigned to the objectives in the **fourth step**. Through the weighting factor, the relative meaning should be expressed which attaches a partner to a single objective. The more important a partner estimates an objective, the higher the assigned weighting factor. Because direct, relative evaluation is extremely challenging–the sum of rates must yield 100%–the estimation can be made on an absolute scale at first. Approved is a 7-point scale of values from 1 to 7. Subsequently, the assigned point values must be set in relation to the total amount, in order to determine the relative weight of the objective.

With the derivation of suitable key figures along with their units, the objectives are prepared for a "measurement of success" (see Figure 8). In order to simplify the search, it is recommended to use existing key figure catalogues. However, until now no specific key figures suggestions have been available which are related to the typical objectives of cooperations. Here catalogues can assist which were developed for other application fields like logistic management or process management. Nevertheless, independent from the type of determination, it should be guaranteed that all partners use the same key figure for the quantization of the identical objective. A prerequisite for that is that the partners commonly agree upon a standardized key figure catalogue. This also includes the scale units in which the measurement of a key figure should result. Their assignation is simple for key figures with which an absolute quantity is measured or for technical or monetary measurements. The preliminary fixing of qualitative key figures is more difficult, which, as for example, are needed to illustrate a know-how adoption. For such key figures, evaluation scales must be set up, into which analogues to scholar mark systems possible parameter values are expressed verbally and then correlated to certain scores. The division of these scales can also take any form.

Due to the complexity of single objectives, it can be necessary to define each objective through more than one performance measure, in order to characterize it sufficiently. In this case the weighting factor of the objectives has to be separated into part-weights for the key figures. To simplify matters, the evaluation can be carried out relatively inside these performance measure groups. In this case, the total sum of the weighting factors below the considered objective amounts to 100%. In order to receive their relative share referring to all of the key figures given, they must be multiplied with the weighting factors of the objective itself. An analogous procedure is to choose, if one has to assign weighting factors in multistage objective-systems (see example in Figure 9).

Alternatively, the concerned objectives can also be detailed in subgoals as long as an 1:1-relationship between objective and key figure is achieved. In this way, only one key figure has to be changed if objectives are modified. As the objective weight equals the key figure weight, a separate weighting of key figures can be avoided. This

Figure 8: Example for the derivation of key figures from objectives

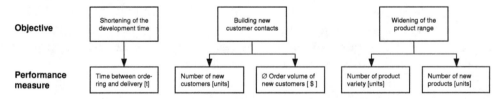

Figure 9: Example for the calculation of global weighting factors

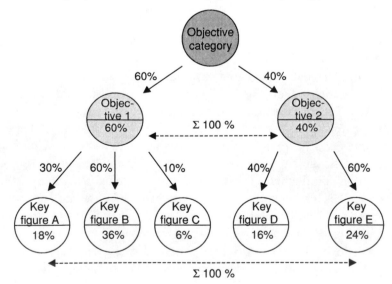

represents a reasonable advantage because in practice an assessment of key figures ought to be far more difficult than that of the objectives. However, this strategy generates further costs because a setback to the first step of the procedure is normally necessary.

After finishing these activities, it seems sensible in the **fifth step** to carry out first analysis on the level of the VC. However, it concerns no compelling condition for the further course of procedures. The premature information about first results ought to motivate the partners to take further part in the evaluation process. A relevant examination comprises the determination of such objectives that would be classified as important by all partners. This is the same as if they have received a weighting factor greater than zero from all participating companies. Together they form the "core set" of common objectives. Besides this, it can be analyzed which objective or objective-segment is especially important for all the partners. To what extent the weighting factors of key figures and objectives between the partners are rated similarly can be examined by correlation analysis like the objective-rank-correlation test from Friedman. Lastly, simple variance analysis allows one to test whether the objectives of the determined cluster of partner companies have significant differences. As cluster criteria, the following come into question: the duration of network membership, the mainly focused cooperation fields, or the class size with respect to the turnover of a partner company.

Stage 2: Determination of the Objective Realization

The second procedural stage can be divided up into four steps. The start of the stage, the **sixth step** of the overall procedure, forms the standardization of the different performance measurement units. This requires the definition of utility functions to describe a well-defined relationship between the possible values of a performance measure and the degree of fulfillment. For all continuous key figures, there must be set limits on both sides. The lower limits represent the tolerated values in the worst case, while the upper limits correspond to reachable values in the best case.

Furthermore, a mathematical function needs to be determined for each measure of performance inside the specified limits. Thereby it is possible that the utility functions begin with a realization degree greater than 0, if the lower boundary value already has a certain benefit for a partner. However, the maximum of the utility functions should correspond to a realization degree of 100%. This restriction makes sense in the view of the additional model of the economic value analysis because a strong compensation between the resulting economic value contributions is avoided. The classification function can take any form. Due to the time needed to complete the specification, linear functions are often used in practice. Besides this there are meaningful application opportunities for nonlinear functions, for example, maximum or saturation functions (for example, Figure 10)

Hereafter the investigation of the fulfillment degrees of every performance measure follows. The course of the economic value analysis allows two variations

Figure 10: Example of a non-linear utility function

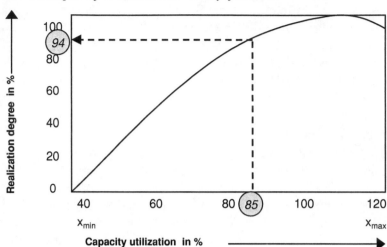

here. On the one hand, the fulfillment degree can be determined retrospectively for a previous period of time. This can be the whole time period in which the company has been engaged if the total success of the cooperation should be specified. Even so, it is conceivable that the inspection refers to a fixed period, if alterations in the concerning time period are of main interest. In order to draw comparisons between the participating companies, the time period must be fixed uniformly for all partners. In this variation, the degree of fulfillment is ascertained through the specification of an actual value using the utility function. Alternatively, it can also be determined directly by the partner, if there are temporal restrictions. If the sequence is applied like this at the outset, the determination of utility functions can be waived. For the structuring of the evaluation process, an explicit specification of planned and actual values should be made for every performance measure. The degree of fulfillment can then be calculated from the formation of the quotient if a linear progression of the utility function is presumed. Quotients greater than 1 have got to be set back to 100% again, in order to bind compensation effects.

The second variant only possesses relevance in periodical evaluations and requires a two-stage action: At the beginning of a particular time period, a required value must be given for all key figures (**step seven**). After the lapse of the period, the actual occurring measurement value has to be determined. Finally, by using the utility function, the fulfillment degree can be derived from the planned and realized values (**step eight**).

The advantages of one variant are the disadvantages of another variant: The usefulness of a retrospective investigation of the fulfillment degree is that in a comparatively short time results can be achieved, because one questioning step can be omitted. Furthermore, the simultaneous determination of both the desired and the actual occurring measurement values alleviates the understanding of the procedure for the partners. It also contributes to better acceptance of the technique. If the naming of the concrete measurement values is not possible or not intended by the partners consciously, the survey can be reduced to the direct specification of the fulfillment degree. However, there also exists the main disadvantage of this strategy: It consists of the possibility that the assessing partner bases his estimates on his present expectancies. Thus, his evaluations describe more the contentment with the actual events, like a "snapshot," than the real development of the cooperations success as measured by his original requirements. As long as planned and realized values are surveyed separately, such "manipulation possibilities" are perspicuously restricted.

The second stage is completed with **step nine** through the analysis of the results, which has to be applied at the partner level first. Here an analysis separated by the key figures is reasonable, in which their relative importance is taken into consideration. For instance, a suitable illustration is made possible through an "importance distance profile" (Lützig, 1982, pp. 158-163). It shows the results in a form in that for each key figure the distance between the planned and the realized value to each other as well as to the upper limit is emphasized in accordance with its relative importance. For the construction of this sort of profile every key figure is assigned a line whose length corresponds to its weighing factor. Next, the lines are arranged, as can be seen in Figure 11. Finally, the planned and realized fulfillment degrees of the key figures are entered on each line and connected with one another. The bigger the distance between both of the profiles, the larger is the gap of the original expectation and the realized results of the cooperation. In cases of retrospective investigations of the fulfillment degree, it has to be taken into consideration that the upper limits of the key figures and the planned fulfillment degree coincide. Therefore it is adequate to plot the present profile. The line that serves as a means of comparison here is the line that connects all 100% points.

An alternative evaluation, which is aimed at all the groupings of the single results with regards to the weighting and fulfillment degrees, is supplied by the "success-contribution-portfolio" (see Figure 12). The fulfillment degrees and the weighting factors of the key figures come in as point positions in a matrix that is divided up into four fields. This division results from the average value of both dimensions. From the resulting position, different recommendations can be derived for the network coordinator and the partner. Key figures positioned in Field 1 have only a substandard fulfillment degree. They can be treated subordinately as long as the number of the key figures positioned there is low. Clearly, higher attentiveness must be given to the key figures that lie in Field II. They indicate an acute call for action, as because of marginal improvements of the fulfillment degrees, a positive outcome of the total success can be realized through the strong leverage effect. Key figures in the Fields III and IV mark the ideal position in the portfolio. Because of their high relevance, the network coordinator has got to maintain and build up the successful position of these key figures in the foreground, which lie in Section III. Here possible cohesions between past developments and the success-judgement should be analyzed in order to deduce recommendations.

Figure 11: Example of a weighted distance profile

Ser. no.	Key figures	Weighting factor	Weighted distance profile
1	Time-span between order and delivery (response time)	0.11	
2	Number of new customers	0.08	
3	Ø order volume of new customers	0.03	
4	Number of product versions	0.09	
5	Number of new products	0.02	
6	Capacity utilization	0.08	
7	Capacity size class	0.04	
8	Debit share at sustenance and maintenance of the resource X	0.10	
9	Information exchange	0.14	
10	Staff rotation	0.05	
11	Exit-options	0.09	
12	Economic independence	0.17	
	Total sum 1 - 12	**1.00**	

Legend: —— realized values ----- planned values

Figure 12: Example of a success-contribution-portfolio

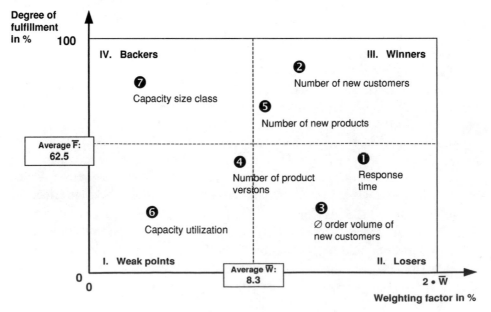

With the aggregation of the partner-specific results, analysis on network-level would also be possible. For an absolute examination, the average values have to be calculated for all individual fulfillment degrees and weighting factors. These average values can be processed with both of the introduced analysis means without difference. From the illustration it can be recognized to which extent single objectives or objective segments are realized by all partners. They deliver important manifestations for the prioritization of fundamental measures.

In order to determine the relative success of the partners in the VC, the fulfillment degrees of the key figures must be multiplied with the weighting factors. Through the summation of these single results an overall indicator for the individual objective realization can be gained. Obviously "dissatisfied" partners are identified through the comparison of these values. General threshold values for this sort of analysis can not be given. It is more important that the benefit-differences between the participant companies stay within acceptable limits. When serious success deficits occur it should be examined whether or not an engagement in the VC is meaningful for the individual company. This analysis is not only necessary to be conducted from the partner's point of view, but also from the VC's point of view. Above all, the potential costs of his elimination must be thereby taken into account. Hence the continuation of these partners in the VC–that are currently or in the future of prominent relevance for the performance of the VC–has to be ensured. This refers to those companies, which have a key position in the cooperation's value chain due to a specific technology or existing capacities.

The entire procedure of a success assessment through CONECT is summarized in Figure 13. Again the broken line around the steps "standardization of key figures" and "fixing of the expected values" ought to refer to their optional character. With the first implementation of the method, the participating companies should be guaranteed that their information will be kept anonymously in order to induce their participation. A disclosure to other partners should be bound within the agreement of the concerned company.

The procedure of the method is principally independent from the type of VC. Specialties could result in focal VCs through the particular influence of the focal partner. His steering claim can induce him not to participate in the success evaluation and to avoid an explicit disclosure of his objectives. This could be with the intent to suppress open objective conflicts between him and the non-focal partners and to prevent own concessions from the outset.

APPLICATION OF THE METHODOLOGY IN THE BUS-VIRTUAL CORPORATION

The BUS-Virtual Corporation in Overview

As a root organization of the present consultation and support network BUS, the BUS Betreuungsverbund für Unternehmer und Selbständige e.V. (registered

Figure 13: Procedural scheme of the CONECT-method

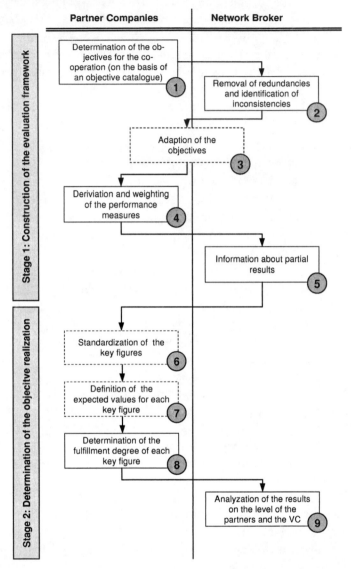

society) was founded in the year 1982 to advise family businesses in different entrepreneurial problems. In order to realize individually negotiated consultation orders, the BUS Betreuungs- und Unternehmensberatungs-GmbH was additionally founded in 1984. Today the VC unites around 60 legal, independent management consultants. The majority of the participating partners are individual entrepreneurs from Germany and Austria.

The strategic business fields of BUS are consultation, support and further training. Partial investments in family companies in the sense of venture capital financing exist in addition. "Consultation" comprises all significant business functions from planning to marketing. "Support" means the consultation during the implementation of the consultation concepts, which is strictly separated from the other services of the VC. Training is offered by the BUS Betreuungs- und Unternehmensberatungs-GmbH, whereas the BUS Betreuungsverbund für Unternehmer und Selbständige e.V. gets in the support of the club members. Beyond that BUS offers its customers different methods of training through the BUS-UnternehmerAkademie, an academy for entrepreneurs. The same is also offered to its management consultants through another academy, the BUS-BeraterAkademie.

Since its establishment, BUS has transacted over 10,000 consultation and support projects for small- and middle-sized companies in Germany and Austria. The consultation and support projects have an average volume of between $ 4,000 and $ 7,000. The basis of the cooperations regarding the internal relationships are permanent basic agreements between BUS and the VC partners.

BUS owns a service center in Munich, which plans in particular the strategic orientation of the VC. Its further tasks are the enlisting of new members, marketing, key-account management, general management, knowledge management and internal education and further training. The services of the center are being deducted together with the consultation achievements.

Course of the Study with BUS

In order to undertake the success evaluation relatively fast, the abbreviated procedural scheme of the benefit value analysis was chosen (see also Hess, Wohlgemuth & Schlembach, 2001). For further simplification, predefined objective and key figure catalogues were laid open prior to the beginning of the investigation. Using the above presented analysis grid of Ebert and after performing individual interviews, altogether 19 cooperation objectives, which are typical for consultation companies, could be identified. They were clustered into five objective categories (see Figure 14).

Based upon this, for each objective exactly one key figure with a measurement unit was defined. These structured objective and key figure catalogues built the framework for the questionnaires in two survey rounds: In round one the partners were being asked to assess the relative importance of the given objectives on a scale from 1 (no meaning) to 7 (key demand). In an analogous manner a communal assessment should be made for every objective category. It was up to the respondents to give further cooperation objectives and likewise to assess them with the standard scale.

With these specifications, the weighting factors of the single objectives could be calculated as follows: First of all the relative weights of the objective categories were determined by setting the evaluation of each objective category in relation to the total sum of all category assessments (A). Then the relative weights of the cooperation objectives contained in each category were figured out by setting the evaluation of each objective in relation to the total sum of all assessments within this category (B). In order to calculate the relative meaning of a single objective in the entire objective system (C), its weight related to the category (B) was multiplied with the weight of the category (A); see Figure 15.

Figure 14: Specific objective catalogue for consultation companies

Objective category	Objectives
Development objectives	1. Raising of the turnover
	2. Lowering of own expenditures through communal use of services and devices (i.e., coordination services, WWW-server)
	3. Acceleration of project execution
	4. Improvement of the service- and consultation quality through external know-how
Sales objectives	5. Widening of the own sector portfolio
	6. Access to multipliers
	7. Participation on large projects through bundling know-how (mutual supplementation of competencies)
	8. Possibility to offer the integrated consultation approach (conception and implementation)
Competition objectives	9. Strengthening of the competition position towards competitors outside of the VC
	10. Strengthening of the negotiation position towards customers
	11. Access to critical market-information/contacts
	12. Access to sales intermediaries through continuity
Learning objectives	13. Continuous updating of the consultation/management knowledge
	14. Development of new consultation fields/core competencies
	15. Gaining of the cooperation experience, raising of capacity for teamwork
Safety objectives	16. Improvement of own capacity utilization, balancing of fluctuations in receipt of orders
	17. Cost- and risk-sharing through communal financing of investments (i.e., product development)
	18. Maintenance of the economical and organizational independence
	19. Reduction of customer losses by temporary absences (i.e., due to sickness)

To avoid "mistakes" at this formal derivation, the weighting factors should be validated in the second survey round by means of individualized questionnaires through the partners. Simultaneously the partners were asked to assess the fulfillment degree of each objective and its assigned key figure for the first half of the year 2000, respectively. The assessment should be carried out from a scale of 1 ("expectations have not been fulfilled [0%]") to 7 ("expectations have been fulfilled completely [100%]"). It was reserved to the respondents to state the concrete realized and planned values of each key figure, in order to derive the degree of fulfillment out of the quotient.

The survey began at the end of March 2000 and was finished at the end of August 2000. All 57 close partners of the VC were invited to participate. In the first

Figure 15: The procedure for the determination of the relative weighting factors

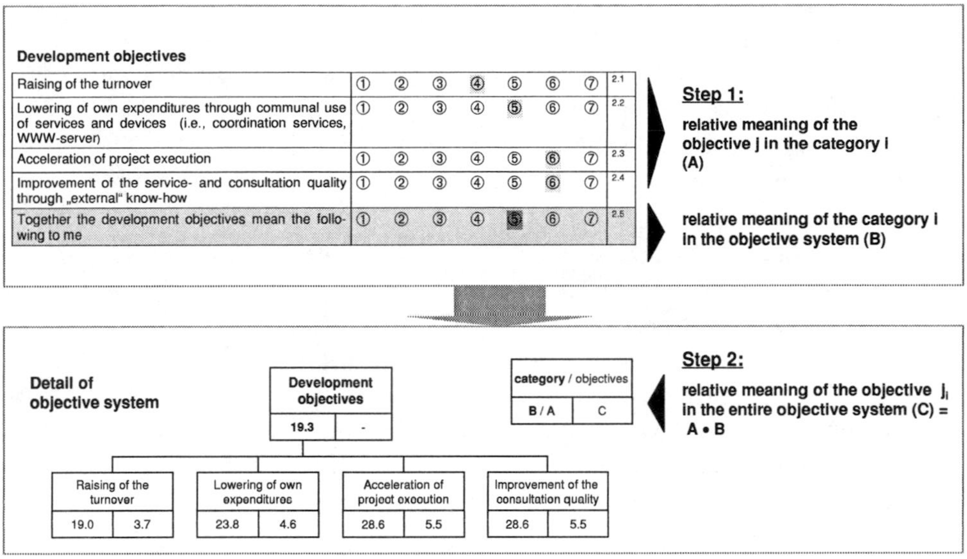

survey stage, altogether 23 management consultants answered; in the second stage, started in the middle of June, 17 answered. The "costs" of the success evaluation for the partners resulted especially from the time exposure to answering the questionnaires. That amounts to around 20 minutes for every stage. The total time exposure for the survey lasted about 45 minutes. The communication between the participants took place primarily by e-mail and mailing and in individual cases by telephone.

The study was carried out through the Munich Central of the VC (the so-called "service center") and the University of Goettingen. The service center served as an interface for the VC members and informed them about the project, tracked the answer behavior of the partners and where required reminded members to return the questionnaires. The task of the University of Goettingen was to create the questionnaires and bring them into agreement with the service center, to collect and to consolidate the partial results, and to calculate as far as possible the concluding success of the cooperation.

Results and Implications

As a significant result of the first survey round, it can be stated that the objective retrieval has led to an overall consistent objective system on the network level. The objective catalogue had been tested before the questioning of internal compatibility of course, but even after completion of further cooperation objectives through the partners no substantial contradictions could be uncovered. Inside the standard catalogue the partners admittedly ascribed only seven cooperation objectives a relative meaning greater than 0: Every one of the remaining 12 objectives was without relevance for at least one member. With it, the "core set" of cooperation objectives is restricted to less than half of all objectives (see Figure 16). Certainly the analysis shows as well that the estimation of the relative objective importance between the partners fluctuates considerably. Hence it can be concluded that possible objective conflicts during the current network decisions are basically the results of differences in priority.

The calculation of the average of the objective weights reveals that the relative meaning of both the cost reduction objective and also the turnover raising objective ranks in the lower third. Learning objectives are at the top of this ranking. This leads to the assumption that "noneconomical" motives are of decisive relevance for the participation in a VC. Therefore monetary parameters possess only a limited validity as success indicators for VCs.

Finally, differences in the agreement of the preference weighting can be identified independent of the duration of the membership. The division of the partners into two clusters with regard to the characteristic "entry of the VC since the 1st quarter of 1995" and "entry until the 4th quarter of 1994," respectively, shows a significantly higher agreement of the weighting in the group of "young" partners. This allows the interpretation that the motives and preferences are comparatively homogenous at time of admission. First in the time course, the priorities of the VC actors shift in different directions.

The comparatively high dispersion of the individual evaluations regarding to the fulfillment of the objectives is counted among the most important results of the second survey round (see Figure 17). These findings underline the necessity to

Figure 16: Core objectives of the BUS VC

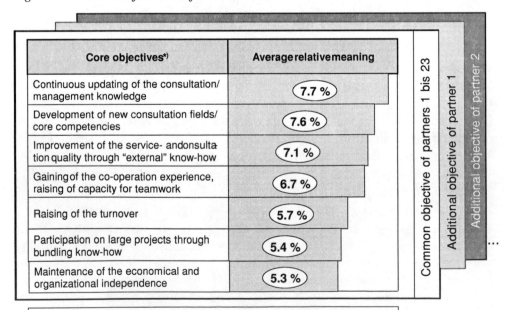

Core objectives*)	Average relative meaning	Common objective of partners 1 bis 23	Additional objective of partner 1	Additional objective of partner 2
Continuous updating of the consultation/ management knowledge	7.7 %			
Development of new consultation fields/ core competencies	7.6 %			
Improvement of the service- and consultation quality through "external" know-how	7.1 %			
Gaining of the co-operation experience, raising of capacity for teamwork	6.7 %			
Raising of the turnover	5.7 %			
Participation on large projects through bundling know-how	5.4 %			
Maintenance of the economical and organizational independence	5.3 %			

*) Core objectives are co-operation objectives which have a relative meaning for all partners greater than zero

include not only the standard variation, but also individual case examinations in a detailed analysis of the success on the network level. Therefore the average success contributions of the objectives can only be interpreted as a prediction of a tendency.

This analysis shows moreover that the middle achievement degrees of the learning objectives take positions in the lower third of the ranking. Referring to the insight gained in the first round, that exactly these objectives possess a higher than average meaning for the VC partners, a concrete management implication can be achieved: such measurements should be taken which work towards an improvement of these expectations (i.e., the intensification of internal education and further training measurements, the improvement of the information and know-how interchange). They serve as a suitable "leverage" for the improvement of the total satisfaction.

As a further result, it can be stated that the most noticeable, worst judgements of the cooperation's success stem from partners that belong to the VC for a long time, partially since its establishment. Different interpretations can be taken from this fact. Firstly expectations might have risen over time; secondly, initially high expectations might also have attenuated through more "realistic" evaluations. Despite an actual fixed reference of time to the last six months, the validity of this "disillusion hypothesis" could not fundamentally be denied, because it can not be excluded that the partners based their evaluation on a total view of the cooperative work up to now. Finally, a third explanation is given by the strong growth of the VC in the recent past, which could have resulted in a strong dissatisfaction of the established partners, perhaps because of their decreased influence or the necessity of splitting customers and orders.

Finally a lower willingness to answer in the second round of questioning can be stated. This result can also be traced back to different causes. A possible

Figure 17: Relative objective achievements of the BUS partners

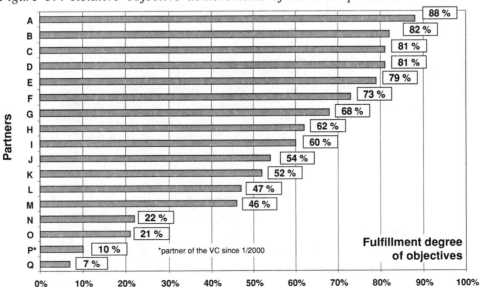

explanation could be that the respondents eschewed the explicit disclosure of their expectations despite of the assurance of anonymity given in advance. Even so it is conceivable that the partners encounter difficulties at specifying their requirements and expectations.

CONCLUSION AND OUTLOOK

The CONECT-procedure as a specific kind of benefit value analysis has been adopted in a pilot project with satisfactory results. With the method, both the evaluations of the partners and the consolidated assessments of the VC's point of view can be ascertained with little expense in installation and transaction. Simultaneously, the procedure allows very sophisticated analysis possibilities through the inclusion of both the main examination levels. The "benefit" of CONECT is the possibility of recognizing early existing dissatisfaction of partners and with that to avoid related costs for the cooperation, like passive or destructive behavior as far as to the withdrawal of the partner. Although the examination was about VCs, the method opens further application prospects in other cooperation forms, like, for example, joint ventures or trade associations.

Insights gained in this survey in comparison to experiences from an earlier practice study confirm that the short version of the procedure has got definite advantages with regards to the amount of answers received. Further examination must show how far the developed objective catalogue possesses a generic character and is applicable unmodified in VCs of other sectors. Demand exists particularly on the refinement of the developed key figure catalogue.

Finally, the hypotheses which could be deduced from the study must be confirmed and specified through long-term documentation. Thereby, the evolution of the expectations of the VC-members over the cooperation's time is definitely an important analysis with elementary management implications.

REFERENCES

Anderson, E. (1990). Two firms, one frontier: On assessing joint venture performance. *Sloan Management Review, 31*, 19-30.

Child, J., and Faulkner, D. (1998). *Strategies of cooperation*: *Managing Alliances, Networks, and Joint Ventures*. New York: Oxford University Press.

Ebert, M. (1998). *Evaluation von Synergien bei Unternehmenszusammenschlüssen*. Hamburg, Germany: Verlag Dr. Kovaè.

Hess, T., Wohlgemuth, O. and Schlembach, H. G. (2001). Bewertung von Unternehmensnetzwerken: Methodik und erste Erfahrungen aus einem Pilotprojekt. zfo. *Zeitschrift für Führung und Organisation*, 70, 68-74.

Lützig, W. P. (1982). *Die vieldimensionale Kalkulation der Kooperation*. Berlin, Germany.

Michel, U. (1996). *Wertorientiertes Management strategischer Allianzen*. Munich, Germany: Verlag Franz Vahlen.

Miles, R. E. and Snow, C. C. (1986). Organizations: New concepts for new forms. *California Management Review*, 28, 62-73.

Rappaport, A. (1998). *Creating Shareholder Value: A Guide for Managers and Investors* (Rev. ed.). New York: Free Press.

Riebel, P. (1994). Einzelkosten–und Deckungsbeitragsrechnung: *Grundfragen einer markt- und entscheidungsorientierten Unternehmensrechnung* (7th ed.). Wiesbaden, Germany: Gabler.

Schaan, J. L. (1987). International joint venture success measurement: Mexican evidence. In D. van de Bulcke (Ed.), *Multinational Enterprises and Developing Countries: A Changing Relationship? Proceedings of the 13th annual meeting of EIBA (pp. 127-144)*. Antwerp, Belgium.

Sieben, G. (1993). Phraseword: Unternehmensbewertung. In W. Wittmann & E. Grochla (Eds.), *Handwörterbuch der Betriebswirtschaft* (5th ed., columns 4315-4331). Stuttgart: Poeschel.

Veil, T. and Hess, T. (2000). Ergebnisrechnung für Unternehmensnetzwerke. Arbeitsbericht Nr. 8 der Abteilung Wirtschaftsinformatik II der Universität Göttingen, Göttingen, Germany.

Zangemeister, C. (1976). Nutzwertanalyse in der Systemtechnik: *Eine Methodik zur multidimensionalen Bewertung und Auswahl von Projektalternativen*. 4th ed., Munich, Germany: Wittmannsche Buchhandlung.

Chapter XVII

What Regulation for Virtual Organizations?

Claudia Cevenini
University of Bologna, Italy

Virtual organizations are a complex subject which requires an interdisciplinary approach. In the absence of specific legislation, consolidated doctrine and case law, jurists can resort to three main cornerstones: agreements between members and with third parties, analogical application of laws in force, and informal rules and trade usage.

The preliminary step is to define the object of analysis as clearly as possible by building a model definition of virtual organizations for the legal research. On the basis of the model's features, the most relevant legal issues can be outlined.

At present, owing to the very nature of VOs, no definitive solutions are possible. However, some basic indications can be provided to enable potential and effective partners of a VO to understand from the start the possible legal implications of their activities.

INTRODUCTION

Rules and regulations are often regarded to as an unfathomable "attorney issue" and somehow feared by the business and IT world.

Projects are started, new strategic lines are followed, breakthrough products and services are brought to the market, and massive human and financial resources are invested only to sometimes discover *a posteriori* that some serious legal problem is acting as a paralyzing bottleneck.

This may be a consequence of thinking–or acting–in watertight compartments. Scientific research, project management and consulting in the fields of legal science, information technology and business organization have for a long time followed separate paths. This is no longer a rational solution in a world where becoming global and networked is the prerequisite for the survival of both large corporations and small and medium enterprises.

Virtual organizations are an extremely complex, cross-section research subject, whose study strongly needs the development of interdisciplinary competencies.

Information technology law is the junction ring between the implementation of new technologies in the economic context and the rules applicable to them–which may constitute either a constraint or an opportunity or both.

Law intervenes in regulating phenomena which arise in social groups and are subsequently consolidated over time. It is the element which binds the members of a community together in their adherence to recognized values and standards.

Before national or supranational legislators deem it necessary to enact *ad hoc* legal frameworks on specific themes,[1] a shorter or longer period of legal uncertainty elapses. This is definitely the case of virtual organizations.

They have been widely studied from the business organization and information technology perspective over the last years but virtually no legal doctrine is to be found on them, nor any specific rules, regulations or case law. On the other hand, conceiving VOs as a legal "no-man's-land" could impair their future development and affirmation in a global market which strongly needs and requires them.

The IT-legal research is presently in the position to offer neither optimal nor definitive solutions but it can start to provide a solid foundation, references, general principles and directives on which to build awareness and case-by-case analyses.

This can be achieved by:

(1)   defining the object of study by developing an "ideal" VO model;

(2)   singling out the most relevant legal issues that may arise from the nature, activities and interactions of the model;

(3)   understanding if the law in force on similar subjects and issues, be it national or supranational, shows some points of connection with the VO model and may be applied by analogy–on the whole or in part;

(4)   analyzing the role of informal rules and trade usage for noncovered or controversial issues;

(5)   discussing unresolved problems.

A TAXONOMY OF VIRTUAL ORGANIZATIONS FOR THE LEGAL ANALYSIS

At present a universally accepted, clear-cut legal definition of virtual organizations is still to be drafted. This is the most important obstacle that has to be faced, as every scientific analysis–first of all–needs an object.

Owing to its nature, however, a monolithic framing of the concept by the legislator would be premature or at the worst preposterous: in the absence of a consolidated experience, exceptions today are often the rule.

As in the scientific studies of complex phenomena, the IT-legal researcher can proceed by building a VO model, that is, by singling out, analyzing and structuring relevant elements, while leaving out irrelevant ones. The model would include the most meaningful features both from the economic and from the legal viewpoint and would make it possible to develop a taxonomy of virtual organizations.

A model is not a picture of reality but rather the way to create a sort of "laboratory"[2]. Secondly, it is the outcome of an arbitrary choice, in relation with cognitive goals. It is not a turn-key solution, but rather a datum point for the VO's decision makers, who would be enabled to preventively assess the legal implications of their actions and strategies.

It has to be stressed that sometimes a blurred image of the virtual organization emerges. Structures and organizations are regarded as or consider themselves to be virtual organizations, while this is not always the case. From Internet companies to business networks, vertical portals and info-mediators, all of them share some traits with VOs and are surely worth of attention; they may be considered virtual organizations at a lower evolutionary stage.

From the confrontation of literature and case studies, a rather long list of characteristics of "real" virtual organizations can be drawn. After having sifted legally relevant traits on the basis of a prevalence criterion, a basic definition of a VO and a taxonomy of its characteristics for the legal analysis can be developed.

Evidently, different or partially overlapping models can be created for different cognitive needs. From the economic viewpoint, for instance, the concentration on core competencies is of fundamental importance, while from the legal one it has barely any relevance.

"A Virtual Organization is a temporary network of legally independent entities which set up business interrelations in order to jointly bring products and services to the market."

Virtual organizations are set up to take advantage of a particular business opportunity and successively be dissolved. Their lifespan can extend over the short, medium or even long term, but not indefinitely. This may bear consequences, for example, as to post-dissolution liability towards third parties in case a dispute arises.

VOs are made up of a plurality of subjects, which always maintain their independence and their former legal status. VOs are mostly made up by companies but may also include other kinds of members, such as universities, local authorities or professionals. In this latter case, different rules may apply; universities and public institutions have to follow strict procedures for the procurement of goods and services, the carrying out of commercial activities, the management of official documents, the hiring of personnel, etc., while members of regulated professions–such as lawyers, doctors or accountants–have to comply with strict rules regarding, in particular, the independence, dignity and honor of the profession, professional secrecy and fairness towards clients and other members of the profession.[3]

The operative goal of virtual organizations is generally for profit–although research and development purposes cannot be excluded in line of principle–and the outcome of the collaboration by the individual partners is the joint provision of products and services, in a way that could not possibly or cost-efficiently be achieved separately. All members have to agree upon rules on how to allocate roles and tasks along the value chain and consequently on how to share profits and losses, also for tax purposes, in compliance with applicable rules and regulations.

"The VO does not achieve its own, separate legal status as a corporation, company group or any other legal institution recognized by national or supranational legal systems."

The Virtual Organization remains legally "virtual." It does not formally achieve a legal status above and beyond that of the individual partners which compose it.

It does not aim to become a corporation, a company group or an association, a trust or a joint venture either under national or under supranational law, although many parallels with these and other existing legal institutions can be drawn. In other words, no exactly matching legal person corresponds to it.

Law in force recognizes and regulates various associative forms which show some points of contact with virtual organizations. It has to be investigated if and to what extent present regulations may be adequate for VOs, as these latter also thrive thanks to their lack of formalities and bureaucratic burdens and the applicability of precise, standardized rules might strongly limit their activities.

"The VO structure is democratic and based upon a peer-to-peer relation; there is no pyramidal hierarchy, nor any central authority is in the position to unilaterally impose 'top down' rules."

In virtual organizations no partner has legally more power than the others and therefore none of them can unilaterally impose or enforce decisions upon another one. Decisions are made on a democratic basis and not imposed by a higher level subject or central authority.

Differences may therefore only arise from *de facto* economic balances or imbalances or from the provisions of contractual agreements; these latter, in any case, only have effect between those who have signed them.

No hierarchical structure is formally created and there is no "owner" or chief executive officer of the VO. It is actually possible that partners decide upon granting particular roles or tasks to one or more partners or even to third parties, but this would always happen in a "bottom up," commonly agreed direction.

"The VO has no own common assets, no personnel, no registered office, no balance sheet, no board of administrators."

Virtual organizations are not corporations, although they may have the same objectives and achieve similar results.

All resources used within the VO value chain formally belong to the individual partners, even if they are committed to a common goal. All tangible and intangible assets as well as all the personnel and consultants engaged in the activities of the VO are never formally "conferred" to this latter.

The Virtual organization does not draw up an autonomous balance-sheet at the end of each accounting year, as it is not included among the legal persons to which an obligation in this sense is imposed by law.[4] Furthermore, not being a corporate group, it is not obliged to draw up a consolidated balance-sheet on the basis of the partners' balance sheets.

The VO does not appoint a board of administrators to manage it, nor does it own any other formal organ.

"The VO may appear to third parties and customers as one corporation with which they believe to interact and transact."

The sharing of resources and as well as the joint provision of products and services may lead customers and, in general, third parties to think that they are in effect dealing with a separate corporation with a legal personality. They may not be aware of the complexity of the structure that lies beneath if an opportune disclosure is not imposed by law or agreed upon by the VO partners.

This may become more evident whenever products and services are offered and/or provided through electronic means–by way of a common interface (i.e., an Internet Web site).

The situation is especially delicate every time the counterpart is not a business entity but a final customer–legally defined as a consumer–to whom, as the weak contracting party, the law usually grants a higher level of protection.

"The VO partners interact and cooperate with the aid of information and communication technologies."

It is generally acknowledged that information and communication technologies (ICT) are extremely valuable tools for traditional companies. In the case of virtual organizations, they are the indispensable basis for their existence and operativeness.

The reasons lie in the very nature of VOs: their various partners may often be geographically dispersed and have to coordinate their activities without being bound by the need for physical presence and possibly also in asynchronous mode, with the aid of videoconferencing, e-mail, simulation techniques, etc. They need, for example, to exchange documents electronically; to be connected to a controlled-access Web-based workspace, in order to share data and information; to create structured electronic databases; to have an external visibility on open networks, especially on the Internet; to provide information and/or products and services electronically; to search for partners or outsourcers via the Web; to interact with customers and provide fast and effective online assistance; and so on.

This may give rise to a myriad of legal problems, such as the legal validity of electronic data and documents and their use as proof in court proceedings; the legitimacy of the use of cryptography for confidential data; the protection of the personal data processed by partners; the ownership, protection and access to shared databases; the liability for the information and data made available on the Web; electronic contracts–validity, time and place if conclusion; the legal implications of the use of software agents for information search and the execution of contracts; etc.

In order to carry on business lawfully, every partner has the duty to check whether its national legislation has enacted rules applicable to the above issues and if and to what extent they are compatible with the rules in force in the other partners' states.

The implementation of ICT in economic relationships has started to be adequately regulated only in recent years and still leaves many areas uncovered.

In the absence of rules and case law on the usage of state-of-the-art technological tools by the virtual organization, reference can be made to the present regulation of similar–although less advanced–traditional techniques, such as fax, telex, telephone and automated devices.

"The contribution of the individual partners to the final product or service may be impossible to distinguish, also because cross-company groups may work on the same project."

In virtual organizations, every partner contributes to the final goal by concentrating on specific competencies. Every ring of the value chain, such as strategic planning, product development, production, marketing, distribution, etc., is taken up by those partners who are best at it. In the end, joint products and services–as mentioned before–emerge as a result.

Moreover, tasks are not rigidly divided, as if the individual partners were the functional divisions of a large corporation: it is possible that one task or function is shared by the personnel and offices of different partners, who work together in transversal, cross-company groups.

Owing to this, it can be very hard–if sometimes not unfeasible–to single out the individual contributions of the different partners and to trace back who is responsible for what.

From a regulation profile, a framework agreement would be the most adequate tool to establish the rules on the basis of which to link individual actions to common results. This could be done also by deciding upon rebuttable presumptions, such as, for example, percentage contributions to certain tasks.

"Partners are often located in different states or continents and may be subject to different legislations.

The different entities which build up a virtual organization may potentially have their main offices or branches in any part of the world. While it cannot be excluded that a VO can be set up and operate only at local, regional or national level, the most common case is that of a transnational/transcontinental organization.

This is another strong point of VOs: they are potentially open to the contribution of any highly competent partner, regardless of its country of origin; this also enables them to enter the right market at the right time for their sector of activity at the global level.

Every partner may be subject to a different legal system and consequently rules may differ substantially.

In addition, it is problematic to assess the location in which electronic contracts are concluded and where intangible products and services are downloaded from the VO e-commerce Web site.

"Information, data, and know-how are generally shared among partners."

In general, as in every initiative in which many different subjects team up for a common goal, it would be advisable for partners to give up any "selfish" behavior that could have negative repercussions on the general outcome of their collaboration.

One of the most precious resources in business today is information. Therefore, all useful data possessed by each partner should be shared.

While this can be quite obvious when they are dealing with publicly accessible information, it can be much more difficult when it has to be decided whether or not a company's know-how built over years or decades of activity should be disclosed and put at everyone's disposal within the VO and on what conditions. Similar considerations can be made in the case of legally protected intellectual property rights, such as copyright and patents.

A cost/benefit analysis should be carried out to understand if and to what extent information sharing is actually feasible. In a legal perspective, partners may decide this by agreement but it has to be stressed that this would only be valid inter partes and that the rights of third parties acting in good faith would usually be protected. As a general principle, if an external subject in good faith–on the basis of a lawful contract–purchases illicitly divulgated data, information or know-how, the contract should remain valid and only a right to damages in favor of the legitimate owner may arise.

The creation of a common information database out of separate databases also implies the delicate issue of data security and the liabilities connected with the ownership of the database builders and the possible noncompliance with technical or legal provisions on data protection.

"Partners may be coordinated by a third party, the so-called 'business integrator' or 'information/network broker.' This may lay down the rules for setting up, operating and dissolving the VO."

Virtual organizations might be born spontaneously or even without any awareness of it. Step by step, companies team up and start cooperating more and more intensely–they create networks; involve suppliers, outsourcers and other stakeholders in the value chain by giving them more responsibilities, also in relation to decision making; set up Web portals, etc.; and finally start acting as a "real" VO.

While this is certainly feasible–and mostly occurs as the evolution of previously consolidated relationships and business practices–more often it is enabled by the intervention of a third party.

This–usually referred to as "business integrator" or "information/network broker"–would act as a catalyst, a sort of "visible hand" of the market, and play an active role in finding the right partners for the right opportunity and then assisting them in setting up the Virtual Organization and later in coordinating its activities throughout its whole life cycle.

In the case of a "spontaneous" VO, every time a new partner enters the organization, conditions and rules have to be necessarily renegotiated (unless existing partners possess such a high contractual power so as to impose their will to newcomers). The presence of a coordinator would simplify this by drawing up templates on which to tailor framework agreements and conditions for the VO and to regulate the relationships among partners.

"The boundaries of the Virtual Organization may be fluid and not clearly show who is in and who is out."

Virtual organizations are dynamic subjects and do not necessarily maintain exactly the same partner composition from beginning to end. Moreover, they interact with a large number of external parties who may in some cases play an active and creative role, and not just act as mere suppliers. In this context, the boundaries of the VO may not be clearly drawn–unlike in traditional groups, networks or corporations.

Some subjects may "officially" contribute, by virtue of bilateral or multilateral agreements, while others may be "unofficial" but nevertheless *de facto* members. From the legal viewpoint, their position could be the most delicate one, especially as regards the proof of their role. Moreover, small enterprises often collaborate in the absence of any formalized agreement.

On the other hand, not all interactions may be foreseen or foreseeable from the start and consequently agreed upon clearly: it would be either unfeasible or at the best uneconomic.

An important point would be to clearly determine the composition of the VO in order to divide its interactions in two main categories: internal and external ones.

SOME RELEVANT LEGAL ISSUES

As a preliminary consideration, every economic activity needs legal certainty for its smooth operativeness.

One the one side, those who wish to become partners of a virtual organization need to be assured that they are not entering a legal land-mine territory and that they are in the position to clearly understand from the beginning the possible implications of their future interactions within the VO.

On the other side, forcing virtual organizations into rigid regulatory schemes would probably stifle their dynamic and informal way of operating, put them on the same level of any traditional company group or some other form of business association and nullify their competitive advantage by imposing severe legal burdens on them.[5]

The Latins said: "*In media stat virtus*," that is, virtue lies in the middle. The perfect solution does not exist, at least not now, so an attempt can be made to draw a balance between the two extremes.

As a general principle, partners can regulate their relationships by agreement, but agreements cannot possibly cover each and every present and future task and interaction of VOs; they may be renewed or rewritten but not continuously– otherwise the stability of rules would be lost. For what is not specifically provided for in the agreements, codes and law in force can be applied, if deemed pertinent.

Identifying and analyzing the legal knots to be untied by virtual organizations are the preliminary steps in order to understand if and how they may be regulated on a case-by-case basis.

Framework Agreement

In the absence of clear, incontrovertibly applicable rules, the VO framework agreement is the strongest tool in the hands of the partners of a Virtual Organization. The principle of contractual freedom allows them to regulate their interactions in the way they deem best, thus leaving the least possible situations to chance.

Agreements are in any case a source of law of inferior level in comparison with formal rules and regulations in force, and unlawful provisions contained in them can be declared null and void. They have the effectiveness of law between the contracting parties but have no effect whatsoever with respect to third parties.

The more detailed the contract is, the less risks the VO may incur. However, a trade-off arises: extremely detailed rules strongly limit the flexibility of the VO structure and actions, as well as the freedom of newcomers, whose alternatives are either to enter and accept the agreement basically as it is or not to enter. Besides, it would be uneconomical and time-consuming to renegotiate a new agreement every time the partnership is enlarged–also on the basis of predetermined templates.

Operational agreements between a restricted number of partners can also be signed to regulate the execution of some particular tasks.

In any case, it would be advisable that a general framework agreement encompassed the following items:

- applicable law and competent court;
- membership rules;
- partners' roles and tasks;
- performance standards;
- allocation of costs and revenues;
- conditions for confidential data disclosure and exchange;
- regulation/limitation of partners' rights to compete with the VO;
- allocation of partners' liabilities;
- alternative dispute resolution procedures;
- entrance of new partners;
- dissolution conditions;
- post-dissolution liability conditions and limitations.

In a more practical perspective, the presence of a coordinating entity, such a business integrator or a network broker, or even a partner with a deep experience in the VO area of business and in the management of company networks would facilitate and speed up the procedure needed to reach a final general agreement. A fast creation phase would enable a virtual organization to seize precious but evanescent business opportunities, which might otherwise be lost if discussions and amendments dragged on for too long.

Applicable Law and Jurisdiction

Virtual organizations are often transnational entities: they may involve partners whose national legal frameworks may differ widely, especially when they include both common law and civil law countries.

Each participant has its registered office in one particular state (and possibly a permanent establishment in other states); it therefore has to comply with the national legislation of that State, as well as with supranational laws and treaties to which the country itself is signatory (while other countries may not).

All phases of the VO's value chain can take place in different locations: production may, for instance, be concentrated in India, quality control in Germany, e-commerce tools development in the US, marketing strategy in Italy, etc. Products and services are then delivered to final customers located in any country, whether by electronic or by traditional means, via a distribution network.

What law applies? What is the competent court? Where does the economic activity take place? Treaties and conventions may contribute to a common legal framework. A basic legal document on these issues is the 1980 Rome Convention on the International Trade of Goods.

In the absence of a clear solution, however, each and every partner might be potentially subject to the law of every other VO member which contributes to the same product or service and also to the law of every country in which products and services are provided.

Moreover, a national court may in particular cases take decisions which spread their effects on residents of other countries.[6] On the basis of the Due Process Clause, the US federal law allows jurisdiction on a defendant in any state in which she/he has had minimal contacts. This principle has been tempered by the US Supreme Court, which has stated some equity factors to be considered, such as the inconvenience caused to a defendant to be sued in a certain jurisdiction; the interest of a certain state in deciding upon the dispute; the interest of the plaintiff in obtaining an effective and useful decision, and the interest of the judiciary system in an efficient composition of interstate disputes; etc.

Liberty finds no refuge in a jurisprudence of *doubt;*[7] jurisdiction has been a controversial legal issue since the invention of cars. What VO partners can do is to reduce the margin of uncertainty as much as possible by signing carefully drawn framework agreements in which both applicable law and competent court are commonly decided upon. They do not necessarily have to choose the national law of one of the partners but can freely opt for another legislation, provided that it best suits the activities and interactions of the VO.

The Legal Identity of Virtual Organizations

In an economic sense, virtual organizations can be seen as a sort of fluid, dynamic meta-enterprise. From the legal point of view, no legal system has yet explicitly defined them as a distinct, legally relevant entity in any of its acts.

It has to be clarified whether and on what conditions a VO can be considered an independent entity, separate from its partners, with its own rights and duties, or if it is merely a sort of "glue" between legally autonomous subjects. This depends much on each individual VO's structure and interrelations.

Virtual organizations may share some similar traits with other institutions recognized by national and supranational legislation; this means that the rules designed for these latter can in some cases be applied by analogy.[8]

For example, in the United States, when no written agreement is signed, most states see the collaboration of companies which team up to do business as a general partnership. In this case, all partners are held "jointly and severally liable": in other words, each of them is liable for the entire amount of all damages owed by the VO, also for the ones caused solely by other partners.

Otherwise, some authors[9] suggest that VOs may be incorporated as traditional corporations, for example, under US law. Their liability would be limited and they would maintain a certain flexibility to regulate new relationships with subcontracting agreements, but at the same time they would bear a higher tax burden at the corporate level.

Taking as an example the Italian legal system, different forms of cooperation among enterprises are regulated, which might be partly assimilated to virtual organizations, in particular:

- *consorzi*[10] (consortia)–With the consortium agreement, a number of entrepreneurs set up a common organization to regulate or to carry out of particular phases of the respective enterprises.[11]

- *associazioni temporanee di imprese*[12] (temporary associations of enterprises)–Associated companies grant a collective special order to act on their behalf and in their name to one of them, the group leader; this latter is allowed to present offers for public procurements for the whole association.

- *EEIG–Economic European Interest Grouping*[13]–It is set up by contract and has its own rights and duties; it can draw up agreements or carry out any other legally valid action, as well as appear before courts; and member states can decide if an EEIG may have legal personality. Its purpose is to facilitate or develop the economic activity of its members, to improve or increase the results of such activity, but not to make profit for itself; its activity has to be connected to the economic activity of its members and may only have an auxiliary character.

- *controlled enterprises*–Enterprises can be considered controlled when they are under the dominating influence of another company owing to particular contract ties with it[14] or in presence of rights, contracts or other legally relevant relationships which give it–together or by themselves–the possibility of having a determining influence on the activities of an enterprise.[15]

On the other side, every time a virtual organization is created or modified, it is opportune to analyze its characteristics and interactions in the light of the applicable law in force and to take adequate measures so that the VO cannot be easily, albeit unwillingly assimilated to one particular strictly regulated legal institute (as recognized by one of the partner's legal system or, still worse, by the applicable legislation chosen in the framework agreement). For instance, in case a dispute arises, the competent court may decide that a certain VO is in fact a particular kind of partnership or corporation–for which the national legislation foresees joint and several liability, or the appointing of a board of administrators or the drawing up a group balance sheet–and ask partners to comply with all these provisions.

Liability

The activities of virtual organizations necessarily involve a complex network of relations, both internally and externally.

Within the VO, different companies and working groups collaborate to produce joint outputs. Outside the VO, several external subjects–such as outsourcers or providers of Internet and telecommunications services–give an indispensable contribution by enabling distance interactions. Sometimes it may be difficult to draw a clear line between who is in and who is out; even a company which is not formally linked to the VO by virtue of an agreement may be considered a substantial part of it. Customers, in turn, purchase the VO products and services often convinced of dealing with a single company. In this context, it may be hard to tell who can be held liable for what.

As to internal relationships, partners should usually agree on a clear allocation of responsibilities and on repressive measures for breach of contract, as well as fix monetary and temporal limitations to liability, such as, for example, a maximum sum for damages and a time beyond which no claim can be stated. In any case, these provisions must comply with the applicable law.

On the external side, whenever third parties provide products and services to a VO, it has to be clearly stated on behalf of whom they are acting in order to be able to reconstruct a possible liability chain and, again, well-defined tasks and responsibilities.

With respect to customers, the VO can propose general contract conditions which contain adequate liability disclaimers. In the case that it is interacting with a consumer, however, its contractual freedom is much more limited than in contracts signed with other businesses. Consumers are the weak contracting party and therefore usually enjoy a much higher legal protection. Some companies even choose to offer higher guarantees than what would be required in order to stimulate trust.

Legal Relevance of Electronic Signatures and Documents

The interactions and information exchanges of a virtual organization mostly take place via information and communication technologies.

It is essential that all documents and data–especially confidential ones–exchanged electronically are not tampered with before reaching the legitimate addressee and that their source can be securely determined. The technical tool which can guarantee the origin, integrity and also the confidentiality of messages sent via an open network is the use of a certified cryptographic key pair for electronic signatures.

Today many countries recognize the legal validity of documents and signatures in electronic form; this makes it possible, at least in theory, to fully substitute paper documents with electronic documents.

In Europe, a number of states[16] have declared digitally signed electronic documents as legally equivalent to paper documents and affirmed their acceptability as a proof before court. The European Directive 1999/93/EC on electronic signatures[17] –which is to be implemented by Member States by July 2001–has confirmed this equivalence, under particular conditions, and laid down uniform principles for electronic signatures and documents.

The United States has passed the Electronic Signatures in Global and National Commerce Act,[18] which similarly affirms the principle that *"a signature, contract or other record [...] may not be denied legal effect, validity or enforceability solely because it is in electronic form.*"

It has to be remembered, however, that in many cases contracts do not need the written form or a signature in order to be valid, however: public-key infrastructures and electronic signatures–where legally recognized–are relevant as they allow the parties to provide the evidence of a contract and to prove before court that an agreement has effectively been concluded.

Data Protection

The collaboration of the VO partners usually requires that all of them have access to personal data contained in other partners' databases or create shared databases.

Each action which involves the processing of personal data, by whatever means and especially in the case of sensitive data, has to comply with applicable legislation on data protection. Even if the partner which first processed a piece of personal information has been duly authorized, also all the other partners which collaborate with him have to comply with the procedures set by law in order not to incur civil or penal liability.

In Europe, the fundamental legal document on this matter is Directive 95/46/EC of the European Parliament and of the Council of 24 October 1995 on the protection of individuals with regard to the processing of personal data and on the free movement of such data.[19]

Considering that most data will travel from one VO partner to another via telecommunications networks, Directive 97/66/EC of the European Parliament and of the Council of 15 December 1997 concerning the processing of personal data and the protection of privacy in the telecommunications sector[20] also needs to be considered.

Basic principles of these norms are information and consensus: the person to whom data refer has to be informed that her/his data are being processed, for what purposes and by whom; except in particular cases, express written consensus is needed for data processing; and data can in any moment be corrected, edited or cancelled upon request.

Intellectual Property Rights

During their history, besides their know-how, companies which join a virtual organization have developed a software or maybe they also have registered patents or trademarks, possess copyrights, and, in general, are holders of a series of rights on immaterial goods.

The well-functioning of the VO would demand the sharing of much of this knowledge with the other partners, but this may clash with the individual needs and policies of each one of them. Moreover, partners may also want to carry on their previous activities as independent business entities and devote only part of them to the VO project.

Before entering a VO agreement, it should be clearly decided what knowledge and rights in possession of every single partner are strictly functional to the life of the organization and upon what conditions and at what cost they can be shared among the members. In the absence of a well-defined set of rules, the mere reliance on trust and economic balances would very much hold back most partners. This is equally true for the sharing of newly acquired information, whose knowledge may favor either the sole holder, if retained, or the whole group, if disclosed.

The Online Provision of Goods and Services

A virtual organization will often offer or provide its products and services via open networks and has to be aware of what practical and legal consequences it implies.

Contracting parties can be located anywhere in the world–sellers must be sure that the provision of a good or a service to a certain country is not prohibited by the national law of the buyer. To avoid any doubt, many online sellers use technical tools which allow customers to buy only from certain countries (e.g., some US sellers only allow US residents to buy) or insert a provision in contract conditions; if customers manage to buy anyway by altering their identity, they will be considered the sole responsible party.

Contracting parties are not visible–somebody could buy in someone else's place (e.g., a person under age or a credit card thief), while an e-commerce Web site might itself be just an interface without any underlying commercial structure; an identification procedure or system is strongly needed. In the case that legally recognized electronic signatures are used, signed documents may–if needed–be used to prove that a transaction between certain parties has effectively taken place.

At present, the basic legal framework in Europe is provided by the Directive on Electronic Commerce.[21] The directive focuses on some basic themes:

- establishment and information requirements for information society service providers–The activity of information society service providers shall not be made subject to prior authorization, except for authorization schemes not specifically and exclusively targeted at information society services; every service provider has the duty to make specific information accessible to recipients, in particular its name and geographic address at which it is established, its details, trade register identification and VAT number.
- commercial communications–They have to be clearly identifiable as such and indicate the natural or legal person on behalf of whom the communication is made, while unsolicited commercial communication by e-mail is made subject to strict conditions.
- contracts concluded by electronic means–Member states shall allow the conclusion of contracts by electronic means and may provide limitations for certain categories (e.g., real estate contracts or contracts governed by family law).
- liability of intermediary service providers–Intermediaries are not liable if they do not start the transmission, do not select the receivers and do not select or alter the information contained in the transmission itself; no general obligation to monitor or to actively seek for illegal activity is imposed on them.

Reference can also be made to other directives which contain some limited provisions on electronic selling, like Directive 97/7/EC of the European Parliament and of the Council of 20 May 1997 on the protection of consumers in respect of distance contracts.[22] Its most relevant feature is the provision of a 10-day term in which the consumer has the unconditional right to return the items she/he has bought–except in particular cases such as the purchase of software.

Alternative Dispute Resolution (ADR) Methods

Bringing a dispute before a court may be a huge problem for a VO, especially if its expected life span covers just a single project. Reaching a final decision may sometimes take many years and this would in certain cases even prevent a Virtual Organization from operating altogether. The VO partners need to reach fast and cost-effective solutions and would profit from agreeing upon submitting possible internal or external disputes to ADR.

These are out-of-court flexible and less formal procedures which give partners a remarkable freedom in choosing the rules to be followed and the persons who will decide on the dispute. These do not necessarily have to be legal counsels but may have a specialized expertise in the VO's area of business or in company networks or in ICT-enabled interactions, etc. In addition, information and data on the procedure are kept confidential, unlike in cases brought before a court.

The relevance of alternative dispute resolution methods is also highlighted by the European Directive on Electronic Commerce, which invites member states not to hamper the use of out-of-court dispute settlement schemes, including electronic means.[23]

There are different ADR techniques, which meet different needs.

For instance, arbitration is a private court decision in which one or more neutral subjects are appointed to make a decision on a controversy. Their powers come from contractual decisions of the parties.

Instead, mediation is a procedure in which the mediator does not have autonomous decision powers but can merely assist the parties, in contrast, to negotiate in order to find an agreement.

Software Agents

Agents may be used by virtual organizations both for partner search (pre-contractual stage) and for the actual conclusion of transactions (contractual stage). The legal status and role of agents still has to be clarified from the legal viewpoint. The most important task is to determine the lawfulness both of their actions and of the set of instructions assigned to them.

In the pre-contractual stage, electronic agents move through a network and search for information. Care must be taken by developers so that this does not in any case infringe upon other parties' rights, such as copyright or privacy or that the agent does not enter protected computer systems against the administrator's will.

In the contractual stage, agents execute contracts on behalf of a human party, be it the VO or one of the partners. The legal implications of a nonhuman transaction have to be considered, in particular in relation to the liability for the agents' actions and to the regulations on error and bad faith.

INFORMAL RULES AND BUSINESS PRACTICES

What happens when a new phenomenon appears extremely difficult to regulate on the basis of the existing legal framework?

In ancient times, law was based upon land property. When commercial transactions started to develop and extend beyond the walls of castles and towns, later even beyond national borders, merchants realized that the rules in force were not at all suitable for their activities. This climate of confusion and legal uncertainty pushed merchants to develop their own code of rules, which later became the *lex mercatoria*. Its importance is confirmed by the fact that today, even in the presence of a well-established international commercial law, the role of the *lex mercatoria* is still kept in high consideration, as witnesses the decision of a French tribunal, which states that in the absence of precise ties with a particular state, the issue has to be submitted to the *lex mercatoria*.[24]

A very similar situation can be envisaged with the advent of new organizational forms such as virtual organizations, the exponential diffusion of global open networks and their use for commercial purposes.

Some authors have coined the term "*lex electronica*"[25] to define the informal legal rules applicable in the framework of electronic commerce; in a broader sense, the concept can be extended to the whole information society, of which VOs are definitely members.

The singling out of the components of the *lex electronica* necessarily moves from the model to which it is inspired, that is, the *lex mercatoria*. This latter traditionally includes five different categories of norms: treaties and international conventions, model contracts, arbitration case law, trade usage, and general principles of the law.

The first three are defined "institutional sources," as they are enacted by authorized organs, while the last two are defined as "substantial law."

In the hierarchy of sources, conventions and international treaties have a dominant position. It has to be stressed that the global nature of virtual organizations contributes to emphasize the importance of informal rules. They are in fact kept in particular consideration at the international level, where the competition of more formal rules is weaker and it is hard for different states to harmonize the reciprocal, often contrasting claims.[26] Informal rules can be the ideal instruments for solving the issues which involve a plurality of jurisdictions and for overcoming the incompatibilities between different national laws.

Therefore, informal rules such as commercial usage, codes of conduct, standards and general principles can be more than mere interpretative tools and actually play a determining role for regulating virtual organizations.

Noteworthy examples are the UNIDROIT principles for commercial contracts and the UNCITRAL Model Laws.

As said before, in some cases, formal legislation in force in the different legal systems can actually be applied by extension; in others, however, it may not be adequate.

Moreover, formal laws and decrees need a long time and a complex procedure to be passed and they can hardly keep the pace with the reality they aim at regulating. Once come into force, they soon become obsolete if reexamination mechanisms are not implemented.

Informal rules, on the contrary, meet the VO need for flexibility, while–to some extent–forcedly sacrificing stability.

The favor for informal rules is supported by further arguments: the sectors of activity with high technological content, due to their very nature, draw substantial advantage by them; regulation in these fields requires a deep knowledge and a practical experience that may escape lawmakers. Therefore, over time these areas will tend to develop a higher and higher level of autonomy from state law.

REGULATION ISSUES IN EUROPEAN PROJECTS ON VOS

The European Commission is presently showing much interest in new collaboration forms among enterprises and is fostering the development of projects on virtual enterprises,[27] in which part of the analysis is devoted to regulatory issues.

VIVE

VIVE[28] (Virtual Vertical Enterprise) is a project within the Fourth RTD Framework Program of the European Commission, which was completed in the first quarter of the year 2000.

Its main objective was to facilitate the creation of virtual enterprises among small and medium enterprises by developing solutions for their setting up and management.

The most relevant results achieved by the VIVE project are:
- the development of a specific methodology;
- the creation of an ICT infrastructure prototype;
- the setting up of two pilot virtual enterprises following the VIVE methodology;
- business metrics to evaluate the benefits of the overall VIVE approach.

From the legal perspective, the VIVE methodology in itself can be considered as a set of norms and provisions to regulate the life cycle of those VEs which are set up and operate in conformance to it, in other words, a sort of normative scaffolding.

The VIVE methodology: (a) determines the role and tasks of the "business integrator," whose presence is deemed essential for the existence of the VE; (b) defines the scope and succession of the different partners' activities; and (c) develops business templates which form the basis for a more detailed regulation of the business integrator's and the partners' actions.

The business integrator negotiates contractual agreements with the partners on the basis of the VIVE business templates. These latter are a support for all activities in the various stages of the VE life cycle, based on previously gained experiences.

VIVE identifies five main phases of the virtual enterprise life cycle, that is: market assessment; VE design; VE constitution; bid process; and VE operation.

After having carried out a market survey and decided upon product requirements, the "market assessment" phase foresees the laying down of the VE business plan, which shall be followed during all successive phases.

The design phase starts with the functional product breakdown, that is, the identification and formalization of the functions and skills needed by the VE; the purpose is to single out the VE categories within which the business integrator will be able to choose the VE partners. This is followed by the initial work breakdown structure, or VE process, to allocate roles, scope of activity and interdependencies of the different partners. Finally, the technological product breakdown is drawn, considering in addition the market product requirements.

Formal technological, organizational, operational and ICT requirements are decided upon in the constitution phase, when potential partners' candidatures are to be evaluated. With the feedback of the successfully qualified VE partners, a final work breakdown structure is drawn and the VIVE virtual enterprise contractual agreement is signed. The contract regulates roles and responsibilities of the VE partners.

The bid process follows, where all specifications for the external offers or requests of offer are determined. To regulate this stage, contract forms are developed.

Finally, during the VE operation phase, orders are executed and the progress is monitored with periodic assessments. The most relevant results of this last stage are the technical document templates and the project progress update and administration templates.

The project has also set up an Interest Group on Virtual Enterprises,[29] composed of over 150 members, including corporations, universities, consulting firms and virtual enterprises themselves. The members participate with different purposes, depending on their nature: some aiming to take up the role of business integrator; others to become users; in other cases, to provide ICT or legal and financial services; or, in case of large enterprises, to build advanced suppliers' networks.

BIDSAVER

BIDSAVER[30] (Business Integrator Dynamic Support Agents for Virtual Enterprise) is a European project in the frame of the IST Call for RTD projects, which was launched at the beginning of 2000. It intends to build a framework to set up and operate virtual enterprises among small and medium enterprises in different business sectors.

The project intends to develop a methodology, processes, models and ICT tools for the cooperative management of projects and the Internet-based dynamic search for partners.

At the beginning, BIDSAVER will identify market requirements for VEs in two particular business areas–space satellites and mechanical equipment– and two VE types–network-oriented and supply-chain-based.

Following a bottom-up approach, a conceptual structure for VEs and their methodology will be identified. This will form the basis to develop the normative framework.

A reference system prototype will be set up; it will include commercial solutions for the different VE activities and three management modules: a business breakdown structure for the cross-mapping of physical and functional items, tasks, resources, timing, risks, etc.; an information-capturing agent for partner search and for the update of information on cooperation opportunities; and a business information integration module to integrate operational functions.

The BIDSAVER methodology and tools will be implemented in pilot applications[31] and applied to real industrial cases. The feedback from the pilots will make it possible to successively revise and improve them.

As to strictly regulatory issues, one of the project's objectives is to define a normative framework, a set of rules to manage both the internal and the external relationships of the virtual enterprise throughout its whole life cycle. A set of templates proposing possible solutions to the most common legal issues will provide guidelines for VE participants in a transnational perspective.

The results of the pilot cases will provide the inputs for the drawing up of best practices and business templates for specific sectors. This knowledge basis is important, as it will allow all VE stakeholders to single out the specific legal problems which affect them and to work on finding possible solutions.

ALIVE

ALIVE[32] is a European project within the IST (Information Society Technology) Program, denominated "Workgroup on the Advanced Legal Issues in Virtual Enterprises." It started at the beginning of 2001 and is presently in progress.

It aims at stimulating the cooperation between the industrial sector and legal and ICT professionals operating in the new economy area.

The project's main objectives are:
- to define a virtual enterprise taxonomy in order to clearly focus the object of research;
- to exchange information and cooperate with external subjects on similar themes;
- to identify and analyze the most relevant legal issues on the basis of the law, rules and regulations in force at the national and European level;
- to create a legal roadmap for VEs on harmonized solutions;
- to formulate proposals for future policies and new RTD actions.

ENDNOTES

[1] This is the case, for example, of the European directives on electronic signatures (Dir. 1999/93/EC of 13 December 1999) and electronic commerce (Dir. 2000/31/EC of 8 June 2000).

[2] Del Bono, F., & Zamagni S. (1999). *Microeconomia*. Bologna: Il Mulino.

[3] In Italy, for example, lawyers are not allowed to be co-owners of a partnership.

[4] However it may be useful to draw up appropriate documents aimed at informing stakeholders of the overall economic, financial and patrimonial situation of the VO.

[5] Such as, for example, the obligations to register, to appoint official decision boards, to draw a balance sheet, to hold meetings following a pre-determined agenda, etc.

[6] A recent decision of the Italian Cassation Court (Supreme Cassation Court, V Penal Section, decision n. 4741/2000, 27 December 2000) has stated that the Italian judge is lawfully competent to deal with defamation coming from Web sites located abroad if they can be reached from Italy; the Italian Court has affirmed the right to impound the Web sites and the contracts signed by the defendant with the Internet provider.

Similar examples are Minnesota v. Granite Gates Resorts, Inc., No. C6-95-7227, SLIP OP., su BNA electronic Info. Policy and Law Report 919 (Ramsey Co. D. Ct. Dec. 11, 1996); Maritz, Inc.v. Cybergold, Inc., 947 F. Supp. 1328 (E.D. Mo. 1996); Inset Systems, Inc. v. Instruction Set, Inc., 937 F. Supp. 161 (D. Conn. 1996); Calder v. Jones, 465 US 783 (1984).

A different orientation is expressed by Playboy Enterprises Inc. v. Chuckleberry Publishing Inc., 939 F. Supp. 1032 (S.D.N.Y. 1996), which has stated that *"[t]he Internet is a worldwide phenomenon, accessible from every corner of the globe. ... [a defendant] cannot be prohibited from operating its Internet site merely because the site is accessible from within one country in which the product is banned."*

[7] Southeastern Pennsylvania v. Casey, 112 S. Ct. 2791, 2803 (1992).

[8] This is only possible for civil law, not for penal law.

[9] See Conaway Stilson, A.E. (1997). *The Agile Virtual Corporation*. 22 Del. J. of Corp. Law L. 497.

[10] Italian Civil Code–Royal Decree 16 March 1942–XX, No 262–Book V–Labour–Title X–Law of competition and consortia.

[11] Art. 2602 Italian Civil Code.

[12] Law 8 August 1977, No 584–Norms to adapt public procurement procedures to the Economic European Community directives.

[13] Regulation EEC No 2137/85 of the Council of 25 July 1985 on the institution of the Economic European Interest Grouping (EEIG).

[14] Art. 2359 Italian Civil Code.

[15] Law 10 October 1990, No 287–Norms for the protection of competition and of the market.

[16] For instance, Italy, Austria and Spain.

[17] Directive 1999/93/EC of the European Parliament and of the Council of 13 December 1999 on a Community framework for electronic signatures (O.J. L 13/12 of 19 January 2000).

[18] Public Law 106-229, 30 June 2000.

[19] O.J. L 821/31 of 23 November 1995.

[20] O.J. L 24/1 of 30 January 1998.

[21] Directive 2000/31/EC of the European Parliament and of the Council of 8 June 2000 on certain legal aspects of information society services, in particular electronic commerce, in the Internal Market (O.J. L 178/1 of 17 July 2000). The Directive on Electronic Commerce shall be implemented in the national law of member states by 17 January 2002.

[22] O.J. L 144/19 of 4 June 1999.

[23] Art. 17 of the directive.

[24] Tribunal de grande instance de Paris, 4 March 1981, Clunet 836, note by P. Kahn.

[25] Gautrais, V., Lefebvre, G. & Benyekhlef, K. (1997). Droit du commerce électronique et normes applicables: l'émergence de la 'lex electronica.' Revue de droit des affaires internationales, forum européen de la communication, 5.

[26] An interesting example is given by the construction of the tunnel under the English Channel; the Anglo-French joint venture in charge of it decided that the contract would be subject to the principles common to English and French law and, in the absence of these, to the general principles of international commercial law, as applied by national and international tribunals. See: Fouchar. (1991). Rapport français. La responsabilité des constructeurs. Travaux de l'Association Henri Capitant, Journées Egyptiennes, t. XLII, Paris.

[27] Virtual enterprises in a broad sense may be seen as a species of the genus "virtual organizations."

[28] The VIVE project's Web site can be found at http://www.ceconsulting.it/ve.

[29] It is possible to register online to the VIVE community at the Web address http://www.ceconsulting.it/ve/default_groups.htm.

[30] The BIDSAVER project's Web site is available at http://www.ceconsulting.it/ve/bidsaver.html.

[31] A value network VE in the micro-satellite sector; a supply chain VE in the mechanical equipment sector.

[32] The ALIVE Web site can be found at http://www.vive-ig.net/default_resprj.htm.

REFERENCES

Bariatti, S. (1997). *Internet: Aspects Relatifs Aux Conflits de Lois*. Riv. Dir. Int. Priv. e Proces.

Bekkers, V., Koops, B. J. and Nouwt, S. (1996). Emerging electronic highways. *New Challenges for Politics and Law*. The Hague: Kluwer Law International.

Berger, K.P. (1999). *The Creeping Codification of the Lex Mercatoria*. The Hague, The Netherlands: Kluwer Law International.

Berwanger, E. (1999). The legal classification of virtual corporation according to German law. *Proceedings of the 2ⁿᵈ Vonet Workshop*.

Bonell, M. J. (1997). The Unidroit principles of international commercial contracts: Towards a new "lex mercatoria"? *Revue de Droit des Affaires Internationales*, 2.

Cavazos, E., and Morin, G. (1994). *Cyberspace and Law*. Cambridge, MA: MIT Press.

Conaway Stilson, A. E. (1997). *The Agile Virtual Corporation*. 22 Del. J. Corp. L. 497.

Cousy H., Van Schoubroeck, C., and Windey, B. (1999). *The virtual enterprise: Techno-legal issues*. Report from the research projects n. 119519 and n. 119520, Commission of the European communities Directorate-general XIII, telecommunications, information market and exploitation of research.

Del Bono, F., and Zamagni S. (1999). *Microeconomia*. Bologna, Italy: Il Mulino.

Edwards, L., and Waelde, C. (1997). *Regulating Cyberspace*. Oxford, England: Hart.

Finocchiaro, G. (1997). I contratti informatici. In F. Galgano (Ed.), *Trattato Di Diritto Commerciale e Diritto Pubblico Dell'Economia* (Vol. XXII). Padova: Cedam.

Fusaro, A., Lapertosa, F., Mongiello, A., and Vaccà, C. (1996). *Associazioni Temporanee di Imprese*. Consorzi. G.E.I.E. Engineering. Turin: Utet.

Gambino, A. M. (1997). *L'accordo Telematico*. Milan: Giuffrè.

Gautrais, V., Lefebvre, G., and Benyekhlef, K. (1997). Droit du commerce électronique et normes applicables: L'émergence de la "lex electronica." *Revue de Droit Des Affaires Internationales, Forum Européen de la Communication*, 5.

Giannantonio, E. (1997). *Manuale di Diritto Dell'Informatica*. Padova: Cedam.

Johnson, D. R., and Post, D. G. (1996, May). Law and borders: The rise of law in cyberspace. *Stanford Law Review*.

Krystek, U., Redel, W., and Reppegather, S. (1997). Grundzüge virtueller Organisationen. Elemente und Erfolgsfaktoren, Chancen und Risiken. Wiesbaden: Gabler.

Mayer, H., Kram, A., and Patkós, B. (1998). Das virtuelle Unternehmen: Eine neue Rechtsform? 16. Dresden: Dresdner Forum für Revision und Steuerlehre.

Pattaro, E. (Ed.). (2000). *Codice di Diritto Dell'Informatica*. Padova: Cedam.

Pérez Luño, A. E. (1998). *Saggi di Informatica Giuridica*. Milan: Giuffrè.

Sommerlad, K. W. (1996). Virtuelle Unternehmen: Juristisches Niemandsland? *Office Management*, (7-8).

Zanobetti, A. (2000). Contract law in international electronic commerce. *Revue de Droit des Affaires Internationales*, 5.

About the Authors

Ulrich J. Franke is a researcher at Cranfield University, England. He has extensive international work experience in the field of logistics management. He has worked for major German blue-chip companies, with his latest position as the head of logistics of a manufacturing company. He holds German degrees in economics and business information systems. Additionally he received an MBA degree from Oxford Brookes University and a PhD in organizational theory from Cranfield School of Management. Presently, he is at Cranfield School of Management and conducting comprehensive research in the management of virtual organizations.

***

Hamideh Afsarmanesh is an assistant professor at the Computer Science Department of the Faculty of Science of the University of Amsterdam in the Netherlands. She has been involved and has directed the research in several European- (ESPRIT, DUTCH-HPCN, DUTCH-SION) and American-funded projects. At the Faculty of Science, she coordinates the research and development in the area of cooperative, interoperable, and federated databases. She has served as the program chairperson in international conferences and workshops in the area of information management and expert systems.

Gianfrancesco Amorosi, who holds a physics degree, started working for IBM after two years as a assistant lecturer. For 10 years he managed internal applications of operational research, simulation and econometric models. Since 1982 he has had technical/commercial responsibility for customers set in the areas of CAD/CAM/CAE, CIM, PDM (product data management), and concurrent engineering. Since 1993 Amorosi opened a consulting office for reengineering of product development process, implementation of concurrent engineering/enterprise and associated methodologies/technologies and recently for collaborative approach in extended enterprise. He is a member of the executive board of ESoCE Italy (European Society of Concurrent Engineering).

Carlos Frederico Bremer is a professor of industrial engineering at the University of São Paulo and one of the coordinators of the Nucleus of Advanced Manufacturing. Before teaching he worked at IBM Brazil and Siemens AG (Germany) performing projects related to information technology. He obtained his doctor thesis in computer integrated manufacturing in 1995 at the University of São Paulo and worked as a visiting researcher from 1996 to 1997 in the field of virtual enterprises at the Laboratorium für Werkzeugmaschinen und Betriebslehre in Aachen, Germany. His current lines of research rely on virtual enterprise, production management and enterprise integration. Furthermore, he develops consulting projects together with international partners like SAP and Deloitte Consulting.

Jacques Brook obtained his master's degree in computer science from the Eindhoven University of Technology. He is working in the Telecommunication Management Department of KPN Research in Groningen, the Netherlands, as scientific consultant. He has been working in projects related to the design of architecture building blocks for telecommunication business processes and network management systems, the design of protocol neutral interface using UML (Unified Modelling Language), and the integration of ATM, SDH and WDM to sustain the growing demand for bandwidth. International activity includes participation in EU-funded projects and the monitoring of ITU-T standardization work within WG4.

Claudia Cevenini is a doctorate candidate in information technology law, CIRSFID, University of Bologna, Italy. She holds a master's degree in Italian and German trade law from the University of Ferrara, Italy, and a degree in business and economics, summa cum laude, from the University of Bologna, Italy, and has completed a graduate arbitration course at AISA, Bologna, Italy. Cevenini is a university assistant, lecturer and scientific collaborator of European research projects in IT law, and a consultant in IT law for public institutions and private corporations. She is a founding member of the nonprofit cultural association InSLA (Information Society Law Association), assistant editor and scientific collaborator of the legal journal *Cyberspace and Law*, as well as author of publications on the legal aspects of e-commerce, electronic signatures, online alternative dispute resolution, taxation and IT.

Ashok Chandrashekar, PhD, is a consultant in the Supply Chain Planning Practice of IBM. He has extensive international work experience in various aspects of supply chain and operations management. He is now involved in developing and implementing advanced state-of-the-art supply chain systems. His publication record includes numerous journal articles, book chapters and other publications. He has taught operations management at the both the graduate and the undergraduate level. His educational qualification includes a doctorate in operations management from Arizona State University and an MS in Japanese business studies.

William Donnelly graduated from University College Dublin in 1987 with a PhD in physics. He worked as a system design engineer in the hydroelectric power industry from 1987 to 1989. From 1989 to 1996 he worked as a technical expert in Broadcom Eireann Research before joining Waterford Institute of Technology, Ireland. Donnelly is the director of WIT's Telecommunications Software and Systems group, which he established in 1997.

Florent Frederix holds electrical engineering (1978) and computer science (1982) degrees, obtained a master's of business administration in 1987 and received a doctorate of philosophy in the field of applied economics (2000) for his work on enterprise network optimization, jointly promoted by the Imperial College - University of London (UK), and the University of Limburg (Belgium). For his achievement to define an enterprise architecture capable to deliver the needed manufacturing capacity in a very short time frame to fulfill the surging market demand for ADSL and GSM devices during the years 1997-2000, he has been nominated for Alcatel's Academy Award.

César Garita obtained a bachelor's degree in software engineering and a master's degree in computer science, both from the Costa Rican Institute of Technology. Currently, he is a senior PhD student at the Faculty of Science of the University of Amsterdam in the Netherlands. In the last years, he has been directly involved in several international R&D projects focusing on the analysis, design and implementation of distributed/federated information management systems to support collaborative virtual enterprise scenarios in different sectors, such as industrial manufacturing and tourism.

Mike Gregory has been responsible for the initiation and development of research in international manufacturing. His early industrial career included responsibilities for manufacturing engineering and manufacturing management. He continues to work very closely with industry and has researched and published in the areas of manufacturing strategy, technology management and international manufacturing. International manufacturing is now his primary research interest. He leads the Institute for Manufacturing and is head of the Manufacturing and Management Division within the Engineering Department of Cambridge University.

L. O. Hertzberger received a master's degree in experimental physics in 1969 and a PhD in 1975, both from the University of Amsterdam. From 1969 till 1983 he was a staff member in the High Energy Physics group, later the NIKHEF-H (Dutch Institute for Nuclear and High Energy Physics). In 1983 he was appointed as a professor in computer science. His current research interests are in the field of parallel computing and intelligent autonomous robotics and their application in industrial automation.

Thomas Hess is head of both the intercompany networks and management accounting research team and the media business research team at the Institute of Information Systems at Georg-August University, Göttingen, Germany. He holds an MA in information systems from the Technical University of Darmstadt, Germany, and a PhD in business administration from the University of St. Gallen, Switzerland. His current research interests include planning and control in intercompany networks, new media and business process management. Hess has published several reviewed articles concerned with planning and control in intercompany networks.

H. P. M. Jägers (Hans) is a professor in the Faculty of Military Management Sciences at the Royal Netherlands Military Academy. He is also a professor of design of information-intensive organizations at the University of Amsterdam. He is a participant in the University of Amsterdam PrimaVera research program (http://domino.fee.uva.nl/PrimaVera).

Wendy Jansen is an associate professor of management information sciences at the Royal Netherlands Military Academy. Her primary field of study is the relation between organization design and the use of information and communication technology. She is also a professor of design of information-intensive organizations at the University of Amsterdam. She is a participant in the University of Amsterdam PrimaVera research program (http://domino.fee.uva.nl/PrimaVera).

Stefan Klein (Stefan.Klein@uni-muenster.de) is a professor for information systems at the University of Muenster, Germany. He has held teaching or research positions at the University of Linz, University of Koblenz-Landau, University St. Gallen (Switzerland), Harvard University, German National Research Center for Computer Science (GMD), and University of Cologne. His research and teaching areas are interorganizational systems, information management and communication systems. He is regularly program committee member or track chair of several international IS conferences and member of the editorial board of several international IS journals.

David Lewis graduated in electronic engineering at the University of Southampton in 1987 and in 1990 received an MSc in computer science from University College London, where he has since worked as a research fellow. He has worked primarily on EU-funded projects, in which he has been responsible for leading teams developing integrated, multidomain service management systems. He has a PhD on a service management development framework for the open services market.

Harris G. Makatsoris holds a degree in mechanical engineering and a doctorate degree in computer systems aided engineering from Imperial College, with a specialisation in production & supply chain management. In 1996 he formed Orion Logic Ltd. in the UK, offering consulting services to manufacturing companies. Since then the company has developed new generation Internet-based software technology for collaborative supply-chain and direct-materials procurement management, targeting European companies in the areas of construction, electronics, metal working/machining and equipment manufacturing. He also led a technical team in an ECU 9 million project that involved three large European semiconductor manufacturing companies. Makatsoris is a partner in a highly successful IT service provider in Greece. He has published a number of papers to date in the area.

Luis Fernando Moraes Marques is a mechanical engineer graduate of the University of São Paulo and currently is ending his master in industrial engineering at the Nucleus of Advanced Manufacturing, an associated laboratory at the University of São Paulo. His current interests lie in virtual enterprise, product development process and management business process research fields.

Hugo Meijers is former Dutch naval officer, helicopter flight commander and Gulf War veteran. After the navy, he became a management consultant and visionary entrepreneur. His academic achievements are in operational research and information management. His main interest is in making unique combinations of multiple scientific and cultural disciplines, resulting in new systemic insights. His key focus is on unorthodox or nontraditional organization models that are emerging through the unconventional usage of technology. He is author of a series of articles. At present, he is manager and managing partner in a number of companies. He can be reached at hmeijers@contraview.com.

Vaggelis Ouzounis is the deputy leader of ECCO (Electronic Commerce Center of Competence) in GMD-FOKUS. Ouzounis managed and participated in several European projects (IST, ACTS, ESPRIT, TELEMATICS, and EURESCOM) and in international standardization bodies. Ouzounis is also involved in the activities concerning electronic commerce and virtual organizations in the European Commission. He chaired a set of strategic and scientific workshops and conferences and gave several tutorials and invited speeches. Ouzounis has published one book and more than 25 reviewed papers in scientific books, journals and conference proceedings concerning electronic commerce and virtual enterprises. His research interests include advanced electronic commerce services, virtual enterprises, and virtual marketplaces.

Howard D. Richards is a consultant with his own company for manufacturing improvement with a large experience in the microelectronics industry, in which he held several senior positions from research to operations management over 33 years employed by the Plessey Company and GEC Plessey Semiconductors. He graduated in physics at Birmingham in 1960 and since his early research became involved in the continuous improvement and management of the manufacture of silicon integrated circuits. He was actively involved in a number of ESPRIT projects and others to improve information, material flow and decision management and has published a number of papers on the subject.

Philip Schary is a professor emeritus at the College of Business at Oregon State University, where he taught marketing and business logistics. He has been a visiting professor at Cranfield School of Management, Copenhagen and Aarhus Schools of Business in Denmark, and the University of New South Wales in Australia. He has also lectured in Chile and China. He holds an MBA from UC Berkeley and a PhD from UCLA in business economics. He has written in professional journals and serves as an editorial reviewer for two journals in logistics management. He has authored or coauthored three books, currently including *Managing the Global Supply Chain,* published by Copenhagen Business School Press.

Dorian Selz (dorian.selz@namics.com) is a member of the management board of namics, overseeing its international expansion. Namics is the leading professional services firm in Switzerland. On joining namics he worked as a senior consultant focusing on the IT, telecom, and automotive industries. His PhD research at the University of St. Gallen focused on emerging forms of network organizations in open electronic networks. During his time at the university he held the executive editorship of *EM–Electronic Markets*, a leading academic journal on electronic commerce and markets.

Yongjiang Shi is research director of the Centre for International Manufacturing in Cambridge University. He is a graduate and former lecturer at the School of Economics and Management of Tsinghua University in Beijing, China. He gained his PhD at Cambridge for work on international manufacturing network configurations and has taken a leading role in the conceptualisation and delivery of the centre's research programme. His research interests are global manufacturing strategy, virtual manufacturing networks, business internationalisation, and technology transfer in developing countries.

Jairo Eduardo Moraes Siqueira works as a industrial integration consultant at the Brazilian aircraft manufacturer EMBRAER S/A – Empresa Brasileira de Aeronáutica. He received his MSc degree in industrial engineering at the Nucleus of Advanced Manufacturing of the University of São Paulo and the degree of mechanical engineer also at the University of São Paulo. His current interests lie in virtual enterprises, product configuration management and business process modeling.

G. C. A. Steenbakkers (Wilchard) is an associate professor of organization sciences at the Royal Netherlands Military Academy. In August 2001 he joined Ordina as an e-business consultant. Virtual and network organizations, e-business and e-learning are the focal point of his current research. He is also a professor of design of information-intensive organizations at the University of Amsterdam. He is a participant in the University of Amsterdam PrimaVera research program (http://domino.fee.uva.nl/PrimaVera).

Roberto Tononi was born in Rome in 1948 and has a degree in nuclear engineering and a master's of science in nuclear safety. At the onset of his career, Tononi collected a 10-year experience in safety of nuclear power plants and was a member of the Scientific Committee for Nuclear Safety, appointed by the Italian government. Afterwards he was an ENEA manager of a program of research on new advanced designs for inherently safe nuclear plants, in cooperation with the Massachusetts

Institute of Technology, where he was a fellow of the Center for Advanced Engineering Studies. Later on, he was the manager of one of the largest international EUREKA research projects, named "Flexible Automation for Ship Prefabrication–EU353." He is currently the manager of ENEA research activities on advanced technologies for SMEs.

Tim Veil is a PhD student and a research assistant at the Institute of Information Systems at Georg-August University, Göttingen, Germany. He holds an MA in business administration, which he received from Georg-August University, Göttingen, Germany, in 1998. Since 1998, his research has been on cost accounting for planning and control in intercompany networks. During that time he has published case studies on planning and control in inter-company networks as well as several working papers on cost accounting in intercompany networks.

Vincent Wade is a head of the Knowledge and Data Engineering Research group in the Computer Science Department in Trinity College Dublin. He received his BSc from University College Dublin, Ireland, and an MSc from Trinity College Dublin, Ireland. He leads research investigating telecommunications and information management systems and virtual environments. He currently leads several EU and industrial research projects in these areas and is author of over 70 technical papers in international conference and research journals.

Malcolm Warner, born in 1937, was educated at Trinity College, Cambridge, where he took his undergraduate and doctoral degrees in the Faculty of Economics and Politics. He was also a graduate fellow at Stanford University, California. He is currently a professor and fellow, Wolfson College and Judge Institute of Management Studies, University of Cambridge. He is the editor-in-chief of the *International Encyclopedia of Business and Management*, Thomson Learning, London: 6 volumes (1996) and 2nd edition, 8 volumes (2001). He has published over 30 books and over 150 articles. As of 2001, he was appointed a co-editor of the *Asia Pacific Business Review*. He recently spent a period as a visiting professor at City University Business School, London, as well as at City University, Hong Kong.

Morgen Witzel is a writer and researcher who works in a number of fields, including virtual and knowledge management, cross-cultural management and historical models of management. He is editor-in-chief of *Corporate Finance Review* and deputy editor of *Mastering Management Online*, published by the *Financial Times* in London. His books include the *Dictionary of Business and Management, Doing Business in China* and the forthcoming *Biographical Dictionary of Management* and *Builders and Dreamers: Historical Models of Management*; with Malcolm Warner, he has written a number of articles on virtual management and their book *Managing in Virtual Organizations* will be published in 2002. Witzel taught for many years at London Business School and remains an associate of the school. He also owns and manages a publishing services company.

Oliver Wohlgemuth is a PhD student and a research assistant at the Institute of Information Systems at Georg-August University, Göttingen, Germany. He holds an MA in industrial engineering, which he received from the Technical University of Darmstadt, Germany, in 1997. Since 1998, his research has been on general management in intercompany networks. During that time he has published reviewed articles as well as several working papers on planning and control in intercompany networks.

Index

W

Y